D-Day 1944

D-Day 1944

Edited by Theodore A. Wilson

Foreword by John S. D. Eisenhower

Published for The Eisenhower Foundation, Abilene, Kansas,
by the University Press of Kansas

Photographs courtesy of Dwight D. Eisenhower Library
Maps by Gary Holman

Published by the University Press of Kansas (Lawrence, Kansas 66049), which was
organized by the Kansas Board of Regents and is operated and funded by Emporia State
University, Fort Hays State University, Kansas State University, Pittsburg State University,
the University of Kansas, and Wichita State University

Library of Congress Cataloging-in-Publication Data

D-Day, 1944 / edited by Theodore A. Wilson ; foreword by John S. D.
   Eisenhower.
      p.   cm. — (Modern war studies)
   Rev. ed. of: D-Day : the Normandy invasion in retrospect. 1971.
   ISBN 0-7006-0673-4 (hardcover) — ISBN 0-7006-0674-2 (pbk.)
      1. World War, 1939–1945—Campaigns—France—Normandy.   2. Normandy
   (France)—History, Military.   I. Wilson, Theodore A., 1940–
   II. Eisenhower Foundation (Abilene, Kan.)   III. D-Day (Lawrence,
   Kan.)   IV. Series.
   D756.5.N6D2   1994
   940.54′2142—dc20   93-42115

British Library Cataloguing in Publication Data is available.

Printed in the United States of America
10 9 8 7 6 5 4 3 2

The paper used in this publication meets the minimum requirements of the American
National Standard for Permanence of Paper for Printed Library Materials Z39.48-1984.

The Eisenhower Foundation wishes to recognize the following
for their financial support of this publication
and the memorials and tributes to the following:

In memory of Dwight D. Eisenhower
and the men and women of the armed forces who served during WW II
Anonymous

In tribute to the men and women of the 1st Infantry Division
1st Infantry Division Museum, Fort Riley, Kansas

In memory of Arthur Eisenhower
The William T. Kemper Foundation

In tribute to Judge Arthur J. Stanley, Jr.,
veteran of the Mexican Border, China Station, WW II (Normandy)
His family

In memory of those comrades of the 10th Mountain Infantry Division
Rocco Siciliano, President, Eisenhower World Affairs Institute

In tribute to the U.S. 8th Air Force
8th Air Force Historical Society

In memory of Fred C. Bramlage
The Bramlage family

In memory of Harry Darby
Edith and Harry Darby Foundation

Eisenhower World Affairs Institute

Ross and Marianna Beach

In tribute to the 30th Infantry Division
30th Infantry Division Association

Contents

Illustrations and Maps

Illustrations

Maps

Foreword

John S. D. Eisenhower

A half century has now passed since June 1944, when General Dwight D. Eisenhower gave the order for the launching of Operation OVERLORD. It has been a quarter century since General Omar N. Bradley wrote the foreword to *D-Day; The Normandy Invasion in Retrospect*. Yet the memories of D-day are still vivid to the generation of people who lived through World War II.

In writing his foreword, General Bradley possessed an authority not accorded to those of us who were not present at D-day. Yet his thoughts, written at the height of the Vietnam War in 1969, were partially distracted from D-day by the scene he was witnessing around him. He saw a nation involved in an unpopular, undeclared war, and he was obviously experiencing anguish over what that war was doing to the fiber of our citizenry.

Shortly afterward, the United States effort in Vietnam ended in defeat. Years of recrimination and national self-doubt followed. By the beginning of the 1990s, however, the world was astonished to witness the collapse of the monolithic Communist bloc headed by the Soviet Union. The Cold War was over! The goal for which the West had striven for half a century was suddenly and unexpectedly attained.

The first Western reaction to the collapse of the Warsaw Pact was one of immense relief. Overnight the nations of the civilized world were delivered from the threat of instant nuclear extinction. With Western Europe no longer threatened by thousands of Warsaw Pact armored formations, our leaders found themselves free to begin converting our economy from one with a semiwartime footing to one based on the expectation of peace.

Yet the post-Cold War world has not simplified the international problems confronting the United States. For one thing, ethnic groups who had never really been at peace among themselves began giving vent to the internecine hatreds that had only been repressed during the years of Communist dominance. Hatreds are now out in the open, presenting the U.S. government with the problem of defining its proper role in a greatly changed world.

Moreover, the new challenge is not confined to the conduct of foreign policy. We Americans, many of us with newly elevated expectations, now find ourselves in the throes of redefining our responsibilities of citizenship: How much do we owe our government, and how much does our government owe us?

All this would seem to have little to do with a book devoted to the study of D-day, the 1944 invasion of Normandy. But the circumstances under which Operation OVERLORD was conducted bear a greater resemblance to the circumstances of today than is immediately apparent. The years 1994 and 1944 are both years of upheaval. Both years find the United States moving forward into uncharted territory.

When one begins a study of the conduct of Operation OVERLORD, one is struck by the degree of imagination and innovation that was required of all the commanders and staff officers, up and down the line, in all the services and of all nationalities. In planning such a vast undertaking as the invasion of Normandy, the participants were breaking new ground, confronting problems for which no book had previously been written.

Where, for example, would one find a blueprint for artificial harbors—those vast, hollow, concrete boxes that were constructed in the ports of southern England and towed to the beaches of Normandy? Where would one find an agreed doctrine on the relationship between air power and land power—a concept on which the entire gamble of invading northwestern Europe with minimum ground divisions was based? Where in history would the OVERLORD logistic commanders find formulas to help them cope with the unexpected success the Allied fighting troops attained at the Falaise Gap? In what dusty file cabinet would one discover the solution to the unprecedented logistic problems that tactical success brought about? Such radical devices as the Red Ball Express—the 24-hour-a-day, circular stream of trucks that supplied the front lines from the beaches of Normandy—were innovations that sprang from the minds of original thinkers. In today's age, where the individual is becoming ever more dependent on gadgetry, the example of individual initiative demonstrated every day during operation OVERLORD serves as a constant inspiration.

Two major problems facing the high command in OVERLORD are still being wrestled with today. One is the relationship between the civilian and military echelons of government during wartime. The other is the concept of wartime alliances among independent powers. Both bear examining.

Our Constitution and our traditions both emphasize the subordination of military power to civilian authority, and throughout the 200 years of U.S. history our military has admirably supported that concept. Our military in World War II was no exception. The experience of the Second World War, however, provides some absorbing and occasionally instructive examples of instances in which the line between the broad direction of the war effort (the idea, propounded by the political) and its execution (the possible, propounded by the military) became somewhat unclear.

The mixing of the political and military areas of responsibility is illustrated by a study of the roles played by British Prime Minister Winston Churchill. Never one to delegate control over anything that interested him personally, the doughty Churchill decided early on to wear two mantles: those of prime minister and minister of war. In that dual capacity, therefore, he sought to manage activities in both arenas, which often caused complications. One example was the controversy over the proposed Allied landing in southern France, which was originally planned to be executed simultaneously with D-day. Its original purpose was, of course, to draw enemy forces away from the main cross-Channel invasion.

When the Big Three (Roosevelt, Stalin, and Churchill) first met at Tehran in November of 1943, Stalin cornered Churchill into agreeing on a date for the execution of OVERLORD; May 1944 was the date chosen. That agreement included a landing in southern France (Operation ANVIL, later DRAGOON). For his own reasons, however, Churchill heartily disliked the idea of a landing in southern France, and he used all the power he could muster to thwart it.

In early 1944, Churchill attempted to persuade President Franklin Roosevelt that changed circumstances called for DRAGOON's cancellation. But Roosevelt considered his promise to Stalin to be sacrosanct, and he refused to consider cancellation. When Churchill pressed on, an exasperated Roosevelt advised him to present his arguments to General Eisenhower, the Allied Supreme Commander for OVERLORD. Roosevelt justified this strange procedure by designating Eisenhower to represent the American Joint Chiefs of Staff.

Churchill was determined to pursue this objective in his role as British defence minister, and he began to hound Eisenhower on the subject of a DRAGOON cancellation. A shortage of landing craft forced a delay of DRAGOON, and Churchill continued to argue against it long after Allied forces had landed in Normandy on June 6.

Churchill's objections to the southern France landings were largely political. The forces for the landing were to be drawn from those fighting in the Mediterranean theater. Churchill did not want to further downgrade that theater, which was so important to the British, in order to bolster the main effort, OVERLORD, which was being conducted largely under American auspices in northwest Europe. But in his role as defense minister, Churchill attempted to make his case for cancellation solely on military considerations, depicting DRAGOON as likely to be extremely costly. Eisenhower, however, was confident that the landings would be easy and highly useful to OVERLORD, and he refused to budge. So the prime minister of Britain was forced to submit to the views of an American general! But a sign of Churchill's greatness was the fact that he bore no rancor; he was, in fact, aboard a British ship near Marseilles on August 15, 1944, to observe the landings himself.

Similar problems arose between Eisenhower and General Charles de Gaulle, provisional president of France, later in the OVERLORD campaign. The clashes between political and military considerations came in the area of civil affairs—specifically, the conflict between the needs of the military in fighting Hitler and the rights of the newly liberated French citizenry. The most dramatic of these conflicts of interest occurred in August 1944, as Allied forces were sweeping across France.

As the U.S. First Army approached Paris, the Americans planned to bypass the city and press the pursuit of Nazi forces retreating toward the German West Wall. But resistance units in Paris rose against the Nazis prematurely, and de Gaulle feared that they would be slaughtered by the thousands and Paris destroyed. Eisenhower gave in to political pressure from de Gaulle and ordered that Paris be taken immediately—by the First French Armored Division. In doing so, Eisenhower may have been stretching his authority as a soldier, but he viewed the maintenance of French goodwill as a military consideration.

An even broader subject for study is the very nature of international alliances during war and threats of war—an issue much in the forefront today. What does World War II tell us about the nature of military alliances? Must the United States, even though suffering economic problems, dominate every coalition that sets about to right every wrong existing on the globe today?

Here the World War II experience is gloomy. Even during the days between 1941 and 1945, when two nations of similar cultures shared a clear-cut objective, the Anglo-American alliance barely worked. Fortunately, the United States, which provided the bulk of resources in men and material, gradually attained the status of senior partner in the alliance, thus avoiding a state of impasse. This is not to say that American strategic wisdom was infallible—perhaps British strategy would have been more successful—but two heads would not have been better than or even as good as one in this case. Eisenhower's opinion was, "An alliance must be directed by the nation supplying the bulk of the forces, both of men and material."

Does this mean that the United States will have to underwrite all police actions in the world from this point on? A study of World War II provides food for thought in addressing this problem.

The men who planned and directed Operation OVERLORD were fallible. All but the occasional eccentric recognized as much. In a conversation with Dr. John Wickman, former director of the Eisenhower Library, General Eisenhower said, "We were not supermen. All we were doing was using the intelligence that God gave us to get a job completed."

This book, *D-Day 1944,* affords the reader a chance to evaluate the performance of the Allies during that critical period of American history. Not only commanders but also planners and combat troops are depicted performing their assigned duties. Despite Eisenhower's modest words, the reader will probably conclude that the men who planned and executed D-day did so with a remarkable degree of ability. They are well worth studying.

Foreword to *D-Day: The Normandy Invasion in Retrospect*

General of the Army Omar N. Bradley

Twenty-five years ago, a global war came to its end. First in Europe, then in the Pacific the armed forces of the two major aggressor nations were defeated and their homelands occupied by forces of the free world. During the intervening years, the dynamics of international politics have brought about many changes that have involved the United States in two more wars. Allies of the past are now estranged, and former enemies are now allies. These changes are not startling or unexpected, and 25 years hence the process of change may again rearrange the relationships among nations—without the upheaval of war, it is hoped.

Following World War II, the United States assumed the position of world leadership among those nations that value self-determination and the rights of the individual—the elusive political-social-economic philosophy known as democracy. During the past 25 years, we have forcefully resisted the spread of totalitarianism and its encroachment upon democracy. In so doing, we have reaffirmed our awareness that democracy will continue to flourish only so long as its foundation is freedom for all.

Today, within our nation, we are engaged in a contest over the integrity of the state and its institutions versus the integrity of the individual as understood by those preoccupied with idealism and disdainful of the practicalities of applying those ideals. There is no disagreement over the value of the freedoms that come from democratic self-government. But from a vocal segment of a generation born and reared to maturity during an era of continuous material affluence and phenomenal expansion of scientific knowledge, there is an impatient demand to do away with all forms and institutions that fall short of democratic utopia. These young people refuse to look back and acknowledge the broadening of freedoms won through laborious effort and the constructive process of evolution of our 200-year history. Never having had to face a need to work to survive, nor really aware that their parents' concern with the accumulation of material wealth and security was born of the Great Depression of the 1930s followed by the upheaval of war, they clamor for destruction of the status quo. Unfortunately, these young people fail to recognize that destruction of the institutions they challenge as imperfect may also destroy the very institutions that provide their freedom to challenge. A democracy such as ours may be threatened from without, but it can be destroyed from within. It can be lost if our young people confuse license with freedom and if their impetuous drive for perfection neglects their personal responsibility for freedom's security.

There can be no thought of extinguishing this youthful zeal. However, part of the solution to our national dilemma may lie in changing the perspective of the adversaries in this confrontation. Reflection on World War II and what it meant as a national effort, reflection on the proposition that a workable solution that gets results is better than an ideal solution that is unattainable, reflection on the personal sacrifice made by so many to defend freedom for the United States and to return individual freedom to Western Europe and the Pacific should all be valuable in changing the perspective of our young citizens.

Historical reflection is not an archaic practice. Examination of World War II, its participants, and its meaning is relevant today. All Americans should pause and look back and learn about ourselves and our responsibilities as free people.

There is a lesson to learn in answering those critics who state that the strategy of World War II was all wrong, or that it would have been much better to have done this or that. There are those who are quick to say how misguided our leadership was, that other plans and decisions would have achieved better results. Perhaps. But the fact remains, we did win the war.

Success was achieved by applying a united effort using available resources in the most practical way possible. Success was achieved through the personal sacrifice of many. Consider two extremes.

In June 1944, I scrambled aboard a landing craft, hitching a ride back to my headquarters afloat after checking on the progress of the second day on Omaha Beach. On the wet, open bottom of the tiny craft, a dozen litters had been loaded. And on those litters a dozen wounded young Americans lay wrapped in blankets already soggy from the spray. All in their raw twenties, they lay quiet, uncomplaining, awaiting transfer to a hospital ship. I was aware that there in the pitching bottom of a landing craft lay the fragments of a generation rashly condemned for being "corrupted" by the ease of democracy and "debased" by the luxury of freedom. But those twelve men learned on a beach in Normandy—as hideously as one can learn—that freedom is not a gift, and that democracy can extract both stern and unequal payment from those who share its bounty. Freedom is neither achieved nor retained without sacrifice by individuals, often in unequal measure. Many of our young men today are learning the same hard lesson in Vietnam.

At the other end of the military ladder, the sacrifice is different, but the burden is still heavy. General Eisenhower possessed the soldier's virtues, the attributes of great leadership—perseverance, determination, and decisiveness—

that enabled him to bear his heavy burden as well as weld together and hold together the Allied Expeditionary Force. This force became the mightiest aggregation of military strength the world has ever known. Eisenhower could make decisions. Presented with the facts of a problem, he had the ability and moral courage to make clear-cut decisions when decisions were required. He always accepted responsibility and squarely faced up to the difficult and frequently onerous decision-making task.

Perhaps the best example of the difficulty of making a decision, the weight of responsibility that can be involved, and the lonely wait to evaluate the results was the decision made in the evening hours of 4 June 1944. Eisenhower had already made the decision not to launch the invasion on 5 June because of adverse weather. But in the dark hours, as 4 June came to an end, he was forced to make a much harder decision. He could chance the unpromising weather and land 6 June. He could wait for the eighth or ninth to see if the weather might improve, but then accept less favorable tide and light conditions (7 June was not available because of a refueling problem if 6 June was canceled). Last, he could delay for two weeks until 18 June. No choice was clearly the best, nor was any even clearly a good solution. As is true so often in matters of national consequence, each possible solution was fraught with unknowns. The agony of the ordeal was obvious as Eisenhower faced the decision that only he could make. "I'm quite positive we must give the order. . . . I don't like it, but there it is. . . . I don't see how we can possibly do anything else." The day for OVERLORD was set.

There is no need to review the terrible responsibility inherent in that decision. To some degree, every leader is faced with the same test, for no decision that involves the lives of others can be taken lightly. Eisenhower made such decisions as a soldier, and he made them as president of the United States. He accepted his personal responsibilities in the continuing defense of freedom.

Freedom is not extended by eliminating the structures of government that protect, however imperfectly, the rights of the individual. Freedom is extended by a self-disciplined commitment of every citizen to defend freedom where it exists and to extend real freedom to all people wherever they may be. These are the principles that free men and women may learn from the study of World War II. These are the principles by which Dwight David Eisenhower lived and by which he served his country so long and so well.

Introduction

Theodore A. Wilson

A noted nineteenth-century historian of the papacy once observed that the aperture through which scholars contemplate the past with a reasonable hope of understanding what actually happened is extremely small, amounting to no more than a fifteen- to twenty-year "window" of comprehension. That aperture encompasses a brief period after the event being chronicled—long enough for the fieriest passions to fade, for essential details and long-sequestered elements of the story to be unearthed, and for a sense of perspective about what was important and what was trivial to emerge, but not so long that the sense of familiarity with time and place, the immediacy of insight derived from personal experience, have been entirely lost.

The fact that the average life span has lengthened substantially over the past 150 years and that historians' access to authoritative evidence has improved suggests that the window of historical opportunity may be extended to between 20 and 50 years after the event. Before that, partisanship and the subjectivity resulting from particular knowledge unavoidably distort any re-creation of past actions. Motives and judgments are thus suspect. Once more than 50 years have passed, the bright perceptions gained from personal experience fade into a uniform grayness, preserved chiefly in musty official records. In addition, the awareness of a multidimensional context for action, that kaleidoscope of both significant and seemingly irrelevant values, concerns, and beliefs framing the event and shaping its "true" meaning, tends to become obscured. Often what emerges is a portrayal that mingles the prejudices of earlier chroniclers and the priorities of historians projecting contemporary issues and value systems into the past. The outcome, although often fascinating and aesthetically alluring, usually bears little relationship to reality.

This collection of essays was created at just that moment when our accessibility to an appreciation—in its fullest meaning—of D-day and related operations is rapidly narrowing. The voices of the generation that lived through those momentous happenings that brought Allied and Axis soldiers, sailors, and airmen to battle for possession of a smallish region of northwest France known for a thousand years as Normandy are inexorably falling silent. The popular memory of this momentous event (insofar as it exists in coherent form) is progressing along a familiar trajectory from actuality to folk legend.

Although the children of the World War II generation willingly accepted the recollections and rationalizations of their parents as unquestionably valid, the grandchildren of World War II survivors view Normandy and other milestones of that global cataclysm much as they do the American Civil War or, for that matter, the Peloponnesian War. The visual and aural evidence of what happened before, on, and immediately after 6 June 1944 is, of course, immeasurably greater and its immediacy and scope far more powerful than similar documentation from previous conflicts. However, unless placed within a meaningful context and ordered as to significance, these images and sounds lose their explanatory power. They may be reality, but to the unknowing observer any truth not explained becomes myth.

Thus, this collection of essays comes in just under the wire. An earlier collection, *D-Day: The Normandy Invasion in Retrospect*, was published in 1971 to commemorate the twenty-fifth anniversary of the Allied invasion of Europe in June 1944.[1] That work manifested the view that sufficient time had elapsed to afford a balanced assessment of the events surrounding D-day. This appraisal was provided by individuals—scholars and eyewitnesses—who had reached adulthood and in some cases held influential positions by the time of D-day. Indeed, *D-Day: The Normandy Invasion in Retrospect* brought together D-day participants and historians, many of whom had taken part in or witnessed the actual events.

Notably, nearly all the chapters in this book were contributed by historians who had devoted their entire careers, or significant portions of them, to writing the so-called green books, the massive history of the U.S. Army in World War II. Working within the confines of the Office of the Chief of Military History (and precursor entities in the Department of the Army), these "official" historians enjoyed unparalleled access to the records generated by the U.S. Army and related federal organizations. During the two decades after World World II, they wrote a series of volumes that were rightly accepted as the standard accounts of their special topics. Individually and collectively, theirs was a remarkable achievement. At the same time, however, the point of view being espoused was limited by the special conditions under which this research was conducted.[2]

Because of this orientation and because the earlier book derived from a conference sponsored by the Dwight D. Eisenhower Presidential Library—then just completing the initial phase of making its holdings available for serious research—*D-Day: The Normandy Invasion in Retrospect* not surprisingly mirrored the concerns and unique expertise of the chief contributors. Grand strategy and, in particular, the question of Anglo-American conflict over opening the Second Front were central to the essays of Maurice Matloff and Forrest Pogue and were featured to a significant degree in several other essays in the 1971 volume. A second important focus was what today would be called the operational dimension of war associated with OVERLORD: mounting the naval effort (Operation NEPTUNE), meeting the enormous logistic challenges of supplying the invasion forces, resolving the controversy over how to prioritize the air campaign, and describing the interaction between technology and military operations. A third emphasis culminated eyewitness accounts, ranging from journalist Don Whitehead's brief evocation of the carnage on Omaha Beach to the complementary recollections of George Elsey and Friedrich Ruge about the navies and Normandy to Forrest Pogue's testimony about his experiences as a combat historian who observed these dramatic events.

In retrospect, one may discern in the chief emphases of the conference and the resulting book several motifs that are more reflective of America in 1969 than of the circumstances of 1944. Anyone who recalls the obsession of policymakers and military analysts with the ongoing trauma of Vietnam during those days will not be surprised by the Janus-like, introspective focus on two questions: How and why did we get it right in the invasion of Normandy? How and why does it seem to have gone wrong in Vietnam? Perhaps the complexities of conference logistics explain the fact that—with the exception of Vice Admiral Ruge—the chief participants were American; nonetheless, the American perspective on the events and controversies of OVERLORD is a notable element of that collection.

A related contemporary influence was the concern with decision making at the national and coalition levels. This emphasis reflected a concentration on national security management—the process of how and why decisions are made within the councils of the U.S. government—in the scholarly environment of the late 1960s. Perhaps, too, the focus on national strategies and high-level military operations reflected a profound lack of interest on the part of the World War II generation (more than eleven million of whom, still living in 1969 and moving through middle age, had experienced military service) in commemorating the traumas of their youth.

D-Day: The Normandy Invasion in Retrospect was deservedly well received, and several of its essays continue to be cited as the authoritative accounts of their subjects. Thus, when the suggestion was first made to me in the spring of 1990 that a new collection of essays be published on the occasion of the fiftieth anniversary of D-day, my initial response blended skepticism and perplexity. What might be achieved by a second collection of scholarly essays on this topic? Had the passage of 25 years wrought truly significant changes in the perspective from which historians were approaching the whys and wherefores of the Normandy invasion?

Extended deliberation and conversations with colleagues engaged in scholarly research on topics related to D-day caused me to conclude that such an undertaking could prove worthwhile. For the reasons enumerated above and as a result of new interpretations flowing from previously unavailable sources, a new go at a collaborative history of OVERLORD and D-day offered an intriguing prospect. Happily, the Eisenhower Foundation and the University Press of Kansas agreed.

Three occurrences in the 1970s opened the way to new approaches to and new insights into the history of World War II: (1) the opening of the vast majority of British official records for the World War II period, (2) the related revelation that a supersecret British signals intelligence operation had been able to decrypt certain high-level German ciphers during large stretches of the war, and (3) the release of hoards of American records under the dual catalysts of mandatory declassification review and the Freedom of Information Act. These events indisputably revitalized the study of wartime Anglo-American political and military relations. For the first time, historians were able to test what I and others have termed the "Churchillian paradigm" against a reasonable approximation of the historical record.[3]

In addition, questions that arose during the 1960s and 1970s—rather than from the long-established orthodoxy promulgated by those who grew up in the environment of the Depression, Munich, and Pearl Harbor and reached maturity as scholars in the early Cold War era of the 1940s and 1950s—produced a significantly different research agenda. The postwar generation of historians interested in World War II—although divided along ideological and cultural-political fault-lines—shared a mistrust about the exercise of power and about the idealism and capacity of democratically elected leaders; an acute awareness of the vital role of partisan, palace, and bureaucratic politics; and a cynical attitude toward the rhetorical banalities of government.

Fortunately, a substantial body of scholarship germane to such an enterprise has been produced during the past two decades. We have been blessed with a number of valuable autobiographies and memoirs by high-level military participants in the events leading to the Normandy invasion and beyond.[4] Continuing the task of delineating the process by which strategic and political decisions were reached, individuals close to the center of affairs have provided diaries and other accounts, and junior figures have offered insightful commentaries about the actions and attitudes of their superiors.[5] These works have added greatly to our understanding of how OVERLORD was mounted. Pivotal biographies of various military and political leaders were completed after the publication of *D-Day: The Normandy Invasion in Retrospect*—for example, Martin Gilbert's exhaustive chronicle of Winston S. Churchill's public career and Forrest Pogue's multivolume biography of George c. Marshall. Such works provided significant insights themselves but also triggered the release of troves of personal papers. A wave of biographies in the 1980s, making full if not always judicious use of this flood of Anglo-American documentation, dealt with various strategic conflicts and clashes of personalities that encumber the history of OVERLORD.[6]

This deluge of biographies has expanded to include military figures at levels below the Army Group Commander on the Allied side (though, regrettably, few careful studies of American, British, or Canadian divisional commanders have yet appeared) and to encompass the principal nationalities participating in a spectrum of military operations. For example, recent works on the Canadian forces taking part in the Normandy battles deal with leadership, military-political relationships, and the combat performance of Canadian troops at all levels.[7] The record is not quite as impressive for U.S. and British forces. A number of full-scale operational accounts of the Normandy battles—Russell Weigley's massive study, *Eisenhower's Lieutenants*, the excellent works by Carlo D'Este and Max Hastings that focus on British policies and performance; several depictions of the factors that inhibited and influenced German reactions to the shock of D-day, and the aforementioned study of Canadian military leadership by John English have appeared.[8]

A tidal surge of memoirs, popular accounts, and studies grounded in substantive research followed the revelation of ULTRA. The flotsam and jetsam left when that wave receded have provided, as Alexander S. Cochran notes in his essay in this volume, some valuable insights into both intelligence and deception operations. Now that the final volume of the history of British intelligence in World War II has been published and it appears that certain categories of American records dealing with ULTRA and other "sigint" operations are being made available, the subject of intelligence and deception's influence on coalition strategy and operations is certain to receive additional attention.

It is also noteworthy that in the past decade, interest in the experiences of individuals and small units during World War II has grown enormously. This is especially notable for those who took part in the cauldron of Normandy battles. In the United States, the fortieth anniversary commemorations of D-day were the impetus for a small flood of individual memoirs, oral history compilations, and unit histories (in some cases, unrevised from the original accounts released shortly after the war). Certainly, the past decade has seen an upsurge in activity among unit associations. No doubt such organizations as the U.S. Army Military History Institute (which is seeking to distribute a detailed questionnaire to the nine million surviving World War II veterans) and the Dwight D. Eisenhower Center at the University of New Orleans (which has created a remarkable archive of D-day oral histories) have played a significant role in making veterans aware of the importance of their experiences and perceptions for the history of World War II. Also at work is the psychological phenomenon of validation, the understandable desire of individuals who have reached a certain point in their lives to explain to others and to themselves the meaning and significance of sharply etched experiences such as wading ashore onto a Normandy beach on 6 June 1944. As yet, few careful studies weaving these various sources into analytical narratives have dealt with the preparation and immersion into combat of American, British, and Canadian soldiers. But such works as Stephen E. Ambrose's *Pegasus Bridge*; his evocative account of E Company, 506th Parachute Infantry Regiment, 101st Airborne, *Band of Brothers*; and Joseph Balkowski's *Beyond the Beachhead: The 29th Division in Normandy* have shown the way.[9]

Recent trends and emerging scholarly perspectives have fashioned this collection, but it must also acknowledge its origins. Although intended to be a coherent narrative that strikes a balance between comprehensiveness and diversity, this collection achieves the former goal by consciously building on those essays in the 1971 collection that are not included in the present work. For example, Roland G. Ruppenthal's detailed portrayal of the logistical buildup before D-day and the supply crisis of August through October 1944 should be viewed as phase two in an overall study of OVERLORD logistics; Kevin Smith's analysis of the policy debate over grand logistics in 1942–43 then becomes phase one of this pivotal if often-ignored story. Similarly, the essays that assess American, British, and Canadian military performance from the launch of OVERLORD to the breakout in late July are to be read in conjunction with Martin Blumenson's skillfully compressed descriptive essay, "Some Reflections on the Immediate Post-Assault Strategy," in the original collection published in 1971.

To grapple with the question of what defines this volume requires a brief explanation of the areas of inquiry and approaches that have been scanted. The thrust of the collection is avowedly Anglo-American (and rather more American than Anglo) on the grounds that the principal issues still attracting the notice of the scholarly community for which this work is intended tend to concern Anglo-American-Canadian relations; the strategic, operational, and tactical choices confronting the Allied forces; and assessment of Allied performance. The German side of this equation is by no means fully explored; consideration was given to including an essay on German military performance to complement Admiral Ruge's semi-autobiographical account of the German navy and Normandy, but the current volume's stress on untapped sources and new perspectives ultimately ruled out its inclusion. Similarly, in a perfect world, an essay treating the relationship between Soviet military operations and the timing and success of OVERLORD would be essential. At present, however, although the history of the Red Army's operations during this period is understood, vital questions with regard to policy in the Kremlin, Soviet assessments of OVERLORD, and long-term logistic and political issues cannot be answered. If and when Soviet records are fully available (potentially a greater watershed for our understanding of World War II than were the ULTRA revelations) and Russian and Western scholars are able to integrate this information with English-language and German sources, an important gap will be closed.

What, therefore, are the goals of this collection? First, the essays in Part One, "The Muster," aim to reconsider long-standing questions from a vantage point sufficiently removed from the fray and with the benefit of a rich palette of evidence. In these pages, the debate over the Second Front, the logistic underpinnings of BOLERO and OVERLORD, and the implications of ULTRA and FORTITUDE for overall interpretations of OVERLORD are considered on the basis of both new sources and the scholarly agenda that has evolved over the past two decades. Part Two, "The Battle," seeks to round out the story of OVERLORD by giving attention to such relatively unexamined topics as the role of special forces (other than airborne and rangers), the unfolding of air and naval operations, the experiences of a Norman population trapped in the maelstrom of battle, and the training and preparation of a small unit deposited on the shores of Normandy. The final part of this collaborative history offers a diverse set of assessments from the perspective of the 1990s about the performance of certain national forces and military leaders arrayed alongside (and sometimes against) each other in Normandy. Finally, it seeks to reach a tentative consensus about the significance of this gigantic military operation and exercise of political will for the outcome of World War II and, thus, for the future of human societies.

Over the past 50 years, innumerable computations of the men and machines available to the adversaries on the eve of their epochal confrontation in June 1944 have made the success of OVERLORD seem inevitable. After all, we know that the awesome buildup of Allied air, sea, and ground forces proceeded without any serious opposition by the Germans throughout 1943 and the spring of 1944. We know that, following a one-day postponement, Ike gave the order to go. We know that an air armada of unimagined size and strength dominated the skies over the English Channel and the invasion beaches. We know that the weather in the Channel approaches cleared sufficiently to permit the naval forces of Operation NEPTUNE to transport the assault troops and their mountains of equipment across the sea barrier to Normandy. We know that the minutely synchronized amphibious operations conformed closely to schedule and that casualties on the beaches were within acceptable limits. We know, too, that Operation FORTITUDE succeeded beyond its inventors' wildest expectations, and that Hitler and the Wehrmacht High Command persisted in viewing the Normandy landings as a diversion until after the beachhead was secure against any feasible German counterattack.

Such introspective certainty, however, is an illusion. The enduring lesson of the essays in this volume is how problematic OVERLORD's predicted outcome was at the time. Given the complexities and uncertainties surrounding the mechanism that Eisenhower set in motion on 5 June, the relative balance of forces, and the dual mysteries of Allied combat performance and rapidity of Axis response, D-day was by no means an inevitable denouement of Allied material superiority. Human beings—individuals and groups—had to subject themselves to that ultimate gamble—battle. For this reason, D-day 1944 remains a subject of enduring fascination.

Editor's Acknowledgments

All books owe debts to an unnameable and, indeed, unknowable throng. This has been an enterprise, however, grounded in the cooperation and enthusiasm of three identifiable groups.

First, deserving far more than these inadequate words of appreciation are the contributors to this volume. I have known most of them through their scholarship and through professional associations for many years, and I count a good many as friends of long standing. I welcomed the opportunity to come to know those I had not previously met as well as the younger contributors to this volume. As a group and as individuals, they showed themselves to be consummate professionals, meeting severe deadlines and accepting my editorial interventions with bemused tolerance and even grace. A scholarly collaboration is in certain respects like an arranged marriage: Both parties enter into the relationship with minimal expectations and sometimes receive unanticipated rewards. The contributors certainly had little on which to judge when they signed on some two years ago to write an essay for a then-unnamed collective history of D-day. I hope that they have found the experience beneficial. From my perspective, the opportunity to work closely with such a talented and cooperative company has been gratifying.

Second, invaluable support came from the staff of the Dwight D. Eisenhower Library. Its director, Dan Holt, played a crucial role in the project's inception, and along the way he performed splendidly as organizer, friendly critic, and hand-holder. The Library's staff contributed in numerous ways, and special thanks are due Gary Holman for drawing the maps under pressure of time and to Kathy Struss, Hazel Stroda, and Robert Paull for their wizardry in reproducing illustrations from the Eisenhower Library's photographic files. A debt of gratitude, too, is owed Deanna Kolling, Michelle Kopfer, and Stacy Meuli for their help with the keyboarding of several essays and the deciphering of my scrawled comments. Thanks, as well, go to Paula Malone and the staff of the College of Liberal Arts and Sciences Word Processing Office at the University of Kansas.

Third, the staff of the University Press of Kansas was unfailingly helpful. The efforts of Mike Briggs, acquisitions editor and a longtime stalwart of the series, Modern War Studies, in crossing all the t's and dotting all the i's to get this book into production deserve special acknowledgment. I also wish to thank Marilyn Holt, who performed splendidly that arcane task of creating the index, and Laura Wilson, who compiled the glossary and gave the entire typescript a final buff and spell-check.

My debt of love and gratitude to Judy Wilson, already beyond redemption, jumped substantially as a result of the tight deadlines and late nights on this project. It rose to dizzying heights when I injected the task of drafting the introduction into a long-deferred British holiday.

Foundation Acknowledgments

Many people were involved in the production of this book. The Executive Committee of the Eisenhower Foundation undertook the project and coordinated the efforts of obtaining the authors and the business arrangements with the University Press of Kansas. The Eisenhower Foundation funded the project with the assistance of those donors listed in the dedication. Ted Wilson, University of Kansas, accepted the often thankless job of serving as general editor. Dan Holt, director of the Eisenhower Library, coordinated the operations among the University Press, the Eisenhower

Foundation, and the Eisenhower Library. Special recognition is given to all the archives staff at the library. Finally, credit is to be given to the University Press of Kansas, Fred Woodward, director, and Michael Briggs, editor, for their foresight in publishing this work.

—Ernest A. Morse, President, The Eisenhower Foundation

Part One

The Muster

1. Wilmot Revisited: Myth and Reality in Anglo-American Strategy for the Second Front

Maurice Matloff

The great assault of 6 June 1944 on the German occupied coast of Normandy represented the supreme effort of the Western Allies in Europe, the culmination of years of planning and preparation designed to liberate the Continent from Nazi domination. Never in the history of coalition warfare had two comrades-in-arms collaborated in a common sustained undertaking more closely and successfully than did the United States and Great Britain in the cross-Channel attack. But behind those landings lay a long history of debate and controversy among the Anglo-American members of the Grand Alliance. These discussions took place in secret councils when the planning staffs met in the capitals and reached into the big international conferences at the summit, a debate that lasted well over two years. Nor did the controversy end with the success of the operation. Scarcely had the fighting on the battlefields of Europe stopped when a great debate broke out in the Western world over the way the war against Germany had been planned, fought, and concluded. Amid the frustration and disillusionment of the Cold War and the growing cleavage between the Soviet Union and its former Western partners in the Grand Alliance, that debate, transferred from secret to public forums, was fed by a flood of books dealing with the controversial issues and decisions of World War II. In the growing body of critical literature that accompanied the search for scapegoats, no work was more provocative and influential than Chester Wilmot's *The Struggle for Europe*, a volume published in 1952, seven years after the surrender of Germany.

Keenly sensitive to the harsh winds of the Cold War that were blowing in the early 1950s, Wilmot, a gifted Australian journalist, looked back on World War II to find out what had gone wrong, to discover "how and why the Western Allies, while gaining military victory, suffered political defeat."[1] In his highly readable, interpretive account of the war in Europe—one of the first attempts at a full-length study of Allied planning and operations and in many ways a brilliant condensation—he stated what were to become almost classic postwar arguments in the criticism of

3

Anglo-American strategy in World War II, focusing on the American conduct of the war in Europe, its conception and execution. Out of his writing emerged a sharp contrast: a naive Roosevelt versus a prescient Churchill, a politically oriented British strategy versus a narrow doctrinaire American military strategy. He viewed "the Second Front controversy . . . not merely in the light of its influence on the defeat of Germany, but also as a political issue the outcome of which was that Anglo-American military power was employed in Western Europe, not in the Balkans."[2] But for American shortsightedness, his portrait suggested, the Western powers would have won the war with a minimum of casualties; would have taken Berlin, Prague, and Vienna ahead of the Russians; and would therefore have found themselves in an advantageous position vis-à-vis the Soviet Union after the conflict. In one way or another, Wilmot's criticisms of American military and political leadership were to find echoes in revisionist writings about World War II on both sides of the Atlantic. His plausible, persuasive account helped shape the stereotypes and images of the American and British approaches to European strategy that became embedded in the postwar literature and that still enjoy considerable popular currency.

My purpose here is to examine the Wilmot thesis in the light of new sources and writings and with the lengthened perspective of the years that have elapsed since the Allies landed in Normandy and Wilmot's work appeared. My focus is on the approach and contributions of the Washington planning staffs and high command to the Allied strategy for the liberation of Europe.[3]

The story begins before Pearl Harbor. Though the United States and Great Britain had become close partners by the time of Pearl Harbor, they had not agreed on a plan to defeat Germany. Indeed, the divergence in British and American concepts of strategic theory emerged early. During the staff meetings at the American-British Conversations (ABC) held in Washington in early 1941, where the future Allies laid the groundwork for the crucial decision to "beat Germany first," the British proposed Italy and the Mediterranean as the proper line of attack on Germany. At the Atlantic Conference in the summer of 1941, the British put forward blockades, bombing, subversive activities, and propaganda as the way to wear down Germany. They stressed mobile, hard-hitting armored forces operating on the edges of German-controlled territory, eventually striking into Germany itself, rather than vast armies of infantry and large-scale frontal ground action. Local resistance would be armed and encouraged to revolt.

When Churchill and his staff advisers came to Washington soon after

Pearl Harbor for the ARCADIA conference, he and President Roosevelt confirmed the "Europe-first" priority, and Churchill elaborated on the British ideas on European strategy. In the Churchillian approach, the emphasis would be on campaigns of speed and maneuverability, on probing soft spots on the periphery of Europe, on a war of opportunity. Although his penchant for the soft underbelly was well known, Norway was also a favorite objective of the prime minister. From the beginning, the British looked upon a cross-Channel operation as the final strike against a weakened Germany. Down to the actual invasion of Normandy, they would continue to hold these two ideas: emphasis on Mediterranean opportunities and a cross-Channel operation as a last blow. The British concept, an amalgam of political, military, and economic factors, reflected the caution bred by huge losses in World War I, the experience at Dunkirk, insular and maritime traditions, widespread imperial interests, a small-scale economy, limited manpower for ground armies, and, last but not least, the prime minister's inclinations. Indeed, that concept appeared more in harmony with their national traditions in war than their traumatic, bloodletting experience in ground warfare in Europe during World War I.

From the beginning, the American ideas developed quite differently. As far back as November 1940, Admiral Harold R. Stark, the Chief of Naval Operations, became convinced that Germany could be defeated only by large-scale ground operations. In the same vein, during the summer of 1941, the army strategic planners concluded that "we must prepare to fight Germany by actually coming to grips with and defeating her ground forces and definitely breaking her will to combat."[4] Here then, even before Pearl Harbor, was the portent of the American theory of a war of mass and concentration, of a decisive war to crush the enemies' forces. In harmony with American traditions, it reflected an optimistic spirit, confidence that the economy could produce the necessary military weapons, and faith in the ability of a large, trained citizen army to achieve offensive purposes.[5]

In 1942, these different approaches to the European conflict were most clearly reflected in the struggle over BOLERO versus TORCH. In the early months after Pearl Harbor, the army's leaders and planners, intent on the Europe-first strategy and a war of concentration, fretted over the scale of deployment to the Pacific. Secretary of War Henry L. Stimson, Chief of Staff Gen. George C. Marshall, and the army planners were disturbed over the threatened dispersion of troops, ships, and supplies to meet immediate crises in the Pacific, Africa, the Middle East, and the Far East. Late in January, Brig. Gen. Dwight D. Eisenhower, then a War Department staff officer whom Marshall had assigned to handle the crisis in the Pacific, worriedly wrote: "We've got to go to Europe and fight—and we've got to quit wasting resources all over the world."[6] Army planners urged that the concentration of U.S. forces in the British Isles for an offensive against Germany should begin. In the middle of March, the Joint Chiefs of Staff (JCS) approved this course of action, which was embodied in BOLERO, the army planners' brainchild.

This plan, as advanced by Marshall, provided for assembling forces for a cross-Channel invasion in the spring of 1943 (called ROUNDUP). With it went a subsidiary plan (called SLEDGEHAMMER) that provided for an emergency small-scale operation on the European continent in the autumn of 1942 in either of two contingencies: the threatened collapse of Germany or the threatened collapse of the Soviet Union. On 1 April, the president accepted the BOLERO plan and sent Marshall and White House intimate Harry Hopkins to London to seek British approval.

Despite misgivings over the proposed emergency cross-Channel operation in the fall, the British approved the American plan "in principle," a phrase that was to cause much trouble in the coalition war. The relief felt by Marshall's staff in Washington was reflected by Eisenhower, then Chief, Operations Division, War Department General Staff, who noted: "at long last, and after months of struggle . . . we are all definitely committed to one concept of fighting! If we can agree on major purposes and objectives, our efforts will begin to fall in line and we won't just be thrashing around in the dark."[7]

To the American staff planners, BOLERO was attractive on a number of counts. To them it offered the soundest strategy for the European conflict: an all-out bombing offensive against Germany's vitals and an attack on the northwest coast of France, using the British Isles as a base. Logistic considerations heavily favored capitalizing on that ready-made and available base. BOLERO represented the shortest route from the United States to the heart of Germany. In the British Isles, the United States could safely land its ground forces without the aid of carrier-based air cover and develop air superiority over the enemy in northern France. The route of attack into Germany via the Low Countries was considered less difficult than any other. The plan would meet the Soviet demand for a second front. It would furnish a definite long-range strategic goal for industrial and manpower mobilization. Above all, it promised decisive action by early 1943 and would fulfill the principle of concentration. For a while, plans went ahead for the second front. On 24 June 1942, Eisenhower arrived in England to assume command in the European theater. American forces began to arrive in considerable numbers.

But the tide soon shifted against SLEDGEHAMMER-ROUNDUP. In June, the prime minister came to Washington and urged a North African operation, as he had at ARCADIA. In July, Roosevelt sent Hopkins, Marshall, and Admiral Ernest J. King to London for further discussions. Out of these negotiations came the decision to launch an attack in North Africa in the autumn of 1942. TORCH thereby replaced BOLERO. The president had overruled the American staff. The Anglo-American agreement over BOLERO had lasted less than three months. Evidently neither Churchill nor Roosevelt had been fully persuaded.

To Marshall and Stimson, the TORCH decision was anathema. To the army's leaders and planners, it meant the adoption of a strategy of encirclement, of periphery-pecking, of what Gen. Thomas Handy of the Operations Division later termed "scatterization." It also meant the inevitable postponement of a definitely scheduled direct thrust against Germany.

In retrospect, the BOLERO plan seems to have been premature. The concept, spontaneously generated by the War Department planners outside the regular Joint Chiefs of Staff–Combined Chiefs of Staff (JCS-CCS) system, miscarried. The British were reluctant, and neither the forces nor the means to cross the Channel were ready. But forces in existence have a way of generating their own strategy, especially when combined with pressure by political leaders for action. There were enough forces and means to undertake TORCH, Churchill and Roosevelt agreed on TORCH, so the Western Allies undertook TORCH.[8]

The landings in North Africa in late 1942 ended the first stage in the Allied search for a strategic plan against Germany. With the Allies still on the defensive, the two approaches to war had had their first conflict, and British opportunism or peripheral strategy had won the first round. New to the art of military diplomacy, the Americans were still thinking in either-or terms—this operation or that one. The one scheme to put Allied planning on an orderly, long-range basis and to achieve the principles of mass and concentration, in which Marshall and the army staff had put their faith, had failed. Fearful of scattering forces and material in what they regarded as secondary ventures, they had yet to find an effective formula.

The decision for TORCH opened a great debate on European strategy between the Americans and the British that endured to the summer of 1944. One Mediterranean operation paved the way for another. The prime minister eloquently urged onward movement: to capture Sicily, land in Italy, secure Rome, go on to the Pisa-Rimini line, then north and northeast. President Roosevelt, himself fascinated by the possibilities in the Mediterranean, seconded these moves, which the American chiefs reluctantly accepted. Marshaling his arguments skillfully, Churchill urged the need for continued momentum and advocated taking advantage of the "great prizes" to be picked up in the Mediterranean and continuing the soften-ing-up process before undertaking the invasion of the Continent across the Channel. The fact that sizable Allied forces were present in the Medi-terranean, providing an immediate opportunity to weaken the enemy, was a telling argument.

At the same time, the Americans, with Marshall as spokesman, gradually made progress toward limiting the Mediterranean advance, directing it to the west rather than the east, linking it directly with a definite major cross-Channel operation (OVERLORD), and winning their way back to the notion of waging a war of mass and concentration on the Continent. Part of their task was to secure agreement from the president, from the British, and eventually from the Soviets. The decisions reached at the 1943 con-ferences—Casablanca in January, Washington (TRIDENT) in May, First Que-bec (QUADRANT) in August, and Cairo-Tehran (SEXTANT-EUREKA) in Novem-ber and December—reflect the compromises of the Americans and British between opportunism and long-range commitments, between a war of attrition and a war of mass and concentration.

Each of these midwar conferences marked a milestone in coalition strategy and in the maturation of American strategic planning. In the course of the debate and negotiation, the planning techniques and meth-ods of the Americans became more like those of their ally, even if their strategic ideas still differed. To meet the British on more equal terms, the American military staff overhauled the joint planning system after Casa-blanca and resolved to reach closer understandings with the president in advance of future meetings. They became more skilled in the art of mili-tary diplomacy, of quid pro quo, or what might be termed the "tactics" of strategic planning. At the same time, their strategic thinking became more sophisticated. They began to think not in terms of this or that operation but in terms of this *and* that, or what one planner fittingly called "permu-tations and combinations." The Casablanca conference, where Marshall made a last vigorous but vain stand for a cross-Channel operation in 1943, represented the last fling for the either-or school of thought among the American staff. Anxious as the U.S. staff was to keep the Mediterranean is-sue under control, Marshall recognized that the Mediterranean offensive could not be stopped completely with North Africa or Sicily and that defi-nite advantages would accrue from knocking out Italy, opening the Medi-terranean further for Allied shipping, and widening the air offensive against Germany.

Beginning with the compromise agreements at the Washington (TRI-DENT) conference in the spring of 1943, the American representatives could point to definite steps toward fixing European strategy in terms of a

Lt. Gen. Sir Frederick Morgan, who, as COSSAC, produced the original Normandy invasion plan.

major cross-Channel undertaking for 1944. At that conference, they gave their assent to the principle of eliminating Italy from the war, which the British urged as the "great prize" after Sicily. At the same time, they won British agreement to the transfer of four American and three British divisions from the Mediterranean to Great Britain. With the British, they approved continuing the Combined Bomber Offensive from Great Britain in four phases to be completed by April 1944 and leading up to an invasion across the Channel. The British agreed that planning for such an operation should start, with the target date of 1 May 1944, on the basis of 29 divisions built up in Great Britain (Operation ROUNDHAMMER, later called OVERLORD).

At QUADRANT, the new pattern of European strategy took clearer shape. There the American chiefs urged a firm commitment to OVERLORD, the plan developed by the British-American planning staff in London (the COSSAC [Chief of Staff to the Supreme Allied Commander designate] planners). The British agreed but refused to give preparations for it the overriding priority over all operations in the Mediterranean area that the Americans desired.

Of all the midwar conferences, Tehran proved to be the most decisive for European strategy. There, for the first time in the war, President Roosevelt, Prime Minister Churchill, and their staffs met with Marshal Stalin, the Soviet leader, and his staff. The prime minister made eloquent appeals for operations in Italy, the Aegean, and the east Mediterranean, even at the expense of a delay in OVERLORD. For reasons of its own, the Soviet Union put its weight behind the American strategy. Confident of its capabilities, the Soviet Union asserted its full power as an equal member of the coalition. Stalin came out strongly in favor of OVERLORD and advocated limiting further operations in the Mediterranean to one directly assisting OVERLORD: an invasion of southern France. In turn, the Soviets promised to launch an all-out offensive on their front to coincide with their allies' moves. Stalin's vigorous stand settled the debate on Western strategy against Germany. The Anglo-American chiefs agreed to launch OVERLORD in May 1944 in conjunction with the southern France operation and to consider these the supreme operations for the year. The final blueprint for Allied victory in Europe had taken shape. Germany was to be crushed by gigantic pincers closing on it from west and east. Roosevelt appointed Eisenhower to command OVERLORD. Preparations for the big cross-Channel attack began in earnest.

The last lingering element in the long, drawn-out debate was not settled until the summer of 1944. In the months following Tehran, the southern France operation came perilously close to being abandoned in favor of the British desire for further exploitation in Italy. Complicating the picture was a shortage of landing craft to execute OVERLORD and the southern France attack simultaneously. But Marshall and the Washington military staff, backed by Roosevelt, remained adamant. The British and the Americans did not reach final agreement on a southern France operation until August, two months after the OVERLORD landings and just a few days before the operation was actually launched, when Churchill reluctantly yielded. In a sense, this concluding phase of the debate represented the last gasp of the peripheral strategy.[9]

Now what of the Wilmot charges, contentions, and conclusions? A number of misconceptions grew up in the postwar period about this Anglo-American debate over strategy, fueled by the sharp distinctions Wilmot drew between the American and British cases. First, it must be emphasized that what was at issue in the midwar debate was not whether there should be a cross-Channel operation. Rather, the question was whether that operation should be a full-bodied drive with a definite target date, as the Americans desired, or a final blow to an enemy critically weakened in a war of opportunity and attrition, as the British desired. It is a mistake to assume that the British did not anticipate a cross-Channel operation from the start. The difference lay essentially in the precise timing and in the extent and direction of preparatory operations. The British insisted on a margin of safety—a margin that attritional operations against the Germans in the Mediterranean would supply—even at the risk of postponing the cross-Channel attack, which they considered a risk worth taking. Once the two sides agreed at Tehran, however, the British stoutly held out for a strong initial assault that would chsum support in the operation. To the Americans, faced with a massive, unparalleled logistic effort at home and abroad and the huge mobilization of men and industry required, precise target dates became more sacrosanct. To them, the cross-Channel attack represented the apex of coalition planning: the concrete embodiment of the Germany-first strategy and the pivot about which their other programs and plans for the global war would fall in logical and orderly place. But to Wilmot and other British critics, this insistence on adhering to precise schedules led to the loss of opportunities in the Mediterranean and a more productive war over the long haul. In other words, both sides agreed on the need for a strong cross-Channel attack. The British believed that planning for it could continue while Mediterranean operations went forward. The Americans insisted that unless a specific date were set and held for the cross-Channel attack and unless Mediterranean operations were limited to those in support of that attack, there was danger that the whole Allied war effort would drag on interminably.

It must be stressed, therefore, that OVERLORD represented a compromise between American and British views, a compromise that evolved out of two years of wartime debate and planning. It was less extensive than the ROUNDUP operation, originally espoused by the War Department in early 1942, and was executed more than a year later than the Americans would have preferred. It was also the end product of a series of preparatory operations in the Mediterranean, and it met the conditions that the British had stressed for success. It is a mistake to assume that the Americans remained opposed to all Mediterranean operations. Here a distinction must be drawn between their planning in the defensive phase of 1941–42, the period of their preoccupation with BOLERO, and in the offensive period, 1943–44. Indeed, much of their planning effort in 1943–44 was spent in reconciling Mediterranean operations with a prospective cross-Channel undertaking.

What of the charge advanced by Wilmot that the Americans were too

GERMAN DEFENSES

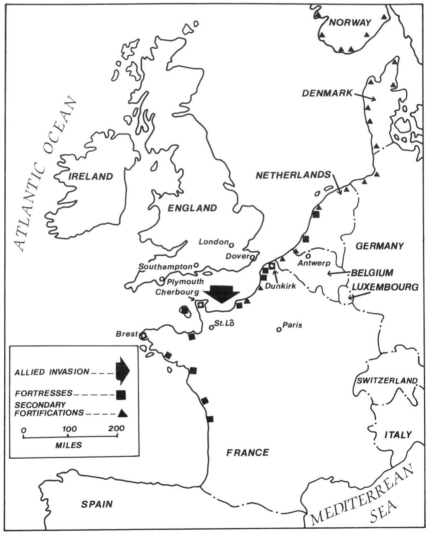

hardware-minded, that they fought a war of organization and material, that they were "militarily unsophisticated and blunt," advocates of the "direct approach and the straight punch"?[10] Wilmot stated: "To Marshall, and indeed to most of America's military leaders, the problem of defeating Germany was one of production, and organization. He thought, as one of Churchill's staff put it, that 'if sufficient driving power were put behind the transportation of American forces across the Atlantic, their momentum would carry them across the Straits of Dover.' It was merely a matter of extending the production-line technique into the field of strategy."[11] To paraphrase Wilmot's view, the Americans had faith that they could fashion, in the camps and factories of America, a gigantic "military steamroller" that they would propel across the Atlantic to crush the hapless Germans at the appointed hour in a massive frontal assault without much thought about the political consequences.[12] "They proceeded on the theory," Wilmot suggested, "that if they made their military machine big enough, they could drive it where they willed."[13] Such views were echoed in Churchill's criticism after the war of the American "logical, large-scale mass production thinking" and J. F. C. Fuller's charge of American "iron-mongering." That the Americans were power minded and sought to take military advantage of their mass-production economy cannot be denied. But the charge of Wilmot and his fellow British critics begs the question whether the Churchillian approach—however suitable to British manpower, economy, and traditions—was suited to American strengths and traditions. If the British improvised from weakness, the Americans organized from strength. This tack was entirely in accord with American experience in large-scale warfare in the Civil War and World War I. It was entirely in harmony with their traditional approach to war and with their capacity to think from the beginning in terms of taking on the main German armies, and the sooner the better. Behind the American staff's fear of attritional and peripheral warfare against Germany in midwar lay their continued anxiety over the ultimate costs in men, money, and time; this anxiety was made all the greater by their growing realization of the ultimate limits of American manpower. It was increased by their concern about getting on with the war against Japan—a war in which they bore the primary responsibility—and about the effects of a long period of maximum mobilization on the home front. All these factors combined to confirm their concept of defeating Germany by means of a direct, concentrated effort.

The question of military sophistication deserves more attention and must be viewed in longer perspective. However doctrinaire Wilmot found the American army's approach to European strategy—an approach he attributed to the singular American experience in the New World, an amalgam of the frontier spirit and a developing machine civilization in isolation from Europe—the Americans entered World War II with a patchwork of military doctrine that was largely European in origin. As in World War I, the Americans began with a strategic framework fashioned out of bits and pieces of European theory and American experience and innovation. Up until World War II, the United States had produced few outstanding military theorists, but the American military shared a common body of strategic thought with Europe. In World War I, Europe provided the basic strategy. The experience in Europe in World War I constituted a significant part of the strategic education of the future American leaders in World War II. Many of the strategic principles gleaned from American deployment in Europe in World War I were reasserted by American leaders in the multitheater context of World War II.

The maturation of American strategic thinking began with World War I and continued in the period between the two world wars. Americans were acquainted with the new theories advanced in Europe by exponents of air power, led by Giulio Douhet, and by such champions of mechanization and motorization as J. F. C. Fuller, B. H. Liddell Hart, and Charles de Gaulle. Reverberations of the European strategic debate were echoed among American theorists. Gradually the offensive overtones in European theory came to be seen as reinforcing the American experience and, in one way or another, the spirit of the offensive became embodied in strategic planning. The army's approach in the interwar period might be termed Clausewitz with refinements. Meanwhile, thinkers in and out of the army air arm advanced a more revolutionary approach to war—the theory of air warfare built around long-range air weapons and strategic bombardment—closely related to that of Billy Mitchell as well as Douhet.

Between 1939 and 1941, American planners sloughed off their earlier preoccupation with academic exercises and began to think realistically in terms of global and coalition warfare. By the time of Pearl Harbor, the services, then virtually three, had begun to reach compromises among themselves and to brush up against British theory. For the first time in its history, the United States entered a war considerably advanced in its strategic thinking on how to fight it.

This maturation did not stop with Pearl Harbor. Once in the coalition war, the army had to learn to adjust to the British notions of operations of opportunity and to deal with the changing patterns of cross-Channel, Mediterranean, and strategic bombing operations. Via the doctrine of concentration, the strategists in the Pentagon and the Kremlin found common ground. Once more, as in World War I, the principles the Americans chose to emphasize—based on the common legacy of strategic thought they shared with Europeans—were entirely in harmony with their own traditions and national policies. Throughout they showed a penchant for quick, direct, and total solutions, trends that had strong precedents in European as well as American warfare. Their planners showed a capacity to grow and to adopt, modify, and incorporate trends in European theory. The staff of planning officers assembled in Marshall's Washington command post, the Operations Division—sometimes called the army's brain trust—was an extraordinary group of men with varied backgrounds, including men of distinguished professional and academic achievement and a number of former Rhodes Scholars. Their flexibility has been vastly underestimated by critics of the American case.[14] The same planners and their chiefs, whom Wilmot accused of a narrow, doctrinaire approach to military strategy in Europe, of overpreoccupation with the hammer blow, could and did support a policy of opportunism in the Pacific not unlike that advocated by the British in the Mediterranean. Indeed, American strategists in World War II came through holding their own with their allies in the councils over European strategy and playing their free hand in the Pacific.

If the contention of lack of military sophistication needs to be examined carefully, so too does the charge that the American staff was completely oblivious to political factors. For example, the prime minister was not alone in his awareness that the defeat of Germany might leave the Soviet Union the dominant power on the European continent. Despite Wilmot's strictures, the U.S. military staff may even have preceded Churchill in this connection, at least as far as the record is concerned. As early as the summer of 1944, the U.S. military staff advised the secretary of state: "While the war with Germany is well advanced towards final conclusion, the defeat of Germany will leave Russia in a position of assured military dominance in eastern Europe and in the Middle East." The planners foresaw that the great historic changes in the international military balance would have important repercussions on the international political situation:

> The successful termination of the war against our present enemies will find a world profoundly changed in respect of relative national military strengths, a change more comparable indeed with that occasioned by the fall of Rome than with any other change occurring during the succeeding fifteen hundred years. This is a fact of fundamental importance in its bearing upon the future international political settlements and all discussions leading thereto. Aside from the elimination of Ger-

many and Japan as military powers, and developments in the relative economic power of principal nations, there are technical and material factors which have contributed greatly to this change. Among these are the development of aviation, the general mechanization of warfare and the marked shift in the munitioning potentials of the great powers.

After the defeat of Japan, the United States and the Soviet Union will be the only military powers of the first magnitude.[15]

In concentrating on the struggle for Europe, Wilmot underestimated the global context of American strategic planning. From the beginning, the Americans had to reckon with the compulsion of the Pacific war. The attack on Pearl Harbor had brought the United States directly into the war, and to many Americans, Japan was the enemy. The margin of safety that the British emphasized in the war against Germany, in the form of Mediterranean operations, the Americans insisted on in the war against Japan, the so-called secondary war. But the limited war refused to stay limited. Despite the Europe-first decision, the war against Japan threatened to catch up with the European conflict. From the beginning, the pressures on Marshall and his staff for resources and manpower for the Pacific were tremendous. The trend toward the Pacific lasted well into 1943. Not until after firm agreement was reached on OVERLORD, and not until well into 1944, did the flow of American troops begin to assume the channels the army planners had originally envisaged for the double war. In order to concentrate forces to meet and defeat the armies of Germany in battle on the Continent, Marshall had sought to put a brake on diversionary deployments in the midwar period. Reversing the trend of 1942 and making the Mediterranean supply a strategic reserve for the cross-Channel undertaking had been part of this aim. Although Wilmot stressed that the Americans were material minded, his work did not take into account the evidence that has accumulated since—that in midwar, they were becoming more and more conscious of the limits of the manpower barrel. To the military, those limits reinforced Marshall's injunction that a democracy cannot fight a Seven Years War.

So much for this brief résumé of Wilmot's thesis and the American strategic case. Now what about Wilmot's picture of the naive Roosevelt versus the prescient Churchill? A few observations are in order here. Wilmot built much of his case for the foresighted Churchill in the European war on the prime minister's early awareness of the Soviet threat. Wilmot had no doubt that in planning the campaign strategy for the Mediterranean in 1943, Churchill had the Soviets at least partly in mind. He stated flatly: "During 1943, although he was still primarily interested in the problem of destroying Hitler's power, Churchill became increasingly concerned about the necessity of restraining Stalin's ambitions. Accordingly, while continuing to put the defeat of Hitler first, the Prime Minister sought to devise a plan of campaign which would not only bring military success, but would ensure that victory did not leave the democratic cause politically weaker in any vital sphere."[16]

Little, if any, evidence supporting this view has come to light. The detailed British official histories of World War II dealing with grand strategy, the products of outstanding British historians, lend no support to the notion that this was actually the case. On the contrary, rather than a coherent politico-military strategy with partly the Soviets and partly the Germans in mind, the British strategy of 1943 appears to have unfolded step by step in accord with the opportunities that arose after TORCH and that Churchill and his military advisers could agree on and persuade the Americans to go along with. Nor is there reason to believe that Churchill was more prescient about the Soviets in 1943 than he had been in 1942. It appears that Churchill went through a number of phases in his prewar and wartime attitudes toward the Soviet Union. During the interwar period, he trumpeted the danger of the Soviet threat loudly and clearly—a note he lowered when the Nazis offered a more direct threat and he wished Roosevelt to join with England and the Soviet Union in the Grand Alliance. In fact, in early 1942, he was willing to enter into a treaty with the Soviets that would have offered them concessions they were seeking, whereas Roosevelt was not. At that time, it was Roosevelt's insistence that such matters be postponed until the end of the war that held the Soviets off. Churchill's anxiety about the Soviets appears to have reawakened late in the war. It is still questionable whether even in 1944 he was fully alert to the threat. Even if we accept the contention that during the debate over the southern France versus Italy and Balkan operations in the summer of 1944 Churchill was looking at Europe with one eye on the retreating Germans and the other on the advancing Soviets, it is still not certain that this was more than a fleeting return to his prewar position.

The contrast in the respective positions of Churchill and Roosevelt on the race to Berlin, on which Wilmot and other writers have focused, also needs a closer look. Much has been made of Churchill's concern over Berlin from the spring of 1945 onward as the Soviet armies advanced on eastern and central Europe, the period when, on the record, he was clearest in his wartime anxiety over the Soviets. Wilmot believed—and many other postwar writers agreed with him—that had the Americans heeded the British, the Western powers would have captured Berlin ahead of the Soviets. Here too, facts that have come to light on the American side since

Wilmot's book appeared need to be examined. We now know that as early as November 1943, when Roosevelt was en route to the Cairo conference, he expressed concern over Berlin during his discussions with the JCS on the zones of occupation in postwar Germany. "The United States," he stated, "should have Berlin." Significantly, Roosevelt added: "There would definitely be a race for Berlin. We may have to put the United States Divisions into Berlin as soon as possible."[17] It is interesting to speculate on what would have happened in postwar Germany had Roosevelt not been diverted from his zonal arrangements by the British. As far as Berlin is concerned, the president, on the record at least, appears to have been prescient earlier than Churchill.[18]

Finally, what about the British strategic case for the war in Europe? Was there a coherent British strategy for the war against Germany, and did it present a better alternative to the American strategy for war and postwar purposes, as Wilmot suggested? To Wilmot, the long British experience with war and with the balance-of-power concept had taught its strategists the value of the indirect approach, which they espoused in World War II. But the question can be raised—as Michael Howard, one of Britain's official historians of grand strategy in World War II, did in his work *The Mediterranean Strategy in the Second World War*—whether there really was a British strategy growing out of their traditions and experience. His work, and the works of the other official British historians writing on grand strategy, suggests that the British strategy in World War II grew essentially in response to changing opportunities and pressures and to compromises among the positions of its leaders. Even Wilmot saw divergences between Churchill and the British chiefs over the Mediterranean. Unlike Churchill, the British chiefs, he pointed out, did not want Balkan or Aegean operations.

For the American historians of grand strategy, this is part of the problem in weighing the British and American cases. There appears to have been not one but a number of British cases for the Mediterranean, depending on whether one looks at the prime minister's position or that of the British chiefs or the Mediterranean commanders. Unfortunately, the official histories—although excellent accounts—do not fully apprise us of disagreements among British planning levels below the Chiefs of Staff. Howard suggested that, however opportunistically the Mediterranean operations were supported by the British in most of 1943 and justified as paving the way for OVERLORD, by the end of that year the Mediterranean strategy appeared to be taking on a direction and rationale of its own. Denying that the British war leaders in 1943 viewed Mediterranean operations "as a way of forestalling the Russians" or that their Mediterranean strategy was based on "prophetic insights," he concluded: "Increasingly they appear to have abandoned their own earlier arguments and to have regarded the Mediterranean theatre, not as subsidiary, but as an end in itself, the success of whose operations was its own justification."[19]

The great fear of the American military planners was that all Mediterranean operations tended to suck in more Allied resources than originally predicted. The so-called soft underbelly of Italy turned out to be a hard-shelled back, and to break it demanded more and more Allied men and means. The great question in their minds was: Were the Allies stretching out the Axis powers to the periphery, as Sir Alan Brooke and the British maintained, or were the Axis powers extending the Allies and diverting them from the main thrust across the Channel? This made the Americans all the more stubbornly persistent in holding the British to the agreed-on strategy.

The controversy that Wilmot's work and Hanson Baldwin's *Great Mistakes of the War* provoked over the question of the Balkans deserves special attention. Wilmot maintained: "The prospect of a Russian advance deep into Central and Southeastern Europe dismayed Churchill, and was one of the main reasons for his unflagging advocacy of those Balkan operations which Roosevelt and the American Chiefs of Staff so persistently vetoed."[20] In popular currency, such writing was sometimes translated to mean that it would have been wiser for the Allies to have invaded the Continent through the Balkans, thereby forestalling Soviet domination of central Europe. But it must be emphasized that the controversy over a Balkan invasion is essentially a postwar debate. No responsible Allied leader proposed a Balkan invasion as an alternative to OVERLORD, and no Allied strategic debate or combined planning took that form. The evidence on this point is clear. In his postwar memoirs, Churchill steadfastly denied that he wanted a Balkan invasion; the evidence offered by him and the British official historians, though not entirely clear on this point, seems to support him. But ambiguities and implications in his position still remain to be explained. The record bears out that he favored raids, help for native populations, and throwing in a few armored divisions and the like for the Balkans. Wilmot interpreted the American staff's unwillingness to agree as inflexibility or blind refusal to recognize the political advantages vis-à-vis the Soviets that would have followed a Balkan operation. Even in British official writing after the war, John Ehrman pointed to the American staff's fear of the "spectre rather than the substance" of the British proposals.[21]

It must be noted that the American staff reaction was only partly anxiety over Churchill's expansive rhetoric. Nowhere in Churchill's wartime or postwar writing, or in Wilmot's popularization, did the leader or the critic face up to the questions that so frightened the American staff: the ultimate costs of an operation in the Balkans, an area of poor terrain and poor communications. Nor did they note that the British were getting weaker, even in 1943, when a Mediterranean strategy was largely being followed. For the Americans, a Balkan operation would be the last intolerable distention of a Mediterranean stretch-out. The thought of being drawn step by step, by design or circumstances, into such an operation was enough to send shivers up the spines of American planners. That they opposed all Mediterranean operations in 1943–44 is a myth. But they were conscious of the fact that the war was wearing on and aware of the high cost of what they regarded as attritional warfare. Moreover, neither the president nor the American staff wanted to get entangled in the thorny politics of the Balkan area. They were determined to stay out. In any event, the Balkan question was never debated by the Allies in frank military or political terms during World War II.

The assumption in the Wilmot thesis that if the Allies had entered the Balkans the Soviets would somehow have been held in check and a more favorable conclusion of the war achieved also needs closer examination. Apart from the question of military feasibility, the conclusion that such a move would have led to a more durable peace is speculative. Had the Western powers entered the Balkans in force to forestall the advancing Soviets, there is no certainty that new embroilments would not have ensued. Certainly American public opinion was not prepared for such a turn of events. It may be argued that in the face of the disarrangement of the European balance of power, the weakening of Great Britain, and the announced American determination to withdraw from Europe soon after the end of the conflict, it would have required far more than the temporary diversion of Allied military power to the Balkans to check the Soviets and ensure a lasting peace in Europe.

In the perspective of the time that has passed since D-day, historians are in a better position to weigh the Wilmot thesis. The contrasts he drew of the American and British strategic cases for the conflict in Europe appear to have been too sharply drawn. The coherent politico-military strategy growing out of long experience in war and diplomacy that he ascribed to the British is simply not borne out by the mounting evidence on the British side. On the American side, he overlooked European precedents in the U.S. staff approach and the common body of strategic doctrine it shared with England, and he seriously underestimated the global texture of American military planning and its own compromises with opportunism. Taking a long view of the British approach, he put the American case in too narrow a framework in context and time. He wrote in a period of grave disillusionment when the West was bracing itself for a possible Soviet ground drive in Europe and seeking to bolster a new alliance, the North Atlantic Treaty Organization (NATO), to restore the balance of power destroyed by World War II. His approach, therefore, led him to look back with a sharp pen to what he regarded as cardinal mistakes in the waging of World War II. He found his scapegoats in the American political and military leaders and the planning staff. Indeed, he concluded his account by flatly saying: "The increasingly heavy international burdens which the American people have accepted since the war . . . have devolved upon them largely as a result of the political and military mistakes of their wartime leaders and especially Roosevelt, Marshall and Eisenhower."[22]

Today, as more evidence accumulates and the perspective lengthens, we are apt to be more charitable about the so-called mistakes made by leaders in the hard-pressed decisions of World War II. Each decision must be put in its proper framework. It is apparent that no single national staff furnished all the answers to Allied strategy; each leavened the other. Each case, British and American, had strengths and weaknesses; each was a product of evolution and internal compromise; each was changed as it met up with its partner's program; and both were molded on the anvil of necessity. This does not mean that one was right and the other wrong. It does mean that the final product was an amalgam of British caution and American directness and perseverance. In strategy, as in politics, there are many ways to skin the proverbial cat. Certainly the Grand Alliance won the war in Europe militarily. It is still a question, and will probably always remain so, whether any alternative course could have produced a faster defeat of Germany and put the West in a fundamentally better position vis-à-vis the Soviet Union. Today we are more conscious of the fact that the balance of power within the Alliance was changing even as the war was being fought; that the cumulative effects of two world wars on Western Europe, combined with favorable geopolitical factors for the Soviet Union and the United States—to which the American staff called attention in the summer of 1944—were leading to the emergence of the United States and the Soviet Union as the superpowers out of the ashes of World War II. It is to the impact of this fundamental change in the power balance rather than to the alleged mistakes of individual Western leaders that historians can most constructively direct their attention. They must ask whether the cards were stacked against the West from the beginning.

Living in a period different from World War II and from that in which Wilmot wrote, we are more conscious of the limits of power, particularly military power, to resolve thorny international questions and ensure last-

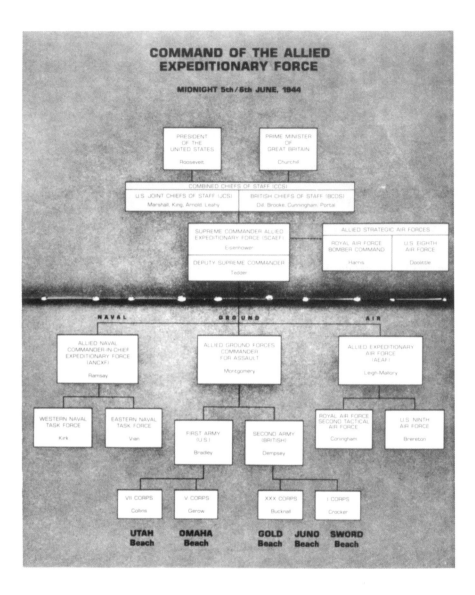

Command of the Allied Expeditionary Force, 5-6 June 1944.

ing peace in tense areas. We are not as sure as Wilmot's generation about the application of force to solve problems, especially between super-powers. The nature of power seems to be changing, and we are under less illusion about the omnipotence of American power. It is even possible that someday a generation weary of war may come to look more favor-ably on what Wilmot viewed as Roosevelt's idealistic but naive proposals to keep the peace. In any event, Wilmot's book must be taken for what it represents—a suggestive, provocative work on the war in Europe written from a British orientation and in a period of disenchantment. As we gain more evidence and perspective on the greatest coalition and the closest partnership the world has yet witnessed in war—really an alliance within an alliance—we have to look behind the popular American and British stereotypes to weigh the similarities and differences and to separate the polemics from the facts. But neither Wilmot's thesis nor the stereotypes that emerged from it should blind us to what Wilmot himself recog-nized—the great common exertion that merged the efforts of the Old and New World to liberate Europe from the Nazi yoke.

2. Biffing: The Saga of the Second Front

Alex Danchev

Characteristically, Winston Churchill took a personal interest in operational codenames. "I have crossed out on the attached paper many unsuitable names," he minuted to long-suffering General Sir Hastings Ismay in August 1943. In the prime minister's judgment, "operations in which large numbers of men may lose their lives ought not to be described by code-words which imply a boastful and over-confident sentiment, such as 'Triumphant,' or, conversely, which are calculated to invest the plan with an air of despondency, such as 'Woebetide,' 'Massacre,' 'Jumble,' 'Trouble,' 'Fidget,' 'Flimsy,' 'Pathetic,' and 'Jaundice.'" Nor should they suggest frivolity. Here he gave as examples "Bunnyhug," "Billingsgate," "Aperitif," and "Ballyhoo." Similarly unacceptable were "ordinary words often used in other connections, such as 'Flood,' 'Smooth,' 'Sudden,' 'Supreme,' 'Fullforce,' and 'Fullspeed,'" and names of living people.

"After all," Churchill observed, "the world is wide, and intelligent thought will readily supply an unlimited number of well-sounding names which do not suggest the character of the operation or disparage it in any way and do not enable some widow or mother to say that her son was killed in an operation called 'Bunnyhug' or 'Ballyhoo.'" What was acceptable to him? "Proper names are good in this field. The heroes of antiquity, figures from Greek and Roman mythology, the constellations and stars, famous racehorses, names of British and American war heroes, could be used, provided they fall within the rules above. There are no doubt many other themes that could be suggested." He urged that all possible precautions be taken when selecting codenames. After all, he intoned, "an efficient and successful administration manifests itself equally in small as in great matters."[1]

It is all the more surprising, then, that the codenames of the Second Front should have slipped through Churchill's fingers. "Our code-words need clarification," he wrote to President Franklin D. Roosevelt in July 1942.

By "Bolero" we British mean the vast arrangements necessary both in 1942 and 1943 for the operation against the Continent. . . . What you have in conversation called "One-Third Bolero" we have hitherto

24

been calling "Sledgehammer." The name "Round-Up" has been given to the 1943 operation. I do not much like this name, as it might be thought over-confident or over-gloomy, but it has come into considerable use. Please let me know whether you have any wishes about this. The "Gymnast" you and I have in view [the Anglo-American invasion and occupation of French North Africa] is, I think, the variant called by your Staffs "Semi-Gymnast." I also use the word "Jupiter" to describe an operation in the Far North [of Norway].[2]

Roosevelt replied with equally characteristic insouciance, proposing

1. That the term "Bolero" be used to designate the preparation for and movement of United States forces into the European theater, preparations for their reception therein, and the production, assembly, transport, reception and storage of equipment and supplies necessary for support of the United States forces in operation against the European continent.

2. That the term "Sledgehammer" be used to designate an offensive operation of the British and American troops against the European continent in 1942, to be carried out in case of German internal collapse, or imminent Russian military collapse which necessitates an emergency attack in order to divert German forces from the Russian front.

3. That the term "Round-Up," or any other name which you may desire, be used to designate an offensive operation against German-dominated Europe, to be carried out by combined American and British forces in 1943 or later.[3]

Such catholicity was clearly a disappointment to Churchill. "I fear that to change the name 'Round-Up' would make the Americans think there was some change of purpose," he minuted. "Therefore we must stick to this boastful, ill-chosen name, and hope it does not bring us bad luck."[4]

ROUNDUP was indeed a curiosity. The codename was foisted on the prime minister, who apparently felt powerless to change it. It was certainly boastful, or at least bombastic; it may possibly have been unlucky; but it was not ill chosen. The name derived originally from a British plan, developed in late 1941, predicated on a prior German collapse.[5] This was an eventuality about which certain members of the British high command remained surprisingly—not to say perversely—sanguine.[6] As conceived in London, the codename described the operation. If all went according to plan, ROUNDUP would be just that. According to this conception, ROUNDUP in 1943 was no more than a later, larger, and presumably more decisive version of SLEDGEHAMMER in 1942. Both operations had an opportunistic cast. In other words, they were contingent on essentially exogenous factors; they depended in the first instance on the exertions of others. If neither Germany nor the Soviet Union collapsed, they would never be mounted. And, one might add, they would never be mourned.

In fact, as we now know, the British always disbelieved in a cross-Channel operation in 1942 and were unalterably opposed to SLEDGEHAMMER. Contemplating the play of the Channel tides, the uncertainties of the weather, and the unresolved problems of beach maintenance from the vantage point of 1943, Churchill struck an unusually sour note in his memoirs: "The fools or knaves who had chalked 'Second Front Now' on our walls for the past two years had not had their minds burdened by such problems. I had long pondered them."[7] In retrospect, the strength of feeling is manifest. What was vouchsafed at the time? In fact, Soviet Foreign Minister Vyacheslav Molotov got a fair redaction of the British position during his visits to London in May and June 1942. Molotov had come to seek assurances about a second front in Europe capable of drawing off at least 40 German divisions from the Eastern Front during the forthcoming German offensive. He sought in vain. Assurances were explicitly withheld. As the prime minister told the War Cabinet, it had been explained to Molotov "that a landing on the Continent this year which was doomed to failure, and resulted in another Dunkirk with considerable slaughter, would do nothing to help the Russians and would, moreover, prejudice the larger-scale operations planned for 1943."[8]

With the Americans, Churchill prevaricated a little longer. Finally and famously, in July 1942 he informed the president that "no responsible British general, admiral or air marshal is prepared to recommend 'Sledgehammer' as a practicable operation in 1942."[9] This blunt pronouncement amounted to an absolute veto. Washington realized that British landing craft and British troops were essential to any operation in Europe for the foreseeable future. At this stage of the war, the Americans were bound by British strategic preferences. SLEDGEHAMMER was laid to rest. Because neither the American Joint Chiefs of Staff (JCS) nor the British Chiefs of Staff (COS) were prepared to countenance JUPITER, GYMNAST held the field almost by default. The following month, Churchill took upon himself the unenviable task of telling Premier Joseph Stalin so in person. His first marathon meeting with "the ogre in his den" was a colossal trial of strength. After much heavy-handed banter and largely negative talk, the prime minister decided that the time had come to divulge the Anglo-American decision. He gave Stalin an outline of the plan. Rather desperately he spoke of the "true" Second Front. He expatiated on the many virtues of the operation. "If we could end the year in possession of North Africa," he argued, "we could threaten the belly of Hitler's Europe." Then, in a spontaneous gesture of mute eloquence, he drew a picture of a crocodile, explaining that "it was our intention to attack the soft belly of the crocodile as we attacked its hard snout."[10] It was an alluring idea. Regrettably, its illustrative possibilities soon outstripped its strategic potential.

Churchillian rhetoric notwithstanding, the hope of a second front in 1942 had been lost. It was always slender. Sledgehammer had posited a maximum of six American and British divisions—the limit of available landing craft at a time when there were some 36 German combat divisions in the west, to say nothing of 178 in the east. In Soviet terms this was as puny as it was precarious, a fact of which Churchill was painfully aware. The British veto was in truth a merciful end. Stalin was bound to be disappointed. The Soviets, however, were in no position to insist, as the ogre himself conceded at the time. Under the circumstances, they showed a remarkable degree of tolerance, or perhaps resignation, when confronted with a stony-faced Anglo-American *non possumus*.

To the Americans, of course, it was a British *non possumus*. The loss of SLEDGEHAMMER was, for some, the cause of deep dismay. General Dwight D. Eisenhower, its putative commander, was heard to lament "the blackest day in history," though he later had a change of heart.[11] His future right hand, Brig. Gen. Walter Bedell Smith, was relieved to see the plan go, "never having felt that it was really on."[12] U.S. Army Chief of Staff George C. Marshall, nominally its principal sponsor, was more ambivalent, propounding SLEDGEHAMMER alternately as a mere possibility and a strict necessity. In reality, he seems to have taken an instrumental view of the operation. When he brought the plan to London in April 1942, the Chief of the Imperial General Staff, General Sir Alan Brooke, was amazed to discover that it "does not go beyond just landing on the far coast. Whether we are to play *baccarat* or *chemin de fer* at Le Touquet . . . is not stipulated."[13] SLEDGEHAMMER was useful to Marshall in two ways: strategically, to orient the Anglo-American war effort toward northwest Europe, and bureaucratically, to counter the strong inertial pull in Washington toward the Pacific (about which he was extremely candid with Brooke). Marshall had an instinctual belief in the overarching strategy of a buildup of forces in England for a decisive cross-Channel attack. As to the duration of the buildup and the timing of the attack, he had reached no definite conclusion. He was not wedded to SLEDGEHAMMER as such.[14]

Roosevelt too was skeptical. Ostensibly, he gave Molotov the assurance that Churchill had refused: "In the course of the conversations full understanding was reached with regard to the urgent task of creating a Second

Front in Europe in 1942." The president had a genius for telling people what they wanted to hear. These words were sufficient to produce a frisson of fear in London, but on close inspection, they fall far short of any concrete commitment, as the artful dodger surely knew.[15]

For many of the key players, therefore, SLEDGEHAMMER was an acceptable loss. Yet an incubus had been created for the future. The suspicion lingered in some quarters that the British position on the Second Front was disingenuous if not downright deceitful. The British, it was said, never intended to carry out SLEDGEHAMMER. What is more, they never intended to cross the Channel. The first of these accusations was true. The second was debatable then and has remained so ever since. The suspicions on which it was based were highly personalized, which is perhaps a sufficient explanation for their remarkable persistence. They focused, and continue to focus, on Brooke and above all on Churchill. Despite the best efforts of the latter, at the time and in his memoirs, they have never been dispelled.[16] In the matter of the Second Front, it seems that "the louder he talked of his honour, the faster we counted our spoons."[17]

Suspicions were aggravated by endemic Anglo-American confusion over ROUNDUP. General Sir John Dill complained in December 1942 that the codename "appears now to have various interpretations ranging from a full-scale frontal attack against [an] unbroken Germany to preparation to take advantage of a sudden crash in German military power."[18] Some of the confusion was incremental. The meaning of codenames tended naturally to blur with time. In this instance, however, there was also something fundamentally at variance. The American conception of ROUNDUP fit the first interpretation suggested by Dill. It was an operation against an unbroken Germany: that was the whole point. As conceived in Washington, the codename did not describe the operation. ROUNDUP was in fact a complete misnomer.

Its successor, OVERLORD, was more apt and reflected the increasing salience of American priorities in the Anglo-American alliance. By all accounts, the codename was selected by Churchill, as one would expect. Can he have been unaware of this association? He was not above making the obvious cracks about DRAGOON, the operation in the south of France to which he was so vehemently opposed.[19] According to the American conception, then, ROUNDUP was profoundly different from SLEDGEHAMMER. This ROUNDUP had a determinist cast.[20] Unlike the British version, it was not a contingent operation, or at least not in the same sense. It was contingent only on Anglo-American agreement (and action) about essentially endogenous factors. Crucially, it depended in the first instance on the exertions of the Anglo-Americans themselves.

Both the Americans and the British conceived of ROUNDUP on a grand scale—grand, that is, by Anglo-American standards—consisting of 48 divisions (usually reckoned as 30 American and 18 British).[21] The assault was still shackled by resource constraints: Of these 48, only five or six could be lifted simultaneously by the available landing craft. The operation was originally touted for April 1943, though May 1943 was almost immediately suggested as a more likely date, and it is clear that as 1942 progressed the British were thinking in terms of what Churchill called a retarded or opportunistic ROUNDUP in August or September 1943. To delay it any further would be to postpone action until the following year, for there was general agreement that the weather prohibited cross-Channel operations during the six months from October to April. Moreover, according to the British COS, the operation would have to be at three months' notice in order to transfer precious landing craft from the Mediterranean to the United Kingdom.[22]

As it transpired, both parties arrived at the comfortable oasis of Casablanca in January 1943 with a proposal to do a ROUNDUP that same year. This may seem surprising. The U.S. Joint Chiefs of Staff had long been of the opinion that a North African operation in 1942 and a cross-Channel operation in 1943 were mutually exclusive; they thought that GYMNAST precluded ROUNDUP. For the Americans, who were determined to cross the Channel in time and in strength, this was intensely frustrating. Their feelings found expression in the July 1942 compromise, designated CCS (Combined Chiefs of Staff) 94, which asserted what Marshall then believed: that "a commitment to this operation [GYMNAST] renders ROUNDUP in all probability impracticable of successful execution in 1943 and therefore that we have definitely accepted a defensive, encircling line of action for the continental European theater, except as to air operations and blockade."[23] Marshall subsequently came to place a less defensive construction on Mediterranean operations. About the consequences for ROUNDUP, however, he had no cause to change his mind, but it was no comfort to be right. The JCS were baffled. They knew they should oppose periphery pecking, but they did not know what they should support. In truth, they had no better idea for 1943 than the one they had already espoused, so they clung to the familiar litany. Their paper for the Casablanca conference recommended what they had previously declared impracticable: "building up as rapidly as possible adequate balanced forces in the United Kingdom in preparation for a land offensive against Germany in 1943."[24]

The British Chiefs of Staff for their part, announced: "We intend to return to the Continent the moment the time is ripe."[25] This was evidently meant to be reassuring. The announcement was more than just a form of words. The concept of time as "ripening" remains deeply embedded in British political culture. F. M. Cornford's comparison of propensity to action with fruit-bearing trees is apt: "Time, by the way, is like the medlar; it has a trick of going rotten before it is ripe."[26] The skill lies in judging the moment. For the COS, the time would be ripe for ROUNDUP when there was "a definite crack in German morale," and not before.[27] On this they were adamant, in spite of Churchill's ceaseless pricking. In fact, the British COS rejected a cross-Channel operation in 1943 as firmly as they had in 1942. At Casablanca they recommended a retarded and opportunistic ROUNDUP at the end of an ambitious program of operations in the Mediterranean—ROUNDUP as residuary legatee.[28] Before the conference, in great secrecy, Brooke laid out their position for his friend and confessor Dill.

Bidden by the prime minister to reexamine once more the feasibility of a determinist ROUNDUP in August 1943, the COS calculated that the maximum force that could be assembled was thirteen British and fourteen American divisions (two of which would have no rear services). To produce these would mean that the capture of Sardinia and Sicily would have to be abandoned, convoys of aid to the Soviet Union canceled, the invasion of Burma postponed, offensive operations in the eastern Mediterranean shelved, and plans for an increased bombing offensive scaled down. The exploitation of TORCH, on the other hand, would allow all these things to come to pass. Brooke and his colleagues therefore concluded that the correct priorities for 1943 were as follows:

(a) To exploit "Torch" to the limit in order to:
  (i) Knock out Italy.
  (ii) Bring Turkey into the war.
  (iii) Give the Axis no rest.
(b) The increased bombing of Germany.
(c) The building up of "Bolero" on the greatest scale that the above operations admit so that *if the occasion arises* we may re-enter the Continent with up to 20 divisions in August or September 1943.

In order to make quite sure that his colleagues grasped the point, he ended: "I am convinced that a 'Round-up' on the scale envisaged by the Prime Minister is impracticable in 1943."[29] Brooke was by nature categorical. Reflecting after the war on his overheated diary entries for December 1942, he penned some characteristic guidance for historian Arthur Bryant:

I was quite clear in my own mind that the moment for the opening of a Western Front had not yet come and would not present itself during 1943. I felt that we must stick to my original policy for the conduct of the war, from which I had never departed, namely, to begin the conquest of North Africa, so as to reopen the Mediterranean, restore a million tons of shipping by avoiding the Cape route; then eliminate Italy, bring in Turkey, threaten southern Europe, and then liberate France. This plan, of course, depended on Russia holding on. Although in the early stages of the war I had the most serious doubts whether she would do so, by the end of 1942 I did not think such an eventuality [a Soviet collapse] likely.[30]

By a strange process of aggregation, therefore, the CCS found themselves in agreement: The time for ROUNDUP was not yet ripe. That conclusion, implicit in the proceedings at Casablanca, was made explicit in the proceedings of the subsequent Washington conference, which set a target date for the cross-Channel operation of 1 May 1944.[31] Plainly, there would be no Second Front in 1943. ROUNDUP had been rolled over. Did it deserve better?

Siren voices, mostly though not exclusively American, continue to answer yes. A full-blown case for 1943 has been made in at least two books, coincidentally published in the same year, and echoed in several others.[32] The main arguments have been recapitulated briefly by Russell F. Weigley:

A cross-Channel invasion a year earlier than the actual "Overlord" invasion could have brought substantial military and political dividends. Fighting earlier in northwest Europe rather than in the Mediterranean area would have permitted the earlier deployment of American divisions already largely formed and trained in 1942. It would have placed the Allies earlier in terrain where, unlike mountainous Italy, they could invoke their strong suit of superior mobility. Politically, an earlier Second Front could have both diminished Soviet suspicions of the West and placed the Western powers in a stronger bargaining position *vis-à-vis* the Soviets in the postwar world.[33]

Sirens are always tempting. This particular temptation should be resisted, however, in the interest of language, logic, and electoral politics. Concern for linguistic precision led Churchill at the time to point out that "our object is the liberation of Europe from German tyranny, that we 'enter' the oppressed countries rather than 'invade' them and that the word 'invasion' must be reserved for the time when we cross the German frontier. There is no need for us to make a present to Hitler of the idea that he is the defender of a Europe we are seeking to invade."[34] On grounds of logic, the dividends adduced by Weigley are *potential* dividends. They posit a successful operation, but the success of a cross-Channel operation in 1943 was by no means assured. In August 1943 there were 44 German combat divisions in the west, and Germany's output of fighter aircraft was still rising.[35] In numerical terms alone, the Anglo-American forces would have been inadequate to the task, even if there had been sufficient assault shipping to lift them, or merchant shipping to supply them, or aircraft to cover them, which is doubtful. Then there was the operational difficulty of staging a full-scale, opposed, assault landing with unblooded troops—and achieving a breakout—against a formidable and as yet undepleted enemy. Without the TORCH landings and the ensuing North African campaign, the encounter in Normandy would have taken on quite a different character, as Eisenhower himself later acknowledged. The British Eighth Army was made by fighting its way from Alamein to Mareth. American troops were entirely without combat experience in 1942. The salutary battle of Kasserine taught lessons that were learned with startling rapidity, but Kasserine did not transpire until February 1943. North Africa was finally cleared only in May 1943. Mobility may have been an Anglo-American strong suit, but pursuit and exploitation were not.

Finally, if the assumption behind a 1943 cross-Channel operation was a standstill in 1942, it put London and Washington in the politically insupportable position of doing nothing of consequence for more than a year while their major ally was continuously engaged in a merciless battle of attrition of epic scale, uncertain outcome, and unimaginable cost. A Second Front presupposed a First Front. Strategic bombing was neither an acceptable nor an effectual expedient. Hoarding for 1943 was a political impossibility. The imperative to do *something* in 1942 was too great —something conspicuous, something graspable, and something that could be represented to Stalin and to Anglo-American electorates as worthwhile. It was to be expected that Churchill and Roosevelt saw this more clearly than their respective Chiefs of Staff. Hence TORCH. Democracies cannot fight a Seven Years War, as Marshall said, nor can they bide their time before engaging the enemy.[36]

ROUNDUP was dead: Long live OVERLORD! Chief of Staff to the Supreme Allied Commander designate (COSSAC) was appointed in April 1943 and instructed to submit an outline plan by August.[37] The operation was to call on available landing craft and involve nine divisions in the assault phase and a further twenty to be moved into the lodgment area. Working toward these requirements, COSSAC proposed a landing in the Caen sector of

Normandy, followed by the early capture and development of airfield sites and the port of Cherbourg. The initial landings would be a three-divisional assault to seize a front of some 30 miles. Concurrently, one airborne division would be dropped on Caen to seize the city.

Here then, was a plan. Unfortunately, it was a flawed one—in Field Marshal Montgomery's magisterial verdict, an unsound operation of war.[38] The three-divisional assault was too small and too thinly spread. To fight from Caen to Cherbourg was to concede to the enemy a natural defensive barrier in the marshes and rivers at the neck at the Cotentin peninsula. The early capture of a port was essential in order to avoid total dependence on artificial harbors. In this plan, such a capture might come too late to prevent logistic debility. Montgomery himself was installed in London as Allied Land Force Commander in January 1944. He came, he saw, and he envisaged a five-divisional assault under the control of two armies, one American and one British, each with responsibility for a front of two corps.[39] The area from Bayeux westward would be American; the area from Bayeux eastward would be British. It was hoped eventually to establish a firm lodgment from Caen to Nantes. The Americans would capture Cherbourg, clear the peninsula, and push on to the Loire and Brest. The British would deal with the main enemy forces, reinforcing Normandy from the east and southeast. The essential strategy was to capture the main centers of road communication (above all Caen) and then, as he wrote to Brooke, "The possibilities are immense: with 700 tanks loosed to the southeast of Caen and armoured cars operating far ahead anything may happen."

Thus the outline plan was cast aside, except for its most interesting feature. COSSAC had boldly insisted that certain conditions be met if the operation was to have a reasonable chance of success. The prime minister extracted three:

1. There must be a substantial reduction in the strength of the German fighter aircraft in northwest Europe before the assault took place.
2. There should be no more than twelve mobile German divisions in northern France when the operation was launched, and it must not be possible for the Germans to build up more than fifteen divisions in the succeeding two months.
3. The problem of beach maintenance of large forces in the tidal waters of the English Channel over a prolonged period must be overcome.[40]

These conditions were reiterated time and again over the next few months to the Americans and to the Soviets. The second condition was elaborated in extraordinary detail. COSSAC prescribed that on the target date, the reserve divisions should be located so that the number the Germans could deploy in the Caen area would not exceed three on D-day, five by D plus 2, or nine by D plus 9. One of the three divisions on D-day could be armored; two more by D plus 2 might be armored or otherwise. Such precise specifications had a dual significance. Since there was never any doubt that the Allies knew whether the conditions were being met, this indicated a truly phenomenal intelligence capability. Less happily, the specifications served to reinforce the view in Washington and Moscow that the wily British were girding themselves to recommend cancellation or postponement of the operation if, for example, the number of German divisions exceeded carefully specified totals.[41]

At the Tehran conference in November 1943, when Churchill reminded him of the three conditions on which the success of OVERLORD depended, Stalin asked what would happen if there were thirteen or fourteen mobile German divisions in France and more than fifteen available from other fronts. Would this rule it out? "Certainly not," said Churchill. Later, as the discussion drew to a close, Stalin caught Churchill's eye across the table and said, "I wish to pose a very direct question to the Prime Minister about 'Overlord.' Do the Prime Minister and the British Staff really believe in 'Overlord'?"

Stalin's question goes to the heart of the matter. It was brutal; but it is also tantalizing, for it is not a question susceptible to definitive answer. In this respect, the saga of the Second Front is a continuing one. As Richard Leighton wrote, "the historian's position is likely to depend largely on where he decides to place the burden of proof—on the Americans, to demonstrate that their suspicions were based on fact, or on the British to show that their professions were sincere."[42] In this historian's view, the burden of proof properly lies with the British. At Tehran, Churchill made a brave reply. "Provided the conditions previously stated for 'Overlord' are established when the time comes, it will be our stern duty to hurl across the Channel against the Germans every sinew of our strength."[43]

How should we interpret what he said and did? Churchill said so much, so sweetly, that it is hard to be sure. The grounds for his presumed hostility to OVERLORD are now well-established.[44] The first was what he called "the hecatombs of World War I" or, more luridly, "the Channel tides running red with Allied blood"—what the unsentimental COSSAC referred to as "the butcher's bill."[45] John Keegan noted wisely that the Churchill of the Second World War was a far more cautious strategist than the Churchill of the First:

Prime Minister Winston S. Churchill in a typically pugnacious pose.

He had lost his belief in Gallipolis and urged prudence on the Americans throughout the discussions of a Second Front, not wholly because of his interest in 'the Mediterranean strategy.' The First World War had killed his youthful belief that war was an adventure—though not that there could be adventure in war—and he knew all too bitterly that great wars kill great numbers, waste the wealth of nations, and despoil the face of the earth. He hoped to win the Second World War at the least possible cost to Britain and her allies.[46]

The second reason dwelt on more recent experience. It was not only the searing memory of the Somme and Passchendaele that preyed on Churchill's mind in 1942–44. So did the soul-destroying passage from Narvik to Dunkirk to the Western Desert—Elizabeth Bowen's lightless middle of the tunnel: "Reverses, losses, deadlocks now almost unnoticed bred one another; every day the news hammered one more nail into a consciousness which no longer resounded. Everywhere hung the heaviness of the even worse you could not be told and could not desire to hear."[47] When Roosevelt heard that Montgomery was going to attack the Germans at Alamein in October 1942, Marshall remembered, "he said stop it: the British always get licked."[48] Not until Montgomery had won that battle and with it his name did it become possible, hesitantly, to counter such well-founded skepticism. Bowen recaptured the moment of exhilaration:

> "Montgomery's through!"
> "Montgomery?"
> "A terrible victory!"
> Sun blinded her from above the roof of the house as she stumbled up the slope, pulling at grass tufts, stopping to shade her eyes. She panted: "A victory in a day?"
> "It's the war turning."
> "How did you hear?"
> "It's all through the country. Come up with you ma'am."
> Donovan reached out to her; their handclasp settled into a grip then a pull upward from him. He had got her alongside him on the coping the better to transfix her with impatient prophetic eyes. "I would give much," he said, "to have a hat to bare my head with: the day's famous."[49]

But the dread feeling of inferiority was not so easily expunged. "I do not believe that 27 Anglo-American divisions are sufficient for 'Overlord,' " Churchill minuted to the COS in July 1943, "in view of the extraordinary fighting efficiency of the German Army, and the much larger forces they could so readily bring to bear against our troops even if the landings were successfully accomplished." He continued: "It is right for many reasons to make every preparation with the utmost sincerity and vigour, but if later on it is realized by all concerned that the operation is beyond our strength in May and will have to be postponed until August 1944, then it is essential that we should have this other considerable operation up our sleeves. We cannot allow our Metropolitan forces to remain inert."[50]

Air Marshal Sir Charles Portal thought that "Churchill was always dying to do the Northern France show but he was afraid—no, he was never afraid—he hated to do it. . . . You must remember that our army had met the Germans at their height, and after they had been pushed around, they began to feel in their heart that they weren't the equals of the Germans."[51]

The third ground for Churchill's disbelief in OVERLORD was the chauvinist strain in his strategic thinking, a strain that grew more virulent as the war progressed and the small British lion was squeezed uncomfortably between a great Russian bear on one side and a great American elephant on the other.[52] At Tehran, the prime minister protested with some asperity that "he could not in any circumstances agree to sacrifice the activities of the armies in the Mediterranean, which included 20 British and British-controlled divisions, merely in order to keep the exact date of May 1 for 'Overlord.' " He was ignored.[53] The correlation of forces was such that Churchill could still secure concessions—in this instance, a postponement of one month—but he could no longer sway campaigns. Fine phrases were no substitute for armored divisions. "Watch the balance of power between us and the British," Marshall cautioned his biographer shrewdly.[54] No one watched more closely than Churchill. Reflecting on the preponderance of American divisions in the allocations for OVERLORD, he minuted: "Now, it seems to me a great pity that we cannot make our quota equal or, if possible, one better. So much depends upon the interpretation given to the word 'division.' I should like to be able to tell them: 'We will match you man for man and gun for gun on the battlefront,' and also that we have made extra exertions for this. In this way we shall maintain our right to be effectively consulted in operations which are of such capital consequence." What he wanted for the twenty British and British-controlled divisions in the Mediterranean (on another occasion, "the most representative Army of the British Empire now in the field") was simply a blaze of British glory. He wrote to his beloved Clementine: "The only times I ever quarrel with the Americans are when they fail to give us a fair share of opportunity to win glory." The letter continued: "Undoubt-edly I feel much pain when I see our armies so much smaller than theirs. It has always been my wish to keep equal, but how can you do that against so mighty a nation and a population nearly three times your own?"[55]

The fourth ground for opposition was temperamental. It was Chur-chill's strategic thirst or, more prosaically, his incurable impatience. Gen-eral Sir Ian Jacob later observed:

> He was a man who required to push away at some concrete project, not a cold, aloof strategist. He had studied battles, and by instinct tended to think of life as a series of conflicts with barriers to be overcome, oppo-sition to be borne down. He hated those periods which are inevitable in a war when operations have come to a conclusion, and there must be a pause for planning and preparation, for regrouping and reorganization. His mind chafed, and he turned always to any project however minor, or however irrelevant to the main theme, in the hope that it would fill the gap. His frequent efforts to get the Chiefs of Staff and the planning staffs to work out an operation in Norway [JUPITER] sprang not so much from a desire to free that country or to close German access to the oceans, but from his wish to have something happen before the next major operation was due to start. One of his favourite phrases was that the enemy must be made "to bleed and burn," everywhere and all the time.[56]

Churchill's thirst for action neatly matched his chauvinism. About this he was quite candid: "We had a preponderance of troops over the Ameri-cans in the Mediterranean. There were two or three times more British troops than American there. That was why I was anxious that the armies in the Mediterranean should not be hamstrung if it could be avoided. *I wanted to use them all the time*."[57] Churchill was miscast in the role of im-perial Machiavelli. Temperamentally, he was, as Marshall said, "a plunger." His true vocation was to play Ben Ritchie-Hook. As Evelyn Waugh ex-plained:

> Tactics according to Brigadier Ritchie-Hook consisted of the art of biff-ing. Defence was studied cursorily and only as the period of reorganiza-tion between two bloody assaults. The Withdrawal was never men-tioned. The Attack and the Element of Surprise were all. Long raw misty days were passed in the surrounding country with maps and bin-

oculars. Sometimes they stood on the beach and biffed imaginary defenders into the hills; sometimes they biffed imaginary invaders from the hills into the sea. They invested downland hamlets and savagely biffed imaginary hostile inhabitants. Sometimes they merely collided with imaginary rivals for the use of the main road and biffed them out of the way.[58]

Taken together, this may all be considered an impressive case for disbelief. Was Churchill only miming obeisance to OVERLORD? It appears not. In the first place, as he himself remarked, British loyalty to OVERLORD was the keystone of the arch of Anglo-American cooperation. And Anglo-American cooperation was, for Churchill, the sine qua non.[59] Five days after D-day, the British Joint Staff Mission (JSM) in Washington warned the COS that OVERLORD was "the last chance we shall have to put across to the American public the magnitude of the British military effort. We must make the most of this since Anglo-American relations in the future will so largely depend on American appreciation of the blood, sweat and tears which Great Britain and the Dominions have shed." It has been well observed that "in the Anglo-American relationship British policy has to pass the test: can the British deliver?"[60]

For all his incorrigible urge to go biffing, Churchill had a grander scheme, conceived in December 1941, that—in spite of the gnawing doubts and dispersionist demons—he consistently pursued down the years. Over a prodigious five-day period on board the HMS *Duke of York*, bound for Washington in the wake of Pearl Harbor, Churchill dictated a four-part conspectus of "the war policy of 1942 and 1943" as he hoped and expected it would develop in every theater. In order of composition, part one dealt with what he called the Atlantic Front, part two with the Pacific Front, part three with 1943, part four with the Pacific once more.[61] Taken together, these papers constitute one of the seminal strategic documents of the war. Addressed to the COS but composed for the president, for himself, and perhaps subconsciously for posterity, they were a purposive blend of rally and entreaty, program, and prophecy.

The most germane section, on 1943, looked forward to a situation in which Turkey, "though not necessarily at war, would be definitely incorporated in the American-British-Russian front," and "the Russian position would be strongly established." In this situation, "it might be that a footing would already have been established in Sicily and Italy, with reactions inside Italy which might be highly favourable." Churchill then considered the necessities of the case. "All this would fall short of bringing the war to an end. The war cannot be ended by driving Japan back to her own bounds and defeating her overseas forces. The war can only be ended through the defeat in Europe of the German Armies." This formulation irresistibly recalled Douglas Haig's often-quoted pronouncement on an earlier war: "We cannot hope to win until we have defeated the German Army."[62]

In 1941, Churchill clung to the vestiges of an alternative road to victory: internal collapse in Germany "produced by the unfavourable course of the war, economic privations, and the Allied bombing offensive." It may be that the British high command never completely lost hope of that outcome, but Churchill himself was not disposed to rely on it. The consequences were spelled out in his paper. "We have, therefore, to prepare for the liberation of the captive countries of Western and Southern Europe by the landing at suitable points, successively or simultaneously, of British and American armies strong enough to enable the conquered populations to revolt." He admitted: "By themselves they will never be able to revolt owing to the ruthless counter-measures that will be employed: but if adequate and suitably equipped forces were landed in several of the following countries, namely, Norway, Denmark, Holland, Belgium, the French Channel coasts and the French Atlantic coasts, as well as Italy and possibly the Balkans, the German garrisons would prove insufficient to cope with both the strength of the liberating forces and the fury of the revolting peoples." More specifically, Churchill envisaged an Anglo-American "liberating offensive" of some 40 divisions, "of which Great Britain would try to produce nearly half," during the summer of 1943.[63]

Some of this did not survive professional scrutiny. On the fanciful suggestion of biffing the Germans everywhere simultaneously, Churchill was forced to yield. Unbeknownst to the Americans, however, on the fundamental conception he and the COS parted company.[64] Churchill's liberating offensive was contingent on essentially endogenous factors—command of the sea and air superiority—both of which were nothing more than pipe dreams at the time he was writing. Contrary to the expressed preferences of the COS, his envisioned assault was not contingent on a prior German collapse. Certainly Churchill wanted first to bomb, blockade, and subvert. "Thus the halter will tighten upon the guilty doomed."[65] He may never have subscribed to "an American-style, all-or-nothing" Second Front.[66] His OVERLORD was no tyrant, but his scheme encompassed much more than mere opportunism. For Churchill, the Second Front was movable but determinate. He knew that OVERLORD was the greatest amphibious biffing ever attempted. Posterity beckoned. He hated to do it, but the impulse to biff on such a grand scale would not be denied. "It may well be that an effort by us and the Americans prepared for 1943 would not in fact come off until 1944, but if we do not begin making plans now it will never come off."[67] The words could have been spoken by the Supreme Allied Commander himself.

3. Constraining OVERLORD: Civilian Logistics, TORCH, and the Second Front

Kevin Smith

Securing and exploiting a D-day lodgment required effective, long-term logistic planning: appraisals that were accurate, hopeful, and prudent of what was needed, who needed it, and when and how it would arrive. Inflated or unwisely attenuated estimates of procurement, transportation, and distribution needs could divert resources, crippling campaigns in Europe or elsewhere. This "art of defining and extending the possible," the essence of logistics, shaped the Second Front strategy that emerged in 1942–44. The argument offered here is that the decision for TORCH narrowed the options available to civilian as well as military logisticians; the Allies' inordinate focus on military requirements mandated several actions that constrained OVERLORD's development. Logistically premature military adventures in the autumn of 1942 diverted shipping and supplies from cross-Channel preparations to the Mediterranean and South Pacific throughout 1943 and 1944. Concurrent neglect of civilian logistic needs (British imports) delayed procurement of vital landing craft, aggravated Allied strategic disagreement, and risked the economic stability of OVERLORD's operational base. Though U.S. industrial capacity eventually proved sufficient to underwrite the Allies' initially excessive global ambitions, OVERLORD's strategic and logistic context had been transformed.[1]

The D-day assault offered tough logistic challenges: immense amphibious landings and subsequent coordination of resupply and reinforcement. U.S. Army official histories clarified OVERLORD's context by detailing the strategic and tactical impact of theater logistics on assault and follow-up operations. Dislike of sending U.S. troopships on dangerous voyages around Britain's east coast as well as limited British port and internal transport capacity dictated deployment of U.S. troops in southwestern and western England. These same factors apportioned French landing beaches and German occupation zones. Supply needs impelled the choice of suitable invasion beaches and the initial axis of operations west toward Cherbourg. Emphasis upon a secure lodgment for an administrative base and the assumption that enemy resistance and logistic problems foreordained slow progress after breakout undergirded the Eisenhower-Montgomery broad front–narrow thrust dispute.[2]

Yet politics had already imposed prior constraints on global logistics—and therefore on local logistics as well. Planning for the cross-Channel logistic dimension of OVERLORD was molded by the diplomatic agreements, domestic political conditions, and strategic goals that inspired the Anglo-American promise of a second front and was configured by the bureaucratic activity and civil-military rivalries that shaped its execution. Strategic quarrels crossed departmental, national, and service lines, magnified by Roosevelt's and Churchill's accent on politics and ignorance of logistics. Difficulties in gauging actual needs and evaluating perceived needs were amplified by the esoteric nature of global logistic calculations, by inevitable exaggeration, and by failures in the American chain of command. Civil-military conflict raged over authority for ship loading and allocation. Conflicting Allied and civil-military logistic priorities threatened alliance cohesion. In particular, political and bureaucratic tangles called into question the chief element in OVERLORD's success or failure—providing needed merchant ships to transport troops and supplies.[3]

How did such conflicts shape Allied efforts to mount OVERLORD? Prior scholarship spotlighted military logistics; Richard Leighton and Robert Coakley thoroughly scrutinized the link between military logistics and U.S. strategy in the classic work, *Global Logistics and Strategy*. Neither their global view nor Roland Ruppenthal's theater-based perspective explored the overall impact of civilian logistics on grand strategy. The official historians do refer to civilian supply needs; Leighton published a seminal article on Roosevelt's resolution of Britain's import crisis. But they lacked access to British archives; their work was grounded in U.S. official records and fulfilled a restricted "official" mission. Incorporating all the elements that influence grand strategy by stressing the relative importance of civilian logistic needs to "grand logistics" provides a startlingly different view of the extended battle over the Second Front's timing, location, and characteristics.[4]

The outlook of these historians is consistent with that of the wartime U.S. Army. While estimating means available for achieving desired ends in Europe and the Pacific, officers and civilians reluctantly recognized that military logistic demands constrained action. General George Marshall, U.S. Army Chief of Staff, noted: "Time and space factors dictated our strategy to a considerable degree. To land and maintain American forces in Australia required more than twice the ship tonnage for similar American forces in Europe or North Africa." Providing lend-lease to the USSR also drained Allied resources. In striving to fight beyond their logistic ca-

GLOBAL SHIPPING ROUTES

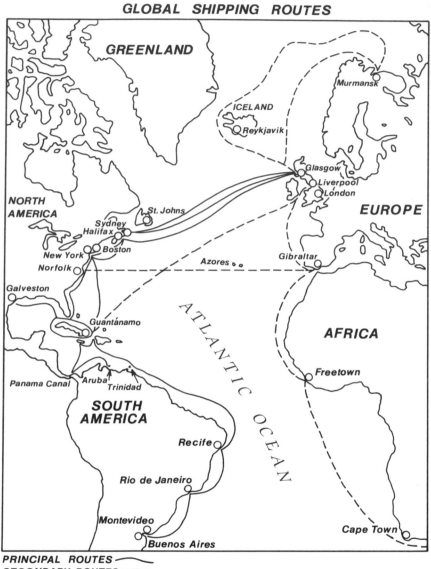

PRINCIPAL ROUTES ⟶
SECONDARY ROUTES --- ⟍

pabilities, the Anglo-Americans only talked about sustaining British imports. General Dwight Eisenhower (soon commander in the European Theater of Operations) recognized British vulnerability to interdiction of their sea communications, but Marshall and influential Generals Brehon B. Somervell (Commanding General, Army Service Forces [ASF]) and C. P. Gross (Chief of Transportation) habitually ignored actual shipping allocations to British civilian logistic needs while they advocated cross-Channel action. This response paralleled army attitudes toward premature calls for reconversion to U.S. civilian production.[5]

London's belated efforts to resist this myopic subordination of British civilian needs to military priorities were handicapped by daily consent to a utopian cross-Channel scheme as well as by its subsequent cancellation in favor of the Mediterranean, a Pyrrhic British victory. Bolstering imports with U.S. shipping also fortified Army distrust of Britons and civilians. Skeptical about any idea that detracted from winning the war, U.S. officers perceived British oscillations as shrewd, crafty, or both.[6] In the absence of the logistic means to fulfill strategic ends, Army planners redefined means and restructured ends at civilian expense.

From its entry into the war, the United States dominated production of the primary determinant of grand logistics: merchant ships. Anglo-American civil-military and bureaucratic struggles over perceiving needs, defining strategy, and controlling distribution converged at this nexus. Amphibious operations relied on ships to move troops and supplies; their availability ruled logistic planning, controlled the arrival of material, and influenced procurement decisions, for it was pointless to order or manufacture what could not be delivered. This scarcity menaced the overextended British Empire's war economy and hampered its offensive planning; it thus relied on U.S. shipbuilders and bureaucrats. Although they acknowledged the abstract dictum that military and civilian needs could not be segregated, U.S. Army planners, who insisted that the crude yardstick of industrial production define military plans, felt no duty to comprehend Britain's import crisis. The origins of this crisis and the ensuing battle for ships are a superb conduit for observing the Allied encounter with the logistic realities of modern war.[7]

Once the German victories of 1939–40 had stripped away allies and illusions, the British began to realize that they had not retained sufficient merchant shipping capacity to wage total war. Britain's shipbuilding industry had not recovered from its 1930s collapse. Italian belligerency closed the Mediterranean to Allied shipping, quadrupling the Middle Eastern front's logistic burden. Wartime circumstances also cut capacity; military needs, convoy delays, extended repairs, port congestion, and North

Atlantic weather aggravated Britain's predicament.[8] Merchant shipping management had been centralized under the control of what became the Ministry of War Transport (MWT), but it could not devise measures to close the gap between capabilities and commitments. British imports of food and raw materials plunged from a peacetime average of 55 million tons a year to 31 million tons in 1941, and military operations demanded more ships. Defeating the U-boats could only mitigate this decline; Britain had to have more American merchant shipping. Stopgap American aid in the spring of 1941 met Britain's immediate needs, but ironically, U.S. belligerency threatened cooperation. Military appetite for control over shipping allocations hampered efforts by U.S. civilian officials in the War Shipping Administration (WSA) to satisfy continuing British appeals for aid.[9]

Britain's merchant fleet absorbed the extraordinary demands imposed by the Far Eastern war, North Cape convoys, and reinforcement of the Eighth Army in Egypt without added U.S. help throughout 1942. But Britain's reserves of vital commodities were dwindling rapidly; experts estimated that imports of vital raw materials and food for the eighteen months ending June 1943 would fall 20 percent below consumption. At any time, British shipping might be unable to meet military needs without cutting imports below minimum levels for essential civilian goods and war production. Churchill's cabinet hesitated to curb British military requests; new U.S. merchant shipbuilding was absorbed by escalating U.S. military demands and could not be allocated to British routes. Thus domestic consumption would have to be cut or minimum stock levels redefined. British officials argued that maximum realistic reductions in stock levels and domestic consumption had already been authorized; more cuts could yield only marginal (if not counterproductive) results.[10]

An industrial society vulnerable to interdiction of its sea communications needed a secure margin of reserve stocks, a large percentage of which would be committed to the "pipeline" between usage and reserve at any given time. If Britain risked redefining minimum stock levels before receiving guarantees of U.S. aid, it might become far more vulnerable later. Even when U.S. shipbuilding could eventually provide enough ships to supply British imports and mount amphibious operations concurrently, Britain's ports and internal transport system would have to handle increased imports while discharging 120 BOLERO ships monthly at the very time when prospective military operations required utmost flexibility from British transport. Such massive convoys would also compete with operations for escort vessels

The British cabinet was also reluctant to deflate civilian morale by inflicting sacrifices in domestic consumption that exacerbated the relative inequity between British and American living conditions; thus British imports had to be boosted before mid-1943 to avoid a choice between restricting the domestic economy and disengaging from overseas obligations. Retrospective skepticism about these minimum stock levels may be warranted; estimates of raw materials consumption proved especially faulty. As shipping capacity and deployment became politicized, expert assessments of possibilities for wheat conservation were overridden by politicians' reluctance to ration or dilute bread; the latter course would divert barley supplies from beer making. Starvation remained unlikely, even when British meal stocks fell to a level equal to two weeks of consumption in early 1943. But confidence in future procurement was an essential ingredient in long-range planning. Just as the Americans demanded an early British commitment to OVERLORD so that their domestic logistic system of procurement, transportation, and distribution could operate smoothly without an excessive dispersion of resources, the Britain demanded a rock-solid, long-term American commitment to Britain's civilian needs so that a healthy British economy and society could supply the staging areas, air bases, food, weapons, and other supplies required for a successful OVERLORD. Although British shipping managers recognized that military operations must retain priority, U.S. Army planners consistently failed to realize the complementary nature of the two objectives: BOLERO and British imports. Their attainment demanded reasonable compromise.[11]

Although civilian needs could not hope for top priority as Allied strategists scrambled to recover from disasters such as Tobruk and to exploit opportunities such as Midway, neither recovery nor advance would be possible without proper attention to British imports. Lord Cherwell wanted military shipments cut to stabilize imports; the Eighth Army could "easily" prune supply demands "if they find the shipping is simply not forthcoming."[12] This argument contradicted Britain's basic strategy of amassing a reserve in Egypt that could reinforce Suez, the Caucasus, or India, but it applied even more forcefully to TORCH—a burdensome adjunct to Middle East strategy that could conveniently double as a truncated second front.

Even as presidential adviser Harry Hopkins, Marshall, and Chief of Naval Operations Admiral Ernest J. King arrived to finalize Allied strategy for 1942, Churchill noted the need for a logistic agreement that would provide substantial U.S. aid promptly. The current level of British resources and U.S. help demanded "retrenchment which would seriously impair" British warmaking from mid-1943.

There is no reason to assume that we cannot get through the present year or that the tonnage position in 1943 will not steadily improve as a result of the prodigious American shipbuilding. But we must be careful not to let our position deteriorate to an unmanageable degree before we have a clear understanding with the United States as to the future. With this object we must now in the next few weeks come to a solemn compact, almost a treaty, with the United States about the share of their new building we are to get in 1943 and 1944. . . . On no account must we run our stocks down to a dangerous level for the sake of getting through 1942, without knowing where we stand in 1943.[13]

British dependence on the United States was obvious. Yet Churchill only talked about maintaining a prudent logistic foundation for grand strategy; the hasty and inadequately examined decision to mount TORCH preceded any such "compact." Premature adventures in North Africa and the southwest Pacific thus obtained unnecessarily disproportionate shipping allocations.

While British imports continued to fall, the Anglo-Americans debated Second Front strategy throughout the spring and summer of 1942. Marshall traveled to London in April and July, seeking accord to avoid further dispersion of effort into defensive action that did not promote a Germany-first strategy. Initial agreement on a cross-Channel attack ensued: Transport and assault planning for BOLERO (deployment of U.S. troops to Britain) would stress ROUNDUP (a heavy 1943 assault exploited by 48 divisions); SLEDGEHAMMER (an emergency 1942 operation mounted mainly by British troops) would be prepared to exploit a Nazi collapse or, alternatively, boost Soviet morale. These plans boasted logistic benefits. Britain's existing bases and its proximity to the United States eased administrative and transport burdens; only in the British Isles could forces build up rapidly along the shortest possible lines of communication. Home defense concerns dictated retention of troops in Britain; only cross-Channel action could utilize such forces. French terrain was logistically and tactically preferable for exploiting an assault.[14]

Yet divergent priorities thwarted Anglo-American strategic agreement in 1942. Soviet collapse appeared imminent as the Nazis drove toward Stalingrad. Churchill and General Sir Alan Brooke, Chief of the Imperial General Staff, insisted that Allied communications through Suez were imperiled by Japanese sorties into the Indian Ocean and by German advances into Egypt and the Caucasus, but Marshall sought a cross-Channel operation and fought Mediterranean diversions. The superficial consensus disintegrated. Public clamor for action to relieve the Soviet predicament in-

fluenced Roosevelt's promise to Molotov of a second front in 1942 and
fortified Allied resolve to engage German troops in 1942 successfully—in
France, if possible. The British and Americans (the Soviets were informed,
not consulted) could not merely focus on the best military plan to defeat
Germany in the west; because victory would be exponentially more difficult without the USSR, military strategy also had to help attain a primary
political goal—preserving the Grand Alliance.[15]

Eisenhower and Marshall argued for SLEDGEHAMMER regardless of its
prospects. Invading North Africa was tantamount to admitting that Soviet
defeat was inevitable and ROUNDUP impossible: "since it is too much to
hope that the Russians can continue fighting unaided, all through 1943,
the final effect would be the abandonment of ROUNDUP . . . a commitment
to this operation renders ROUNDUP in all probability impracticable of successful execution in 1943." They contended on strategic and diplomatic
(not logistic) grounds that GYMNAST (rechristened TORCH) would postpone
cross-Channel action indefinitely. But Churchill's cabinet rejected these
arguments. Tactical, logistic, and political constraints dashed hopes that
Allied forces could seize, hold, or exploit a French beachhead in 1942. Air
cover was inadequate, landing craft were scarce, and U.S. troops were
largely unavailable. Britain insisted that any landing must aim at permanence; a sacrificial campaign would not be tolerated. SLEDGEHAMMER's implications for British imports were not seriously examined, but both civilian and military logistic limitations meant that Britain's adamant rejection
of SLEDGEHAMMER was predicated upon and dictated a patient buildup for
ROUNDUP.[16]

Since waiting was politically and diplomatically untenable, Churchill
and his strategic advisers advocated TORCH as their only serious alternative
to the still less desirable Pacific. Tobruk's fall accented tenuous Allied control of global communications; Brooke was convinced that TORCH would
save shipping by opening the Mediterranean. Logistic needs thus seemed
to bolster arguments for TORCH. But what would be the logistic effect of
adopting TORCH? A current and prospective shortage of landing craft
helped cancel SLEDGEHAMMER but did not imply approval for TORCH.
Rather, it suggested building strength in Britain and mounting ROUNDUP in
1943. Although the Americans' primary objection had been TORCH's irrelevance to the Soviet battle for survival, they also disparaged its logistic
cost: It duplicated administration, was vulnerable to interdiction, and
wasted resources on indirect action from a new operational base. British
shipping official Sir Arthur Salter, absent from these discussions, also criticized the Allied focus on narrow political goals and neglect of logistics.
He protested the assignment of separate U.S., British, and combined the-

aters that prevented effective combined strategy and need-based allocation of shipping. There was not sufficient shipping to sustain current and projected action in widely separate theaters without considering logistic necessities, especially available cargo tonnage. Logistic resources could not mount Mediterranean and French campaigns in 1943, so TORCH precluded a 1943 ROUNDUP.[17]

Allied military and civilian leaders glossed over logistic questions. The British Chiefs of Staff (COS) had asked MWT to assess SLEDGEHAMMER's cost to imports, but Churchill peevishly rebuffed MWT concern about the larger BOLERO buildup: "This must await the decisions pending on strategic questions. Bring up next week." Even as he admitted the need for "a solemn compact" ensuring U.S. shipping aid, he stressed German U-boats' threat to Allied military plans far more than their impact on imports. Obsessed with offensive action, he overstated British power and miscalculated the price of premature action that jeopardized Britain's war economy. Though Marshall had argued that TORCH would be costly and ineffectual, he later confessed that in the rush to strategic decision, "the logistic situation had been given only cursory examination." TORCH was intended to rally the Anglo-Americans to a common Germany-first objective, but unrealistic political and diplomatic goals dictated a logistically untenable strategy that inspired continued strategic debates and civil-military competition for scarce shipping; these battles risked fragmenting the alliance instead.[18]

Politics overruled strategic and logistic facts to dictate halfhearted U.S. support for TORCH. Roosevelt's intervention in favor of TORCH was decisive; Allied troops would land in North Africa, shaping Allied strategy thereafter. British peripheral strategy's greatest victory was a major disaster for Britain's logistic freedom of action because Churchill and Roosevelt had imposed impracticable political and diplomatic conditions on grand strategy—and logistics. Britons had argued that, given limited resources, evicting the Germans from North Africa was an essential prerequisite to—not a diversion from—a successful ROUNDUP. But because they pursued the Germany-first strategy in a way contrary to the American approach, Britons could not spurn TORCH's offspring—and indeed legitimized them—adopting Sicilian and Italian invasions and pressing exploitation all the way to northern Italy in 1945. Brooke's ritualistic invocation of the traditional, peripheral, indirect, British way of war depended on sincere American consent to maintain it. Although Britain lacked the landing craft, the manpower, and perhaps the resolve to cross the Channel, it also lacked the shipping resources to implement a peripheral strategy. Reviewing the costs of TORCH makes this limitation abundantly evident.[19]

Why did TORCH have a pernicious impact on British imports? It was intended to save shipping by opening the Mediterranean, but its hasty and partial approval, shoddy design, and weak exploitation accelerated initial shipping costs intolerably. Marshall had not ruled that SLEDGEHAMMER's rejection was irrevocable and, indeed, briefly withheld final endorsement of TORCH while monitoring the Soviet front. Early BOLERO shipments had been badly labeled, and Eisenhower lacked the time to reorganize carelessly managed supply depots. He had to reorder supplies, wasting shipping. Confusion lingered about TORCH's objectives and scope. British desire to trap Rommel's Afrika Korps and clear the southern Mediterranean inspired advocacy for landings at Algiers and points east, American concern about Spanish or German interdiction of vulnerable lines of communication through the Strait of Gibraltar to Oran motivated insistence upon a tactically dangerous and logistically nightmarish landing at Casablanca. Ingrid Bergman had an easier time leaving Casablanca than did Patton's First Armored Corps. Command disputes and general U.S. dislike of Mediterranean landings hamstrung preparations. Though U.S. commanders were concerned that TORCH's apparent irrelevance to the Eastern Front might render ROUNDUP strategically impossible, their haphazard contributions to TORCH planning helped ensure ROUNDUP's logistic infeasibility in 1943. In September, the disorganized Allied strategists finally agreed: Casablanca, Oran, and Algiers in November. Brooke's initial plan might have saved shipping and justified Mediterranean operations; compromise hampered effective exploitation. TORCH could not quickly clear the Mediterranean and did not relieve Britain's shipping burden; despite other arguments marshaled in its behalf, TORCH in its final form was logistically unjustifiable.[20]

TORCH cut imports by altering cargoes and rerouting escorts. MWT normally scheduled ships carrying military cargo outbound to load civilian cargo on their return. But convoy cycles were shortened to hasten TORCH's buildup and maximize vessels' use on military missions; scarcity of useful cargo (except phosphates) in North Africa also cut potential reimbursement. Escorts and cargo ships were diverted from imports to operations. Twenty-four cargo ships that would normally have been escorted were sunk while sailing independently in the autumn of 1942. Belated acknowledgment of defense's precedence over offense dictated priority for merchant and escort shipbuilding over landing craft, reducing strategic flexibility and threatening Allied capacity to mount OVERLORD.[21]

TORCH also increased British shipping commitments, with consequences that were not fully seen until the deployment was irreversible. Adhering through August to an absurd target date of 7 October wasted ships by holding them idle. Despite a heavy disparity between U.S. gains and British shipping losses, the United States had supplied no extra aid, and Britain provided half the ships carrying U.S. equipment in the first assault wave. Hitler's choice to fight for Tunisia encouraged Mediterranean battles, pressuring the Reich in ROUNDUP's absence, but unexpected, constant improvisations in equipment supply and troop assignments were required, mirroring the difficulties experienced in planning TORCH. French rearmament, special truck convoys, and demands for more signals and salvage equipment, aviation gasoline, tanks, and antitank weapons dislocated Allied logistics throughout early 1943. These demands deferred a scheduled cut in TORCH shipments from 66 to 20 British ships monthly and provided a useful warning that increased safety margins would be essential to a successful OVERLORD. Yet by imposing unforeseen immediate burdens and unknown long-term costs on global logistics, TORCH rendered such margins increasingly unlikely. The TORCH theater did not reach maintenance basis until June 1943, when supplies for the Sicilian invasion (HUSKY) flooded North Africa.[22]

Amid this unending drain, imports into Britain plummeted below an expected 25 million tons to the lowest wartime level: 23 million tons for 1942. From November 1942 to February 1943, imports totaled just 4.98 million tons: an annual rate of 15 million tons. TORCH was costing Britain 500,000 tons monthly—30 percent of current imports. This prompted action: In December, Churchill reversed course and halved shipments to military and civilian programs in the Middle East and India, despite Army protests. He also ordered a severe cut in domestic raw materials use, which ensured that prior consumption estimates would prove excessive but also required larger subsequent weapons shipments from the United States at heavy shipping cost.[23] Such drastic measures could not bridge the gap between capabilities and commitments; indeed, they heavily mortgaged the prospective shipping dividend from TORCH, since those ships would have to be replaced in order to mount further operations from the Middle East (such as HUSKY). Only U.S. aid could rescue Britain. The decision for TORCH had rested squarely on the expectation of U.S. help, but because it preceded the necessary logistics diplomacy, the result was depletion of imported raw materials and food stocks.

Was U.S. help likely? Confronted with British estimates that 25 and 27 million tons were the minimum acceptable imports for 1942 and 1943, respectively, WSA Deputy Administrator Lewis Douglas contemplated U.S. aid but rejected a firm obligation. Bitter U.S. civil-military conflict obstructed thoughtful attention to British requests. Early WSA organizational problems had alienated the Army, and British input into Douglas's restructuring had nurtured mistrust of civilian interlopers. Somervell and the U.S. Joint Chiefs of Staff (JCS) also opposed aid to British imports because that would cut military deployments. Despite WSA's direct access to Roosevelt, Somervell and Gross rejected WSA oversight, exasperating Douglas:

> If the War Department and the Generals would not try to run production, shipping, and transportation, in which they have no experience and for which their restricted and limited intellectual lives make them unfitted; if they would stop trying to grab more and more power, leaving to the civilian the things that are civilian; and if they will only stick to . . . organizing a fighting machine, we might have a better chance of winning sooner.

Army officers eventually reciprocated civilian disdain by refusing to attend committee meetings with WSA officials.[24]

Britain would wait no longer for an authoritative definition of U.S. aid. Churchill hoped to buttress waning British power with U.S. help; he sent his Minister of Production, Oliver Lyttelton, to America in November 1942 to resolve several resource allocation disputes and to ask for a "fair share" of ships from America's "vast" output. Lyttelton asked for enough shipping to augment imports to 27 million tons in 1943 by carrying 7 million tons of cargo in U.S. ships. Banking on U.S. shipbuilders' surpassing current production estimates, on 30 November Roosevelt offered Lyttelton and Churchill the "definite assurance" that the WSA would allocate from America's expanding merchant fleet the tonnage needed for import and Imperial needs in 1943: 300,000 tons allocated monthly, retained cumulatively on British routes to compensate for early allocation shortfalls, carrying 7 million tons of cargo. He designed and conveyed his response to retain maximum maneuverability. He could divert tonnage to military purposes in an emergency; he hoped for a "substantial reduction" in aid thanks to Mediterranean clearance for shipping traffic, and he expected economies in military and civilian shipping management. These loopholes could encourage cuts in the level of U.S. aid.[25]

Roosevelt's general aversion to confrontation also exacerbated Allied logistic challenges; he neglected the bureaucratic chain of command, sidestepping Allied and civil-military conflict over resource priorities. He guaranteed sizable, consistent allocations for 1943 without consulting his military advisers and then "forgot" to tell them. British officers provided some enlightenment for a bypassed JCS, but Roosevelt deferred official confirmation until just prior to JCS departure for the Casablanca conference, impeding thorough military review of his pledge and distorting Somervell's grasp of some crucial details. His cover letter (dated 8 January) forwarding his 30 November letter to Churchill offered no hint of the shipping bombshell within, emphasizing equipment allocations instead. Thus Somervell misconstrued the premise and scope of Roosevelt's pledge; U.S. aid was designed to augment British imports substantially, not merely replace shipping losses.[26]

Roosevelt compounded the confusion by appointing Somervell as his sole shipping negotiator at the Casablanca conference. Douglas and Somervell's enduring dispute over cargo vessels' assignment, control, and loading had exploded in December 1942. Douglas had attempted to deny military claims to decide all destinations arbitrarily and conserve scarce shipping so that Guadalcanal and TORCH convoys could be mounted without causing calamity elsewhere. He provocatively reaffirmed WSA's charter of civilian control, contending that its responsibility for ship operations included mixed loading of cargoes where needed to save shipping space. Confrontation proved counterproductive. Somervell adamantly rejected British aid requests and WSA dominion: "I don't want to load any civilian cargo," he stated bluntly. Roosevelt told Douglas to meet with Gross daily until 1 February and seek compromise. Douglas thus remained in Washington during the Casablanca conference, unavailable to comprehend or to plead Britain's case.[27]

British optimism that imports would now be secure contrasted with the U.S. Army's total ignorance of the abysmal current state of British imports and the consequent inevitability of massive U.S. aid. British civilian needs were irrelevant to Army planners; because Somervell thought that British import needs were being met, he underrated the level at which guaranteed U.S. aid to British imports would continue and demanded British cargo shipping aid to BOLERO at Casablanca (to complement troopships already allocated). BOLERO had nearly ceased. Less than 4,800 troops would reach Britain during February to April 1943. Overall troop strength stagnated at around 100,000; over 1 million were needed. Somervell's logistic fixation complemented Marshall's doubts about British intentions: Even if ROUNDUP was impossible in 1943, assent to and support for BOLERO was a litmus test of British intentions for 1944. Somervell thus exploited British preoccupation with an overall agreement that would permit specific promotion of the British-sponsored Mediterranean strategy.

Both sides agreed that the "first charge" on Allied resources would be ending the "stranglehold on all offensive operations" caused by shipping shortages by protecting British sea communications. Nevertheless, Somervell pressed for British cargo shipping to fulfill BOLERO by carrying

1,600,000 tons in 1943 and, most importantly, 500,000 tons in the second quarter. Thus British civilian needs would be greatest at the very time that their sacrifice on behalf of Army deployment plans was deemed most necessary. Somervell lacked the perspective to see that military convenience could not endanger the sustenance of BOLERO's base society.[28]

Britain's shipping negotiator, Minister of War Transport Lord Frederick Leathers, knew of Roosevelt's evasion and moved warily. Perhaps reluctant to risk the hard-won strategic agreement that depended on a shared perception that available ships could both supply Mediterranean operations (Britain's hope) and implement BOLERO (the U.S. demand), Leathers saw that querying whether both could be accomplished while U.S. ships carried 7 million tons of imports might jeopardize Roosevelt's support. He offered British shipping for BOLERO, with provisos, including an early end to TORCH's buildup phase and a predictable insistence that ships could not be taken from British imports.[29]

TORCH steadily demanded more resources. Discrepancies between the Allies' calculations of shipping availability and assumptions about shipping priorities emerged as Casablanca's exaggerated hopes toppled. Strategy had outrun military and civilian logistic capabilities. BOLERO virtually stopped as Kasserine ended dim hopes for a quick victory and mandated TORCH's reinforcement; British imports plummeted far below 1942's awful yearly rate of 23 million tons, inspiring a British plea for additional and more rapid aid.[30]

As this plea reached Washington, U.S. Army planners finally sorted out the muddle that their Anglophobic avarice had helped promote. When Gross asked Douglas to help force British fulfillment of the Casablanca "commitment," he discovered Leathers's provisos and the full portent of Roosevelt's letter. Gross assumed that as chief shipbuilder, America should exercise its logistic power to decide strategy and British import levels. Meeting Britain's request would halve U.S. overseas deployment, so Gross sought to impose an import program of 16 million tons (11 million below the declared minimum) in 1943. He bitterly reproached WSA and the British for hiding information and allocating ships without JCS knowledge or approval: WSA should consult the JCS "before complying with a directive of the President." Bureaucratic failure fed civil-military conflict over civilian logistics' priority and threatened Allied harmony.[31]

Roosevelt had ignored military advice to choose TORCH; he did so again to commit U.S. ships to British imports. Douglas insisted on 30 March that the United States could and must honor Roosevelt's November promise. Strategic necessity and alliance cohesion called for immediate action. Though Roosevelt's procrastination had worsened the crisis and forced drastic if belated measures, the delay had providentially postponed a decision until the two necessary conditions for adequate allocation to *both* British imports and U.S. military deployments were nearly met: a stupendous increase in U.S. merchant shipbuilding, and the codebreaking successes that helped bring victory in the Battle of the Atlantic. Technological and manufacturing advances rescued the Allies from the consequences of meager attention to logistics. Balancing American capabilities and commitments would still require Douglas's skeptical attitude toward exaggerated Army shipping assessments; they had wasted ships as floating depots in the South Pacific. He thus correctly perceived the potential solution for Allied conflict: a real commitment to both British imports and BOLERO. Roosevelt agreed that sufficient shipping allocations to British imports would be a top priority and ignored a JCS plea for revision. By doing so, he embittered U.S. military leaders and aggravated their deep-rooted mistrust of British motives.[32]

Yet even in this redefined logistic situation, BOLERO could not provide the balanced force necessary to sustain a 1943 ROUNDUP. Priority for the air offensive dictated a retarded buildup for the Army contingent, which numbered just 60,000 in September 1943. But what would occupy Allied forces until spring 1944? U.S. suspicions about British intent continued; believing that "we have never had tangible intent that the British intend to launch cross-channel operations," Army planner General Albert C. Wedemeyer was receptive to Navy arguments that landing craft construction should not be allowed to interfere with naval shipbuilding programs keyed to Pacific plans. Landing craft that did exist were diverted to the Pacific, and the higher shipping losses caused by TORCH required greater production of escort vessels at the expense of landing craft. Meanwhile, British pressure for Mediterranean action only encouraged U.S. attempts to emphasize Pacific strategy: "Each side wanted a loophole permitting it to carry on its own favorite sideshow while talking of the major effort against Germany."[33]

Combined Chiefs of Staff (CCS) conferees met again in May to reconcile strategic ideas. Britain's pledge to cross the Channel in 1944 inspired JCS consent to more Mediterranean operations after Sicily. Although Somervell and Leathers had hoped that strategy and shipping would be "related fully," the CCS resolved strategy on 20 May—before shipping availabilities were determined. Brooke's diary for 23 May noted: "We started with a C.O.S. meeting to which we invited Lord Leathers and Cherwell, and discussed the whole of the shipping situation in relation to the plans we had been making. Luckily the shipping worked out all right and covered all our plans."[34] Thus strategic and logistic plans remained discordant.

Logistic agreement remained elusive. Though British planners were confident that fewer losses and more building would balance needs and shipping, a sizable deficit arose. Douglas admitted that the U.S. Army's figures showed an "unreal . . . paper deficit," but feared confrontation and further demands. Leathers worried that operations might be canceled or postponed needlessly. When the British erased their deficit with credits for fewer losses and improved cargo carriage, Somervell responded with increased bids for shipping. At an all-night session to complete shipping talks before a 23 May CCS meeting, Gross predictably argued that the "very big deficit on U.S. Army account . . . could only be met by inroads on the U.K. import program. The British were still living soft and could easily stand further reductions." Douglas and Leathers objected: A sound British economy was necessary to mount BOLERO. Stiffly resisted by Douglas, Leathers, and British officers, Gross and Somervell abandoned their efforts to escalate demands without inducing the Britons to assume their deficits—though these retained freedom from detailed civilian supervision. Somervell and Leathers agreed that the remaining deficit, "if properly spread, is not unmanageable."[35] Thus even as victory in North Africa and the Battle of the Atlantic beckoned, Allied logistic planners struggled with TORCH's legacy of distrust.

From May 1943, the primary grand logistic challenge remained finding a proper balance for shipping allocations among the European, Pacific, and Mediterranean theaters. Despite enjoying a relative abundance that enabled buildups imperative for both OVERLORD and Pacific offensives in 1944, the Allies never fully parried TORCH's repercussions. Civil-military bickering and bureaucratic infighting had shaped strategic implementation during logistic scarcity and continued to do so as shipping became relatively sufficient.

The changed situation challenged both civilian and military logisticians with a difficult adjustment. Increasing U.S. shipping allocations and victory in the Battle of the Atlantic flooded the North Atlantic with temporary shipping gluts that rendered British demands for explicit aid levels anachronistic. Both MWT and the U.S. Army had difficulty adjusting to the sudden feast after such a long famine, for lend-lease and Army procurement had slowed to match previous shipping availabilities. But MWT "anticipated" certain cargoes, carried BOLERO cargo on import ships, imported second-priority cargoes, and diverted refrigerated ships to the southern Dominions for meat. Increased loadings and arrivals and severe consumption cuts had also augmented British stocks, even though imports did not reach 27 million tons in 1943. But U.S. officials suspected that British shipping officials were either wasting ships or had deceived

Americans into excessive ship allocations and were now chiseling extra cargoes. Import and stock-building contingency plans for countering German interdiction of British communications now raised Americans' suspicions as they discerned British attempts to prepare for postwar recovery before Britain lost lend-lease procurement facilities and access to U.S. ships.[36]

TORCH's strategic and logistic legacy hampered the U.S. Army's response to "surplus" ships in the summer of 1943. At Quebec in August 1943, Brooke stressed the role of Mediterranean operations in OVERLORD's success by dispersing German army and air strength. Marshall approved the invasion of Italy and Eisenhower's request for 66,000 troops diverted from BOLERO. Yet port capacity was already "a despotic factor governing the buildup rate." The contest between military and civilian needs for British port facilities in the months before D-day was heightened by underemployment of port capacity before the autumn of 1943—even after the general shortage of shipping had ended. Simultaneous U.S. Army opposition to ship allocations for civilian needs and suspicion that allocating Army troops and equipment to Britain would be counterproductive without assurances regarding their eventual use in France were the prime causes. This continuing uncertainty and memories of disorganized supply depots in 1942 limited "preshipment" of vital equipment that could have eased British ports' later burden and ensured adequate supply of ammunition. The War Department assented to ASF's request that BOLERO's low priority (eighth for ground equipment, fourth for air equipment) be revised only in December 1943 (after Tehran settled U.S. doubts about British devotion to OVERLORD); this affected theater arrivals from March 1944. Ships meanwhile mounted Pacific operations that required reinforcement, and BOLERO dictated U.S. military access to British ports at imports' expense.[37]

Although BOLERO cargo and troop shipments accelerated in autumn, 1943, residual suspicion of opportunistic British diversions and of inflexible American "contracts" continued to haunt post-HUSKY operations. Since shipping was ample in the Atlantic and scarce in the Mediterranean, Britain sought flexible application of promised aid, but such shipping demands contradicted a chief justification for TORCH. Though Douglas agreed that U.S. ships would help supply Italian operations, Americans resented being "lured" there: Why send Liberty ships to risky waters and clogged ports to satisfy "Imperial" needs while British ships stayed in the Atlantic? This dispute beset shipping talks throughout the autumn of 1943. While Britons resented U.S. demands for an authoritative commitment to OVERLORD, Americans were angry that Britain had received explicit logistic pledges and then tried to alter allocations to British advantage.[38]

British demands for flexibility and increased import aid for 1944 during the December 1943 talks at Cairo were resisted because the Army needed access to British ports to unload BOLERO ships. Denied access to U.S. calculations, British officials suspected that the Americans pitched their demands just high enough to reduce British imports for 1944. But Leathers wearily agreed that imports would not obstruct BOLERO's access to British ports.[39]

Earlier delays now dictated a rushed effort to fulfill BOLERO. Cargo and troop shipments reached their full potential only in midwinter, as reduced shipping losses enabled the Army to overcome its backlogs and assemble 1,527,000 men in Britain by May 1944, double the number present just five months before. Cargo handling recorded similar achievements; 40 percent of all U.S. tonnage discharged in British ports between January 1942 and May 1944 was handled between January and May 1944. This effort caused one more conflict between British imports and BOLERO just two weeks before D-day. British ports were inundated with preparations for handling cargoes outward bound to France and with civilian imports; they could not handle incoming BOLERO cargoes that exceeded previously stated maximum levels. Yet Allied armies had to have these supplies. Eisenhower noted: "We have simply developed one of those bottlenecks (for no one is at fault for it) incident to big operations." This politic, simplistic evaluation ignored the entire logistic and strategic context of OVERLORD's development since the Allies had decided for TORCH and Roosevelt had deferred the decision on British imports in 1942. Eisenhower cashed in Leathers's pledge, appealing to Churchill to postpone discharge of ships carrying 500,000 tons of imports so that final preparations for D-day could be expedited. Of course, Britain would not jeopardize OVERLORD; Churchill assented. British rebuilding of reserve stocks in 1943 prevented the recurrence of an import crisis when 1944 imports fell short of 1943 totals.[40]

The strategic controversies surrounding OVERLORD in early 1944 were inextricably linked to logistic obstacles; though strategic success coincided with the advent of relative shipping sufficiency in 1943, OVERLORD's execution was haunted by prior logistic and strategic compacts. Balanced allocation of resources between BOLERO and Mediterranean exploitation remained elusive in 1944. Churchill demanded retention of landing craft for Anzio; deficient port facilities compelled their prolonged use there. Thus the Italian theater's ability to spare troops to invade southern France (ANVIL) was questioned. Just as Roosevelt's pledge to Molotov in 1942 had eclipsed logistic details and led to a premature TORCH, his vow to Stalin that ANVIL would accompany OVERLORD plagued rational balancing of ends and means in 1944. Diplomacy also meshed with logistic constraints, in that Atlantic port capacity dictated that a prominent French contingent had to deploy through Marseille.[41]

ANVIL posed another logistic quandary: allocation of landing craft. Because its fate would affect OVERLORD's assault component, ANVIL dominated the OVERLORD-Mediterranean debate during the spring of 1944. Civilian supply needs no longer risked strategic stalemate, but prior insistence on offensives during 1942's shipping crisis now jeopardized a 1944 OVERLORD. Shipping losses had diverted production priorities from landing craft to merchant and escort vessels; resentment of Mediterranean operations had inspired the U.S. Navy to send the landing craft it controlled to the Pacific. Victory in the Battle of the Atlantic and U.S. production enabled the fulfillment of demands by Eisenhower and operational commander General Bernard Montgomery for a bigger OVERLORD assault, but only at the expense of ANVIL's temporary postponement due to landing craft shortages. That action merely delayed recriminations; the strategic uncertainty that had aggravated procurement problems also caused continuing shortages of landing craft and ammunition, which hampered OVERLORD's execution and follow-up. Any discussion of the controversial Allied failure to end the war in 1944 must therefore begin by examining the long-term logistic context.[42]

American leadership in World War II has often been castigated for a naivete that failed to see the political consequences of its obsession with military objectives. America's growing pains also included the consequences of ignoring a balanced approach to civilian and military logistics: an endangered OVERLORD. Emphasis on political and diplomatic goals and failure to relate logistic demands and civilian supply needs to strategy aggravated strategic conflict, poisoning Allied strategic execution with bureaucratic mismanagement and civil-military strife. Regardless of any other constraints, Allied decisions in 1942 had logistic consequences that made a 1943 ROUNDUP infeasible and rendered a 1944 OVERLORD more difficult. Thus the Anglo-American allies, and specifically U.S. military leadership, pursued narrow objectives in their haste to engage the enemy—willfully risking British detachment, German technological breakthroughs, or Russian collapse in 1943 that might well have rendered OVERLORD impossible.

OVERLORD's local and global logistic challenges derived from Roosevelt's hasty 1942 decision for TORCH and his handling of Britain's import crisis. Military strategy among democratic allies is always influenced by

LSTs, grounded on beaches in Normandy, disgorge their cargoes.

diplomatic and political factors; yet pressure to reassure their Soviet ally dictated a premature, implausible pledge of a second front in 1942 beyond their logistic capacity. It magnified Soviet distrust, paid lip service to giving British sea communications priority, and encouraged mutual deceit. Roosevelt may have displayed political mastery by deferring an honest pledge to underwrite British imports, but he thereby exacerbated conflict. Americans and Britons thus faced the Second Front's logistic challenges in an atmosphere of mutual suspicion, battling for two years over proper priority for cross-channel, Mediterranean, and Pacific operations. British and U.S. civilian shipping planners disagreed with U.S. Army officers about proper priority for British imports. These disputes converged as Roosevelt's bungling caused Somervell's ignorance and encouraged Leathers's duplicity, delaying universal recognition of Britain's desperate need for U.S. shipping. U.S. shipbuilding saved British imports, but the civilian logistic crisis enhanced mutual suspicion of British chicanery and U.S. obtuseness, thereby slowing the BOLERO deployment and clogging British ports.

Churchill could not reverse Roosevelt's pledge to Molotov; he proved a willing, unwise accomplice in the strategy of illusions that substituted TORCH. This strategic "victory" brought a severe shipping burden that cost Britain logistic independence. It straitjacketed British strategic options and forced British cargo shipping aid for BOLERO as a quid pro quo for Sicily to head off possible U.S. threats to try a Pacific-first strategy. While British logistic dependence eventually helped produce the strategic servility that ensured an end to British resistance to a second front in 1944, U.S. Army rapacity meanwhile endangered the logistic fulfillment of its preconditions. Determined to launch a cross-Channel operation in the teeth of German defenses, U.S. planners claimed that British "muddling through" with inferior resources was no longer permissible or necessary. Yet although U.S. industrial output proved able to sustain the logistic support that finally energized the Second Front in 1944, setting aside many of the Allies' self-inflicted logistic challenges, Allied leaders still struggled in the final months of preparation—and in the immediate aftermath of the assault—with strategic and logistic disputes. These disputes flowed inexorably from their unwillingness and inability to take sufficient notice of logistic factors when opting for TORCH and postponing a decision on British imports in the waning months of 1942.

4. ULTRA, FORTITUDE, and D-day Planning: The Missing Dimension

Alexander S. Cochran

Appreciation of intelligence and deception as vital components in Anglo-American planning and prosecution of the 1944 cross-Channel invasion of northwest France has undergone a remarkable development over the past decade. This evolution came about primarily through the addition of the missing dimensions in OVERLORD planning—ULTRA and FORTITUDE. The former was the successful British codebreaking operation that gave Allied decision makers and planners priceless access to German military radio traffic from 1939 onward, an accomplishment of which Hitler and his planners remained oblivious throughout the war.[1] The latter was a cover and concealment plan for the OVERLORD landings that effectively convinced Hitler and his Third Reich planners that the major Allied landings in mid-1944 would be in the Pas de Calais area rather than on the Normandy beaches, a scheme that relied extensively on ULTRA-derived information.[2]

Before British official acknowledgment of the intelligence operation and the subsequent opening of archival documents on deception planning, some official historians who knew about it simply left this dimension out of their assessments; most lacked the background to discuss its overall implications for both the planning and the landings. The result was a serious flaw in our understanding of OVERLORD.

This startling shift in historical perspective—amounting to a new paradigm for assessing OVERLORD and related operations—calls into question the authoritativeness of the official histories of this conflict. Those histories supplied the foundation and much of the scaffolding for several generations of scholarship dealing with World War II. Winston Churchill's influential history and memoir, *The Second World War*, has been cited by numerous historians in recent years as having set a tone and an agenda for postwar scholarship.[3] Churchill's six volumes only hinted at the ULTRA secrets (and then only for those who knew what the codenames BONIFACE or MOST SECRET SOURCES really meant). Other less-informed scholars who sought, as J. H. Plumb once advised, "to move down the broad avenues which he drove through the war's confusion and complexity" were following a road map that not only lacked details but deliberately left out important thoroughfares and intersections.[4]

Of special relevance are the distinguished volumes in the monumental enterprise, The United States Army in World War II.[5] The scholarship of those official historians who wrote on high-level strategy in general and operations such as OVERLORD in particular (including Maurice Matloff, Forrest C. Pogue, and Gordon Harrison) is still considered basic and generally authoritative; but what has become increasingly evident is the degree to which the Army and War Department chroniclers lacked access to key intelligence records.[6] Admittedly, the pivotal works in the Army's green books that bear on Normandy were published long before the ULTRA secret was divulged, but the American official history community has made no effort to redress the problem. Making this lacuna more remarkable is that their British counterparts apparently appreciated the contribution of intelligence and deception, as evidenced in the History of the Second World War: United Kingdom Military Series.[7] Not only did British official historians of OVERLORD such as John Ehrman and L. F. Ellis write in greater detail about intelligence planning,[8] but a subsequent work published over the past decade, British Intelligence in the Second World War, fully documents and integrates the critical role played by intelligence in planning for OVERLORD.[9]

For reasons that remain unclear (perhaps reflecting the sensitivity of intelligence authorities in Washington), discussion by U.S. official historians concerning either intelligence operations or deception as a part of OVERLORD planning was minimal. Maurice Matloff's volume on grand strategy published in 1958 briefly noted an agreement reached among the Soviets, British, and Americans at the Tehran conference for OVERLORD operations to include "a cover plan . . . to be concocted by their staffs."[10] In Supreme Command, Forrest Pogue's discussion of OVERLORD planning from the perspective of General Eisenhower and his staff mentioned a diversion plan involving the Pas de Calais envisioned by the Chief of Staff to the Supreme Allied Commander designate (COSSAC), but the three chapters about the intense planning efforts from early January through late May 1944 make no mention of deception planning.[11] Gordon Harrison's Cross-Channel Attack, which remains the most detailed U.S. official treatment of OVERLORD planning, correctly noted that COSSAC planners had always been conscious that "everything possible should be done before the invasion to reduce the enemy's capability to resist"; yet Harrison's account said nothing about specific intelligence operations to achieve this goal.[12] According to all three official historians, the essential issues in OVERLORD planning, regardless of level, were numbers of assault troops, availability of landing craft, arrangements for joint and combined coordination, and the relationship between ANVIL and OVERLORD landings.

Likewise, memoirs by American military leaders written in the first two decades after the war had little, if anything, to say about deception planning. Dwight D. Eisenhower's *Crusade in Europe*, the standard source for early historians of OVERLORD, made brief mention of "thoroughly considered means of deceiving the enemy as to the point and timing of attack" as well as "the wide variety of measures we took for convincing him."[13] His aide's memoirs suggest that there was almost total naivete in London, with Eisenhower wondering at one point in the deliberations about OVERLORD, "Do you suppose the Germans really are such suckers as to think we will attack through Norway?"[14] Steven Ambrose, who was Eisenhower's biographer and enjoyed the additional advantage of working on the edited volumes of Eisenhower's papers for the war years, made no mention of deception planning.[15] Neither did Marshall's biographer, Forrest C. Pogue, who possessed full access to the papers of the Army's Chief of Staff.[16]

Not surprisingly, popular American renderings of OVERLORD have been more concerned with the actual operation, quickly skimming over the planning phase. When such accounts do describe the events leading up to D-day, they rely on those works cited above and thus have nothing to say about deception operations.[17] In June 1969, a scholarly conference was convened to commemorate the twenty-fifth anniversary of D-day.[18] For this gathering, Pogue made brief mention of the "amassing of intelligence material which would be necessary for final planning"; Maurice Matloff, primarily concerned with countering the Chester Wilmot thesis regarding Anglo-American strategy, had nothing to say about intelligence or deception planning.[19]

British official historians—whose accounts were, for the most part, published several years after those of their American counterparts and cited them lavishly—dealt with OVERLORD deception planning, though only circumspectly and in the sparsest of detail. In *Grand Strategy: August 1943–September 1944*, John Ehrman noted in the section on the Tehran agreements that the Allies "should consult each other on complementary plans of deception for the summer's operation." A short (several paragraph) discussion later identified this plan as BODYGUARD, noting that it "in essence was a British plan."[20] The volume in the British official history that dealt specifically with OVERLORD, *Victory in the West: The Battle of Normandy* by L. F. Ellis, contained two chapters on planning. Ellis briefly mentioned that COSSAC's responsibilities included intelligence and deception plans and noted the Supreme Headquarters Allied Expeditionary Force (SHAEF) plans "to disguise their intentions and mislead the enemy—a plan based on a fiction . . . to mislead the enemy into the belief that the Normandy assault was but a diversionary attack." This was to be accomplished "by artificial and indiscreet wireless traffic and . . . dummy craft."[21] It seems likely that such tidbits would have caused historians to ask awkward questions about what the Germans knew or were made to believe about Allied intentions, but that did not happen for another decade.

British memoirists also made explicit mention of deception planning for OVERLORD. In Churchill's history of the war—which was to be used for some 25 years as a primary source—the prime minister quoted verbatim from the Tehran agreements for "a cover plan to mystify and mislead the enemy as regards these operations." As to the actual deception planning for OVERLORD, Churchill flatly stated that "it would not be proper even now (1951) to describe all the methods employed to deceive the enemy" and then proclaimed that "the final result was admirable."[22] Eisenhower's intelligence officer, Britisher Kenneth Strong, who had staff responsibility for deception planning, referred in passing to "a carefully thought out and brilliantly executed deception plan [that] persuaded the Germans that the landings on 6 June were subsidiary," but one of the senior British War Office planners made no mention of what we now know as FORTITUDE.[23] Alan Brooke's self-righteously edited recollections of OVERLORD planning referred only briefly to "cover plans" being discussed at Tehran, and Montgomery's authorized biography made no mention at all of deception schemes.[24] Their circumspection stood in stark contrast to Chester Wilmot's outright reference to the XX Committee (though not by name) in the few sentences he accorded deception efforts—"report of spies who surreptitiously provided [the Germans] with appropriate data"; however, Wilmot's indiscretion went unnoticed by historians."[25]

Appreciation of the role played by intelligence and deception began almost two decades ago with the publication of four seemingly unrelated books on intelligence operations during World War II. The breakthrough work was J. C. Masterman's *The Double-Cross System in the War of 1939 to 1945.*[26] Masterman, an ordinary British academic with an undistinguished career, offered a first-person account of his rather extraordinary wartime experiences as a member of a British wartime intelligence operation that had "turned" German spies.[27] This double-cross operation gave the British the capability of supplying the Axis with what we now call disinformation. Though the greater part of Masterman's narrative deals with setting up this operation in the early stages of the war and then a portrayal of how the captive German agents were used through 1943, the most startling disclosure of the book is in the chapter "Deception to Cover the Normandy Landing and the Invasion of France," in which he outlines a heretofore unknown aspect of the OVERLORD plan. The gist of Masterman's revelations is that the double-cross system and turned agents had been used to deceive the Germans about the exact location of the expected Allied invasion of northwest France. While chary of giving specific information, he noted provocatively that "we were able to state with confidence what the Germans did *not* know about our preparations as well as what they did know."[28]

In the United States, Masterman's book became an immediate focus of popular speculation, and it soon worked its way onto various national best-seller lists—a remarkable feat for a university press book. British popular interest in Masterman's book was as intense as that in America. "No better book on wartime intelligence" trumpeted an anonymous reviewer in the *Times Literary Supplement*.[29] However, its revelations were ignored by scholarly reviewers in both America and Britain.[30]

Several years later, another book on World War II intelligence, also a wartime memoir, was published. The subject was one that had not been treated in any of the official histories or World War II memoirs. In *The ULTRA Secret*, F. W. Winterbotham, a British Royal Air Force intelligence officer, revealed for the first time the existence of an Allied signals intelligence operation—ULTRA—that had given senior British and American leaders, high-level planners, and selected commanders access to intercepted German wireless (radio) traffic at both the strategic and operational levels throughout the war.[31] The book focused on Winterbotham's personal experiences carrying those intercepts directly to Churchill and other senior Allied military leaders. He had precious little to say about what was revealed or what resulted from this capability to peer inside the Reich. He had even less to say about the utility of ULTRA intelligence in planning for OVERLORD. But once the existence of World War II's greatest secret was disclosed, the implications for the historical interpretation of such pivotal junctures as OVERLORD began to be realized.

It became obvious that most of the British official histories were written with the knowledge that ULTRA had been a factor in Allied calculations. So far as is known, none of the American official historians privy to this operation. Shortly after reading Winterbotham's book, Forrest Pogue recalled having a sentence in the draft manuscript that would become *Supreme Command* removed after review by G-2.[32] The sentence read: "It was almost like planners were reading the enemy's mail." Pogue had thought nothing of the deletion at the time. But now, knowing that the Allied high command had access to German communications at the highest levels triggered a stunning shift in perspective.

Winterbotham's disclosures on ULTRA set off a flurry of reaction on both sides of the Atlantic, much of it negative. One former ULTRA officer noted that "the Group Captain is far too careless about facts and dates to make a serious contribution."[33] Others correctly noted that *The ULTRA Secret* was written from memory rather than documents. British historian A. J. P. Taylor noted that "ULTRA certainly contributed something to the war . . . [and that is] very different from saying it won the war."[34]

Although Winterbotham could be dismissed for being short on details, the next work to appear moved the debate to another plane. *Bodyguard of Lies*, by British journalist Anthony Cave-Brown, was a massive tome of over 900 pages that substantiated the ULTRA operation in remarkable detail.[35] Cave-Brown's rich narrative focused on World War II intelligence operations in Europe that included not only selected ULTRA operations but also others arguably determined by the French Resistance movement and the German conspiracy movement against Hitler.

Most important for considerations of intelligence and OVERLORD was Cave-Brown's focus on the deception plans that had been agreed upon (and briefly mentioned in the British official histories) at Tehran. At that tripartite summit, Churchill called for a "bodyguard of lies"—hence the title of Cave-Brown's book—to cover both the Anglo-American invasion of France and the Soviet offensive through Byelorussia into Eastern Europe. A large section of the book, entitled "Cover and Deception—January to June 1944," detailed the actual OVERLORD deception operations, FORTITUDE NORTH and FORTITUDE SOUTH—designations that had not been used in either the official histories or wartime memoirs.[36] He also depicted the activities of XX Committee and showed how ULTRA had formed a vital part of this operation, a relationship with which none of the official historians had dealt.

Popular reaction to *Bodyguard* in both the United States and England continued the pattern established by Masterman and Winterbotham. British reviewers, such as Michael Howard, who had prior knowledge of ULTRA and deception operations, were measured and cautious.[37] One skeptical American analyst compared Cave-Brown's story to those told by novelist John LeCarre.[38] But for the first time, there was a surge of interest on the part of the American academic community. Writing in *Military Affairs*, Roger Spiller wondered about "a need for complete reassessment of the history of the Second World War."[39] Harold C. Deutsch, a German historian at the Army War College, noted the importance of ULTRA to the outcome of World War II but cautioned historians to render balanced assessments.[40]

In retrospect, what proved most significant for scholars of World War II were Cave-Brown's sources. His initial knowledge of deception planning as well as ULTRA came from interviews; his research during the mid-1960s in the U.S. National Archives and the British Public Records Office (PRO) on both subjects had drawn a blank. By following his instincts and with a journalist's dogged persistence, Cave-Brown ultimately discovered a treasure trove after the initial disclosure of ULTRA. Interestingly, access to primary documentation about both ULTRA and FORTITUDE eventually came through the National Archives and the U.S. Army Center for Military History rather than the PRO. Thus Cave-Brown's citations in *Bodyguard* were to American military records regarding what were essentially British intelligence operations.[41] That may explain his assertion that "two (US Army) official historians . . . had tried and failed to include chapters on cover and deception in their work"—a generous but possibly unwarranted endorsement of the perspicacity of the U.S. official military history enterprise.[42]

While scholars were contemplating the fallout from Cave-Brown's bestseller, another wildly successful book on World War II intelligence operations appeared: William Stevenson's *A Man Called Intrepid: The Secret War*.[43] The focus of this undocumented narrative was on events totally unrelated to OVERLORD deception, such as the Heydrich assassination and individual spies in France and Germany. But Stevenson did confirm the importance of ULTRA as well as the degree of American participation in coalition planning beginning early in the war.

The publication of these immensely popular books had dual implications for World War II historians. First was the opening of previously buried records in both the National Archives and the PRO. Archivists in Washington now made available records dealing with MAGIC, the American equivalent of ULTRA.[44] Though MAGIC involved U.S. codebreaking operations directed against Japan, one dimension—reading the dispatches of Japanese Ambassador Oshima Hiroshi from Berlin to Tokyo—had great importance for the success of OVERLORD.[45] They also released a series of reports by U.S. Army officers who had served in the ULTRA operation during OVERLORD planning and execution.[46] Making up for lost time, British archivists at the PRO opened massive numbers of raw ULTRA evaluations sent from intelligence analysts to decision makers at all levels—so-called flimsies—for selected time periods during the war, along with detailed indexes.[47] They likewise made available documents that had been withheld from previously released files because they dealt with ULTRA material.

The second harbinger of the maturing approach to the role of intelligence and deception was a wave of books.[48] Some were ULTRA memoirs written by those who had participated in the operation but had remained silent for 25 years.[49] Others represented attempts by both participants and trained historians to integrate ULTRA into overall perspectives on World War II.[50] With respect to OVERLORD, most important were two British works: Ralph Bennett's *ULTRA in the West: The Normandy Campaign, 1944–45* and Ronald Lewin's *ULTRA Goes to War.*[51]

Ralph Bennett, a retired historian who had worked as an OVERLORD and ULTRA analyst before and during the Normandy invasion, confirmed—in numbing detail using actual ULTRA flimsies—the degree to which Allied planners and commanders knew German dispositions before the landings. *ULTRA in the West* also portrayed the indecision of some German leaders as to exactly where the Allied landings would be.[52]

Ronald Lewin was a British military historian who benefited from being in the confidence of his country's official historians with respect to ULTRA. Drawing on published books and numerous interviews, Lewin was the first to integrate signals intelligence fully into World War II planning and operations. Even so, he was well aware that his efforts were only a "first cut," with much spade work still to be done.[53] His chapter on D-day planning laid out how the double-agent network had provided the Germans with misinformation about the FORTITUDE plans and how this effort was subsequently coordinated through Anglo-American channels set up prior to Pearl Harbor and duly verified by ULTRA. Fully developed by the spring of 1944, the system was used to deceive the Germans about the exact number of Allied troops and divisions in the United Kingdom and those slated to take part in the impending invasion.[54]

Sensing that a major revision of World War II history might be at hand, scholars undertook full-scale research in the newly opened records. In the mid-1980s, scholars reported preliminary findings at several academic conferences.[55] Some historians were compelled to revise themselves. Former U.S. Army official historian Charles B. MacDonald, in a revised edition of his book *Mighty Endeavor: The American War in Europe*, noted that "without ULTRA, the clever Allied deception scheme probably would not have succeeded."[56] Eisenhower biographer Steven Ambrose revised his earlier assessments of Eisenhower to include ULTRA and a discussion of FORTITUDE planning based on newly opened sources at the Eisenhower Library.[57] In his biography of Alan Brooke, which updated Bryant's earlier version, Sir David Fraser noted Brooke's appreciation of ULTRA as "rendering ultimate victory possible."[58]

Picking up on these general assumptions, historians writing on OVER-

LORD sought to include the intelligence dimension. British historian John Keegan admitted in his 1982 study of the OVERLORD battlefield that "ULTRA was to play a major, and towards the end, perhaps the decisive part in winning the Battle of Normandy."[59] A year later, American historian Carlo D'Este briefly discussed the OVERLORD cover operations and concluded that "the masterly conceived and enormously successful FORTITUDE deception plan and ULTRA, which kept the Allied commanders informed of German problems, troops strengths, dispositions, and intents" was of pivotal importance.[60]

In the absence of compelling documentation, other historians shied away from sweeping generalization, in particular with respect to OVERLORD planning. Russell Weigley, a distinguished American military historian, dismissed the value of ULTRA for OVERLORD planning as having "somewhat waned" since North Africa.[61] British military historian Max Hastings wrote that ULTRA information "was erratic and incomplete . . . ULTRA could seldom provide decisive intelligence for Allied troops"; he concluded that the assumption "that ULTRA provided the Allies with absolute knowledge of enemy deployments, and capabilities is a travesty of the truth."[62]

What explains these diverse judgments? Most World War II historians were frustrated not so much by a lack of sources (by the mid-1980s, a small mountain of documents was opened) but by the difficulty in working with them. Scholars tended to dismiss Masterman, Stevenson, and Winterbotham as writing only from memory. They were suspicious of Cave-Brown for using American sources to document a British operation. They were skeptical about Lewin's reliance on secondary sources supplemented by interviews. In their view, Bennett's pathbreaking work proved an unsatisfactory compromise between recollections and low-level documents. The "smoking guns" that linked ULTRA intercepts to decisions made at the highest level affecting OVERLORD had not yet been discovered—if, indeed, they existed.

Those who worked with ULTRA documents in the National Archives quickly discovered that the so-called American ULTRA reports were more administrative histories than primary source materials.[63] The links between information and action were tenuous; although senior leaders such as Roosevelt, Marshall, and Eisenhower might have used ULTRA in a substantive way, they died without recording any specifics on how and when that intelligence had been used. Those researching in the British records confronted an overwhelming mass of raw data that lacked any chronological rationale or worldwide perspective.[64] They now recognized that codewords such as BONIFACE in Churchillian memos or references to MOST

SECRET SOURCES or MOST SECRET in correspondence from the War Office, the Admiralty, or the Air Ministry was ULTRA-derived information, but that did not carry their inquiries very far.[65] The question continuing to elude even the most dedicated researcher was how such intelligence factored into OVERLORD planning.

The opening of archives also gave historians a tentative explanation of why the records on both ULTRA and deception operations had been withheld so long—fears that Cold War enemies might learn of Anglo-American capabilities.[66] Still lacking was an official interpretive study on signals intelligence operation and deception planning for OVERLORD. A major step toward filling this void occurred on the British side of the Atlantic in 1979. A new volume in the official British series, History of the Second World War, appeared. It bore the title, *British Intelligence in the Second World War*. Intriguingly, the first volume of what was projected to be a five-volume work was subtitled, *Its Influence on Strategy and Operations*.[67] This first volume dealt with intelligence from the interwar period through 1941. The primary author was Professor F. H. Hinsley, who, along with several coauthors, had worked in the ULTRA operation during the war and was thus able to understand the nuances and import of the documents. As the Hinsley team stated in the Preface of this initial work, the goal of the subseries was "to produce an account of the influence of British intelligence on strategy and operations during the Second World War," emphasizing two contextual goals: to outline the intelligence dimension of the conflict without retelling the history of the war, and to deal with the many-faceted aspects of intelligence operations, embracing such obvious subjects as spies and codes but also lesser-known, amorphous topics of deception and counterintelligence. Hinsley and his colleagues asserted that they had enjoyed "unrestricted access to intelligence records"; this claim was substantiated when unofficial researchers at the PRO attempted to see documents specifically cited by Hinsley and associates only to be informed that they were still restricted.[68]

Two more volumes were published over the next five years: Volume 2 focused on 1942 through mid-1943, and volume 3, part 1, dealt with selected aspects of intelligence, including the V-weapons, from mid-1943 through mid-1944.[69] These volumes quickly established themselves in the tradition of previous volumes in the official British series on World War II as exhaustively researched, meticulously presented, and thoroughly documented. Unlike the popular works cited earlier, these works gained attention and general acceptance by the scholarly community. As had their predecessors, Hinsley and his colleagues exercised restraint with regard to assessing the roles and influence of specific individuals. Interestingly and somewhat out of character, however, they specifically countered claims about alleged previous knowledge of the Coventry bombings that had been sensationalized by Winterbotham, Cave-Brown, and Stevenson and dealt with the detailed contributions of both the Poles and the French to ULTRA.[70]

Hinsley's first volume focused on the bureaucratic process established to ensure that intelligence was included in the planning for and prosecution of the war. In doing so, he documented the degree to which intelligence and planning were initially integrated by the British and eventually the Americans. This volume and the two subsequent ones used case studies to outline instances in which strategy and intelligence were combined, and they included assessments of the importance of intelligence. What became clear was that from 1940 through mid-1943, the insights from intelligence—an appreciation of German intentions—were largely negated by the operational and strategic inability of the British to do anything with this information. In North Africa, the Mediterranean, and the Atlantic through 1942 (which coincided with American entry into the war), British intelligence merely informed. With regard to pre-OVERLORD planning (then subsumed under COSSAC), intelligence merely validated the level of German preparedness in northwest France, an exercise that convinced planners of their inability to mount an invasion in 1943.

Because of their emphasis on the process, Hinsley and his colleagues had very little to offer historians concerned with OVERLORD and deception. An exception was conclusive documentation regarding both the process and the substance of the ULTRA operation. Both Winterbotham and Cave-Brown insisted that by late 1943, signals intelligence had made significant contributions at the strategic and tactical levels and in both planning and execution. Its accomplishments were impressive enough to have gained the confidence of Anglo-American leaders, military commanders, and planners—to a degree not previously appreciated. From 1943 onward, ULTRA reported on the number, location, and operational status of German divisions in the area where the Allied landings were planned. These appreciations were regularly funneled to the British chiefs as well as Churchill through the Joint Intelligence Committee (JIC). From the outset, COSSAC planners were conscious of two factors. One was the critical threat posed by German panzer divisions to the amphibious assault during the most vulnerable period following the landings. These fears had been vividly illustrated in 1942 by the ill-fated Dieppe raid.[71] Second was the need to deceive the Germans as to the time and location of the main (and, as it turned out in OVERLORD, only) landing. As Hinsley correctly noted, "Tactical surprise was [a] prerequisite."[72] Thus intelligence in general and ULTRA in particular formed an essential part of COS-SAC planning that was taken up by SHAEF. COSSAC's conclusion that the Germans would not collapse without an Allied invasion of Europe was based on ULTRA, "our most important source of intelligence."[73] SHAEF appears never to have questioned that conclusion.

The first volume of the British intelligence subseries to address OVER-LORD planning was volume 3, part 2, published in 1988.[74] As Hinsley had noted earlier, a key aim was to deceive the Germans as to exactly where the invasion was to be launched along the French coast (everone now accepted that the Germans knew that an invasion of northwest France was inevitable). This volume documented the details of the deception plan that became known as FORTITUDE, a scheme that eventually became essential to OVERLORD's success. Planners envisioned feinted landings in both Norway (FORTITUDE NORTH) and the Pas de Calais (FORTITUDE SOUTH). But would the Germans take the bait? Hinsley and his colleagues observed, "The feasibility of FORTITUDE rested heavily on the knowledge . . . to be confirmed through sigint [that] the Germans were convinced that the Pas de Calais was the most likely invasion area."[75] They went on to trace through specific intercepts as well as JIC appreciations the degree to which knowledge of German assessments was passed to Anglo-American planners. As the JIC reported on the eve of OVERLORD, thanks to ULTRA, "there has been no intelligence during the last week to suggest that the enemy had accurately assessed the area in which our main assault is to be made. He appears to expect several landings between the Pas de Calais and Cherbourg."[76]

A second category of intelligence involved some sense of how the German commanders intended to oppose the expected Allied landings. Did they intend to meet the invading Allies on the beaches, as they had at Dieppe? Or had they decided to hold back, massing their forces for a decisive counterattack later on? As we now know, this was a matter of considerable debate between Hitler and his commanders.[77] However, ULTRA was less than satisfactory in answering this question for the simple reason that to do so required going inside the minds of Third Reich leaders, a feat that signals intelligence, however penetrating, could not accomplish. ULTRA analysts were able to document indecision on the part of the German high command, and that uncertainty led to "continued anxiety" among OVERLORD planners.[78] Several weeks before the landings, British intelligence confirmed for Churchill and OVERLORD chiefs that a "maximum of thirteen divisions . . . might be brought against OVERLORD."[79] Considering that the maximum number of Allied divisions projected to be ashore dur-

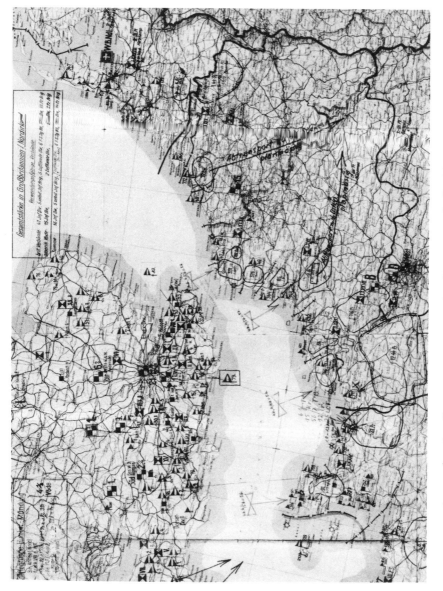

A map showing German guesses as to the disposition of Allied forces in Britain.

ing the first few days was considerably fewer, Eisenhower and his advisers were left in a precarious situation. ULTRA held no magical solution to the "fog of war," which Clausewitz had spoken of a century before and military commanders had faced for ages.

The precise details of the actual deception operation and how intelligence dealt with this problem of German reactions was dealt with in volume 5 of the British intelligence series, Michael Howard's *Strategic Deception*, not published until 1990.[80] Howard, a distinguished military historian, documented from a British perspective both the process by which deception operations were conceived and planned and the substance of specific operations. In the first case, he showed how double agents and the XX Committee were used to deceive Berlin. He also discussed the London Controlling Station, charged with the overall coordination of deception policy, which had first been revealed in *Bodyguard of Lies* and *Man Called Intrepid*.

The most revealing comments with respect to OVERLORD planning in this long-anticipated study were found in a chapter devoted to FORTITUDE. Noting that "deception becomes possible only when operational intentions have been determined,"[81] Howard made the obvious but often-ignored point that COSSAC intelligence planning for the cross-Channel invasion was academic in 1943 because there was simply no capability to launch such an invasion. However, with the appointment of Eisenhower as OVERLORD commander and the establishment of his headquarters in January 1944, everything was changed. The task for Allied planners became to mislead the Germans as to the precise nature and location of the invasion. That plan, FORTITUDE SOUTH, involved the creation of a notional invasion force whose mission was to seize Pas de Calais after the Allies had feinted landings at Normandy. To do so, the First United States Army Group (FUSAG), with the redoubtable George S. Patton in command, was established. Although the existence of such a diversion scheme was common knowledge (thanks in part to the popular movie *Patton*), totally unknown was the critical role played by the double agents who planted the information. As Howard commented, "Over 500 such transmissions were made between January and D-day: a daily average of about four."[82] Agents such as Garbo, Brutus, and Tate—first discussed by Masterman—"not only deceived the Germans to where the assault was coming but sow[ed] doubt as to whether it was coming at all."[83] Their messages were far more influential than the elaborate camouflage and indiscreet FUSAG radio traffic.

As the actual landings grew closer, there was a close integration of de-

ception planning and the OVERLORD operational plan. "Double agents . . .
mixed with their misinformation about the bogus structure of FUSAG
some true information about units serving with 21st Army Group," Howard stressed.[84] Also involved were very strict operational security measures instituted by the Allies. These included restriction of unauthorized
travel into areas where British and American armies were massing prior to
boarding transports and an almost total ban on diplomatic message traffic
out of the British Isles, with any exceptions requiring the approval of
Churchill, Roosevelt, and the War Cabinet. Although official historians as
well as popular chroniclers had mentioned such precautions, the precise
details as to how deception and counterintelligence operations were conducted and coordinated in the weeks before D-day were revealed in full
only in the final volume in the British intelligence series, *Security and
Counter-Intelligence.*[85]

As a result of deception schemes aimed at protecting OVERLORD, "At the
beginning of June, the Germans had no greater insight into Allied intentions than they possessed six months earlier. They had never altered their
perfectly correct belief that . . . the main attack would be launched across
the channel, with or without diversionary attacks elsewhere. But as to the
exact date and place, they remained completely uncertain."[86] Thus the deception operations pursued by the XX Committee and the reporting system facilitated by ULTRA gave Allied leaders such as Churchill, Eisenhower,
and the invasion commander, Field Marshal Bernard L. Montgomery, great
if not inevitable confidence as they approached the date of the landings.
Unfortunately for historians, those who made and executed the OVERLORD
plans in June 1944 went to their graves without revealing the degree to
which these MOST SECRET operations influenced their thinking and decisions. All that remain are platitudinous references that acknowledge without providing specifics.[87]

The details of American participation in ULTRA and deception planning
remain unexplored. There is no intelligence volume in the U.S. Army
green book series. This lack tends to support the British sense of American skepticism about such operations. Pogue's sections on deception
planning were subsequently declassified for researchers; however, little
use has been made of these sections or the supporting documentation.[88]
In 1984, responding to the positive reaction of the historical community
to Hinsley's volumes, the National Security Agency submitted a proposal
to cooperate with the Center of Military History on a joint history of
American World War II intelligence operations. This effort apparently
foundered on the rocks of institutional turf battles and the splintered in-

terests of the U.S. intelligence community. The Office of Air Force History subsequently commissioned a study of World War II intelligence of all types as it influenced Army Air Force operations during the conflict; however, that study, when published, will have little to say about the impact of FORTITUDE on OVERLORD planning.[89] In 1986, the U.S. Army War College hosted an international conference on "Intelligence and Military Operations." The lone paper on FORTITUDE at this gathering was a rehash of an official British Army report written in 1947 and subsequently confirmed in Howard's volume. Nothing was said about the American perspective.[90]

Regardless of continuing silence from the official history community in Washington about deception and OVERLORD, the British have provided historians with the missing dimensions of ULTRA and FORTITUDE—major components to be integrated into our overall understanding of that momentous undertaking. As they make clear, prior to the substantive OVERLORD planning effort of January to May 1944, signals intelligence intercepts under ULTRA, along with the intelligence operations of double agents under the XX Committee, gave British planners (and their military and civilian chiefs such as Churchill and Montgomery) a priceless sense of confidence about the capabilities and intentions of their adversary across the Channel. Roosevelt, Marshall, and a few others, including Eisenhower, became privy to the secret in 1942. What remains unclear and undocumented is the degree to which the American planning staff shared that assurance. Second, for those who devised OVERLORD, a critical—some might maintain essential—element of success hinged on their ability to deceive the German high command as to the exact time and place of the landing. Only deception on that scale would allow the Anglo-American invasion force the requisite time to build up and then absorb the expected Axis counterattack. FORTITUDE accomplished this mission.

In retrospect, negative assessments such as Weigley's and Hastings's of intelligence's role in the outcome of OVERLORD are incorrect. ULTRA did make a significant difference to the struggle for Normandy, as the British official historians document. What is not substantiated is precisely how and to what extent it provided the critical margin of victory from the American perspective, as the works of Matloff, Pogue, and Harrison did not consider ULTRA. Also, the official American accounts lack any authoritative discussion of FORTITUDE.

Thus the American official history of World War II remains unfinished. Historians can make a strong argument that by the spring of 1944 the Americans had taken on the dominant role in Allied planning—but only from the logistic perspective. Not until the role of American intelligence—both analysis and operations—is fully integrated into assessment at both strategic and tactical levels will there be any consensus regarding the hierarchy of American contributions to the overall Allied victory and the thought processes of leaders on both sides. This dimension is still missing.

5. Technology at D-day: Allied Weapons Old and New

Robin Higham

D-day took place some 29 years after the Gallipoli-Dardanelles landings of 1915. This fiftieth-anniversary essay is appearing almost twice that number of years after D-day. Have the changes in warfare been proportionately as great in the second interval as in the first? There were amphibious assaults before Gallipoli at places and times as diverse as Cartagena in 1741 and Walcheren in 1809, to cite but two British examples. And in these past actions, as in the case of Wolfe at Quebec in 1759, assaults against fortified places were generally allowed to come ashore without opposition on the beaches. The decisive action took place more formally, as on the Plains of Abraham.

In 1915, the British assault on the Gallipoli peninsula lacked any concept of surprise. Battleships had sailed up the Dardanelles, engaged the forts, and even sent landing parties ashore to spike the guns that the Turks had abandoned. However, the Turks got their revenge when some of the battleships ran into an Ottoman mine field and were sunk. Surprise was also lost by careless talk in London, and by the fact that after the invasion fleet arrived in the Levant it had to be sent to Alexandria to be combat loaded. Even when the assault force finally arrived off Gallipoli and began to land on 25 April 1915, it was put ashore in ships, boats, and other conventional transport. Debarking and deploying infantry were subjected to machine-gun and rifle fire and at once took casualties. Insufficient planning, lack of initiative on the part of officers, and the appointment of indecisive commanders all caused the objective to be lost sight of—namely, Constantinople and the opening of a supply route to Russia as well as a diversion of the Central Powers from their assault on the czarist forces.

Gallipoli eventually ended in failure coupled with high casualty rates both from the enemy and from disease. Technology played a role on both sides of the struggle. From out at sea the guns of the new battleship HMS *Queen Elizabeth* and of monitors pummeled defenses inland, guided at times by reports from primitive spotter planes launched from the precursors of aircraft carriers. Closer in, there was little gunfire support from warships because the flat trajectory of their guns prevented them from hitting the targets, which were mostly hidden from view by folds in the terrain. The infantry and artillery battle was largely fought close above the beaches with rifles, machine guns, and some barbed wire. Though the British Gallipoli commander, General Sir Ian Hamilton, was a hero who had been sent to watch the Japanese learn how to penetrate barbed wire and assault dug-in Russians in 1904–1905, the majority of his troops were either veterans of colonial wars or rank amateurs. On the Turkish side were veterans fighting on their home terrain, led and inspired by the German Limon von Sanders. The technology and tactics available were close to what the Turks had used in the defense of Plevna in 1877.

Gallipoli probably exhibited more continuity than change because it came early in a major war, before the contestants became serious and had to think about changing their tactics in order to break a stalemate. The precedent of the Russo-Japanese War of 1904–1905 had not sunk in any more than Petersburg, and the lessons of the American Civil War had begun to penetrate the European military mind early in the twentieth century.

D-day, 6 June 1944, occurred in rather different circumstances. In the first place, it came after almost five years of war as well as four years of increasing rearmament. D-day took place at a time when much new and improved equipment was available in quantity and special material had been developed and tested. D-day also occurred near the end of a decade of revolutionary developments in the technology used at sea, on land, and in the air.

At sea, the Germans were using welded-hull U-boats that could go as deep as 600 feet, magnetic mines, and acoustic torpedoes that were chemically propelled, so they left little or no wake. These torpedoes could be fired from below periscope depth and could be preset to run particular patterns. But one problem with using them in the Channel was the plethora of old wrecks in relatively shallow water, which could be misleading. Closer to the shore, the Germans had been able to erect all sorts of beach obstacles, given added punch by attached explosives. Backing up the beach obstacles were numerous guns either sited in bunkers on top of the cliffs or set into the cliff faces so that they could enfilade the beaches. However, except for the extension of obstacles from the land battlefield into the sea and the development of more sophisticated explosives and waterproof fuses, German naval defenses in the Channel consisted mostly of items used in the First World War or in the Western Desert of North Africa, where the German anti-invasion field commander, Field Marshal Erwin Rommel, had learned to use mine fields effectively. But he was unable to sow his sea mines.

On the Allied side of the war at sea, the revolution was more profound but still a continuation of methods developed by scientists in the 1914–1918 war and applied by the Royal Navy after 1934. Bigger and better depth charges that were able to sink deeper and faster were achieved by 1942, when it was realized that attacks were keeping U-boats down but not sinking them.

The real breakthrough for both escorts and hunter-killer groups as well as for aircraft came with the development of electronics, primarily in the 1930s. This meant the appearance of asdic and sonar (the British and American names for underwater sound-ranging equipment). What had been learned by mid-1944 were both the wonders and the liabilities of this equipment, though the Germans still had a better understanding of the way in which currents and temperature gradients deflected electronic pulses under water. Nevertheless, lessons learned and applied through training and battle practice had made the British, Americans, and Canadians much more adept at antisubmarine warfare (ASW) tactics. This was an excellent case of applied technology and an example of the lessons learned from the North African landings of 1942, when a few U-boats disrupted anchorages and resupply. The war at sea pitted applied science and training working in harness to defeat a technological menace. In essence, however, human strengths and frailties determined its outcome.

After mid-1943, the war at sea had a very important air side; subsequently, more than half the enemy submarines destroyed were the victims of aircraft. These not only ranged on much wider patrols, thanks to the arrival of the very long-range (VLR) B-24 Liberators, but had also been fitted with the sophisticated 10-centimeter radar and the Leigh light for illuminating U-boats on the surface at night. The development of low-level bombing techniques, in which the pilot rather than the bomb-aimer dropped the bombs; an understanding of U-boat strengths and weaknesses; and the development of suitable arms to exploit those weaknesses while avoiding their quad 20-mm guns gave the surface navies the upper hand after mid-1943.

All this meant that the Allied navies were able to protect the amphibious and support forces from U-boat attacks much better than they had off North Africa. Not only did they have the numbers to accomplish the task, but they had the technology and the know-how to use it effectively.

The whole amphibious operation owed a great deal to Gallipoli. The U.S. Marines had studied that disaster and determined how to turn a bad example into a workable operation. Although much of what they learned was applied in the design and development of new landing craft, ship-to-shore trucks called DUKWs, and methods of transferring infantry and artillery from ship to shore, it was essentially designed for the Pacific in an atoll-smashing campaign against the Japanese.

The successful Nazi campaigns of 1940 transformed the war situation; suddenly, as in the days of Napoleon, Britain faced 1300 miles of hostile coast. The trenches had become the English Channel. To cross no-man's-land would now require an amphibious operation such as the Germans had tried to mount in the third quarter of 1940. And it was only when one of the British defensive sector commanders, General Sir Frederick Morgan, set his staff to work to see what the Germans would have to bring against Britain that the islanders really had a true measure of what an enormous and hazardous operation a cross Channel attack would be. This gave impetus to demands for landing craft tanks and landing ship tanks (LCTs and LSTs).

Even these marvels of shipbuilding—especially the LST, with its cavernous hold and deckload, flying-off platform for spotter aircraft, and priceless ability to bring its cargo to within feet of dry beach—were not in sufficient supply. Thus operations in Italy canceled another end run around the Germans at Salerno and Anzio so that the necessary landing craft would be available in Britain for practices and D-day. And that demand meant that the invasion of southern France had to be postponed until August rather than being simultaneous with D-day.

When the multitude of ancillary craft had been loaded and were ready to be escorted across the Channel, they had to be protected en route by ASW vessels, and then their target shoreline had to be made as safe as possible, which was not easy. Thanks to the work of Captain Jacques Cousteau in the development of underwater breathing apparatus, frogmen were able to go in ahead of the invasion fleet and attempt to defuse and even destroy many of the obstacles that low-level photographic reconnaissance unit (PRU) aircraft cameras had revealed.

Much credit must be accorded to the training given to the largely amateur sailors and marines who manned the landing craft; this enabled them to do their jobs. Craft were lost to enemy fire and to accidents due to lack of sufficient seamanship. The latter was a case of technology being only as good as the man in command, his helmsman, and crew.

Protection of the invasion fleet and of the troops it put ashore might have been particularly difficult if a way had not been found to deal with the enemy guns hidden in the cliff faces and firing along the shore. It was true that the emplaced artillery and naval guns on top of the cliffs could be handled by bombers, once it was light, and by naval gunfire. But the guns in the cliffs were another matter, for they did not always show up in PRU shots, and the Germans were careful not to reveal their positions prematurely. Fortunately, in spite of the failure of radio communications through wet and lost sets, by this stage of the war the destroyers were commanded by bold, experienced captains. They took their fragile grey-hounds of the sea close into the beaches, sometimes bumping the sandy bottom, and delivered effective 4.7–inch (British) or 5–inch (U.S.) gunfire in rifle-like aimed shots at the offending German guns. With depth sounders and other modern gear, they gave an excellent demonstration of fearless supporting seamanship.

Meanwhile, further out to sea, the older battleships such as *Queen Elizabeth*, sister ship of Gallipoli's *Warspite*, and six other capital ships provided heavy gunfire support using radar for station-keeping. Two World War I monitors also assisted. This was a case of an old weapon being combined with a new weapon to do the job. The difference from the Dardanelles in 1915 was not only electronics but also the suite of antiaircraft guns with which all warships had been fitted by 1944.

Unlike Sicily in 1943, when the invasion fleet had to protect itself from both Allied and enemy bombers because insufficient care had been taken to coordinate movements of aircraft and shipping, D-day planners made great efforts to suggest to naval forces that aircraft were likely to be their friends. There were forward air controllers aboard ships, and the troops had been equipped with radio-telephones so that they could talk to their colleagues above. Great care had also been taken to paint black and white "invasion stripes" around the wings and fuselages of all Allied aircraft, an evolution from the practice of painting the undersides of Typhoons with black and yellow stripes to enable them to be distinguished from the German FW-190 in dogfights. Greater speeds meant that lookouts and gunners had less time to identify friend and foe in spite of the fitting of aircraft with a radar-imaging identification friend or foe (IFF) set. But not all surface vessels were fitted with such sensitive radar.

In the invading armies there was much that was old, but also many things that were new. Again, it was typical of the continuity and change in war. Going ashore, the British infantry carried the same rifles they had used at Gallipoli; their helmets had been developed at about the same time on the Western Front. Their webbing was of the same vintage, but their battle dress had been redesigned into a much more comfortable, practical, everyday combat uniform instead of the nineteenth-century tunics, trousers, and puttees worn until the eve of the Second World War by the Army and Air Force. The Americans carried newer rifles and also wore modern battle clothing, but their pack was still 1918 style because of the resistance of the Quartermaster Corps to a new design (even in wartime it took 18 months from the inception of an idea to an acceptable piece of equipment). U.S. tanks were fitted with a modification of the 75–mm French artillery piece of World War I; the Sherman tank, like its British counterpart, was a modified 1942 design that was still not equal to the then-current German Tiger and Panther tanks. The Sherman won by numbers, an example of U.S. mass-production abilities—technology in the factories.

The British Bren-gun carrier was a derivative of the infantry tankette of the interwar years and carried the very accurate .303 Bren automatic rifle. The accompanying infantry carried 9-mm Sten guns, which were developed to use up captured Axis ammunition in North Africa and were known, for their tinny construction, as "Woolworth guns." Like many sound weapons systems, the Bren-gun carrier remained in service throughout World War II. By D-day it had been modified to take a 40–mm Bofors antiaircraft gun. It was used against pillboxes, where its cliploading and accuracy enabled fire to be poured through the gun opening.

To meet the German mine field problem, various "funnies" were developed under the direction of that pioneer tankman Maj. Gen. P. C. Hobart of the 79th Division. One of these was the "flail," which carried a revolving drum on arms ahead of it. As the drum revolved, chains attached to it beat the ground to explode German mines. The German reaction, of course, was to reconfigure the fuse and mine so that when the flail detonated it, the charge was under the tank.

Both the Allies and the Germans had learned a good deal from the disastrous Dieppe raid of 1942. That raid had shown that the British could put tanks ashore but that they needed a means to get over the shingle; they needed to be protected, as did the infantry and the combat engineers, by massive fire support and tactical airpower, and the overall tactical commander had to have waterproof communications so that he could get the picture in his command ship offshore and be able to direct the battle. The landing attempt had also shown that complacency among the intelligence staff was deadly. Finally, and of much influence on D-day, was the lesson that any attempt to capture a port was likely to be counterproductive for two reasons: The Germans would assume that the port was the vital objective, and the resulting fighting would make a successful attack useless—a classic Pyrrhic victory.

For the Germans, the lessons of Dunkirk were that an assault could be stopped on the beaches and that their defense had worked pretty well. The result was that their victory, as is often the case, made them complacent. As far as their equipment was concerned, the German soldiers carried weapons developed from the First World War supported by better artillery and well-developed tanks. Although the German army had always studied defense because of the problems of a two-front war, until mid-1943, the Germans had been so successful that blitzkrieg ideas had taken hold. Their biggest problem, apart from the high command system, was the haphazard nature of the fortifications developed along the French coasts by the Todt Organization.

In between the Army and the Royal Air Force were the airborne parachutists and glider troops. Here again, there was a combination of continuity and change, as well as lessons learned from the enemy. The German use of paratroops, gliders, and air transports in the Norwegian, Dutch, Belgian, and French campaigns of the spring of 1940 had compelled British and later U.S. military authorities, including Churchill, to pay attention to developments the Russians had used in 1934. The commander of the Royal Flying Corps in France, Sir Hugh Trenchard, had even proposed air landings in 1917 as a way of stopping the German bombing of Britain.

After their successful, but Pyrrhic, assault on the island of Crete in May 1941, the Germans gave up airborne attacks while the Allies adopted their ideas wholesale. The Allies first used gliders and paratroopers in Sicily in 1943, with variable success. The Germans, as it happened, also used paratroopers to reinforce the garrison there, and the two groups landed on the same dropping zones (DZs) within minutes, creating a deadly confusion.

By D-day airborne operations were in much better condition thanks to several electronic developments. The first was Gee, which enabled a navigator with nimble fingers to get two different readings off his scope and plot these on Mercator charts overprinted with parabolic lines from the main station and the two slave stations. A competent navigator working fast could get a fix within five yards. With that sort of accuracy, he could drop loads into small DZs, enabling, in theory, paratroopers and their supplies to arrive close together. Moreover, even greater accuracy for dropping paratroopers or for landing gliders could be achieved, again in theory, by the use of the Rebecca/Eureka beacon system. The trouble was that the whole signal system relied on the advance drop of small teams to set up the Eureka beacon, which could be read on a direction and distance cathode ray tube (Rebecca) at the navigator's station on an incoming aircraft. With 100-, 50-, and 10-mile scales, a plane with a well-coordinated crew could home accurately right onto the beacon.

In addition to IFF, the Mosquito and Black Widow nightfighters had airborne indicator (AI) radar, which by 1944 was much improved over the primitive sets the Beaufighters had been equipped with in the summer and fall of 1940. These British and American nightwatchmen could patrol the beachhead area at night and could either be vectored onto any "bogey" not transmitting an IFF signal or seek them out themselves. In general, they cooperated with sector controllers on command ships with the invasion fleet offshore.

The air forces' technology at D-day was largely the product and refinement of four revolutions in material that had developed after rearmament began in 1934. The first was the technological revolution in engines, airframes, fuels, and ancillary equipment led by both the Germans and the Americans. The second was the manufacturing revolution in all-metal aircraft construction (even the wooden Mosquito was revolutionary in the De Havilland manner, using wood and other less essential raw materials and new glues for bonding and including only two aircrew). The third revolution was in electronics, which suddenly began to proliferate from its radar base on both sides of the Channel as well as more slowly in the United States; by the time of D-day, however, the Americans were well advanced with both radar-controlled guns on the German model and the highly important and secret VT proximity fuse.

The fourth radical development was the transformation of airfield construction. The Air Ministry Works Department in Britain built some 444 between 1934 and 1944, and the advent of concrete runways starting in 1939 both enlarged the size of the fields themselves and demanded new engineering methods. The heavy bombers that undertook the spring 1944 transportation plan destruction of the French railway weighed four times as much as the standard bomber of 1934 and twice as much as that of 1939. Concrete runways were essential and required a revolution in building techniques. The Germans also built all-weather airfields, but for them it was less essential because so many of their aircraft were designed in the 1930s to operate off grass fields in support of rapidly advancing blitzkriegs. The Allies had learned in North Africa and Italy, not to mention the Pacific, the necessity of being able to establish airstrips as soon as possible in advanced locations. From 1940 on, the United States had developed and made available Marston mat, which soon became known as perforated steel plate (PSP). This could actually be flown in and laid by inexperienced crews with little supervision, as it locked together simply and provided an ideal landing strip for everything from Typhoons, Mustangs, and Thunderbolts of the Tactical Air Force to C-47 Dakotas and disabled heavy bombers. Although slippery when wet, it was durable and can still be seen today around the farms of Normandy.

There was also a fifth revolution of the decade 1935–44 involving the jet engine and aircraft. But the German ME-262 did not become operational until 1944, with the British Gloster Meteor following shortly thereafter; both were reserved for home defense. The radical and unreliable ME-163 rocket-propelled fighter appeared shortly before D-day, but it was a high-altitude interceptor that would have done little to help the forces under Field Marshals Rundstedt and Rommel against the assault of Allied tactical air forces or even the heavies when used in low-altitude attacks after the lodgment had been made.

The same may be said of the atomic bomb. If the British air raid on the heavy-water plant in Norway had not been successful, Hitler might have had a bomb, and he might have used it against London. However, to use it in the West might have created a Pyrrhic victory because the fallout would have drifted back over Germany, given the prevailing winds, and its use in France would have been a hazard to his own troops. Given his hatred of the Soviets, a more likely use might have been against Moscow. But who knows? Gas might have been as effective, since by D-day no one was carrying gas masks. Gas disabled more people in World War I than it killed, thus requiring more personnel to take care of the wounded.

Another sort of applied science was one of the eventual objectives of the Allied armies as they broke out of the beachhead—to clean out the launching sites for the German V-1 buzz bombs and V-1 ballistic rockets along the northeast French coast. These weapons, which were aimed at that immense target of metropolitan London with its almost 50-mile diameter, were not very accurate but had some psychological impact. More effective from the military point of view were the 5-inch aircraft rockets carried by Allied fighter bombers, devices reinvented in the Second World War.

Military services reflect the societies from which they come. Anglo-American societies had believed in volunteering until late in the First World War and had reinstated conscription for the Second. The result was that their armies were much more democratic. They were also a multicultural mix of the races and cultures of the Commonwealth in the British case and of the ethnic melting pot of America. In addition, there were the forces of the governments-in-exile in London. All these personnel were welded together by commonality of uniform and equipment, by the technological marvels of modern production. More than this, by agreement and through lend-lease, there was a certain amount of interoperability of weapons because things like Sherman tanks and Mustang aircraft were used by various Allies.

The command system, evolved from the First World War, had become one of alternating nationalities to ensure that everyone focused on the Allied purpose and not on individual national aims. Thus officers were compelled to think, plan, and act for the good of the cause. As compared to Gallipoli, one Allied advantage was that the admirals, R. Kent Hewitt (USN) and Sir Bertram Ramsay (RN) had experienced all the landings in

Europe—North Africa, Sicily, and Italy—and Ramsay had also managed the Dunkirk evacuations in 1940.

At the lower end of the spectrum, medical supplies and rations came increasingly from joint sources. Drugs came from both sides of the Atlantic, and the ubiquitous C, D, and K rations were shared.

For the Germans, there was also a mixing of ethnic groups as their armies became manned by people from all over Europe and as organizations such as the Todt construction gangs contained more and more forced labor. But whereas the Allies agreed on Europe first, the Germans focused on the Soviet Union, so Rommel was unable to get the manpower, the concrete, and the mines he needed to build the West Wall into an impregnable Maginot or Siegfried Line along the shore. This placed him at a severe technical disadvantage against the Allies. In addition, he suffered greatly in the air, since Great Britain had been sealed off against German PRUs. Thus he could not see the other side of the hill, and when the great day came, his superior, Rundstedt, was hamstrung by the successful Allied deception, which made it appear that U.S. General George S. Patton was going to land the First Army near Cap Gris Nez on the shortest route across the Channel.

That deception was a masterpiece of technological planning. A leisurely advancing circle of heavy bombers flying low over the Channel, dropping the radar-reflective window, convinced German radar operators that a large fleet, simulated by motor gunboats, was slowly making its way across the narrows just as the Germans expected it would.

That deception on the morning of 6 June 1944 was but the end of a long program of technical planning that had begun almost as soon as the British had successfully withdrawn from Dunkirk in June 1940 and had been forced to think about protecting the United Kingdom from a threatened German invasion. Attack on a defended coast was more complex than the nineteenth-century promoters of invasion scares had realized.

Once Sir Frederick Morgan's group took a serious look at the problem and began to calculate the size of both the necessary initial wave and the follow-up requirements to make good wastage and keep an invading force ashore supplied and mobile, it became obvious that even putting only three to five divisions (10,000 men) ashore was a major operation. Gallipoli had clearly shown that unloading onto beaches was a time-consuming and vulnerable enterprise. Dunkirk and subsequent operations such as Dieppe in 1942 had shown the absolute necessity of air cover, which meant that no cross-Channel assault could take place beyond the range of fighter cover from airfields in southern Britain. It was also necessary to get forward airstrips ashore as soon as possible in order to have quick-reaction fighter and fighter-bomber forces within close range of the enemy, as opposed to having to maintain wasteful standing patrols or endure the delay while aircraft were launched from Britain and crossed the Channel, assuming that orders were approved and transmitted in the shortest time possible.

Morgan's calculations quickly showed that there were only two or three ports available on the north coast of France. Unlike in the November 1942 TORCH operation, these would not be immediately available and were likely to be heavily defended, for the Germans knew that the Allies needed them. Thus Le Havre at the mouth of the Seine and Cherbourg on the Cotentin peninsula were desirable. But before they could be taken, the armies ashore would have to be supplied over the beaches or through very small, easily congested, and vulnerable ports. In actuality, Le Havre was not taken until July 1944, and the Germans did an excellent job of containing the beachhead and then delaying the capture of Cherbourg until 27 June, by which time they had demolished the docks, creating a further delay. The stubborn defense of Brest and Lorient had also denied access to those U-boat lairs on the western coast. So the Chief of Staff to the Supreme Allied Commander designate (COSSAC) planners were correct when they decided that they would have to create artificial harbors so that the necessary tonnage of supplies could be put ashore directly in support of the beachhead.

Thus the Mulberries—the Phoenix floating caissons and obsolete ships—were to be taken across the Channel and sunk to form a breakwater for an artificial harbor. Later critics with the benefit of hindsight and without informed firsthand knowledge of the situation in Britain in 1940–44 have criticized the money and time wasted on the Mulberries, little realizing the incredibly short time for actual construction. Their criticism has been sharpened by the great and unusual summer storm that hit on 18 June and in three days partially wrecked the American artificial harbor. However, unloading over the open beaches, even with a plentiful supply of LSTs and other landing craft, would have been insufficient to maintain the forces ashore. Moreover, the severe rise and fall of the tide on that coast (more than 20 feet), coupled with the uncleared beach obstacles, made artificial ports essential.

The technology used was not new, for concrete ships had been built during the First World War, and concrete caissons of a smaller size had been used in the interwar years in various construction projects. What was bold and new was to make such large ones as those taken across to France. Yes, they were awkward to tow, yes, they were not sunk in perfect position in the difficult conditions of wind and sea on the day of their ar-

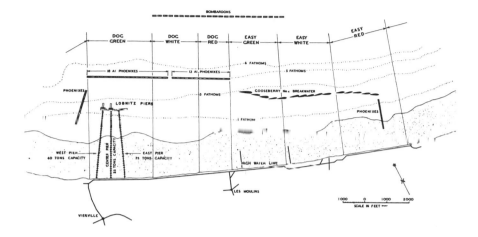

A diagram of Mulberry A, one of two artificial harbors constructed offshore.

rival; and yes, they did not stay in place. But no military operation in wartime goes perfectly, and the Channel has always been noted for the variability and difficulty of its weather. That the caissons shifted in the great storm was due in part to no one having allowed for such high waves. Those rolling in were sufficient to cause the caissons to bump up and down across the bottom and to incapacitate the Gooseberry floating breakwaters. But with their port facilities and the rolling roadways, the ports created at Arromanches and St. Laurent were able to do their job. And Arromanches was still there in 1981.

Weather was a constant natural problem that had faced the German planners in 1940 and was eventually a factor in Hitler's calling off the invasion of Britain. The COSSAC team was equally aware of the problem, and when Supreme Headquarters Allied Expeditionary Forces (SHAEF) came into being, a special Allied weather team was created in February 1944 by Eisenhower's order. This combined team proceeded to gather historical data and enter it on Hollerith cards, a pre-IBM system. They would forecast the weather for the coming week on the basis of the past, and at the next weekly briefing they would measure their accuracy. This gave both the forecasters and the senior officers who listened to them confidence. Thus, when the critical judgments had to be made from 3 to 5 June, Eisen-

Mulberry-Gooseberry harbor displaying storm damage.

hower had great confidence that his weathermen were giving him the most reasoned predictions for such a fickle subject. That the meteorologists could provide such accuracy was due to the great buildup of scientific data through human observation, recording instruments, and sounding balloons that could provide data from the upper atmosphere, as well as observations made by aircraft crews and the special instrumentation that Meteorology flight aircraft carried.

To get the invasion fleet across the Channel, radar-reflective buoys were laid that could be read on screens through the sea clutter that "snowed" on the sets of the day. But getting ashore in France was complicated by the fact that the charts of those shifting bottoms and wayward currents were 50 years out of date. As a result of wind, tide, currents, and the accidents of night operations in war, various parties found themselves in different places from those they had planned. The demolition of Belgian gates, Tetrahydra, and C elements was hindered by the dislocation of underwater teams in the dark, by the loss of the boat carrying the poles to mark the safe passage through the obstacles, and by the sinking in the rough weather of eight out of nine Grasshoppers, with their ripple salvoes of Hedgerow rockets designed to clear paths through the obstacles and up the beaches. In other words, no matter how good the technology, men had to make sure that everything went right, including making allowances for the roughness of the sea and the fickleness of its unplotted currents. And there was always chance. One path through the obstacles was not blown because at the moment the officer went to trigger the fuse for the demolition charges, he was shot and killed.

But that human side of technology happened not only on the Allied side. Rommel got only a small proportion of the mines he wanted to lay at sea, and air attack prevented the placement of those. The Luftwaffe suffered from an overabundance of men per aircraft (100:1) and had a serviceability rate of only 32 percent for the 500 aircraft in the command, versus, for instance, the 75 percent that Sir Hugh Dowding had been able to count on in RAF Fighter Command in 1940's Battle of Britain.

Maintenance and wastage are essential components of technology that are much overlooked. In this case, the ineffectiveness of the Luftwaffe against the D-day landings can be explained in part by that low serviceability rate. Obviously the Germans had the men but not the spares with which to keep their aircraft operational. In contrast, by 1944, the Allies had become selective enough in types and experienced enough in maintenance and in calculating wastage to be able to operate continuously. In fact, the reserves for wastage on D-day and thereafter were, it turned out, well above those needed.

Wastage and maintenance were not merely air force problems. The Anglophobe Admiral Ernest J. King, Chief of Naval Operations in Washington, was reluctant to assign landing craft to the European theater in part because he had a Pacific agenda but also because those that had been assigned in 1942 had not been used. He was also irritated with the British Admiralty because it would not spend money on dockyard overtime to repair landing craft damaged in training accidents. Not until February 1944 was it agreed that OVERLORD's needs would be met in part by transferring 242 landing craft of various sizes from the Mediterranean and that the admiralty would repair those that had been damaged. In addition, the shortage was overcome by agreeing to allow heavier loadings and to delay ANVIL in the south of France for two months. Moreover, the turnaround of landing craft was improved by the building of hardstands sloping into the water so that the craft could be loaded directly from beaches instead of having to lie alongside a dock and be loaded by crane. Off the Normandy beaches, the smaller craft that shuttled between ships and shore were loaded with infantry via "helter-skelter" canvas chutes within which fully loaded infantry could slide into the boats instead of precariously scrambling down cargo nets in the choppiness of the Channel.

Getting tanks ashore was another interesting technological problem. In the first hours, many tank landing craft would not be able to beach, yet the infantry badly needed the physical and moral presence of armored fighting vehicles to help them get off the beaches and break out into the countryside in back of them. In addition to tanks, it was necessary to get ashore DUKWs carrying 75-mm and 105-mm guns and mat-laying tanks that would, in effect, pave the ball-bearing shingle so that tracked and wheeled vehicles could reach the exit roads.

The Dieppe raid in 1942 had seen the first attempt in Europe to fit tanks with "snorkels" so that when they dropped off the ramps of LCTs and sank to the bottom, they would still be able to keep their engines running and the crew alive while they climbed ashore. Unfortunately, the idea did not work very well, and a number of tanks and crews were lost. The solution to this operational dilemma was provided by a Hungarian in Britain who proposed a duplex-drive (DD) tank that had not only the usual tracks but also propellers in the rear. Some 30,000 launchings of these beasts, fitted with canvas aprons similar to the temporary bulwarks used in ancient sailing ships, had taken place around Britain, with only one fatality. The planners and designers had simply not anticipated the waves of 6 June.

On D-day, a number of DDs simply sank out of sight when they plunged off the ramps; others, after a successful launching, were swamped on the way ashore. Part of the problem was the limited experience of the landing craft crews, who dropped the Shermans and Churchills as far as four miles offshore. Another part was the failure to take counteraction to the sea state. At Omaha Beach, only 5 of 32 DDs launched four miles out made it ashore, and three of these were delivered on shore by an LCT that was unable to lower its ramp at sea. At Utah, 28 out of 32 reached the beach because they were dropped only two miles out. The success rate at the British beaches was much higher due to the protection provided by the Calvados Reef, which calmed the waters. Two DDs were lost when rammed by LCTs that evidently did not see their low profile. Some of these tanks may have been lost because of human nature; tank crews discovered that they could store additional gear and other items in the sponsons, thus reducing their buoyancy. Unfortunately, someone always has to think of what people may do, especially when technology is handled by ingenious amateurs and not by automatons.

A further example of the need to think through the use of equipment may be seen in the essential bulldozers. Those in General Sir Bernard Montgomery's sector were armored against small-arms fire, but those that landed at the American beaches were not. Yet these beasts of burden were essential for making roads so that troops and vehicles could clear the beaches.

Obviously, there is not enough space to cover all the developments mentioned in the recent literature. This includes the whole question of the technical side of ULTRA. Suffice it to say that the technological marvel, Enigma machine, was in fact a prewar Polish commercial invention used on merchant ships. Although cracking it was a technical-mathematical achievement, it was only a continuation of the constant battle that was being fought long before the First World War, in which technology began to play a much greater role in codebreaking and intelligence gathering.

Like ULTRA, technology was really more than the icing on the cake; it was a very important ingredient. But no matter how great the production and availability, and no matter how many ingenious solutions actually got to operational units, success at D-day was due to successful conceptions of grand strategy, strategy, tactics, planning, and training on both sides. In other words, technology was the sword and the armor, the bow and the arrow, but it was useless without trained personnel who comprehended its advantages and limitations and had worked with others to create a well-guided force.

Rommel and Rundstedt started with the disadvantage of Hitler as their commander, a man who did not like or understand the sea and its technology. They also had the disadvantage of Hitler's megalomaniacal attitude toward the USSR, as compared to Franklin D. Roosevelt of the United States, who agreed that it was Europe first, the Pacific war and the Japanese second. And even if Churchill was as General Sir John Kennedy said—the man with whom and without whom the British won the war—at least he had a wide grasp of war, especially naval warfare.

The Germans were slow to appreciate the seriousness of the Allied threat of a cross-Channel invasion and did not appoint a commander to prepare their response until Rommel arrived in 1943. By then the Todt Organization, lacking strategic guidance, had expended its energies where it saw fit and where the work was easiest. It had largely fortified Cap Gris Nez at the shortest crossing point without sitting down and gaming out the role and thoughts of the COSSAC team. Thus, when Rommel was placed in command of the defenses, with Admiral Friedrich Ruge as his naval adviser, he was handicapped by vast lengths of shoreline that were incompletely defended, he was short of concrete and mines, and he was hamstrung ultimately by Rundstedt's failure, like that of the Turks, to see that the vital thing was not to allow the enemy to make a lodgment and expand it into a beachhead.

Yet history was there for both sides to study. D-day was not the first Allied landing since Gallipoli 29 years before, nor were the Germans without experience. They had demonstrated in Crete that a successful airborne invasion depended not so much on equipment as on the training and guts of those dropped and on an understanding of the advantages, limitations, tactics, and essence of such operations.

By 1944, the Allies had the benefit of considerable experience in two theaters of amphibious assaults and had largely developed the equipment and trained the people to command and use it. What made D-day special was the apparent gamble of finally landing back on the Continent in northern Europe, the apparently formidable nature of the defenders, and the reputation of their commander, as well as the many gadgets developed for the assault, which made great copy. Indeed, one of the things that made D-day special were the combat cameramen and journalists who recorded it for both contemporaries and posterity. That too involved a technology that was much improved since Gallipoli in 1915.

Last, the reader may wish to know how D-day relates to the Gulf War, some 46 years later. Inchon, Korea, in 1950 was merely another replay of Pacific war tactics by veterans of that affair. Lebanon in 1958 was merely a positioning operation. Vietnam saw some of the same equipment, notably LSTs and some smaller landing craft, used, but it never saw a full-fledged assault against a defended area. The Falklands was a storm in a teacup in 1982.

The Gulf War saw the threat of an amphibious attack used as a feint to pin Saddam Hussein's forces. The real legacy of D-day in that 1990–91 conflict was in the advanced technology—especially air transport, radar, and satellite coverage—and the use of sophisticated helicopters (just becoming available in 1944) and ground vehicles, including tanks. But perhaps the most important legacy from 6 June 1944 was the enormous sea transport and logistic planning. Containerships, among other means, were used to mobilize overwhelming power to launch an attack from well-prepared bases in Saudi Arabia and from aircraft carriers in the Red Sea and the Persian Gulf. Cruise missiles were fired from refurbished World War II battleships.

The Gulf War also saw technology ballyhooed, but 87 percent of the bombs dropped were the old "iron" ones not too dissimilar from those used in pulverizing the Normandy defenses, though the means of delivery was largely from high-tech aircraft, descendants of the ME-262 and the Meteor.

D-day was made possible technologically by the revolutions that were taking place in material as a result of both the great jump forward in the First World War and the revolutions unleashed when disarmament failed and rearmament for the next war opened the coffers.

Part Two

The Battle

6. The Navies and NEPTUNE

Max Schoenfeld

Navies are traditionally ambivalent about amphibious operations, and the greatest one of modern times was no exception. NEPTUNE, the naval operation to place the armies of the Western Allies ashore on the continent of Europe, posed enormous difficulties. Doctrinally, both the United States Navy and Britain's Royal Navy embraced the Mahanian concept of the decisive clash of fleets. Amphibious operations, with the attendant problems of working with armies and their different ways of thinking, were an unwelcome intrusion for "blue-water" seamen. German defenses would pose formidable obstacles, and scarce resources would have to be mustered from across half the world. Thus neither Allied navy was eager to tackle an early operation. Each had a full plate throughout 1942 and 1943: the U.S. Navy in the Pacific and the Royal Navy in the North Atlantic, Mediterranean, and Indian Ocean. When the American Joint Chiefs of Staff requested their Joint Strategic Committee to assess in early 1942 the possibility of carrying out such an operation in mid-1943, the committee's affirmative reply was ill received by the leadership of the U.S. Navy. That service viewed the prospect of transporting needed men and material across the Atlantic as problematic at best until the U-boats had been mastered. Nonetheless, the Navy embarked in early 1942 on the task of building sufficient landing craft for such an undertaking.[1]

Following an extended and at times bitter debate during the spring of 1942, Admiral Ernest J. King, the American Chief of Naval Operations and Commander-in-Chief, U.S. Fleet, had accepted the North African operation, TORCH, advocated by Prime Minister Churchill and insisted on by President Roosevelt for the end of 1942. But King had stipulated that there could be no second front in northwest Europe until 1944. Although that point was suitably fudged on paper, King henceforth acted as if it were accepted coalition policy and shifted his attention once more to the Pacific. An early victim of the priority for TORCH was the landing craft building program. Given the highest construction priority in the spring of 1942, it was cut back in the summer.[2]

Following TORCH and the Casablanca conference of January 1943, Lt. Gen. Frederick E. Morgan was appointed Chief of Staff to the Supreme Allied Commander designate (COSSAC), and planning gathered momentum. On 15 July 1943, Morgan reported to the British Chiefs of Staff that a cross-Channel invasion of Europe was a feasible operation. His report stressed two major concerns, however. First was the problem of supplying Allied forces across the beaches until regular port facilities became available. His second concern was the availability of landing craft and ships to put the armies ashore and sustain them there.[3] COSSAC had thus identified two of the three main problems that would affect the naval operations to support OVERLORD. The third, of course, was German countermeasures. These, as the painful rebuff at Dieppe had indicated, would be formidable.

The Royal Navy assigned to Morgan's staff one of its brightest stars, Rear Adm. George Creasy, a future First Sea Lord, as well as the experienced Commodore John Hughes-Hallett from Lord Louis Mountbatten's Combined Operations staff. In contrast, the U.S. Navy assigned a pair of captains as its senior representatives.[4] The U.S. Navy preferred to maintain an autonomous organization in England, the 12th Fleet, whose Task Force 122, under Rear Adm. Alan G. Kirk, was responsible for the American part of the cross-Channel operation being planned by COSSAC. Separate American organizations also dealt with amphibious forces and landing craft and bases. Not until April 1944 would the U.S. Navy come under operational control of the Allied Naval Commander for NEPTUNE/OVERLORD. The U.S. Navy's tradition of maintaining maximum independence from joint and combined organizations gave rise to British suspicions that it was deliberately dragging its feet in regard to NEPTUNE. That service, for its part, was just as suspicious of British intentions regarding the operation. At the Washington conference in May 1943, King was openly skeptical about the British commitment to any full-scale attack across the Channel. Had the U.S. Navy held itself less aloof, one suspects that many of these misunderstandings could have been avoided.[5]

At the second Washington conference (TRIDENT) in May 1943, Anglo-American leaders set 1 May 1944 as the tentative date for the invasion of northwest Europe. With the question of when resolved, it was necessary to decide on where. Possibilities fell within the 300 miles of coastline opposite England between Flushing and Cherbourg. The two chief contenders were the Pas de Calais, from Dunkirk to the mouth of the Somme, and the Bay of the Seine, from Caen west along the coast of the Cotentin peninsula of Normandy. General Morgan and Admiral Mountbatten were convinced that the latter was not only preferable but was, in fact, the only satisfactory place. However, it took a meeting at Mountbatten's headquarters in Largs, Scotland, at the end of June 1943 to convince the doubters. The Normandy beaches were at least equal to those of the Pas de Calais, and the beach exits were more numerous and wider. Also, the Pas de Calais was more heavily defended and more easily reinforced. Of particular note for the navies, Normandy offered a better chance of early capture of a major port. One calculation proved false; weather records showed that bad weather in the Channel during the summer months came from the south and west. The Normandy beaches were much more sheltered from such weather than was the Pas de Calais. Unfortunately, against all the odds, 1944 turned out to be the year of a freak June gale out of the north-east.[6]

When the next Allied conference convened at Quebec in August 1943, Morgan was able to present an outline operational plan focused on Normandy. At least one person at Quebec was uneasy about the COSSAC plan. Prime Minister Churchill called for at least a 25 percent increase in the strength of the initial assault, which had been set by the Combined Chiefs at three divisions, with two in immediate follow-up. Churchill's proposal revived concern about landing craft. COSSAC estimated a large deficit of these vessels. How was it to be made up? American production was being increased, but the effect of this would not be felt until April 1944. Thus, COSSAC calculated that it would also be necessary to reallocate craft from the Mediterranean and elsewhere, comb out training facilities, and increase both serviceability rates and loading.[7] At the Tehran conference, under Stalin's prodding, the invasion scenario took firmer shape. Returning to Cairo following this meeting, President Roosevelt announced on 3 December 1943 the choice of General Dwight D. Eisenhower as Supreme Allied Commander. The Cairo conference also reallocated some landing craft to NEPTUNE but continued the plan for a simultaneous landing in southern France, which required keeping other craft in the Mediterranean.[8]

Eisenhower arrived in London on 14 January 1944 to take up his duties, and COSSAC was absorbed into Supreme Headquarters Allied Expeditionary Force (SHAEF). Eisenhower's naval deputy, Allied Naval Commander, Expeditionary Force (ANCXF), was already in place. Admiral Sir Bertram Ramsay had been appointed in October 1943. He had carried out with distinction the Dunkirk evacuation in 1940 and later served as Deputy ANCXF for TORCH. His appointment as naval commander for NEPTUNE was the result of Churchill's intervention when another name was proposed at the Quebec conference. Ramsay proved to be one of the prime minister's better picks. Rear Admiral Creasy from COSSAC's staff became Ramsay's Chief of Staff.[9] From the time he first examined the COSSAC plan, Eisenhower asserted the need for a larger initial landing, a view shared by his ground forces commander, General Montgomery. This view prevailed. The decision to expand the assault required finding more shipping. One step toward that goal was to set back the date for D-day by one month to gain additional production. In the actual event, all of COSSAC's earlier recommendations had to be accepted. Most notable was postponing the landing in southern France to permit reallocation of landing craft to OVER-LORD. The primary loss was one month of good campaigning weather in Western Europe.[10] Ramsay also proposed that his bombardment force be increased. Any additional warships, however, would have to be American. Transatlantic squabbles ensued, but late in the day the U.S. Navy sent more ships than Ramsay had requested.[11]

On 26 April 1944, ANCXF moved into his battle headquarters at Southwick House, seven miles north of Portsmouth and less than a mile from Eisenhower and Montgomery. Southwick House became the center for executing Operation NEPTUNE. Morgan had succinctly described Ramsay's task some months before: "It was the crossing of the water's edge that demanded almost the greatest concentration of thought and ingenuity, first to ease the passage of the assaulting troops themselves, then to widen the greatest of all bottlenecks in the supply lines to be laid behind them."[12]

ANCXF's Naval Outline Plan provided that the British Second Army would be landed on the three eastern beaches—Sword, Juno, and Gold—by the British Eastern Task Force (Rear Adm. Sir Philip Vian). The U.S. First Army would be landed on the two western beaches—Omaha and Utah—by the U.S. Western Task Force (Rear Admiral Kirk). Each of the five beaches had its own force, designated by the first letter of the beach's name. The five landing forces were responsible for putting ashore the U.S. 4th Infantry Division (Force U), U.S. 1st and 29th Infantry Divisions (Force O), British 50th Infantry Division and 8th Armored Brigade (Force G), Canadian 3d Infantry Division and 2d Armored Brigade (Force J), and British 3d Infantry Division and 27th Armored Brigade (Force S). Also at sea would be two immediate follow-up forces to land the U.S. 2d, 9th, 79th, and 90th Infantry Divisions (Force B) and the British 49th and 51st Infantry Divisions, 7th Armored Division, and 4th Armored Brigade (Force L). The transport and escort for this immense force would employ 4,126 ships and craft, excluding the minesweeping and bombardment forces. Each landing force was composed of several convoys, and each of these was coded by its country, place of departure, nature of cargo, and number in order of sailing. A special organization was set up to manage the complex convoy movements involved.[13]

A major concern of the planners was how to sustain the armies until captured ports could be brought into use. The solution was to create artificial harbors, the famous Mulberries.[14] One would be erected for each of

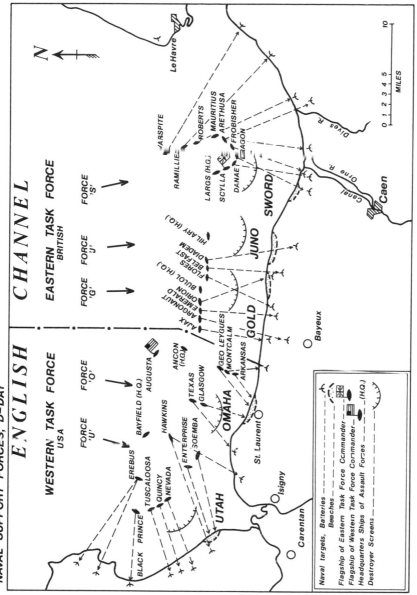

NAVAL SUPPORT FORCES, D–DAY

One small component of Task Force 125.

the two Allied armies. Building them required an immense commitment of labor and resources in Britain. In Correlli Barnett's words, they were "triumphs of the British genius for improvisation and adaptation using essentially 'low technology' components, materials and engineering methods."[15] When the great June storm destroyed the western Mulberry, it proved possible to unload across the American beaches at a rate exceeding that planned through the artificial harbor. This raised the issue of whether the great effort to construct them was worthwhile. Those who take this view miss the point that the soldiers were not prepared to go ahead with the landings unless they had assurance of adequate supply, which only the Mulberries seemed able to promise. More open to question was laying pipelines under the ocean (PLUTO), a project to get motor fuel across the Channel expeditiously. It had more than its share of problems, and Morgan, among others, doubted that it was worth the effort.[16]

Getting the various parts making up the Mulberries—some 400 units weighing 1.5 million tons—across the Channel and into their correct places was no less enterprising a task than their construction. It would take 158 tugs two weeks to carry this out. ANCXF gave Rear Adm. W. G. Tennant (R.N.) the chore of moving and emplacing the artificial harbors. He had previously served with Ramsay and had distinguished himself in the Dunkirk evacuation.[17] On Tennant's initiative, breakwaters composed of obsolete ships ("corncobs") that were sunk stem to stern were provided for each of the five beaches.[18] These would prove their worth and, according to Vice Adm. Brian Schofield, "saved the situation when the great gale occurred."[19] These massive undertakings constituted only part of Ramsay's task, which he believed required a detailed plan, given the scale of the operation and the limited sea room available. This led to production in mid-April of a naval plan that, with annexes, exceeded 1,000 pages. The U.S. Navy, led by Kirk, believed that the plan should have left more initiative to Ramsay's subordinates. In view of the magnitude of the task, Ramsay's judgment seems sound, and the lack of rapport between him and Kirk may have had something to do with their disagreement.[20]

The naval plan's success depended largely on how well the navies could cope with German defenses that stood between England and a secure lodgment on the coast of Normandy. That challenge took several forms— active and passive. Although the planners received a prediction in March that 75 U-boats could arrive in the Channel area by D plus 4, the German submarine threat never assumed serious proportions. Very different was the threat from mines—weapons that wait. Field Marshal Erwin Rommel and his chief naval adviser, Vice Admiral Friedrich Ruge, had a good appreciation of the mines' potential to provide an effective defense. Rommel had declared that "the main battle line will be the beach," and he was lavish in planting mines in coastal waters and along likely landing areas. Ruge was one of the Kriegsmarine's foremost experts in the use of sea mines. The greatest handicap the two faced was an insufficiency of weapons, and on numerous occasions since the war, Ruge has described the various problems that led to the German mine fields being of limited effect on D-day.[21]

The mines nonetheless constituted a serious problem. They were of four basic varieties: contact, magnetic, acoustic, and pressure. The last, often called the "oyster" mine, came in two varieties and was planted on the sea bottom. It was activated by a change in water pressure created by the hull of an approaching ship. Its acoustic subtype could be swept under ideal conditions, but its magnetic subtype required countermining. Oyster mines had not been used before D-day, so they would come as an unwelcome surprise to the Allies. However, the Germans could not use surface minelayers, which were unable to penetrate the Allied naval defenses. That left air-dropping by the Luftwaffe, which mounted a considerable effort. By 6 July, some 600 oyster mines had been laid, all by air, and proved extremely hazardous to shipping.[22]

The considerable tides along the Normandy coast, typically twenty feet, and the shallow gradient of the beaches, which made them accommodating to landing craft, combined to give Rommel a way to extend the depth of his defensive system by projecting it onto the broad tidal flats.

Contact mines were attached to steel piles and wooden stakes driven into the beach sand, where they were interspersed with other obstacles designed to impale, tear, or blow the bottoms out of landing craft. Mines were also buried in some beach areas. Ramsay correctly evaluated the danger when he wrote that "the mine threat is our greatest obstacle to success."[23]

The German scheme of beach defenses affected the landings' timetable. As night was desired for crossing the Channel and daylight for the landings themselves, H-hour (hitting the beach) should come soon after daybreak and about three hours before high tide. The landing craft could then disgorge troops short of most beach obstacles. Special parties would clear the obstacles ahead of the rising tide. The optimum tidal conditions at sunrise would occur for only two three-day periods in June 1944, the fifth through seventh and the eighteenth through twentieth. H-hours on the five landing beaches were spread over an hour and a quarter to meet different conditions on the various beaches, which extended some 50 miles from Sword to Utah. The eventual times set were 0630 on Utah and Omaha, 0725 on Gold and Sword, and 0735–0745 on Juno.[24]

The Germans had a third defensive weapon in addition to U-boats and mines: the fast torpedo boat forces, or *schnellboote* (the Allies called them E-boats), which actually inflicted the first casualties on the amphibious forces. At the end of April, following Operation TIGER, (a landing exercise by the American force assigned to Utah Beach), several U.S. tank landing ships (LSTs), escorted by a single corvette, were returning to harbor when *schnellboote* caught them, sinking two LSTs, damaging a third, and inflicting over 700 casualties.[25]

On 28 May 1944, Ramsay issued the order to carry out Operation NEPTUNE. This directive assumed a D-day of 5 June. NEPTUNE had to be put in motion this early because of the time required for the convoys sheltered in distant ports, notably the corncob ships, to reach the invasion area. On 31 May, the business of loading and movement began in earnest. A remarkable rate of combat readiness was achieved in the landing ships and craft, 99.3 percent for the Americans and 97 percent for all the others. No less remarkable, given the vast movement of shipping under way, was that German air reconnaissance did not detect what was afoot.[26] Eisenhower's decision to postpone the landings a day, promulgated at 0500 on 4 June, caught many ships at sea, and these had to be turned around. Convoy U2A, comprising 140 vessels bound for Utah Beach, was recalled only with difficulty. It had managed to pass through a mine field without loss, but one tank landing craft (LCT) later became a casualty. Ramsay's operational plan passed its first stern test. The day's delay failed to cause serious disruption to the naval forces, and the whole process remained undisclosed to the Germans.[27]

In the vanguard of the invasion force came the minesweepers, some 255 strong.[28] At the tip of this armada were 36 Royal Navy 112-foot minesweeping launches, three or four of which were to carry out a skim sweep ahead of the senior officer's vessel of each minesweeping flotilla. This was perhaps the most dangerous post in the whole procession of over 2,700 vessels.[29] A first step in the great minesweeping operation was to clear a circular area south of the Isle of Wight through which most invasion convoys would be routed. Out of this area five miles in radius, designated Position Z but promptly nicknamed Piccadilly Circus, ran eight channels as far as the German mine field in the middle of the English Channel. From there to the assault area, ten channels were swept, ranging in width from 400 to 1,200 yards. To assure accurate reference points for the sweepers and following forces, sonic buoys were laid at the entrances to the channels. Dan buoys were then laid every mile by the minesweepers to mark the edges of the swept channels, which were cut on the night of D minus 1.[30]

Because the sweep down to the French coast would cut through strong Channel tides, first running eastward and then westward, the minesweepers would have to carry out an intricate ballet in mid-Channel, turning their sweeps over as the tide turned, in the dark and in upswept water. This was executed by each vessel taking in its port sweeps in succession and forming a single line ahead. The senior officer's ship in the van and the motor launches ahead of him would keep their sweeps out. Then each would turn in succession, and they would sweep themselves back into the newly cleared channel. When far enough north, the vessels turned again to the south, streamed their sweeps to starboard, and took up cutting the new channel where they had left off. Only the highest standard of training permitted this evolution. Admiral Kirk correctly summed up the accomplishment when he said: "Minesweeping was the keystone of the arch of this operation . . . and minesweeping plans of unprecedented complexity were required. The performance of the minesweepers can only be described as magnificent."[31]

As they approached the beaches, the minesweepers coming down the channels split up, some to clear areas for assault transports and lanes for the bombardment ships, others to clear boat lanes to the shore just ahead of the landing craft. Once these essential lanes were open, the minesweepers would expand the swept areas and keep these safe waters clear of new mines. Hard on the heels of the minesweepers came the bombardment forces, led by six battleships, two monitors, 23 cruisers, and 68 de-

Operation NEPTUNE represented the largest naval armada ever assembled.

stroyers. Behind these were the leading assault forces. In all, some 195,000 Allied seamen and merchant mariners were at sea on 6 June, manning an invasion force carrying 130,000 soldiers, 2,000 tanks, and another 12,000 vehicles. There were in all 59 convoys, 21 for the American beaches and 38 for the British or Canadian beaches.[32]

Although massive bombing began at midnight and three airborne divisions began dropping behind the landing beaches at 0130, not until German coastal radar reported the approaching mass of shipping around 0300 did Naval Gruppe West decide that an invasion was under way.[33] German shore batteries, subjected to intensive air attack before the assault, were able to open fire on approaching ships off the American beaches as early as 0500.[34] However, the most serious threat to the American ships came from an unexpected field of magnetic mines laid at the end of April on the Cardonnet bank, over which the Utah Beach landing forces needed to move. The destroyer USS *Corry* became its first victim, but before D-day was over, sixteen landing craft were lost to this field. The next day the fleet minesweeper USS *Tide* was sunk, with heavy casualties.[35]

A major naval bombardment is a spectacular sight; it appears to the observer that nothing possible can survive the massive firepower deployed. Experience from the Pacific war indicated, however, that its destructiveness seldom approached appearances. Well-sited reinforced-concrete gun emplacements could be disabled only by a direct hit on the gun embrasure itself by a heavy-caliber shell. The Germans had such gun emplacements both to fire seaward and to enfilade the beaches while presenting no direct target to naval guns. The latter sites evidently had not been uncovered by photo analysts.[36] On D-day, history only repeated itself: Naval bombardment proved to be among the least efficient of military activities.

A key factor in naval bombardment is the law of averages; the more shells fired at a target, the higher the probability of a disabling hit. Here the Americans were less wise than the British, the former opting for a 30- to 40-minute bombardment before H-hour. The British preferred two hours, which was better but still not sufficient. Most German gun emplacements emerged largely unscathed. The bombardment accomplished two functions. First, it forced German gunners to "keep their heads down" during the critical period when the first assault waves moved toward the shore. Then, when the Germans tried to move up infantry or armored forces against the Allied lodgments, naval gunnery—notably the long-range battleship rifles—proved effective at breaking up German concentrations. In this respect, naval gunfire was most valuable in the days immediately following D-day itself. On that day, it fell largely to the ground forces to clear the fixed German gun emplacements. Naval bombardment would have to be assessed a modest contribution to Allied success.[37]

Tidal conditions at sunrise dictated that the earliest assault come on the westernmost landing area, Utah Beach. Rear Adm. Don P. Moon (USN), commanded Force U. The Americans had placed the lowering positions for their attack transports eleven miles offshore, as compared to eight miles for the British, to be out of range of German heavy batteries. Ramsay's judgment in thinking this overlay too cautious now appears correct. The American attack transports had to begin unloading in darkness, and the first wave began a difficult two-hour journey to the shore at 0430.[38] Dieppe and Sicily had taught that tanks needed to come ashore with the first infantrymen. Accordingly, eight LCTs, each with four duplex-drive (DD) tanks, were included in the initial assault on Utah. However, rough weather delayed the LCTs, which reached the transport area half an hour late. Their control officer, a lieutenant (junior grade), realized that they would be too late if the tanks were floated off the LCTs at two and a half miles from shore as planned, so he led the vessels into calm water just a mile offshore before discharging the tanks. Although one LCT was mined crossing Cardonnet bank, the 28 surviving tanks got ashore just behind the first infantry. This display of initiative by a junior officer contrasted sharply with the decision of Rear Adm. Morton L. Deyo, commanding the bombardment squadron. Although German shore batteries had opened fire at 0505, he waited until 0536, only fourteen minutes short of the scheduled time, before deciding to reply. Since the reasoning behind a short bombardment was to preserve "surprise," Deyo's inaction seems otiose.

As the first wave approached the beach, a massive rocket salvo was unleashed against the defenses by specially equipped landing craft. This and gunfire produced a heavy cloud of dust that obscured landmarks, and the strong tidal current carried the landing craft a mile south of the designated landing beaches. This proved fortunate, for that site was almost undefended, and the beach obstacles were less formidable there than to the north. The first landing craft appears to have touched down at 0635, only five minutes late. Naval demolition teams and army engineers landed with the second wave and rapidly cleared beach obstacles. A communications interruption and poor visibility led to the rumor that one of the landing sites for Utah was under heavy fire, and Admiral Moon delayed the departure of several waves for that beach. With Moon was Maj. Gen. J. Lawton Collins, VII Corps commander, who soon prodded the cautious sailor into lifting the suspension.[39] Fortunately, the delay led to nothing worse than some avoidable congestion later in the day. Part of the problem was too narrow a landing front. One of the two beaches could accept an average landing wave of only seven mechanized landing craft (LCMs), five LCTs, or six infantry landing craft (LCIs); the other beach could accommodate even fewer. As the experience of the first wave indicated, a much broader area could have been used. Overall, the Utah landings ran smoothly, and casualties were light.

Omaha Beach presented a more formidable obstacle. Although the beach itself was well-suited to receive landing craft, it was fronted by cliffs through which there were only four suitable exits. The eastern end of the landing area was only four miles east of Pointe du Hoc, where the Germans were believed to have a battery of six 155-mm (6-inch) guns, the primary reason for placing the transport area eleven miles off the beaches. This decision, in Samuel Eliot Morison's words, "turned out to be a big mistake."[40] When captured by Rangers, the battery was found to mount only wooden dummies. Because the Omaha assault area was more exposed to the weather than the Utah beaches, rough seas added to the difficulties experienced by the landing force.[41]

Unlike at Utah, mines were absent from the Omaha approaches. At 0430 the first wave moved toward the beaches. It was promptly swept off course by a strong tidal current. The landing craft became scrambled, and units arrived at the wrong places, which made it difficult for senior commanders to get a grip on their units. This proved unfortunate, for the German defense of Omaha was the most intense encountered on D-day. As at Utah, the Germans had skillfully sited guns to enfilade the beaches without being visible from the sea. Naval bombardment was thus of marginal assistance in reducing these strong points. Under such circumstances, the infantry needed immediate help from tanks. But the DD tanks on the left flank of Omaha were launched two and a half miles from shore, and all but five of 32 sank. On the right flank, all 28 DD tanks were wisely landed on the beach. Of 50 howitzers to be landed, 32 were lost when their amphibious vehicles foundered in the rough seas. The rocket barrage had been fired too early, and the projectiles fell short of the German defenses. Thus the assault force was seriously short of firepower. Primary compensation was provided by American destroyers in the bombardment force. As it became clear that a crisis was developing on the beach, the destroyers moved in as close to shore as possible to employ their five-inch guns in direct support. Here, also, problems of coordination arose. One destroyer captain later observed that he could employ only about 20 percent of his fire support capability because he lacked reliable communication with the shore.[42]

Beach obstacles also took a toll of landing craft. The sixteen underwater demolition teams who were to blast boat channels through the Omaha obstacles were scattered all over. Two teams were wiped out at once by enemy fire. The remaining teams raced against a rapidly rising tide, clearing only a third of the boat channels at the cost of heavy casualties. At 0830, the beachmaster halted all landing efforts while hundreds of craft, large and small, milled about in rough water. Yet by 1030 some sort of rough order was restored to the landing process. In no small part, this achievement resulted from LCTs and LCIs, riding the high tide, butting their way through those beach obstacles they could not clear. Fortunately, not many obstacles were mined on Omaha Beach.

As the tide receded, the demolition teams returned to their clearing effort; by evening, five large and six small boat channels had been opened. At nightfall, five regiments had been landed on Omaha Beach, and they had secured a narrow beachhead roughly five miles wide and a mile deep. In retrospect, it seems clear that the landing plan was inadequate. The battery at Pointe du Hoc had been allowed to dictate the location of the assault transport zone, which was too far from shore. There was poor judgment shown in allowing some LCTs to lower their ramps too soon. Ship-to-shore communication for gunfire support was not resilient enough to withstand the confusion of a tough battle on the beaches. The naval contribution to success at Omaha was, on balance, indecisive. The shore was won by the courage and tenacity of the soldiers.

The British Eastern Task Force was responsible for the landings on three beaches. Running west to east these were Gold, Juno, and Sword. All landings began at least an hour after the American landings, and all beaches received a two-hour naval bombardment. The British set their transport areas eight miles from shore, an advantage in the prevailing weather. The easternmost of the three British assault forces was the only one to encounter German naval interference during its approach. German torpedo boats from Le Havre sank a Norwegian destroyer but failed to reach the transports.

Some ten miles east of Omaha lay Gold Beach, where landing began at 0725. The British 50th Division got off to a rough start. Many DD tanks were knocked out as they arrived on the beach, and communications for direct gunfire support quickly collapsed. Gun embrasures that did not face directly toward the sea had largely escaped detection and plagued the troops as they tried to move off the beaches. A rapidly rising tide and stubborn beach obstacles combined to retard the clearing of boat lanes. Gold proved to be more heavily mined than Omaha, and this too impeded progress and increased casualties. As at Omaha, the troops needed the aid of destroyer gunfire to eliminate German strong points, notably at Le Hamel. The limitations of such gunfire are illustrated by the fact that this strong point was not finally suppressed and overrun until 4 p.m. Still, the German defense at Gold did not compare to that at Omaha; by evening, five British brigades had a firm beachhead established.[43]

Juno Beach was the Canadian target for D-day. Because of a suspected reef just offshore, H-hours on the western and eastern parts of Juno had been set for 0735 and 0745 respectively. Although there had been some navigational errors in the approach channels, no vessel was lost to mines during the approach. It was necessary to postpone the stipulated H-hours by ten minutes to sort out mixed-up elements of the landing forces. Since the H-hours were already set late, this meant that many beach obstacles were covered with water by the time the landing craft arrived in the tidal zone. Troops had to be discharged into several feet of water to make their way ashore. The obstacles, combined with strong tides, extracted a high toll of landing craft. Although the Juno landing was messy, the Germans were unable to prevent the Canadian 3d Division and part of the British 51st Division from securing a lodgment some six miles deep by the evening of 6 June.[44]

NEPTUNE planners had anticipated that the hardest fight would be for the easternmost landing area, Sword Beach. It lay just west of the Caen

Canal and the Orne River, which constituted the eastern boundary of the invasion area. A strong thrust east from this area posed the most direct threat to the Germans, and they were certain to mount a powerful counterattack here as early as possible. Hence it was vital to get a strong force established ashore quickly. The British 6th Airborne Division had been dropped during the night to secure essential water crossings and needed prompt reinforcement and the support of heavy weapons. Nonetheless, the actual landing beaches were narrow, allowing only a single brigade front. Speed in clearing obstacles and in moving forces off the beach was thus urgent.[45]

The landings here got off to a good start, with most of the DD tanks getting ashore promptly at 0730 to support the infantry. Opposition on the beach was generally light, except at the eastern end. By 0943, or only eighteen minutes behind schedule, the entire assault brigade of the British 3d Infantry Division was ashore, and the follow-up brigade began to land. At this point, the narrow frontage of the landing began to tell. It proved impossible to get forces off the beach rapidly enough to prevent serious congestion. Clearing the exits proved sticky, and the pile-up continued, presenting a tempting target to enemy fire. Meanwhile, a combination of weather, mines, obstacles, and shelling caused significant losses of landing craft.

In the ensuing disorder, the D-day timetable went by the board. The planned ambitious thrust south to seize the city of Caen failed, with the formidable 21st Panzer Division blocking the British advance on this key objective. In retrospect, it is hard not to attribute this failure to the narrow beach frontage. Sword could not sustain the sort of force that the capture of Caen would require in the face of strong German reaction; the landing force had done what was possible under the circumstances.[46] Despite all the shortcomings, the initial landing phase of Operation NEPTUNE was a success. However imperfectly, the navies had put the troops ashore everywhere in sufficient force. The defenders had failed to defeat the landings on the beaches. By nightfall on 6 June, the Second Front was a reality.

Operation NEPTUNE now entered its second phase, that of sustaining the buildup on the Continent. This proved not much less challenging than the landings. The Allied assault area constituted a deep bowl of water south of the line 49°40' north latitude, running some 60 miles from Pointe de Barfleur on the Cotentin peninsula to Bruneval, north of Le Havre. There needed to be a steady flow of shipping into and out of this area, and German forces had to be excluded. In fact, the main danger to shipping was within the assault zone in the form of German mines. The field over Cardonnet bank proved hard to sweep, and from the night of 9

June onward, German aircraft began dropping the new oyster mines in the transport area. Mines, mostly of the magnetic variety, claimed four destroyers and two minesweepers and damaged 25 other vessels in the exposed Utah sector during the first ten days of NEPTUNE. Newly sown oyster mines were chiefly responsible for five warships and four other vessels being lost off the British beaches between 22 and 29 June. The only safe procedure for vessels was to move at no more than four knots in shallow water.[47]

Sweeping had to be continuous, yet there was no assurance that mines resistant to sweeping were not still lying in wait. Nighttime spotting pinpointed the splashes of mines dropped from aircraft. These hot spots were then avoided until the mines were known to have been swept. The difficulty of doing this is suggested by the case of one mine observed to have fallen close to the bombardment cruiser HMS *Hawkins*. It was eventually detonated eleven days after being laid and during sweep number 52 over its known location.[48] Only the eruption of the Allied ground forces out of the Normandy peninsula, forcing German airfields and mine depots farther from the assault area, reduced the mine problem from a major threat to a nagging nuisance. By comparison, the use of glide-bombs by German aircraft was never anything but an annoyance.[49]

At first, fast German surface vessels threatened to impede the Allied buildup. On the nights of 7–8 and 8–9 June, *schnellboote* operating out of Cherbourg and Le Havre managed to sink or damage shipping. Torpedo boats from Boulogne were successful on the night of 9–10 June. There were more Allied losses the following night. Thus, when a concentration of enemy torpedo craft at Le Havre was reported to Admiral Ramsay, he called on RAF Bomber Command to reduce the threat to his shipping. On the night of 14 June, over a thousand tons of bombs fell on Le Havre harbor, sinking three fleet torpedo boats, ten *schnellboote*, fifteen mine and patrol craft, and several other small combatants. The following night, the German craft in Boulogne harbor received similar treatment. The German surface forces never recovered from these twin blows, and thereafter their activity was not a significant problem for the Allies.[50]

The only German destroyer force in the west was located in the Bay of Biscay. When it sortied from Brest on the night of 8–9 June, two ships of the flotilla were sunk and a third heavily damaged in a brisk naval engagement. With their surface forces all but eliminated by the end of June, the Germans turned in July to using a sort of human torpedo named the Marder. This was a regular torpedo suspended from another one, without a warhead, that provided propulsion. It had a human operator enclosed in a watertight casing, with his head above the surface. Their greatest limitation was their slow speed, about four knots, until the active torpedo was fired at a target. In early July, these devices managed to sink three mine-sweepers and damage an old cruiser. The cost to the Germans was heavy; 30 of the human torpedoes were lost in two nights. A variety of other special weapons were employed with even more limited success. These efforts largely ended by mid-August.[51]

The Kriegsmarine's elite, the U-boat force, attempted to succeed where mines and surface forces had failed. Earlier in the war, this proud force had threatened to render the Second Front impossible; by June 1944 it was only a shadow of its former self. Over 30 boats were held in their Biscay bases awaiting the invasion, but landing craft were approaching the assault beaches before the U-boats were ordered to sortie, too late to impede the landings. Only nine of the Biscay boats were equipped with snorkels, and without these underwater breathing devices, the majority of the German submarines had little hope of survival against air and surface patrols. The nonsnorkel boats were largely lambs to the slaughter, fighting simply to survive.[52] The snorkel boats pressed on. Two British frigates were sunk, one by a snorkel boat from Norway, in mid-June. On 29 June, a spectacular success was achieved by one boat, sinking three merchant ships and damaging a fourth in an attack off the English coast. By then an LST had been sunk off Cape Barfleur. This amounted to little, given the scale of the NEPTUNE shipping; the U-boats achieved almost nothing in exchange for heavy losses.[53] The naval effort against NEPTUNE was a failure, with mines the main impediment to Allied shipping. The power of nature itself was able to do as much to discommode the Allies as the Germans.

Once the troops were ashore, the navies had to ensure that the armies received a steady flow of additional forces and supplies to sustain them, which would permit the buildup of a force powerful enough to fight its way out of the beachhead and across the Continent. The small ports of Courseulles and Port en Bessin, captured early on, proved able to take about 1,000 tons a day each. Unfortunately, the Build-up Control Organization (BUCO) proved too weak to cope efficiently with organizing the follow-up shipping schedules, and some confusion resulted before it got into stride.[54] The armies pressed for selective unloading of ships to meet priorities defined by the battle's progress. This threatened to create unmanageable congestion in the roadstead and on the beaches, but the soldiers proved difficult to sway. Admiral Ramsay insisted that if all arriving ships were promptly unloaded, "the priorities will take care of themselves."[55] Eisenhower supported Ramsay's view. As the alternative to this common-sense approach was not working, the field commanders acceded. As Ramsay had predicted, problems quickly got sorted out.

Under pressure for speed in unloading, the navies adopted the practice of beaching vessels as large as LSTs. These would "dry out" on a falling tide, when they could be unloaded. As the tide flooded, they were then floated off. Initially, this saved a lot of time in transshipment, but it meant tying up the big LSTs for about twelve hours, when it took only about an hour to unload one directly onto the beach. When the first floating pier went into service, eleven LSTs were able to discharge onto the pier in the first day. This yielded a significant savings in turnaround time for these valuable ships.

The artificial harbors were considered an urgent part of the Allied buildup, and the first convoy of corncob block ships arrived off Normandy on D plus 1. The ships were sunk in five groups, one off each landing beach. Two of these would be incorporated into the more elaborate Mulberries. By D plus 4 all the block ships had been sunk in their designated positions. They provided a valuable breakwater for small vessels when the great storm came. The floating roadways that would constitute the tidal piers within the artificial harbors proved difficult to tow across the Channel, and after some losses, efforts were made to bring them across in landing ship docks (LSDs). Sinking the caissons, which would complete the major breakwaters for the two artificial harbors, began on D plus 3, and by D plus 10 the outlines of the two harbors, each the size of the naval port at Gibraltar, were discernible.[56]

By nightfall on 18 June, nearly 630,000 troops had been landed from the sea, along with 95,000 vehicles and over 200,000 tons of supplies. At this point the weather intervened. Most unusual for the time of year, the prevailing wind on 19–22 June blew out of the NE/NNE. Although wind velocities rarely exceeded 25 to 32 knots, waves were able to build up over a reach of 90 to 125 miles before they exploded against the northern coast of the Cotentin peninsula. Nearly 35,000 men a day had landed during 16–18 June, but the 19–22 June average fell to under 10,000. Supplies—most seriously ammunition—dropped from 25,000 tons a day to just over 7,000 tons. Large parts of the artificial harbors gave way under the storm's impact. The American harbor, more exposed, was so badly damaged that it was not repaired. What could be salvaged from its wreckage was used to restore the British harbor. All told, some 800 craft were driven ashore.[57]

Despite this savage blow, which was more damaging than anything the Germans had been able to inflict on the flow of supplies, recovery from the storm was remarkably rapid, although the supply deficit it caused was not made up until 26 July. On 29 June, supplies began landing over the main stores pier of the surviving Mulberry, and by 19 July, that artificial harbor was essentially complete. Even more impressive was the ability to land supplies directly on the American beaches. Pontoon piers extending off open beaches proved sufficient, requiring only the shelter provided by the sunken block ships.[58] Admiral Ramsay wound up NEPTUNE shortly after the great storm, on 24 June. By that date, the Allied navies and merchant marine had put ashore 715,000 men, 111,000 vehicles, and 260,000 tons of stores. On 5 July, the millionth Allied soldier stepped ashore. The naval aspect of D-day was by itself an unequaled accomplishment.[59]

Military planners are cautious souls, apt to choose safe options. These are not always the best choices. Landing frontages in Normandy were too narrow, and wider landings could have been achieved with minor adjustments. The naval bombardment was too brief, notably on the American beaches. The time problem here seems to have been manageable and would not have posed serious negative consequences. The U.S. transport areas were too far from the beach. A more determined attack on resolving the traditional problem of ship-to-shore communications would have yielded large benefits on D-day. Strategic surprise paid the highest dividend and, indeed, ensured the operations' success. The NEPTUNE plan and the enormous muster to effect it proved adequately robust to overcome all obstacles. The navies got the troops ashore in sufficient numbers and sustained them during the critical assault phase of the invasion. When Admiral Ramsay wound up Operation NEPTUNE, the Allied armies were on French soil to stay.[60]

7. German Naval Operations on D-day

Friedrich Ruge

On 7 June 1919 I was a very young naval officer preparing to scuttle a German destroyer interned at Scapa Flow. Twenty-five years later, on the morning of D-day plus 1, I realized that the Allies had established a permanent beachhead and that the war was definitely lost. I had been appointed naval adviser to Field Marshal Erwin Rommel in November 1943, when he received instructions to examine the defenses in northwestern Europe. He had orders to begin in Denmark (why, I don't know). From there we moved over to France around 20 December 1943. From my previous appointments, I knew the coast very well, as I had swept and laid mines practically everywhere in those waters.

Rommel immediately made extensive tours of inspection to get a personal view of the situation. Soon it became evident that the defenses were weak in men and materiel. The only hope of beating off a large amphibious operation lay in integrating all the available forces in one common plan, which held some prospect of success. When we arrived in France, there was no such plan for the defense; Rommel, however, soon developed one. The infantries were comparatively numerous, but only very lightly motorized. At first, there was only one combat-ready armored division in the west, but more were organized or sent to France, until there were ten in all. Our air force was extremely weak—only a few hundred bombers and fighters. Of course, they were unable to support mobile operations. Rommel, realizing this at once from his experiences in North Africa, came to the conclusion that the best plan was to put the infantry and every single man, including the staffs, bakeries, supply trains, and so on, into a belt of field fortifications. These strong points were to be protected by as many land mines, as much concrete, and as much barbed wire as possible. This "Rommel Belt" was to be about three miles deep all along the coast, with the armored divisions stationed behind it in such a way that the guns of their forward units could shell the beach. In addition, as much artillery as we could assemble was to be put into and behind that belt. In this way, when attacked, the infantry would quickly have armored and artillery support, and the divisions on either flank of the attacked area would form the reserves. With the good road-net in France, they would be available almost as rapidly as when stationed farther inland.

Rommel was a great believer in close cooperation between infantry and armor. But he did not believe in the rapid, large-scale operations visualized by other generals such as Field Marshal Gerd von Rundstedt and Leo Freiherr Geyr von Schweppenburg. He knew from Africa what it meant to fight without an adequate air force. He foresaw that the mobile operations would be slowed down so much that they could not be effective, particularly after the Allies had established a beachhead with landing strips for fighters. He realized and unmistakably stated that it would not be possible to eliminate such a beachhead once it had been formed. A third front in France, with our forces in Russia and Italy retreating, would mean disaster everywhere. In Rommel's opinion, the only hope for a tolerable end to the war was to beat off the attack either before or at the time it reached the beach.

Incidentally, this coincided with Hitler's Directive No. 40 of March 1942. It said, literally, that the aim of the defense was "the collapse of the enemy attack before, if possible, but at the latest upon the actual landing." Directive No. 51 of November 1943 repeated Directive No. 40 in greater detail and in more urgent tones.[1]

In view of normal army experience, Rommel's defense system had the disadvantage of too little depth. This could be improved, however, by extending the defenses far into the sea—putting obstacles in shallow water and placing various types of naval mines in deeper water. Because of the great differences between high and low tides (up to twenty feet in the Seine bight), putting obstacles all along the foreshore required an immense amount of work and material.

If we had known where the attack would come, work could have been concentrated there. After the raids on Saint-Nazaire and Dieppe, the ports themselves were fortified to such an extent that they could be ruled out. Rommel first expected the Allies to strike astride the Somme River, but he later favored the Seine bight, where they actually came. However, Oberkommando der Wehrmacht (OKW) and Oberbefehlshaber West (OB WEST), under Rundstedt, did not agree with his reasoning. They were of the opinion that the invasion fleet would take—indeed, had to take—the shortest way, and consequently expected the attack between the Somme River and the Schelde estuary. Therefore, infantry divisions were stationed there in two rows—even in the Boulogne-Calais area, which was well defended by heavy batteries protected by concrete or armor. Further west, infantry and artillery were spread out rather thinly. In the western part of the Seine bight, between the Orne and Vire rivers, precisely where

Field Marshal Erwin Rommel (left) in a captured German photograph.

the attack came, there was only one weak division and no heavy battery. Along excellent landing beaches we found only observation posts, with nothing between them for three-quarters of a mile in places, and little behind them. This would not have mattered too much if we had had some naval strength. However, for offensive purposes, the navy had become the weakest of the three services.

By the Treaty of Versailles, the German navy had been restricted to six armored ships of 10,000 tons, six light cruisers of 6,000 tons, some minor craft—no submarines or airplanes—and 15,000 officers and enlisted men. When Hitler started rearming in 1935, he did not expect a war against England and concluded the London Treaty, which fixed the German navy at 35 percent of the Royal Navy. In any case, the situation required that the army and air force be created first.

Grossadmiral Erich Raeder understood sea power and did not want a war against England. He was satisfied with a small, balanced fleet. Only in 1939, after Hitler had revoked the London Treaty, did Raeder examine the possibilities of a war with Great Britain as an opponent. Hitler assured him, even then, that there was no danger of war before the middle of the 1940s.[2]

In 1939, Raeder embarked upon the Z-plan, which meant the creation of strong task forces of great endurance. These, together with submarines and raiders, were to attack British shipping in all oceans and compel the Royal Navy to disperse its strength. However, not a single one of the larger ships of that program was ever finished. When war broke out, the few surface ships that existed were used for commerce raiding until the submarines took over about a year and a half later. These operations were quite successful, but the surface ships were practically used up in the process. The last event was the *Bismarck* affair.

The submarine war caused the Allies heavy losses, but in 1943 it broke down almost completely. The submarine staff had realized the implications of technical developments on the Allied side too late. They did not believe that Allied escort vessels could take bearings on the high-frequency messages that the submarines were ordered to send when shadowing a convoy. Many submarines were thus lost by direct attack. Those that attempted to escape by diving were too slow underwater to elude the improved sonar. The "snorkel," a breathing tube, was then installed to enable them to proceed submerged with their diesel engines. Although this diminished the danger from radar and direction finders, it made surface attacks in wolf packs impossible.

Only a new type of submarine with a much greater underwater speed had any prospect of evading the antisubmarine warfare forces of the Allies. Two types, XXI and XXIII, were scheduled to be built but could not be ready before the winter of 1944–45. I was Director of Naval Construction from the fall of 1944 to 1945 and oversaw their development.[3] As things turned out, only five of type XXIII, the smaller one, became operational. Early in 1945 they undertook seven operations near the English coast, sank some ships, and came back unharmed.

There were about a hundred submarines, mainly type VII, in the submarine bases on the Bay of Biscay. Some had been improved by snorkels and others were being converted, but it was an open secret that in case of an invasion, little could be expected from them. No submarines whatsoever were stationed in ports on the Channel.

It should be mentioned that there was no naval aviation. When Goering began to build up the German air force, he claimed everything that flew. Only a few naval aviators were trained for the small planes carried by battleships and raiders. The two aircraft carriers under construction never reached the operational stage. Reconnaissance for submarines was flown by air force units when and if it was flown. The same situation had existed in the Mediterranean. Knowledge of the necessities of naval war was scanty in the air force commands.[4] Consequently, the only naval forces available in France were destroyers, torpedo boats (that is, very small destroyers), and, for offensive operations, motor torpedo boats (MTBs). In addition, there were minesweepers, escort vessels, patrol boats, and subchasers. The destroyers had a standard displacement of about 2,500 tons, which meant a maximum displacement of about 3,500 tons. They were armed with four or five 6-inch guns and eight torpedo tubes. In June 1944 there were only four destroyers operational in the Bay of Biscay, where they escorted submarines, raiders, and merchant ships.

In the case of torpedo boats, two types were stationed in the west. At the beginning of 1944 there were four so-called fleet-torpedo boats of the Elbing class, so named because they were built by Schichau in Elbing, West Prussia. They had a displacement of 1,300 to 1,700 tons. T-21 was severely damaged by a fighter-bomber, went into dry dock in Le Havre, and had just been repaired when the invasion began. The other three were used for laying mines in the Channel. In March they were sent to the Bay of Biscay. On the way back, at the end of April, they were intercepted by superior British forces. T-29 was sunk, and the other two were slightly damaged. After repairs in Saint-Malo, they had another fight with British destroyers. T-21 was sunk along with the British *Ashanti*. T-24 reached Le Havre, where it joined the Fifth Torpedo Boat Flotilla, consisting of five old torpedo boats of 900 to 1,300 tons. Ten days before the invasion, one torpedo boat was lost off Le Havre and two others were damaged. Fifth

Flotilla, therefore, consisted of two old and two new torpedo boats on 6 June 1944.

The MTBs were better suited for operations in the Channel. They displaced about 100 tons and were armed with two torpedo tubes and two light guns each. In theory, their speed was 40 knots, but in practice it was much less. Five squadrons of eight boats each were stationed in the west. Early in 1944 there were two squadrons in Ostend, one in Boulogne, and two in Cherbourg. Early in May, one squadron was moved from Boulogne to Le Havre. In January 1944 they carried out nine operations in the Channel, on one they sank five ships (1,200 gross tons) off Land's End. In February they undertook thirteen operations, four of which were to lay mines. They sank or damaged a number of vessels with a loss of two boats. Thirteen operations in March were unsuccessful because the MTBs were located too early by the British for an attack. In April they carried out fourteen operations with one loss. They sank two tank landing ships (LSTs) and damaged one in Lyme bight. On another occasion they claimed to have sunk a floating dock. In May there were twelve operations devoted mainly to laying mines. It became impossible to reach the English coast undetected. Over and over again they were attacked by planes and destroyers that chased them almost into Cherbourg. Two were lost, two others damaged. When the invasion started, only 35 MTBs were ready for action.

The defensive forces were far more numerous. Four hundred fifty-eight small craft operated on D-day. But their actual fighting value was low, in spite of the great experience and bravery of their crews.[5] The types of vessels used were minelayers, minesweepers, and larger minesweepers of 500 to 600 tons with one or two 105-mm guns and some other lighter guns. There were normally six squadrons of eight ships. They were most frequently used in the Bay of Biscay and in the western Channel; in the narrows, R-boats[6] played the main part. They were motorboats of 100 to 200 tons, containing one or two light guns and possessing a speed of about twenty knots, very handy for sweeping and also for minelaying. They could each take eight of our large mines.[7] We had five squadrons of twelve R-boats each. There were 200 trawlers and drifters that had been converted into patrol vessels and auxiliary minesweepers; one squadron of subchasers consisting mainly of small whaling vessels, which my good friend Captain Ernst Felix Krüder had captured in the Southern Polar Sea and sent to France; and a number of large and small steamers that were equipped as big magnets for sweeping magnetic mines. For local sweeping purposes, we had commandeered fishing vessels, pilot steamers, tugs, and even lobster boats for use in the Bay of Biscay. A new development was the so-called gun carriers, small landing craft with one or two 105-mm guns. Altogether, they were a motley crowd. They had one thing in common, however: All were armed to the teeth with small guns (some of which were taken from unprotected air force fields) and heavy machine guns, and their crews knew how to use them.

As to the coast defense proper, the navy's contribution in men and material was considerable. Coastal artillery was installed in several steps. The first step was to erect a group of heavy guns in the Calais-Boulogne area, the narrowest part of the Channel, where they were to protect Operation SEELOEWE, the planned invasion of England in 1940–41. When work was finished, there were four naval batteries there, each with three to four 280- to 406-mm guns and all heavily protected by concrete. Moreover, there were some army coastal batteries placed there with calibers up to 280-mm, plus a great number of smaller guns.[8]

Protecting these places was the next step. In 1940–41, no large-scale British attacks were expected, but raids were considered possible.[9] One or two heavy batteries and two to three medium ones were enough to defend each main port, but this program nearly exhausted naval resources and reserves, which were extremely low because Hitler gave priority to two other large programs.

It was one of Hitler's "intuitions" that Norway would be attacked again, and he gave orders to fortify the main ports there. Narvik and Bergen received seven heavy batteries and about 30 to 50 medium and light batteries each. There was something to be said for erecting batteries at places where the long channel between the islands all along the coast was open to attack from the sea, but 350 batteries with guns ranging from 88 to 406 mm was too much of a good thing for Norway. Another plan of Hitler's was to convert the Channel Islands into a kind of heavily protected and unsinkable carrier. By 1944, eleven batteries with 38 heavy guns up to 305 mm were erected there. Every month, 90,000 tons of material were carried to the islands, and 32,000 workmen were engaged in the project.

Because the navy could not produce all those batteries and train their crews, the Army Coast Artillery (Heeresküstenartillerie) was founded in 1940. Within a year they had either set up or placed under construction over 200 batteries, more than half of them in Norway. However, many of the guns were obsolete, protection was lacking, and their crews had yet to learn how to hit targets moving on the water. The commando raids on Saint-Nazaire and Dieppe had shown that isolated batteries outside the port defenses could be eliminated from the rear. This led to the next step: moving batteries of that kind closer to the ports; integrating them into the system of defense there; and, at the same time, setting up more guns for the protection of those ports. Owing to the lack of reserves, this took a long time. Therefore, two heavy batteries of three 380-mm guns, one west of Cherbourg and one at Le Havre, were not ready on D-day. The final step—putting batteries behind the threatened parts of the coast between the ports—started late, and the program was not very far advanced.

In the winter of 1943–44, the navy somehow found four more batteries: two 210 mm and two 150 mm. OB WEST simply gave one of each type to the Fifteenth Army and the Seventh Army, without any regard to the actual situation. Therefore, one 210–mm battery was erected not far from Calais, where there was already a surfeit of guns. The other was sent to Fort Saint-Marcouf and was the only heavy naval battery that made itself felt in the invasion proper. The same applied to one of the two 150–mm batteries that was erected at Longueville, not far from Bayeux. The other one went to a place south of Le Havre and was too far away from the operations to be effective.

The army was in favor of placing the guns behind the coast and camouflaging them. The navy, however, wanted them forward and under armor or concrete. This was better for firing at moving targets, but concrete was in short supply, and fixed concrete embrasures restricted the arc of fire to an angle of a little over 90 degrees. Too late, navy engineers hit upon the bright idea of revolving turrets made of concrete. Taking everything together, naval coast artillery contributed greatly to coast defenses in general but did little to defend the coast of Normandy against the invasion.

Another naval contribution to the defense was a chain of radar stations all along the coast. At that time, German radar was not as good as the Allied radar, but it had discovered and reported the landing fleets about three hours before the first troops arrived on shore. Our radar stations were attacked many times in the last weeks before the invasion, but on D-day almost all of them were in working order again.[10]

A distinct asset was our monitoring service. Early in May it found out from an Allied landing exercise on the southern coast of England that the landings would begin about two hours after low water. In previous years it had monitored the British radar results so exactly and quickly that we were able to give our small convoys their correct positions from English radar and warn them of impending MTB attacks, which was of considerable help.[11]

The net of naval communications was excellent. We had teletypes to all the main ports, whereas the army relied mostly on telephones. Nobody could listen in on teletype messages, and we always had in print what had been communicated. The only problem that arose was training our people to condense their reports, questions, and so on.

Finally, German naval contributions to the defense included providing motorized units for transporting ammunition, torpedoes, and so on and making available a number of naval training units that could serve as infantry battalions under certain conditions. They were transferred from Germany to places behind the coast where they relieved army units for the defense proper.

The organization of the three armed services in France had simply happened after the campaign of 1940 and had never been streamlined for defense purposes. Basically, the navy was to fight the enemy on the sea and the army was to defend the coast. But it was complicated by the fact that the enemy might arrive by sea and then fight ashore. After long discussions, orders were given that the Sea Commandant, a naval captain or rear admiral responsible for 100 to 200 miles of coast, would be in charge as long as the enemy was on the water. As soon as the landing began, control of the fire direction went over to the army division that held the sector under attack. All the batteries were under the orders of the senior coast artillery commander of that sector. On the whole, this system worked quite well, although there were some complications. Local commanders tended to switch fire too soon from the ships to the infantry units that had already disembarked and could attack them directly.

Let us now turn to the subject of obstacles and naval mines. The army was in favor of constructing underwater obstacles on the beaches and foreshore between high and low water. Although time was far too short to finish this task in any thorough way, the obstacles hampered the Allies considerably and caused the loss of about 200 landing craft. It was a different tale with the naval mines, which were to extend the Rommel Belt seaward. By 1944, I had spent nine years in mine development and ten years in command of minesweepers at various levels, so I think I can say that I knew that weapon. It was not difficult to explain its possibilities to Rommel. He was an expert on the use of mines in land warfare, and we soon agreed that tactically there were great similarities. However, it proved impossible to convince Navy Group West of the urgency of the situation and the necessity to lay mines immediately.[12] From August 1943 to January 1944, sixteen minefields had been laid in the Channel between Boulogne and Cherbourg, a bit south of the old fields. There were also a number of smaller fields at various locations but, unfortunately, Navy Group West insisted on using mines with a time mechanism, and our time mechanism was limited to 80 days. Consequently, most of the mines were already ineffective on D-day.

One small victory for German defenses: an LCVP on fire offshore on D-day.

A simple mine for shallow water that could be produced locally, the coastal mine A (KMA), was laid in the Dieppe area and south of the Gironde River. At neither location was it particularly urgent. Navy Group West wanted all other mines laid by torpedo boats and large minesweepers, despite the fact that MTBs and R-boats had been used for the same kind of work in previous years. The larger vessels suffered heavily from air attacks. The first excursion of these smaller boats had been planned for the night before D-day, but it was canceled on account of weather conditions.

Under the name of *Blitzsperren* (lightning fields), Navy Group West prepared a system of mine fields to be laid by all vessels as soon as the attack was imminent. Considering the lack of reliable reconnaissance and the short distance between the coasts, this was a plan of doubtful value. As things turned out, most of these fields were laid on D-day, but not a single one was laid off the landing beaches. The Allies were there before the minelayers, just as we had predicted. Shortly before the invasion, MTBs laid some mines near the Isle of Wight. But oyster mines, the pressure mines, were not laid because their use was not allowed by OKW until after the invasion. On the whole, it must be stated that much could have been done with naval mines.

As to the actual events, the navy did very little on D-day. As far as I remember, the last air reconnaissance was on 26 May. The large Allied minesweeping operation on 5 June was not recognized and evidently not sighted, although at least two squadrons approached the French coast so closely that they could make out details ashore. In any case, no report reached the various headquarters. The landing force was reported by radar between two and three o'clock on the morning of D-day—at about the same time the first alarm was given because paratroopers and dummies had landed in several places. Our meteorologists had predicted continuing bad weather. They had no news of the approaching area of high pressure that enabled General Eisenhower to come to his momentous decision. No German patrols were at sea, and the minelaying excursion had been canceled. Only the four torpedo boats at Le Havre and one MTB squadron at Cherbourg were ready at short notice.

The torpedo boats, under the command of Captain Heinrich Hoffman, left Le Havre and attacked the Allied forces screening the landing fleet to the east. They torpedoed the Norwegian destroyer *Svenner* but left the battleships HMS *Warspite* and HMS *Ramillies* unharmed, even though they were immediately behind *Svenner*.[13] Hoffman attacked again in the following nights, but without success. The first night, patrol vessels from Le Havre tried to clarify the situation and suffered some losses. Two squadrons of MTBs went to sea from Cherbourg but were unable to find any targets. They had been alerted rather late, and evidently the radar reports had not been evaluated when they were told where to search. The following night one MTB was lost on a mine. They had their first success on the night of 7–8 June, sinking two LSTs in the Bay of the Seine and one infantry landing craft (LCI) and one tank landing craft (LCT) to the west of Fécamp. During the following nights, the MTBs attacked repeatedly, had some successes, and suffered considerable losses. In some of their operations they laid mines. From 9 June on, the German air force also dropped mines in the Bay of the Seine. At least 43 Allied vessels were sunk or damaged by mines.

On the night of 8–9 June, the German destroyers stationed in the Bay of Biscay tried to penetrate into the western Channel. However, they were intercepted by Allied destroyers. Two German destroyers were lost, and one Allied destroyer was heavily damaged. The two remaining destroyers returned to Brest and did not make another attempt.

On the evening of 14 June, 325 Lancaster bombers attacked Le Havre. The German antiaircraft batteries had orders not to fire because an attack with radio-controlled glide-bombs was planned at the same time. Consequently, the British attack was a full success. Three torpedo boats, ten

MTBs, and numerous minesweepers, patrol boats, and other vessels were sunk or damaged. There remained only one operative MTB in Le Havre. The following night, a similar attack was directed against Boulogne, where a considerable number of minesweepers and other craft were destroyed. By that time the Allies had a large bridgehead ashore, and there was no possibility of throwing them back into the sea. However, the fight went on.

As for the naval batteries, the 210-mm battery at Fort Saint-Marcouf to the east of Cherbourg initially fired at targets at sea and sank one destroyer, the U.S. *Corry*.[14] When visibility permitted, it turned its fire toward Utah Beach. Several ships, among them two battleships, tried to silence it. One of the guns was put out of action by a direct hit, and the two others were damaged. However, the crews succeeded in repairing one; when it was damaged again, they repaired the other. In this way they continued to fire for two days, although the battery was already under infantry attack and cut off from the German main force. Nevertheless, it defended itself for three more days. By that time all the officers and petty officers had been wounded or killed. Those who could walk retreated through inundated country and reached the German line five miles back.

The other naval battery, four 150-mm guns at Longues, north of Bayeux, was not quite finished, but all four guns could fire. Its commanding officer and crew evidently were inferior to those at Fort Saint-Marcouf. Heavy air attacks before D-day did not harm the guns but destroyed much of the fire control equipment. On D-day the battery took several ships under ineffective fire. It was bombarded by battleships and cruisers until three guns were knocked out. The fourth fired for the last time on the evening of D-day. The next morning the crew surrendered to British troops after an infantry company, which was to defend it, had been ordered back to the defense of Bayeux.

The difficulties of cooperation between the army and the navy on the German side are illustrated by events at Sword Beach in the British sector. For the British, it was imperative to get supplies to their paratroops east of the Orne River, and they occupied the bridge across the river at Bénouville close to the sea before it could be blown up. At an inland shipyard between Bénouville and Caen, some patrol boats and minesweepers were under repair. They raised steam and went downstream, only to find the way out to sea blocked at the bridge. As the situation was not at all clear, they went back. When they were told about the importance of the bridge, they formed a party of volunteers and, together with army engineers, proceeded to try to blow up the bridge. The sailors reached it, but the engineers who carried the explosives did not make it. Thus, the bridge remained unharmed and in British hands, although it could have been destroyed right at the beginning.

So far, I have not mentioned any submarine activity. Of course, they were alerted on D-day, and 36 left their bases on the Bay of Biscay within 24 hours. It was soon realized that submarines without snorkel equipment could not operate in the Channel. Eighteen formed a group in the Bay of Biscay. They did not find any targets, and some of them were lost by attack from the air. The submarines with snorkels attacked the 12th Support Group with T-5 (wren) torpedoes, homing on the noise from the propellers.[15] It was 14 June before the submarines reached the Allied shipping lanes in the Channel. The following day they sank an LST, a frigate, and a destroyer escort. Operating in the Channel was most difficult. Losses were high and results meager. Without intending to get there, one of the submarines found itself in Spithead Roads off Portsmouth. But there was no target in sight that merited a torpedo, and the submarine crept out again and reached one of the bases on the Bay of Biscay.

A group of submarines left Baltic and Norwegian bases to take up a defensive position off the Norwegian coast. Five were sunk by planes, and five others were damaged. One was sunk by a submarine. Four more were sunk in the Atlantic and two were damaged. Submarines with snorkels laid mines off Plymouth and Land's End. One attacked a U.S. battleship off Cherbourg, but the torpedoes detonated too early. Altogether, the submarines arrived far too late to be of any influence, and their losses were so high that the operation was a complete failure. From D-day to the second half of August, at least 36 submarines were sunk and fourteen damaged in the Channel, in its western approaches, and in the Bay of Biscay on the way to and from the submarine bases.

A few days after the Allies had landed, Army Group B, commanded by Rommel, was informed that the navy intended to attack the invasion fleet with small assault craft. This new arm had been organized by my classmate Vice Admiral Hellmuth Heye. At that point, it consisted of one-man torpedoes and crash boats. The former was a torpedo used as a carrier and operated by a man inside with some sort of navigational aid. He carried another torpedo that he could maneuver and launch.[16] The crash boats had an explosive charge in the bow and were meant to ram the target. The pilot, with a watertight suit, jumped overboard after putting the boat on a direct course toward the target. He was then picked up by a following boat. It worked better than one would have expected. Two-man submarines were not yet ready to be placed into operation.

This plan had been kept top secret. If we had known it earlier, I could have contacted Heye and we might have moved some men and these new weapons to France in time. It took exactly one month until they began to operate in the Bay of the Seine. On the night of 5–6 July, 26 one-man torpedoes proceeded against the ships off the mouth of the Orne River. They sank two minesweepers while losing nine of their own. Two nights later, a midshipman succeeded in damaging the old British light cruiser *Dragon* so heavily that it had to be beached, forming part of the artificial port at Arromanches. Later, one-man torpedoes sank a destroyer and a minesweeper, but their losses increased. When they attacked for the last time on 16 August, they lost 26 out of 42 and sank only one small steamer of 700 tons. At the same time, MTBs used long-range torpedoes for the first time with some success. There were also many bitterly fought engagements between Allied and German small craft, with losses on both sides. The German patrol and minesweeping forces suffered heavily.

Perhaps one further incident is worth mentioning. A naval transport battalion carried torpedoes and ammunition to Cherbourg with almost no losses. Part of the battalion was in that fortress within the Cotentin peninsula that was cut off by American troops. By using small country lanes, however, they cut through the line the following night. The battalion carried ammunition through to the western part of the German front and on to a wooded hill south of Pontorson, where they established a well-camouflaged forward depot. After the American breakthrough at Avranches, the battalion commander and his men observed the American columns rushing to the west in the direction of Brest and to the south-southeast in the direction of Rennes. They kept under cover the whole day. During the night they again traveled on country roads until they were south of Rennes, the capital of Brittany. Then they retreated to the east, reaching Fontainebleau with nearly all their vehicles and men.

On 4 September the last thirteen MTBs left their bases on the Channel and went to ports in the Netherlands. The German armies were in full retreat. France was lost. Navy men took part in the defense of the few ports that were held until the end of the war. What remained of the navy was concentrated in the Baltic, where ships of all types did good service until the last days of the war, ferrying over 2 million people fleeing from the Russians.

In the attempt to counter the invasion, the German navy lost heavily without corresponding results. This was due partly to material weakness but also to a lack of insight into the problems involved. Before the war, nobody in the German armed forces had examined these problems. Consequently, they were not understood, and there was not enough cooperation between the services, which alone could have brought better results. But that is a different story.

8. The Air Campaign

Alan Wilt

Despite the many controversies surrounding OVERLORD, there has been little disagreement about the effectiveness of Allied air power. Commanders of the vanquished and victors alike have attested to its overwhelming success. The German general, Baron Heinrich von Luttwitz, commander of the 2d Panzer Division, reported soon after the invasion that the Allies "have complete mastery of the air. They bomb and strafe every movement, even single vehicles and individuals . . . and during the [bombing] barrages the effect on inexperienced troops is literally 'soul shattering.' "[1] On 9 June, General Gunther Blumentritt, chief of staff to theater commander Field Marshal Gerd von Rundstedt, observed that "all sources are emphasizing again and again the numerical superiority of the enemy air forces as their strongest component during the battle."

One day later, the celebrated field commander Erwin Rommel, then head of Army Group B, wrote to his wife: "The enemy's air superiority has a very grave effect on our movements. There's simply no answer to it."[2] On the eleventh, he went further and indicated to Armed Forces High Command headquarters in Berlin that "movement of our troops on the battlefield by day is . . . almost entirely impossible, while the enemy can operate without hindrance. In the country behind, all roads are exposed to continual attack, and it is therefore very difficult to bring up the necessary supplies of fuel and munitions." One day earlier, an Allied bomber attack effectively put Panzer Group West's headquarters out of commission by destroying 75 percent of its communications equipment and numerous vehicles and by killing seventeen officers, including the chief of staff. The operation led its commander, Gen. Baron Leo Geyr von Schweppenburg, to declare that the enemy did not possess "air superiority, but rather air supremacy" over the battle area. The testimonials could go on and on.

On the Allied side, with the exception of a few army commanders—mainly those whose soldiers had experienced so-called friendly fire—almost everyone had praise for the air effort. No better evidence can be adduced than that of General Eisenhower himself. On 24 June, he and his son John, then a recent graduate of West Point, were being driven through a portion of the Normandy beachhead. The road was clogged with vehicles, and the younger Eisenhower remarked to his father, "You'd never get away with this if you didn't have air supremacy." The elder Eisenhower's terse reply was, "If I didn't have air supremacy, I wouldn't be here."[3]

Therefore the question to be posed is not whether the Allied air campaign succeeded, for that is a given, but rather what factors allowed the Allies to achieve success? Four possible answers stand out: British and American air leadership and organization, doctrine, tactics, and numerical superiority. One or a combination of these factors goes a long way toward explaining why the Allied effort more than fulfilled their expectations in the sky over Normandy.

Although perhaps no worse than the clashes between Anglo-American naval and army leaders, those involved in the air campaign do not present an edifying picture. In spite of their acknowledged abilities and subsequent renown, many British and American officers simply did not get along.[4] Among the top commanders, Air Chief Marshal Sir Trafford Leigh-Mallory, commander-in-chief of the Allied Expeditionary Air Force (AEAF), did not like his countrymen Air Chief Marshal Sir Arthur Tedder, Eisenhower's deputy, and Air Marshal Sir Arthur "Mary" Coningham, Leigh-Mallory's subordinate and head of the Second British Tactical Air Force. Coningham, in turn, disliked Leigh-Mallory, and one of Tedder's functions was to mediate between Coningham and the AEAF commander.

Lt. Gen. Carl "Tooey" Spaatz, named head of the U.S. Strategic Air Forces in December 1943, was also not favorably disposed toward Leigh-Mallory and resisted every attempt by the tactical commander to gain control over Spaatz's strategic forces. The same situation applied to Air Chief Marshal Sir Arthur "Bomber" Harris, who at times ran Bomber Command (BC) as if it were his own personal fiefdom. Even the Eighth U.S. Air Force commander, Lt. Gen. James Doolittle, who enjoyed good relations with nearly everyone, had run-ins with fellow air leaders when they tried to divert his fighters from escorting Eighth's bombers to carrying out tactical missions instead. In short, these hard-driving, strong-willed officers were a difficult group to keep in tow. They were not by inclination team players.

Relationships between many of the air and army commanders were also far from cordial. The usually diplomatic Eisenhower could not stand Leigh-Mallory and had difficulty holding himself in check when the two were together. According to Lt. Gen. Walter Bedell Smith, Eisenhower's chief of staff, "other than Montgomery, no one on the Allied side could rile Eisenhower quicker than Leigh-Mallory, whose personality and manner rubbed the Supreme Commander the wrong way."[5]

The First U.S. Army commander, Lt. Gen. Omar Bradley, got along well

Air Chief Marshal Sir Arthur Tedder (above) and General Carl "Tooey" Spaatz (right), overseers of the Anglo-American air campaign.

enough with his American fliers, Ninth Air Force's Maj. Gen. Lewis Brereton and Ninth Tactical Air Command's Maj. Gen. Elwood "Pete" Quesada.[6] But the prickly head of Twenty-First Army Group, Field Marshal Sir Bernard Montgomery, hated the critical Coningham, even though they had worked well together in North Africa and Italy. Montgomery, in fact, would not locate his headquarters on the Continent with Coningham's, as was normally done; at one point, Field Marshal Sir Alan Brooke, Chief of the Imperial General Staff, volunteered to go to Normandy to assist in handling Montgomery. This did not prove necessary, but it was not until September 1944 that Montgomery and Coningham located their headquarters side by side, and the two never completely overcame their mutual antipathy.

Thus, personal relationships were not what they might have been, and—partly as a result—the organization of the air campaign was also far from optimal. For some months prior to D-day, the British had been led to believe that the Americans would be reluctant to place their strategic forces under British command, and, for his part, Harris did not want Bomber Command under the tactically oriented Leigh-Mallory. The peculiar compromise that was worked out still defies rational description.[7] Leigh-Mallory was supposedly the overall air commander, but at first the strategic bombers and fighters were nominally under Chief of the Air Staff Sir Charles Portal, though actually under Spaatz and Harris. On 14 April 1944 (unofficially, earlier), command of all the pertinent air forces officially reverted to Eisenhower as theater commander. But his deputy, Tedder, in effect supervised the strategic forces, with operational control still under Spaatz and Harris; Leigh-Mallory oversaw the tactical air portion of the campaign. This compromise overcame some of the animosities that had grown up among the various commanders, but it certainly did not make for clear lines of command authority.

There were, to be sure, mitigating factors.[8] Below the higher levels, relations between British and American group commanders were generally good. Air Vice Marshal Harry Broadhurst of 83 Group got on well with his U.S. counterpart Quesada, and Quesada and Coningham were also on friendly terms. Moreover, the top air commanders or their representatives—normally the actual commanders, including Leigh-Mallory, Tedder, Coningham, Brereton, Spaatz, and Harris—met daily to supervise the air war. At these 11 a.m. meetings, they took stock of what was happening and set targeting guidelines for the next day's operations. The meeting minutes further reflect that everyone involved well understood the overwhelming importance of OVERLORD and the need to cooperate to get the job done.[9] Nevertheless, the relationships between the commanders and the organization of the air campaign were obviously not the key elements in the Allies' success.

More promising are the three other factors—air doctrine, tactics, and numbers. British air leaders during the North African campaign had developed a sound doctrine for conducting tactical operations, but not until mid-1943 did the Americans follow the British lead and codify the basic air principles by which they would engage the enemy. The relevant field manual (FM 100–20) stipulated that the first priority for air forces was to gain air superiority over the battle area. Only when this was accomplished were interdiction of the combat zone and direct support of the ground forces feasible. The latter two principles were undoubtedly significant, but the aviators considered air superiority the fundamental prerequisite for a successful campaign.[10]

The Allies diligently worked to accomplish all three principles throughout the air phase of OVERLORD, approximately from April through July 1944, but the air superiority dimension was especially evident prior to the invasion. During this time, the primary consideration for air leaders was to engage and defeat the German air force in every way possible— from attacking airfields to downing aircraft to bombing aircraft factories and facilities. In this regard, they were ultimately successful, for by D-day, the sky was virtually clear of enemy aircraft. To pinpoint exactly when this occurred is difficult, since it was an ongoing process. It is certainly safe to say that sometime in May the Allies achieved air superiority.

British and American air leaders therefore did not disagree as to the desirability of gaining air superiority. What led to often violent disagreements were other air responsibilities, namely the strategic mission and its relationship to OVERLORD. By 1944, long-range bombers were heavily involved in striking targets in Germany. Should they give up that mission to assist with OVERLORD? Strategic bombing advocates realized that they would eventually be called upon to help out, but the question was when? They wanted to put off this diversion of resources as long as possible, especially since they believed that the Combined Bomber Offensive was beginning to have a real impact on German war production. But those commanders associated with OVERLORD understandably wanted the increasingly formidable strategic forces under their control.

These differing approaches led to what has become known as the transportation-oil dispute. The question of how to take advantage of the heavy bombers and their escorts had been discussed for some months, and the discussions intensified once Eisenhower's Supreme Headquarters came into being in January.[11] By then, Sir Solly Zuckerman, Tedder's scientific adviser, had come up with a transportation plan. Zuckerman argued that air raids on rail centers, especially maintenance and repair facilities, in northern France would help cripple Germany's ability to provide for its forces once the invasion took place. Tedder concurred, but in early March, Spaatz countered with a plan of his own, known as the oil plan. Backed by extensive documentation, his view was that the best way to get at Germany was to attack its oil-refining capacity inside the Reich. Spaatz stated that airfields, synthetic rubber plants, and rail centers within Germany would also be targeted, but by making the oil industry the top priority, he predicted that German gasoline supplies could be reduced by 50 percent within six months and that OVERLORD ultimately would be helped in the process.

Although rail center missions had already been undertaken, a final decision regarding the argument between Tedder and Spaatz was not reached until 25 March.[12] At a high-level meeting called specifically to discuss bombing policy, Eisenhower opted for the transportation plan. He said that everything he had read convinced him that, apart from the attack on the German air force, the transportation plan was the only one that offered a reasonable chance of the air forces making an important contribution to the land battle during the first vital weeks of OVERLORD; in fact, he did not believe that there was any real alternative. He realized that it would not be possible to provide an estimate in figures of the reduction in military traffic that might be achieved, but in his opinion it was only necessary to show that there would be some reduction—however small—to justify adopting the plan, provided there was no alternative available. Eisenhower's statement had embedded within it a number of important points. He did not see the oil plan as a viable alternative to the proposed transportation plan. He fully supported the aim of air superiority, of reducing the German air force to impotence. Nor did he expect the transportation alternative to be totally effective; he merely hoped that it would be of some help.

Spaatz was beaten, and he knew it. He did not present his case at the meeting until after Eisenhower had rendered his opinion. Even Harris backed off from actively opposing the transportation plan. Spaatz continued to be upset for some time, and at one stage in April he even threatened to resign. But following Eisenhower's promise that attacks on oil targets would be permitted as soon as possible—they started again in May—Spaatz remained at his post. Toward the end of the 25 March meeting, Chief of the Air Staff Portal brought up another point: He feared that the transportation raids would threaten the lives of French civilians (estimated at 80,000 to 160,000 casualties) and believed that this matter ought to be looked into. Before long, Lord Cherwell, Churchill's scientific adviser, enlisted the support of the prime minister for such an inquiry. Although Churchill harbored concerns about how the bombing would affect British-French postwar relations, he also had genuine qualms about the possibility of additional French civilian casualties. Throughout April and into early May, the issue was debated weekly at British Defence Committee meetings.[13] The meetings conformed to a pattern. Evidence would be presented that the previous week's attacks on rail centers had not killed as many civilians as expected, and after some discussion, Churchill would give his approval, with some restrictions, to continue the bombings for another week. Finally on 2 May, an exasperated Eisenhower said that the restrictions were hurting the execution of the overall air plan. The prime minister then turned to President Roosevelt for his support, but the American president backed Eisenhower's right to make the final decision. At that point, Churchill went along.

In fact, the transportation plan—and attacks on other targets—had yielded such impressive results that on 3 May, Tedder called a meeting of the air commanders to look into other alternatives besides concentrating on the rail centers.[14] They decided that, in addition to the railway targets, they would emphasize strikes on rail and road bridges over the Seine and Meuse rivers, airfields in the area, and enemy artillery batteries along the coast, subject to the proviso that the attacks not tip off the location of the invasion—always a prime consideration. Allied planners, to be sure, had already considered missions against bridges, airfields, and coastal batteries as viable priorities, but Tedder was indicating that in his opinion the raids on the rail yards were far enough along that other targets could now be brought into the targeting scheme.

Results were indeed impressive.[15] By 6 June, all 80 rail centers in the targeting plan had been attacked. Seventy-three of them were thought to be severely or moderately damaged, and analysts estimated that military traffic on the French railroads was now only 37 percent of what it had been in March. Moreover, the Allies had damaged an estimated 475 locomotives and cut rail lines at 150 points, thus hindering rail movement even farther east. Although postwar critics have claimed that the attacks on the rail targets did not make the best use of Allied air power prior to the assault, the raids obviously did some damage and certainly justified Eisenhower's hopes.

As for the other main targets, the results also exceeded expectations. On 26 May, the bombing of the Seine bridges began, and by D-day, all twelve railway and fourteen road bridges had been cut or otherwise rendered impassable. The Allies had greater difficulty with the coastal batteries, but eleven of 24 (both inside and outside the invasion area) had been partially or totally damaged, and all 24 targeted radar stations in the projected combat zone were considered inoperable. Although not top-priority missions, Allied fighter-bombers and fighters had also flown numerous sorties against enemy command posts, repair and ordnance depots, expected troop concentrations, and naval shipping.

Most important from OVERLORD's standpoint were the 50 German airfields and satellite landing grounds within 130 miles of Caen, although again the Allies attacked airfields across northern France so as not to tip off OVERLORD's location. Raids on them began in earnest on 11 May. By D-day, 36 of the nearby airfields had been attacked, and though the number rendered totally unable to function was small, it rose dramatically shortly after the invasion. The attacks on airfields near the invasion beaches tell only part of the air superiority story. Eighth and Fifteenth Air Forces (the latter based in Italy) also struck numerous runways and airfield facilities throughout the rest of France; British and American heavy bombers attacked targets inside Germany, including aircraft factories and oil refineries; and fighter escorts strafed airfields and other air-related targets on the way back from the bombing missions. The effects of these operations were substantial.

The oil offensive had another benefit: It forced the Luftwaffe to concentrate fighters in eastern France and in Germany to defend its industrial base. Although both the Allies and the Germans suffered heavy casualties during the bombing raids, it hurt the Germans more because they did not have nearly the number of aircraft or aircrews for replacements that the British and Americans possessed. As a result of the constant bombings, German fighter losses for those commands directly involved—Air Fleet 3 and Air Fleet Reich—jumped from 733 aircraft in January 1944 to 1,267 in May, and Luftwaffe operational fighter strength for all theaters (despite increased production) declined from 1,361 on 30 June 1943 to 1,114 on 30 April 1944.[16] With respect to raids on the oil industry, which intensified after 6 June, by the end of July, 98 percent of Germany's capacity to produce aviation fuel had been destroyed. The long-term effects thus vindicated Spaatz's contention that hitting the oil targets would eventually pay a handsome dividend.

According to statistics compiled toward the end of 1944, for the preinvasion phase from 1 April through 5 June, the Allies dispatched 200,639 aircraft (the number of effective sorties was approximately 20 percent lower, though no exact figures were given) and dropped 195,380 tons of bombs at a cost of 1,987 aircraft and 13,120 aircrew casualties.[17] Although not all the sorties were OVERLORD related, Allied air power had obviously become a vital component of the war effort, and even more devastating air operations were in the offing.

As in so many other respects, D-day opened a new phase in the air war. Despite the difficulties in coordinating an operation of OVERLORD's magnitude, thousands of airborne troops were dropped behind the coast; Bomber Command, Eighth Air Force, and naval gunfire pummeled coastal defenses and landing beaches; and heavily armed fighters provided cover for the ships and the troops that were coming ashore. By the end of the day, a lodgment had been secured; although not as extensive as had been projected, it was a considerable lodgment nonetheless.

By any calculation, the air contribution had been massive.[18] Twelve thousand eight hundred thirty-seven aircraft (including transports and troops carriers) had flown 14,674 sorties and dropped 11,912 tons of bombs, with only around 120 aircraft lost. By contrast, and accentuating the degree of air superiority the Allies had achieved, the Luftwaffe had a mere 520 aircraft with which to repel the invaders, and only 175 of these were fighters. It had flown at best 100 sorties during the day (Tedder had expected at least 600), and only two Focke-Wulf 190s managed to penetrate the Allied air cordon to the beaches but did no damage. Nor did the approximately 175 medium and torpedo bombers that had set out at dusk to harass Allied shipping have any effect. All in all, army, naval, and air force commanders had to be pleased.

Having already accomplished the first major objective—air superiority—Allied air forces could move on to additional tasks. They still had to guard against losing their hard-earned air advantage, but they could now emphasize more than ever before support of the ground and, to a lesser extent, the naval forces. This emphasis on tactical operations and on developing new tactics began on D plus 1.

When describing the second major factor that led to Allied success in the air—tactics—one must keep in mind that the effort did not start during the postinvasion phase. Although General Quesada has admitted that the Allies still had a lot to learn, they had derived a good deal of experience with tactical operations during the North African, Sicilian, and Italian campaigns, and a number of the OVERLORD commanders had served in the Mediterranean theater.[19] In addition, during the preliminaries to OVERLORD, British and American pilots and crews had attacked numerous tactical targets and thus had firsthand knowledge of Germany's air defense system in the west. The Allies were also helped by the fact that ULTRA, Britain's decryption of German radio messages, was now providing almost unbelievable amounts of information about the enemy—information that

ALLIED AIR COVER FOR THE ASSAULT ON D-DAY

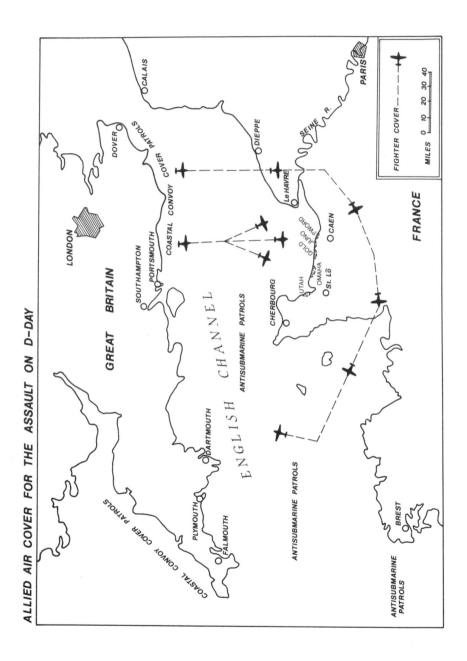

on occasion was timely enough to be of tactical use, as in the 10 June attack on Panzer Group West's headquarters.[20]

The main air units involved at the tactical level were Brereton's Ninth U.S. Air Force, Coningham's Second British Air Force, and Air Marshal Sir Roderic Hill's Air Defence of Great Britain (renamed from Fighter Command). The strategic air elements included Harris's Bomber Command and Doolittle's Eighth Air Force. Carrying out the air plan at times blurred the strategic-tactical distinction. The strategic bombers on occasion struck what might well be considered tactical targets; tactical aircraft, especially fighter bombers flew sorties against what might be construed to be strategic targets. Whatever the mission, and however it was accomplished, the outcome was impressive.

The types of missions usually accorded with tactical air doctrine. Some were to maintain air superiority. Others, in fact a great majority, were to interdict the battlefield and thus cut off supplies and personnel from the rear. Still others, though not well developed, were to provide close air support for troops near the front. There were, of course, additional priorities, such as missions for strategic bombing and their escorts and for photo and tactical reconnaissance, but the wonderful advantage of air power was that the aircraft involved could often be used for more than one purpose.

Many of the mission requests reflected targeting priorities from before the invasion.[21] Airfields were a particularly important concern, and between 6 and 27 June, the Allies flew 6,278 sorties and dropped 14,816 tons of bombs on 65 of them. The primary purpose was to render them unserviceable, but the secondary purpose was to destroy as many enemy aircraft on the ground as possible. Bridges were another continuing priority, and during the same period, between D-day and D plus 21, heavy, medium, and fighter-bombers flew 5,390 sorties and delivered 9,055 tons of bombs and 256 rockets on the Seine and Loire river bridges. The latter were especially difficult to knock out, since they were often of masonry construction, but they were now within the range of fighter-bombers, whose accuracy made them the best type of aircraft for that particular mission.

Rail targets were also attacked, though the emphasis switched from hitting marshaling yards and repair and maintenance facilities to bombing rail junctions, switching points, and locomotives and rail cars as they moved along the tracks.[22] To get an idea of the allocation for the attacks, in the 21 days after D-day, tactical air forces flew 2,581 sorties and dropped 2,302 tons of bombs, while the strategic forces flew 4,097 sorties and dropped 15,055 tons, for a total of 6,678 sorties and 17,357 tons. For

A high-level bombing attack in support of the Allied advance from the Normandy beachhead.

both the rail and the bridge targets, analysts found that after the invasion, the time required for the Germans and their workers to complete repairs lengthened considerably.

Other priority targets included V-weapon sites, whose importance re-emerged when flying bombs began to wreak havoc on London on the night of 12 June. During the next several weeks, Bomber Command also subjected enemy shipping to devastating raids at Le Havre, Boulogne, and the Brittany harbors.[23] Still, throughout June and July, one-half to two-thirds of all sorties on any given day were not directed against specific targets but consituted what might be described as search-and-destroy missions; they included convoy patrols, beachhead cover, and especially armed reconnaissance. These targets of opportunity were also part of the mosaic, and the pilots and crews taking part in them attempted to hit every train, vehicle, troop concentration, ship, or airplane that moved. The aircraft on preplanned missions also attacked targets of opportunity when

possible. In this atmosphere, it is little wonder that enemy morale was severely shaken in D-day's aftermath.

The system featured much more than free-lancing, however. It was set
in motion as follows: Each evening at a Combined Operations Center, a
committee of two air and two army officers allocated the requests they
had received, usually from army but also from air force sources.[24] Taking
into account the number and types of aircraft available, they then assigned a variety of missions for the next day. These were called planned
missions. The center also received subsequent requests, which were to be
executed the same day but for which there was no special urgency, which
were termed ordinary requests. There was also a third category, immediate requests; in this case, army divisions or corps contacted the center directly to get assistance for an immediate problem that had arisen during
the course of battle.

On D-day, requests had been handled at a center in England, but as
early as the next day it was recognized that assigning targets, particularly
for immediate requests, had been either too slow or nonexistent because
the radios being used on the beaches had insufficient range. Therefore,
the task was moved to control ships offshore.[25] The first urgent request
was filed by the 8th U.S. Infantry, 4th Division, on D plus 1. On 19 June, a
fully-developed center, co-located at the operation headquarters of the
First U.S. Army and the advanced headquarters of IX Tactical Air Command, came into operation in the American zone. In the British sector, the
same system was put in place at the headquarters of the Second British
Army and its supporting air unit, 83 Group.

Co-location was replicated down the line to division level (with armored formations down to the combat commands).[26] Air and army representatives evaluated each request; those that were considered legitimate
were passed up to the Command Operations Center, which then put the
request aside for planned or ordinary missions or, if urgent, assigned it to
aircraft on the ground or already aloft. The division or corps center,
called Fighter Control Centers by the Americans and Visual Control Posts
by the British, then relayed the assignment to the appropriate aircraft. At
this point, the Fighter Control Center or geographically appropriate
Fighter Director Posts took over. Air Support Party (ASP) officers at the
Control Center or at the Director Post used radios and radar to guide the
aircraft to the target area. Radio contact with the flight or squadron leader
was maintained until about five minutes before the attack. During this interval, the ASP officer briefed the pilots on any special characteristics of
the target, the location of friendly troops, and whether the targets had
been marked by smoke, flares, or other means.

In some cases, the ASP officers actually directed the aircraft to the target, but it was more usual for the strike aircraft leader to communicate with the air-ground coordinating party that had originated the request for final details before initiating the attack. Using this system, the response in a few instances was as rapid as three minutes, but ten minutes to an hour was more normal. In this way, not only were interdiction targets hit in a timely manner, but the system also increasingly embraced close air support missions.

When the Allies turned to the use of contact cars (half-tracks) or armored column cover—in which pilots or army personnel in fast-moving situations were placed in lead vehicles on the ground and in direct contact with aircraft overhead to provide support—the rudiments of effective close air support were laid down on the Normandy beachhead. In fact, if one does not limit close air support to direct support of ground forces and includes attacks on any enemy target in close proximity to the front lines—ammunition dumps, storage depots, troop concentrations, headquarters, gun positions, rail junctions, tanks, armored fighting vehicles, and the like—between 6 and 28 June, Allied tactical air forces flew 11,255 sorties against such targets, and strategic forces chipped in with another 3,424.[27] When close air support is combined with the air superiority and interdiction sorties, it is clear that these tactical innovations brought about substantial results.

Among the many aircraft utilized, those best suited for interdiction and close air support missions proved to be the American P-47 Thunderbolt and the British Hawker Typhoon.[28] Both were formidable aircraft. The P-47 mounted three .50-caliber machine guns and used mostly 500-pound bombs and 260-pound fragmentation bombs (and later rockets) to accomplish its tasks. Though notorious for its fuel consumption, its air-cooled engine made it less susceptible to enemy fire than its liquid-cooled counterparts among Allied fighters. The Typhoon had four 20-mm cannons and was best known for its armor-piercing rockets, although it could also carry conventional ordnance. Spitfires, P-38 Lightnings, and P-51 Mustangs were other frequently used fighters, but they were not as effective as the P-47 or the Typhoon for close-to-the-battlefield missions.

Among the medium and light bombers, the Allies depended primarily on B-25 Mitchells, B-26 Marauders, Bostons, and highly reliable Mosquitoes. For heavy bomber missions, the Eighth Air Force relied on B-17s and B-24s; Bomber Command had turned mostly to Lancasters. Despite some limitations, all these aircraft presented the Germans with an almost insuperable challenge.

The rosy picture being sketched of Allied air power during the post-invasion phase does not mean that the various air forces did not experience problems. One was the matter of airfield construction.[29] Allied air commanders were well aware of the need for airfields on the Continent. They further realized that capturing those used by the enemy would be insufficient—hence, the need for large numbers of trained construction teams to build them. But the airfield program fell behind schedule from the start. Part of the problem was that on the first day, Montgomery's British and Canadian forces failed to liberate Caen and, more particularly, the open country south and southeast of the city. Failure to take over this area severely handicapped the air engineers, for it meant that they did not have sufficient space or the type of terrain needed to accomplish the massive construction program. Another part of the problem was that all the supply demands of the various military components and the destruction of the artificial Mulberry harbors by a storm in mid-June made it difficult to get the necessary materials on time.

The engineers did their best. They had completed an emergency sod strip by the evening of D-day in the Utah Beach sector and an airfield for transports near Omaha by D plus 2. The British overcame the difficulty of a silica dust unique to Normandy, which caused maintenance problems for the Typhoon and Spitfire engines, by fitting them with special air filters and by watering down the runways. As early as 11 June, the RAF had four landing strips in operation, and the Americans had finished three. Still, by 30 June, planners had expected to have twelve airfields built in the British sector, but the best the engineers could do—at times in the face of enemy artillery fire—was to finish ten and have one more under construction. Of the fifteen projected for the American zone, only seven had been completed, with four under construction by month's end. The number increased substantially in early July, but not until the end of the month were sufficient fighter-bomber and reconnaissance groups in place on the beachhead.

A second problem was whether fighter aircraft should be used against enemy targets that were within range of ground artillery.[30] Both army and air force commanders felt uneasy about relegating fighters to an artillery role. However, there were more than enough fighters to undertake such a task, and on occasion the fighter-bombers could attack a target more quickly and more accurately than the 240-mm howitzers or the 8-inch guns or howitzers. Although the issue was never completely resolved, the air dimension of close support was here to stay.

Third was the question of how best to use the strategic bombers for tactical missions. Before the invasion, the controversy had been settled by delegating the heavy bombers to strike transportation and other tactical targets, even though they were not prohibited from launching some raids against strategic targets inside the Reich. After the amphibious assault succeeded, strategic air chiefs were more anxious than ever to return to their "proper" mission.[31] But Supreme Headquarters Allied Expeditionary Force (SHAEF), having benefited earlier from the heavy bomber forces, was reluctant to part with them. Consequently, air leaders continued to assign them to attack primarily enemy harbors, rail junctions, airfields, and V-weapon sites in and around Normandy.

While the Eighth Air Force and Bomber Command continued to bomb targets in Germany, on 14 June a crisis seemed to be in the offing on the eastern flank of the beachhead. The 7th British Armored Division was reported to have suffered a severe setback. At a commanders' conference that day, SHAEF and air leaders thought that a "terrific air punch" might help and would bolster troop morale. The next day, while Eisenhower and Tedder went over to Normandy to investigate, Leigh-Mallory at the air commanders' meeting produced a scheme to use the heavy bombers against tactical targets in support of the 7th Armored. During the discussion, someone murmured "CASSINO," thus conjuring up memories of the strategic bombing disasters on the Italian front earlier in the year. In the face of opposition from other air representatives, Leigh-Mallory agreed not to call upon the bombers. It happened that the decision was overtaken by events, because Eisenhower and Tedder discovered that the 7th Armored was not as threatened as had been thought.

A door had opened nonetheless. From this point on, the idea of using heavy bombers to open up a front or to overwhelm enemy forces was in the ascendancy, and during July, Doolittle's and Harris's bombers undertook a number of tactical raids.[32] On 7 July, as part of Operation CHARNWOOD, 467 Bomber Command Lancasters, Halifaxes, and Mosquitoes as pathfinder (marking) aircraft dropped 2,276 tons of bombs north of Caen to assist British and Canadian troops in taking the city and the area beyond. The bombers hit their targets, but they were too far in front of the Allied soldiers to have much effect. On 18 July, the British launched a much more extensive operation, Operation GOODWOOD. Prior to the ground attack, 2,016 British and American heavy, medium, and light bombers dropped over 7,000 tons of bombs in an effort to help British armor clear the region and reach high ground east of Caen. Despite the effectiveness of the bombing run, an antitank gun line was not targeted, and this oversight, combined with a tenacious German defensive stand, stopped the offensive after only slight gains. Less than a week later, on 24 and 25 July, 2,022 of Doolittle's Eighth Air Force heavy bombers and 382 of Brereton's Ninth Air Force medium bombers undertook two missions to set the stage for Operation COBRA, the attempt to break out of the bridgehead near Saint Lô. In the end, American ground forces succeeded in breaking out, but it remains controversial as to how much strategic air contributed, since in both attacks some bombs fell short, killing 126 and wounding 631 soldiers and slowing momentum. In fact, General Quesada, the tactical air commander, went so far as to protest the heavy bombers flying perpendicular to the front line rather than parallel to it, as his planes had done.

The Saint Lô bombing incidents did not stop the Allies from continuing to use heavy bombers in a tactical support role, but they do point to a fourth problem for the British and Americans: air attacks on friendly forces.[33] Between 8 and 18 June, IX Tactical Air Command reported that its aircraft bombed and strafed American troops on thirteen separate occasions, and there were numerous incidents elsewhere. For instance, on 21 June, Ninth Air Force and Second Tactical Air Force planes tried to open the way to Cherbourg but hit U.S. soldiers in the process.

Nevertheless, all these problems pale in comparison with the overall Allied success in fulfilling their tactical air missions. The American official history stated that the interdiction portion of the campaign was the most significant Allied air contribution to victory in the Battle of Normandy; the close air effort, though lacking in certain aspects, also became an increasingly potent element in the air arsenal.[34] These achievements resulted from sound tactics and other factors, but the Allies also possessed a final advantage that was probably the most important of all: enormous numerical superiority.

The Allied figures for the air effort in June and July 1944 are shown in Table 8.1.[35] Even though the July effort did not equal that of June, 328,445 sorties dispatched and 287,907 effective sorties over the two-month period is truly an astounding effort. To be sure, these figures were rivaled and even surpassed before the war was over, and not all the sorties were directly related to OVERLORD. (The true number of OVERLORD sorties is difficult to separate out, since fighter escorts returning from bombing raids often attacked targets of opportunity in France.) Still, Allied air produced a remarkable achievement. The loss rate of only about .9 percent for both months is also amazingly low, especially when compared with the 10 to 20 percent loss rate sustained on some heavy bomber raids earlier in the war.

The remaining elements of the table offer few surprises. As one would expect, AEAF, the tactical and air defense component of the Normandy air armada, flew more sorties than both of the strategic air forces combined, but the heavy bombers dropped a far greater tonnage of bombs. What is

Table 8.1. Allied Air Effort, June–July 1944

	Aircraft Dispatched	Effective Sorties	Tons of Bombs	Aircraft Lost
		June 1944		
AEAF	102,546	94,202	28,424	745
BC	20,589	17,166	57,267	285
8AF	55,727	46,653	60,505	534
Total	178,862	158,021	146,196	1,564
		July 1944		
AEAF	83,945	75,598	19,808	551
BC	22,253	18,544	57,615	321
8AF	43,385	35,744	45,697	488
Total	149,583	129,866	123,102	1,360
Grand Total	328,445	287,907	269,298	2,924

Sources: AEAF, "Monthly Statistical Summary of Operations," Jun–Dec 1944, 506.308, USAFHRA; 8AF, "Statistical Summary of Eighth Air Force Operations, European Theater, Aug 17, 1941, to May 8, 1945," 5, 19, 520.308-1, USAFHRA; and Martin Middlebrook and Chris Everitt, eds., The Bomber Command War Diaries: An Operational Reference Book, 1939–1945 (London: Penguin, 1985), 517–54.

not apparent from the figures are some of the less heralded missions that were, nonetheless, risky and part of the total effort.[36] For example, air-sea rescue aircraft saved 1,245 pilots and crew members between 6 June and 31 August, transport aircraft evacuated 98,247 casualties out of the battle zone between D-day and the end of September, and Allied planes flew in supplies and personnel to assist the resistance movements in their increasingly valuable activities against the German enemy.

In comparison, Luftwaffe activity was meager at best. Between 6 and 30 June, Air Fleets 3 and Reich flew only 13,829 sorties and lost 1,181 aircraft.[37] During the same period, the Allies flew approximately 159,676 at a cost of 1,508 aircraft. In the month after D-day, the Germans were able to augment the 520 aircraft at their disposal at the time of the invasion with an additional 1,105 planes, but this number was more than offset by the losses incurred. To obtain an idea of the numerical disparity between the two sides, consider that the Ninth Air Force alone had twice as many aircraft available (over 2,000) on any given day as the applicable German air fleets had at their disposal. Moreover, the Allies had subjected Luftwaffe airfields in France to such incessant attacks that their use was severely curtailed. On 12 June, the Germans gave up any pretense of using their fighters for bombing missions and had the pilots concentrate on attacking enemy aircraft. German bombers remaining in the theater went exclusively to minelaying activities.

These caused the Allies difficulties but were never a major problem. The Luftwaffe was in no position to contest Allied control of the air.

The British and Americans possessed another great advantage—their aircrews.[38] Through June and July, sufficient pilots and crews were available for all the ready operational aircraft on any given day, and they were better trained than their German counterparts. By 1943, the number of British pilots being trained began to decline, but the Americans took up the slack. During the year, Army Air Forces' training schools in the United States turned out a phenomenal 82,700 pilots. Whereas German pilots during training averaged 170 hours (40 in combat-type aircraft), Americans averaged 310 hours (with 170 in suitable trainers).

Overall, Allied aircraft might not have been of better quality than their German equivalents, but in terms of the variety of missions, number of aircraft, and training of aircrews, there was no comparison. The once-vaunted Luftwaffe was a spent force, and OVERLORD contributed to its further deterioration. With regard to the Normandy air campaign as a whole, Allied success can be attributed to air superiority, tactical achievements, and numerical predominance. Allied air and numerical superiority combined to overwhelm the enemy, while tactical superiority came about primarily because of their own efforts.

The success of the air element of OVERLORD brings to mind several other observations. Allied control of the sky was gained only shortly before the invasion, suggesting that—at least in terms of the air war—the summer of 1944 was the proper time to launch the assault on Festung Europa. A year earlier, in 1943, the Western Allies were not ready for such a complex undertaking. They did not have the numbers to achieve air superiority; the Combined Bomber Offensive was only beginning to hit its stride; and, despite progress in North Africa, the Allies had not developed the tactical capabilities to give effective support to ground and naval forces. By May 1944, however, the British and Americans had reached a point where they could take advantage of what John Terraine called their "crushing air power."[39]

In an even broader sense, it might be contended that Britain's long-term strategy of sapping German strength before invading the Continent was achieved with regard to the air campaign. To be sure, some British leaders had never been enthusiastic about an OVERLORD-type operation, but by the time it was launched, the Luftwaffe had been so weakened that it barely had to be taken into account as a combat factor. The German air force occasionally inflicted substantial air casualties (over 5 percent) on Allied bombers and fighters over the Reich, but, for all intents and purposes, in Western Europe the Allies owned the sky. Air superiority had become air supremacy. Nevertheless, the fact of air supremacy should not lead to the conclusion that air power alone was decisive. The Wehrmacht was not defeated solely by attacks from the air. That was a task for the Allied armies, and British and American military leaders followed sound doctrine by having their land forces meet and defeat the enemy in ground combat. In the end, the victory in Normandy was a joint and combined effort.

9. Special Operations and the Normandy Invasion

David Hogan

What are "special operations"? The phrase has defied precise definition, despite numerous attempts by military lexicographers. Before World War II, service manuals, in giving examples of special operations, listed such missions as stream crossings, trench raids, night operations, and amphibious landings. During the conflict, the British Special Operations Executive (SOE) and the American Office of Strategic Services (OSS) both defined special operations as "subversive warfare," which, roughly translated, meant sabotage, support of resistance movements, and guerrilla warfare; at different times, the OSS also included commando raids and psychological operations in the concept. Recent definitions have not been much more helpful. The Department of Defense (DOD) has defined special operations as "operations conducted by specially trained, equipped, and organized DOD forces against strategic or tactical targets in pursuit of national military, political, economic, or psychological objectives," a definition that could encompass such varied activities as B-52 bombing raids or airmobile operations. Indeed, to many observers, special operations has come to mean almost any military mission, and some nonmilitary missions, that does not fit the pattern of big-unit, conventional warfare.[1]

Lacking any satisfactory alternative, I define special operations as what special operations forces do. In the United States, those forces consist of sea-air-land (SEAL) teams from the navy; air force special operations units; and Rangers, Special Forces, psychological operations groups, civil affairs detachments, and special aviation units from the army. Their missions include raids and the capture of especially critical points by commandos, aid to partisans, psychological operations, sabotage and subversion, escape and evasion, civil affairs, beach reconnaissance and demolition, and air support of these activities. This definition will not even be acceptable to all elements of the special operations community, but it furnishes a starting point.[2]

As amorphous as the concept of special operations is today, it was much more so at the start of World War II. Much of the American experience with what we now call special operations—notably the exploits of

Rogers's Rangers, Morgan's riflemen, and the partisans of Marion and Mosby—lay in the distant past. Interest in commandos among military officers was limited to mess-table discussions about German storm troopers in World War I and an occasional nostalgic article in a professional journal about George Washington's light infantry. Except for the oft-strained alliance of convenience with Cuban rebels during the war with Spain, the services' background in partisan warfare lay more in terms of fighting guerrillas than supporting them. In the Philippines, Central America, and the Caribbean, the army and marines had dealt with problems of native insurgencies and military government, and service schools in the 1920s and 1930s had devoted some time to so-called small wars, examining operations in deserts, mountains, and other "undeveloped regions." During World War I, the army and navy had some exposure to propaganda through the army's Military Intelligence Service and the Committee on Public Information. Such activities, however, were exceptions to the dominant orientation toward big-unit warfare forged by the experiences of the Civil War and the Western Front in World War I, changes in the American economy and culture since 1865, and the identification of professional officers with the armies of Europe.[3]

The British background in special operations was more extensive than that of their American counterparts, but it was similarly lacking in continuity. Britons could point to a long tradition of raids by expeditionary forces that capitalized on British maritime supremacy, notably the famous descent on the U-boat base of Zeebrugge during World War I. British governments had supported feudal lords against their French monarch and Spanish guerrillas against Napoleon, and the legendary T. E. Lawrence had led Arab insurgents against the Turks. In Africa, India, and the rest of the empire, the British had accumulated substantial experience in military government and civil affairs, and British propaganda in World War I had acquired so powerful a reputation for effectiveness as to be credited by many Americans with having drawn the United States into the war. Still, by the mid-1930s, a lack of ongoing organization, doctrine, and trained personnel had largely dissipated British expertise. Only as the shadow of Nazi Germany loomed over Europe in early 1938 did the Foreign Office and the War Office establish sections to investigate subversive warfare. These investigations produced the wartime Political Warfare Executive (PWE) for propaganda and the SOE for support of resistance movements.[4]

When war came in September 1939, the Germans proved more ready than the Allies to use special operations, perhaps because defeat in World War I had made so many in the SS and the Abwehr, Germany's intelligence service, more receptive to such activities. Propaganda had played a major role in Hitler's rise to power, with the Nazis taking full advantage of the latest advances in group psychology and mass-marketing techniques. Through radio, film, and other media, they employed themes of German military might, the injustices of the Versailles treaty, the perfidious British, and the Nazi-Soviet pact to inspire fear, sympathy, and divisiveness among enemies and neutrals. In the campaign of 1940, such methods proved stunningly effective in combination with the use of elite parachutists to seize the "impregnable" fortress of Eben Emael and disguised infiltrators to cut phone wires and seize bridges, road junctions, and other key points in the Wehrmacht's path of advance. The actual accomplishments of the Nazi "fifth column" were much exaggerated, but stories of nuns in hob-nailed boots, airdrops of poisoned chocolates for children, and mysterious accidents in munitions plants created an atmosphere of terror that greatly contributed to the French collapse in the summer of 1940.[5]

Alone except for their dominions and a few exile governments, the British, having left much of their army on the beaches of Dunkirk, turned to special operations as one of the few ways to hit back at the enemy following the fall of France. A propaganda campaign by the Ministry of Information (MOI), British Broadcasting Corporation (BBC), and, later, PWE was already under way despite bureaucratic rivalries and Winston Churchill's dislike for psychological warfare. The prime minister showed considerably more enthusiasm for descents on the French coast by elite raiding units, known as commandos. An interservice Combined Operations Headquarters (COHQ) was created in July 1940 to plan and execute raids and to carry out experiments in amphibious techniques and develop landing craft for an eventual cross-Channel attack. Given the long period that had to pass before such an invasion would be possible, British planners somewhat wistfully hoped that a three-pronged strategy of economic blockade, aerial bombardment, and subversion within the occupied territories would eventually bring the Germans to their knees. Under the loose supervision of the Ministry of Economic Warfare, SOE sought to encourage passive resistance and sabotage in the occupied areas and, as the movement grew, to supply arms and equipment for a vast underground army that would rise in a general insurrection when the invasion came. Because of disputes over strategy, however, SOE did not start infiltrating agents into occupied France on any scale until 1941.[6]

On the other side of the Atlantic, special operations had caught the attention of William J. Donovan, a World War I hero, corporate lawyer, and friend of President Franklin D. Roosevelt. Visits to Europe and discussions with the British during the summer and winter of 1940–41 convinced Donovan that the United States must overcome its distaste for fifth-column activities and develop its capability in this field. When he returned, he convinced the president, in July 1941, to authorize formation of the office of Coordinator of Information (COI), later the Office of Strategic Services, for collection and analysis of data and such other "supplementary activities" as the president might direct. The corollary was significant, for Donovan, following the British lead, was already developing his concept of special operations as a tool to soften rear areas for eventual invasion. He regarded propaganda as the initial "arrow of penetration," to be followed by a campaign of sabotage, subversion, and small-unit guerrilla warfare by partisans, assisted by commandos. Donovan would need time to work out this concept, create an organization to support it, and sell it to superiors. In the meantime, he had the field to himself, except for preliminary army investigations into propaganda, General Douglas MacArthur's efforts to form an underground movement in anticipation of a Japanese attack on the Philippines, and marine experiments with the rubber boat companies that later became the Raiders.[7]

When Pearl Harbor thrust the United States into World War II, American strategists soon turned to special operations as part of a "preliminary active front" in northwest Europe. Although the Americans advocated the soonest possible cross-Channel attack, they reluctantly recognized that it would take at least a year to assemble in Great Britain the resources for such an effort. At the London conference in April 1942, General George C. Marshall proposed, and the British accepted, a plan for a series of air and coastal raids preparatory to an invasion in April 1943. Nevertheless, in early 1942, execution of any special operations strategy had to be, for the most part, a British show. COI had established an office in London, but during 1942 that agency was undergoing a reorganization into the OSS as well as jurisdictional disputes with the army and, in the field of propaganda, the new Office of War Information. Not until 1944 would the OSS exercise much influence on policy relating to subversive warfare in northwest Europe. Meanwhile, to ensure American participation in future raids, Marshall ordered the formation of a provisional Ranger battalion of volunteers from American units in Northern Ireland. The Rangers would train and raid under COHQ and then take their combat experience back to their formations.[8]

Over the ensuing year, the raiding strategy fell far short of expectations. From May to September 1942—the prime raiding season—COHQ conducted only the disastrous Dieppe raid, canceling five others at the last moment and nine at some earlier stage of planning. Bad weather proved the greatest obstacle, but the program also suffered from complexities of planning among the three services as well as competition for scarce planes, landing craft, and other resources. Even the Dieppe raid showed the limitations of a raiding strategy. The origins of the debacle remain the subject of much controversy, but the desire of Anglo-American strategists for some diversion in favor of the hard-pressed Soviets dovetailed nicely with COHQ's desire to put on a showy, large-scale raid after the frustration of canceling several smaller ones. Its benefits, however, appear dubious next to its costs. Although it may have raised the level of anxiety of enemy coastal forces, it also revealed to the Germans some weaknesses in their defenses. Its diversionary value for the Soviets was negligible, and the Royal Air Force, seeking to draw out its German adversary, actually lost twice as many planes as the Luftwaffe. Whatever the Allies might have learned about amphibious assaults—and by most accounts, they learned a great deal—they could not continue to sacrifice whole divisions to obtain them.[9]

Even as the raiding program languished, amphibious landings in the Mediterranean were not only featuring the use of commandos and Rangers to seize key points in support of the main attack but also spawning a new series of special units. In North Africa, Sicily, and Italy, Rangers and commandos captured coastal batteries and terrain features dominating the invasion beaches. Teams of British canoeists, later known as the combined operations assault pilotage parties (COPPs), reconnoitered the beaches in North Africa and used beams to guide in the invasion fleet. As for the Americans, the exploits of U.S. Navy demolitioneers near Port Lyautey helped inspire the formation of naval combat demolition units (NCDUs). In the Mediterranean, the Allies faced a major task in reaching agreement on a proper control structure for civil affairs, providing for equal partnership. After that, the real problems of disorder and chaos in Sicily and Italy must have seemed tame. Also in the Mediterranean Allied Force Headquarters's Psychological Warfare Branch learned much about the value of psychological warfare and the difficulty of coordinating different propaganda agencies, each with its own approach based on its own ideology.[10]

Thus, as planners began to work out the details of OVERLORD—the cross-Channel invasion and the biggest challenge yet for the Allies—amphibious landings in the Mediterranean indicated several areas where special operations could contribute. Reconnaissance by special teams could inform the Allies of the best landing sites, and demolition teams could remove German obstacles from beaches. Commandos and Rangers could carry out raids to gather information, divert the Germans from the true landing beaches, and, on D-day, seize key points, notably the German battery at Pointe du Hoc that dominated Omaha Beach. With Allied help, the

French resistance could provide intelligence and, through sabotage and guerrilla operations, hinder the German response to the invasion. Propaganda might weaken the German will to fight and encourage the French to resist. Well-conducted civil affairs could enable the Allies to focus on the main front without concern for rear areas. Through such missions, special operations might provide the margin needed to surmount the assault's two main challenges: mustering enough force, supported by naval and air power, to crack hardened defenses on dominating ground with a basically frontal attack; and enabling the force, once ashore, to build up enough strength to withstand counterattacks by panzer divisions.

Nevertheless, to utilize special operations properly, the Allies had to overcome some major obstacles. One notable problem was the difficulty of conducting such operations in France. Although France contained some forested terrain and mountains—in particular the Vosges, Jura, Massif Central, Alps, and Pyrenees—that could provide cover and concealment for a guerrilla force, these lay in the eastern, south central, southeastern, and southwestern regions of the country, far from the OVERLORD invasion beaches. Much of France, including the invasion region, consisted of settled, relatively open farmland, which forced the partisans to disperse and focus on sabotage and intelligence gathering. As for Normandy, the Germans had cordoned off the coastal area to a depth of 30 to 40 miles, within which they carefully screened the local population, their labor force, and strangers. Given the dense concentration of antiaircraft batteries, it would be difficult to supply the weak, scattered resistance elements that did exist there. Any major aid from the resistance had to come from outside the beachhead area.[11]

A second obstacle lay in the divergent policies of the Allied governments toward the French, who were themselves badly divided. Rifts within the resistance reflected the deep cleavages in prewar French politics and society. The adherents of General Charles de Gaulle were largely concentrated in Armée Secrète, which de Gaulle hoped would form the nucleus for a nationwide army of liberation and a base of political power in postwar France. The Gaullists often clashed with the rightist Armée de l'Armistice, which drew its followers from the demobilized army of the collaborationist Vichy government, and with the Communist Francs Tireurs Partisans, who had their own postwar agenda and were based largely in industrial areas. The Maquis, young men who fled to the mountains to escape forced labor drafts by the Germans, contained elements of all three groups. By 1943, the Gaullists were gaining in strength, largely through the efforts of Jean Moulin, who had brought several groups together in a Committee of National Resistance. Gestapo arrests in the summer of 1943 shattered this nascent organization, but the resistance displayed surprising powers of recovery. Although the Gaullists were attaining supremacy among non-Communists by the winter of 1943–44, the resistance was hardly a unified movement, and the Allies possessed the ability to influence this power struggle by their distribution of arms and equipment to the warring factions.[12]

The Allies, however, could not agree on a common policy toward the French. Although Churchill and other British leaders often clashed with de Gaulle and did not want to recognize outright his Committee of National Liberation (FCNL) as the French government-in-exile, the British government and public could not forget his support during the dark days of 1940, nor did they doubt that the general truly embodied the spirit of French resistance. The British foresaw the need for some sort of provisional authority in France, and, under the circumstances, they saw no alternative to the FCNL. Although the U.S. War Department was inclined, on grounds of military expediency, to agree with the British to some extent, Roosevelt and the State Department were not ready to confer such a lofty status on de Gaulle nor to take any step that might impair the ability of the French to choose their postwar government. They often expressed their desire to cooperate with "all patriotic Frenchmen," including former Vichyites, and backed conservative General Henri Giraud as an alternative to de Gaulle. Vague and idealistic, the American policy underestimated de Gaulle's support among the French people by late 1943. It also complicated Allied efforts to work with the FCNL and to develop civil affairs agreements that would leave most governmental burdens to local French officials while assuring access to French resources for the war effort.[13]

Even if a common policy had emerged, the Anglo-Americans would have found the FCNL a difficult ally. Eager to erase the memory of 1940, de Gaulle was seeking not only to position himself for the postwar political struggle but also to preserve French status as a great power, independent of the British and Americans. His actions to sustain his concept of French honor, as well as his proud and sensitive personality, aroused Roosevelt's dislike and even irritated the more understanding Churchill. De Gaulle's FCNL, although eager to work with the Allies in the liberation, raised the hackles of their counterparts on several issues. The existence of SOE's F Section, which operated agent nets separate from those of the FCNL, annoyed de Gaulle, who had to be persuaded to offer commissions to French officers who served in SOE. The FCNL also wanted to develop a highly centralized organization to enhance its control over the resistance; the British, remembering the disaster of summer 1943, wanted greater decentralization, with regional nets reporting directly to London. French plans for partisan action, including the seizure and defense of key ground, seemed dictated more by the demands of French honor than by practical guerrilla tactics, which warned against being pinned down in defense of fixed objectives. Given French independence and separate FCNL communications, the Allies could not be sure what precise course the French would take when the moment of liberation came.[14]

Disputes with the French contributed to a third major obstacle for special operations planners: the problem of organization and control. As a relatively new field, special operations was plagued by conceptual problems, a menagerie of often duplicative agencies, and different nationalities. When ten new NCDUs arrived in England in the late autumn of 1943, they lacked even a commanding officer to provide direction to their training. As for raids and reconnaissance, the Chief of Staff to the Supreme Allied Commander designate (COSSAC), the headquarters established in 1943 to plan OVERLORD, supposedly controlled such activities in the invasion area, but COSSAC's reliance on COHQ to staff such missions and on an interservice committee to coordinate them limited its real authority. COSSAC was also supposed to have enough control over SOE's special operations activities to ensure their conformity with OVERLORD plans, but reliance on liaison rather than a formal command structure left SOE with ample freedom in its operations. When they looked at psychological warfare, OVERLORD planners found a veritable jungle of rival agencies, each with its own philosophy: the PWE, MOI, and BBC on the British side; the New Deal idealists of the Office of War Information (OWI) and the hard-boiled realists of OSS on the American side. For civil affairs, planners had to decide between the Mediterranean model of separate military government or a structure closely integrated with the military chain of command. Lt. Gen. Sir Frederick Morgan would later point to civil affairs as the most vexatious command problem faced by his COSSAC.[15]

If, by some miracle, Allied special operations planners sorted out these problems of organization and jurisdiction, they faced the matter of command, control, and communication with the resistance. From bitter experience, SOE had learned the impracticality of canalizing control through a single communications channel and had taken steps to establish independent communications with the separate groups. The tenuous links with these groups improved over time, but SOE still needed to deal with the limitations of radio technology as well as the delay involved in running couriers to and from the field. The possibility was ever present that the Germans had infiltrated some or most of these circuits and were using their call signs in an effort to mislead the Allies. Thus, the Allies could

General Eisenhower, Prime Minister Churchill, and General de Gaulle confer just before the invasion.

never be sure that they had an accurate assessment of the strength of the resistance.[16]

Competing demands for scarce resources, especially aircraft, presented a fourth major obstacle to the special operations effort. When SOE appealed for the diversion of a few more planes from the bombing offensive in the spring of 1943, it met strong opposition from Air Chief Marshal Sir Charles Portal, who remarked to an SOE official, "I cannot divert aircraft from a certainty to a gamble which may be a gold-mine or may be completely worthless." In the end, SOE could secure only a slight and inadequate increase. The OSS encountered similar problems in convincing Lt. Gen. Carl A. Spaatz of the U.S. Northwest African Air Force to divert a few planes to special operations. After a fruitless appeal to the Joint Chiefs of Staff, Donovan finally persuaded Spaatz's chief of staff, an old comrade from World War I, to allot three B-17s for special missions into France. In London, the OSS, after considerable lobbying, managed to pry loose from the Eighth Air Force the B-24s of the 479th Anti-Submarine Warfare Group, later the nucleus of the CARPETBAGGER project to drop supplies and agents to the resistance. Despite these efforts, only a minuscule number of planes were conducting special operations in France by the end of 1943.[17]

Permeating special operations, as it did practically every other aspect of OVERLORD, was a fifth major obstacle: the need for secrecy. The Allies had developed a secrecy mania in their efforts to hide the time and place of the invasion and to convince the Germans that the blow would fall on the Pas de Calais. With regard to special operations, this obsessiveness becomes more fathomable when one remembers that SOE was just recovering from the breakup of the PROSPER circuit in the summer of 1943, a disaster that resulted in large part from agents' carelessness about security. Despite SOE's efforts toward decentralization and greater isolation of circuits, other agencies were understandably concerned. As late as the winter of 1943–44, War Office officials restricted infiltration into France by SOE's British officers on the grounds that the security of the invasion would be endangered. Would special operations advocates be able to convince doubters that their missions into France would produce benefits that justified the risk to perhaps the most important secret of the war?[18]

Such obstacles could only reinforce the natural skepticism of OVERLORD's military leaders toward special operations. The big-unit warfare toward which most were inclined was based on different assumptions, notably the notion that the destiny of nations was decided by the clash of mass formations. A mind-set shaped by World War I, Leavenworth, Camberly, and the genteel atmosphere of interwar British and American military culture could not help but see special operations as an odd sideshow, a series of pinpricks without tangible effect. Both leading ground field commanders of the Normandy invasion, General Sir Bernard L. Montgomery and Lt. Gen. Omar N. Bradley, were careful tacticians, schooled in their armies' doctrines of applying overwhelming force. They were therefore somewhat skeptical of the claims of special operations advocates. Nor did Supreme Headquarters Allied Expeditionary Force (SHAEF) offer more fertile ground. Although Morgan, now the deputy chief of staff, possessed a more open mind, the chief of staff, Lt. Gen. Walter B. Smith, cherished a visceral dislike for special operations, particularly psychological warfare. Still, in a total war against an enemy who had often used such methods, discomfort with "butcher and bolt" raids or "mind warfare" was less a factor to such leaders than the hard-headed question of whether they could contribute enough to justify the diversion of resources.[19]

In part, the skepticism can be traced to the nature of the special units. Lacking a prewar history for the most part, they appeared as Johnny-come-latelies, improvised in response to events. When the first NCDUs arrived in England, naval commands had little idea of their mission and often assigned them to "collateral duties," such as serving as officer of the day at a hotel. Rangers and commandos, at least, had recognizable unit organizations, but few knew what to think of the six-man NCDUs or SOE's three-man Jedburgh teams, which consisted of an American or British officer, a French officer, and a wireless operator. Just as unconventional, special operations training could embrace anything from cliff climbing and demolition of beach obstacles to the study of the legal principles of military government. Trained in high-level daylight bombing, American pilots assigned to special operations duty needed to learn to fly modified B-17s and B-24s on low-level solo missions at night. Finally, special operations units included graduates of elite English universities, Spanish Civil War veterans, a former czarist army officer, and "tough little boys from New York and Chicago" whose one great ambition, according to an instructor, "was to get over to the old country and start throwing knives." Orthodox soldiers did not know what to think of such mavericks.[20]

The man who would have the biggest say in determining the role of special operations in the invasion was himself an orthodox soldier. Like other American generals, Dwight D. Eisenhower had been schooled in mass warfare at Leavenworth, the Army Industrial College, and the Army War College. His background as trainer, aide, staff officer, and high-level planner hardly disposed him toward special operations, and he probably did not understand them. Nevertheless, Eisenhower possessed a mind that was more capable of grasping complexities than some of his detractors would admit. His political skills have received general acclaim. He knew how to deal with people; even de Gaulle trusted the plainspoken American. Nevertheless, Eisenhower could get impatient with political considerations when he believed that they stood in the way of his mission. Such an attitude might have led to grief in some circumstances, but in 1944 it was not out of line with the overall American policy to win the war and worry about politics afterwards. As Supreme Commander, Eisenhower had to balance special operations against other priorities, but he realized that the Allies could not afford to neglect any means, including guerrilla warfare or psychological operations, that might ease their formidable task.[21]

Eisenhower's tact and prestige, as well as Roosevelt's deference to military considerations, were largely responsible for SHAEF's ability to work out a modus vivendi of sorts with the FCNL. From the first, Eisenhower took the view that he badly needed the support of the resistance; he also needed to have an arrangement with a constituted French entity that would permit him to avoid embroilment in French politics and allow him to turn over to local authorities those areas that were not essential for military operations. He argued repeatedly to his superiors that the FCNL provided the only viable means for achieving those goals. Roosevelt responded by authorizing Eisenhower to hold informal discussions with representatives of the FCNL regarding the resistance's contribution to the invasion. In a 15 March directive, the president allowed Eisenhower considerable discretion in deciding when, where, and how civil affairs in France were to be administered, but the document also contained the proviso that contacts with the FCNL by no means constituted recognition. Roosevelt's directives at least enabled SHAEF to open several working relationships with representatives of the FCNL at the nonpolitical level, for both resistance work and civil affairs. Nevertheless, the lack of a formal agreement prior to D-day complicated planning in several areas.[22]

Political complications hindered the establishment of proper command and control over the resistance. By early 1944, SOE special operations had formed an integrated organization that would eventually become Special Forces Headquarters (SFHQ). SFHQ reported to SHAEF, which had received from COSSAC responsibility for coordinating, through its G-3 section, underground resistance in France in direct support of OVERLORD. This command arrangement did not leave room for the French—not a surprising development, given continuing confusion over what contacts were permitted with the FCNL and doubts within Allied command circles about French competence and operational security. Under pressure from the FCNL and its representative, General Pierre J. Koenig, the Allies finally created the Etat Major, Forces Francaises de l'Interieur (EMFFI) in May to supervise resistance activities, but SHAEF resisted subordinating SFHQ to this agency. This chaotic, improvised structure would cause numerous problems for SFHQ operatives in the field.[23]

Command and control over propaganda and civil affairs were in only a slightly better state. After an initial attempt to combine press relations and psychological operations in a single section, SHAEF established a separate psychological warfare division under Brig. Gen. Robert B. McClure in April 1944. Drawing on his North African experience, in which the civilian agencies had sometimes worked at cross purposes with Eisenhower's headquarters, McClure moved to subordinate them under military control. SHAEF Operations Memorandum No. 8 stipulated that the army groups, operating under SHAEF directives, would control frontline propaganda; consolidation propaganda—psychological warfare directed toward rear or liberated areas—would be conducted directly by SHAEF or would be decentralized to the army groups when desirable and practicable. The OWI, OSS, PWE, and MOI enjoyed freedom in the field of strategic propaganda against enemy rear areas, but their activities were subject to SHAEF coordination and the approval of the Combined Chiefs of Staff in Washington. After a prolonged debate, SHAEF also opted to integrate civil affairs more closely into the military chain of command than had been the case in the Mediterranean. Each command level down to corps added a G-5 section, which would plan and coordinate the conduct of civil affairs within its command area. Under the policy control of SHAEF, 21st Army Group would delegate its powers to the armies, which would supervise the civil affairs detachments in the field.[24]

Although SHAEF might have wished to tighten the command structure over special operations to enhance its own control, it proved more reluctant to divert scarce aircraft to special operations. To carry out leaflet drops, Morgan arranged a compromise; CARPETBAGGER would handle the bulk of the missions while the tactical air forces covered any shortfalls by carrying out drops in the course of their normal operations. For drops of supplies and agents, SHAEF proved more intractable, causing advocates to turn to political leaders. Through a personal appeal to Churchill, including eyewitness reports from agents, the FCNL's Emmanuel d'Astier persuaded the prime minister to increase the British allocation of aircraft to SOE and other clandestine agencies. As British supply drops to the resistance mounted to a level ten times that of the American program, Donovan and the State Department warned the Joint Chiefs of Staff that the disparity could be a source of friction in postwar relations with

France. The Joint Chiefs passed the warning on to SHAEF. In response, in early May, Eisenhower directed the Eighth Air Force to furnish another 25 aircraft to CARPETBAGGER, producing a dramatic rise in supply sorties to the resistance.[25]

Special operations advocates might have overcome SHAEF's reluctance to divert aircraft to their activities, but they could never entirely reconcile the need for secrecy with operational requirements. The problem of security had an effect on several aspects of special operations planning, from the decision not to drop uniformed Jedburghs, ordnance groups (OGs), and special air service (SAS) troops before D-day to the propaganda plan to avoid a pre-D-day barrage of leaflets and broadcasts focused on Normandy. It also had an impact on the already complicated task of ensuring the cooperation of the resistance. In early May, Eisenhower notified the Combined Chiefs of Staff of his desire to inform Koenig of the approximate time and place of the invasion in order to facilitate advance coordination with the resistance. Suspicious of FCNL security, the British vetoed the proposal, but SHAEF pressed the point. In the end, the dilemma was resolved only by inviting de Gaulle to London on the eve of the invasion to make a broadcast. Even then, the French leader refused to read the statement the Allies had prepared for him. As events showed, concern about security was not unjustified, for German security services later claimed that a broken SOE circuit alerted them to the imminence of the invasion.[26]

Security breaches—real or potential—would have added to the skepticism of field commanders and staff officers who, despite the efforts of advocates such as Morgan and McClure, remained largely unconvinced about the benefits of special operations. After a few commando and Ranger raids early in 1944 had been aborted by rough weather, Montgomery, despite Morgan's arguments, had SHAEF cancel the remaining missions, claiming that to continue the program would only aggravate the shortage of landing craft and might alert the Germans without providing any new information. Morgan, at McClure's instigation, queried Montgomery's chief of staff, Maj. Gen. Sir Francis de Guingand, about 21st Army Group's preparations for psychological warfare. De Guingand replied that much frontline propaganda was not worth the cost and that not until long after D-day could the Allies afford to grant shipping space for such comparative luxuries as propagandists with their bales of leaflets and radio equipment. At First U.S. Army, prejudices against civil affairs officers were endemic, and Bradley raised civil affairs to the status of a G-5 section only under pressure from SHAEF. Although they appreciated the immediate benefits of commando assaults against key points or reconnaissance by COPP teams, field generals by and large were too concerned with the problems of the assault to bother with such remote issues as partisan warfare, psychological operations, and civil affairs.[27]

SHAEF was more receptive to the resistance's potential, but given the uncertainties surrounding the subject, planners were inclined to view any contribution from the movement as a bonus. SHAEF's directive to SOE on 23 March 1944 stated that resistance groups, in preparation for the invasion, should attack German aircraft, lower German morale by sabotage and "kindred methods," keep German forces as dispersed as possible, and prepare to assist Allied forces. As for the resistance's role after D-day, several SHAEF planners found the prospect of a popular uprising alluring, but SHAEF decided that a levee en masse would be hard to control and might backfire on the Allies if the Germans instituted massive reprisals. Nevertheless, SHAEF's directive of 23 May called for an all-out attack on D-day by the active resistance and Allied special units on German communications and troop movements. Plan Vert, prepared by the French under SOE's general direction, allotted targets on key stretches of railroad lines in France to resistance teams; Plan Tortue provided for groups to harass road traffic through roadblocks, mines, and ambushes. The 23 May directive also called on the French to interfere with German reserves, especially motorized forces in northern France, and hit enemy telecommunications, command posts, airfields, and supply dumps. Jedburgh teams would deploy to coordinate and help supply the resistance, and OGs and SAS troops would provide operational nuclei and perform missions that the resistance could not handle.[28]

Psychological operations for OVERLORD posed an especially formidable challenge. Along with security restrictions precluding a specific focus on German troops in Normandy before the invasion, propagandists were under orders not to make any commitments about Allied postwar policy toward Germany, not to suggest that the German army would be absolved from responsibility for German aggression, and not to hint that German militarism would survive. SHAEF's psychological warriors had to convince a German soldier hardened by discipline, comradeship, professional pride, and the Allies' unconditional surrender policy that the war was lost. They decided to achieve this goal by exploiting the shaken German confidence in their leadership, the Luftwaffe, and their own invincibility and by building trust in the reliability of Allied statements. Through leaflets and broadcasts, the Allies would drive home the theme that—with the invasion—Germany would be facing a four-front war against a united coalition possessing superior resources, a war it could not win. Allied "black" or covert propaganda would emphasize the "enemy within": the growing weakness of German war production, the impotence of the Luftwaffe, and the breakdown in authority on the home front. After D-day, the Allies planned to focus on foreigners in the German army, offering amnesty to those who had been coerced into service. Although SHAEF did not formally issue its directive on psychological operations against the Germans until after D-day, its general principles were known and applied by the army groups in the early days of the invasion.[29]

The absence of a final directive also caused SHAEF to improvise in civil affairs. Lacking an Anglo-American agreement on policy toward the FCNL, planners worked from the basis that the FCNL would be recognized at some point as the provisional national authority and that an agreement would be concluded along the same lines as those with other governments, allowing military control of critical regions and leaving other areas to the FCNL. In general, SHAEF was able to work out satisfactory arrangements for purging local administrations of Vichyites, maintaining law and order, restricting traffic on roads needed for troop movements, and distributing relief supplies, but not without some conflicts. At least one civil affairs officer encountered problems obtaining space in scarce shipping from a harassed First Army supply officer, and an Anglo-American proposal to use francs issued under the authority of the Supreme Commander drew a predictable blast from the FCNL, which saw the supplemental currency as an infringement on French sovereignty. Still lacking an agreement with the FCNL, SHAEF issued an interim directive on civil affairs on 25 May. This document substantially approved existing plans but also provided that SHAEF intended to work entirely through local officials and not to institute a military government in France.[30]

In comparison with the complexities of planning for other special operations, the issue of how best to employ special units in the assault seemed relatively simple. Their missions, however, were vital. In the American sector, three companies of the 2d Ranger Battalion were to climb the cliffs of Pointe du Hoc on the west side of Omaha Beach and capture a battery of 155-mm guns that dominated the approaches to Omaha while another company seized Pointe de la Percee, flanking the beach. If the assault on Pointe du Hoc were unsuccessful, the 5th Ranger Battalion and two other companies of the 2d would land on Omaha and move overland to the position. Joint teams of NCDUs and army engineers would follow the first assault wave onto the beach and blow gaps through the exposed obstacles before the rising tide engulfed them. On the British beaches, 41, 47, and 48 Royal Marine Commandos were to land on the flanks and drive inland, while the commandos of the 1st Special Service Brigade landed on the left of Sword Beach, took the port of Ouistreham at the mouth of the Orne River, and moved inland to link up with the 6th Airborne Division and secure bridges over the Orne. Ten landing craft obstruction clearance units would clear lanes through the obstacles for the British invasion fleet.[31]

Even as final plans were being completed, preliminary special operations had begun. Through leaflets, including daily newspapers with the latest war news, and broadcasts by the BBC, Voice of SHAEF, "black" stations, and OWI's American Broadcasting Station in Europe, Allied propagandists drove home their theme of the "year of doom," stressing Allied strength, the inevitability of invasion, and the failings of the Nazi leadership and Luftwaffe. At first, COSSAC and SHAEF used commando raids to gather data on the invasion site, but even before the cancellation of the raiding program, SHAEF increasingly relied on the stealthier COPPs. In mid-January, the COPPs carried out two critical missions, first to the British and then to the American beaches, where they collected soil samples and noted the types of obstacles. With more aircraft, SOE increased drops of weapons, ammunition, medical supplies, explosives, and agents to the resistance. Field agents, or country sections at SHAEF, sent their requests to SOE, which figured priorities, pinpointed drop areas, and sent a list to the Eighth Air Force for approval. Once the air force approved, SOE sent the list to CARPETBAGGER. Given the means, resistance operatives went to work, sabotaging 808 locomotives in three months and preparing derailments in anticipation of D-day. As the tempo of sabotage in France accelerated, Rangers, commandos, landing craft obstruction clearance units, NCDUs, OGs, SAS troopers, Jedburghs, and civil affairs units were training for their roles on 6 June.[32]

For special operations units taking part in the assault, 6 June 1944 proved to be a bittersweet day of heroic feats and heavy losses. At Pointe du Hoc, the Rangers scrambled up the cliffs under fire only to find that the Germans had removed the guns to protect them from bombardment. A Ranger patrol later found and destroyed the pieces, and the small force held for two days until relieved by the 5th Ranger Battalion and 29th Infantry Division from Omaha. On the British beaches, the commandos seized Ouistreham and made their linkup with the 6th Airborne. Even with help from tanks, 41 Royal Marine Commandos on the right flank of Sword could not overcome stiff resistance at Lion-sur-Mer, and the other two Royal Marine commandos on Gold and Juno suffered heavy losses while capturing their objectives. NCDUs on Utah encountered light opposition and were able to complete their mission by 8 a.m., but the NCDUs on Omaha had a very difficult time. Currents and haze carried them off their proper course, leaving them in many cases on the beach ahead of the assaulting infantry. Not surprisingly, the soldiers often took cover behind obstacles that the NCDUs had rigged for demolition. In the confusion, under heavy fire, the NCDUs made only six of the sixteen scheduled gaps during the first low tide. British frogmen had a somewhat easier time, in part due to the presence of significant numbers of armored vehicles to provide fire support.[33]

D-day represented a peak for special assault units, which thereafter performed relatively unimportant and often unsuitable missions, but it was only the beginning for the civil affairs personnel and propagandists. Before the assault, Allied aircraft saturated Normandy with leaflets, announcing to German soldiers the opening of the "Fourth Front" and warning civilians to evacuate. During the first days, Allied leaflets and "safe conduct passes" assured the German soldier that he had fought with honor and could surrender without shame, while other leaflets and broadcasts urged Poles and Russians serving in German coastal units to surrender and not be sacrificed by the Herrenvolk. Once ashore, the Allies used radio, magazines, and newspapers, such as news sheets in Bayeux and Isigny, to counter rumors and inform the French about how to help the Allied armies. Civil affairs personnel, including three officers who arrived in gliders with the 82d Airborne Division, found their task simplified by the absence of large towns, the proximity of a rich agricultural area, and the presence of an able local administration. Except for some looting, the French maintained law and order, and civil affairs officers could limit their activities to contacting the local mayor and resistance leader, providing any necessary help with law enforcement, turning over captured German papers and material to the appropriate staff sections, and arranging for establishment of refugee camps and distribution of flour, wheat, and soap.[34]

While civil affairs personnel worked to maintain order in liberated areas, reports that were coming into SHAEF's G-3 division from behind enemy lines indicated an uprising of greater dimensions than even SFHQ had anticipated. From Lille in northeast France to the Pyrenees, resistance operatives sabotaged railroads and highways, blew bridges, and cut telephone wires while partisan bands harassed German troop and supply movements. Thanks to Allied air power, sabotage, and ambushes, the 2d SS Panzer Division took sixteen days to cover a three-day journey to the beaches, and the 11th Panzer Division, which had reached the Rhine from the Eastern Front in a week, needed three more weeks to travel the remaining distance to Caen. In cooperation with the air forces, SFHQ stepped up its program of supply and agent drops; the U.S. Army Air Force alone expanded from 288 missions in May to 442 in June. Most of the Jedburgh teams and SAS troops dropped by the air force in June deployed into Brittany and the Loire valley, where they found the resistance to be stronger than expected. The Jedburghs provided liaison with the Allied high command, trained resistance groups, and boosted French morale by their presence. The SAS cut railroads, armed the Maquis, harassed German troop movements, and made certain provinces nearly uninhabitable to enemy troops. Most OGs parachuted into southern France, but a few took part in the operations in Brittany.[35]

The problems that SFHQ and other special operations forces encountered showed that all the efforts of SHAEF and its subordinate echelons had not completely eradicated the obstacles that had worried planners from the beginning. A jury-rigged, inexperienced special operations command structure drew complaints from Jedburgh teams, among others, for its "unrealistic planning, inadequate briefings, confusing command and liaison arrangements, and an embarrassing lack of response to repeated requests for supplies." SOE operatives in the field received little guidance about handling political factions, and they often found that Allied tactical commanders disregarded their intelligence reports and showed little respect for the fighting abilities of the partisans. Many complained that by the time they deployed to the Continent, the resistance was already fairly well organized and Allied forces were often just a few days away. These difficulties and such problems as the need for better intelligence on Pointe du Hoc, the unrealistic mission assigned to NCDUs, equipment glitches plaguing the propaganda services, and continuing political imbroglios regarding civil affairs indicated that the Allies still had much to learn about special operations.[36]

Few would deny, however, that special operations played a valuable role in OVERLORD. To be sure, observers found it difficult to measure achievements in such areas as factory sabotage and black propaganda, and the extravagant claims made by special operations advocates moved Lt. Gen. George S. Patton, Jr., among others, to evaluate special operations in the invasion as "better than expected and less than advertised." Nonetheless, special operations delivered much in civil affairs, beach reconnaissance, Ranger and commando operations, tactical propaganda, and, as SHAEF itself admitted, sabotage and guerrilla activities. A SHAEF memorandum in July 1945 as to "the value of SOE operations" emphatically stated that "the major cause of delay to enemy troop movements was action by the Allied strategic and tactical air forces," but SHAEF admitted that sabotage enabled the Allies to achieve a scale of destruction that could have been reached only by devoting the entire weight of Allied air power to the task. SHAEF cited delays in the movement of German reinforcements, the diversions of German troops to guard duty and punitive operations, the confusion in German communications, and the value of the resistance for intelligence collection, flank and rear guard support, and maintenance of French morale during a difficult time. Eisenhower himself later equated the worth of the resistance to fifteen divisions.[37]

Taking into account all the problems faced by special operations in the Normandy invasion, the wonder is that they came out as well as they did. In future years, their successes would be used by special operations advocates as a model and an opportunity to castigate skeptics. Actually, the doubts of skeptics prior to the invasion were by no means unreasonable. Unfavorable operating conditions, political complications, disorganization, problems of communication and control, demands for scarce resources, questions of security, and overall lack of comprehension of such activities presented real obstacles, and the prospective benefits lay largely in the realm of the moral or intangible. Nevertheless, a total war of peoples and ideologies, a war in which the Allies were attempting to liberate a conquered nation seeking to regain its self-respect, conferred special importance on moral factors. In addition, the challenge of OVERLORD, involving an amphibious landing that included several unique tasks, caused commanders to grant greater attention to special operations than would otherwise have been the case. As Supreme Commander, Eisenhower, who did not have a complete grasp of the potential of such operations, was nevertheless willing to consider their possible contribution and to act on it. His open mind and leadership ensured that SHAEF took the steps that enabled special operations to contribute morally and materially to the success of the Normandy invasion.

10. D-day 1944

Forrest C. Pogue

At 0645 on the morning of 6 June, off Omaha Beach, a young lieutenant of the 16th Regiment, 1st Division, John M. Spalding of Owensboro, Kentucky, was swimming for his life. His section of 32 men had unloaded from a larger craft into landing craft for vehicles and personnel (LCVPs) some ten miles out nearly four hours earlier and joined other small boats as they headed for their appointed beaches. Loading in very rough sea, many men became seasick immediately, and others joined them as they moved toward shore. Shortly before 0600, they saw the first flashes of fire but were uncertain whether they represented Allied bombardment along the beaches or German artillery. Fifteen or twenty minutes later, they caught sight of land through mist and smoke and dust stirred up by heavy naval fire. At 0630 the boat halted and the skipper ordered the ramp dropped and the men to go ashore. The lieutenant jumped and found himself up to his waist in water. Assuming that shallower water lay ahead, he commanded his section to follow him in. He found, as did many others that morning, that the crews had been fooled by sandbars. After a short time, they were in water over their heads.[1]

With a strong undercurrent carrying them toward the left, the men were soon floundering and in danger of drowning because of the heavy equipment most of them were carrying. They ended up abandoning most of it in the water or at the water's edge. An 18-foot scaling ladder, a 72-pound flamethrower, a useless walkie-talkie, a mortar and its ammunition, and one of their two bazookas were cast aside.

The lieutenant recalled later that as he was going in he saw two sergeants struggling in the ladder. As he reached out, as if to help them, one said, "We don't need any help." He replied, "Hell, I am trying to get help, not give it."

By amazing good fortune, they made it to the shore without casualties, but at the beach's edge a rifleman was hit in the foot by small-arms fire, and a few minutes later a Browning automatic rifle (BAR) man was hit in the shoulder by a shell fragment. The lieutenant was not encouraged to find that he was 1,000 yards to the east of his supposed landing place and that the men of his company as well as those who were supposed to be on either side of him were now confused, uncertain of the landmarks, and often bunched in areas where they made good targets. His salvation lay in the prompt decision to start off the beaches as soon as possible. Stopped by wire, one of his men with a bangalore blew a hole large enough for them to pass through. Rushing ahead to a demolished building, they took shelter behind it and a nearby pile of rubble, exchanging fire with enemy snipers. Machine-gun fire dotting the wall they hid behind accounted for the first man of the section killed on D-day.

Looking back at the sea, the lieutenant sought to locate other sections of his company. Instead, he saw boats in flames. They reminded him of the men he had seen struggling in the water, who had escaped from the duplex-drive (DD) tanks that had sunk on their way to the shore. At last he saw a tank on the beach at about 0730 but even that was not reassuring. "After a couple of looks back," he recalled, "we decided we wouldn't look back anymore."

Meanwhile, one of his men had found a small defile several hundred yards away, running toward the top of the hill. The lieutenant called his men to come up on the right, and they pressed upward in the face of small-arms fire, which, although heavy, cost few casualties. Worried about the machine gun above him, he forgot to examine the path until his sergeant warned, "Watch out for the damned mines." The place was supposed to be infested with small box-type mines, but no one was hit, although the company that followed them a few hours later suffered several casualties. "The Lord was with us and we had an angel on each shoulder on that trip," the lieutenant later explained.

But their luck did not always hold. Trying to take out the troublesome machine gun above them with a bazooka, one of the sergeants was shot in the arm. A private first class was shot next as he tried to fire. Another sergeant who had picked up an automatic rifle was hit in both legs. But one machine gun could not cover them all, and other members of the section, who had moved up, charged the position. The one enemy soldier, who turned out to be a former Polish prisoner now enlisted in the German static defense force, suddenly surrendered.

By dint of luck and leadership, the lieutenant reached the top of the hill between 0900 and 1000. He believed—and later investigation showed that he was probably correct—that his was one of the first units of the 16th Regiment to hit the top. Once they reached it, the men had an advantage over the enemy in bunkers or individual positions that were now below them toward the sea. Methodically they began to flush the enemy out of bunkers and the communications trenches. Throughout that morning and afternoon, the lieutenant was conscious of the close-in navy support that helped silence enemy fire.

Soon other squads and sections came up the same or similar paths and

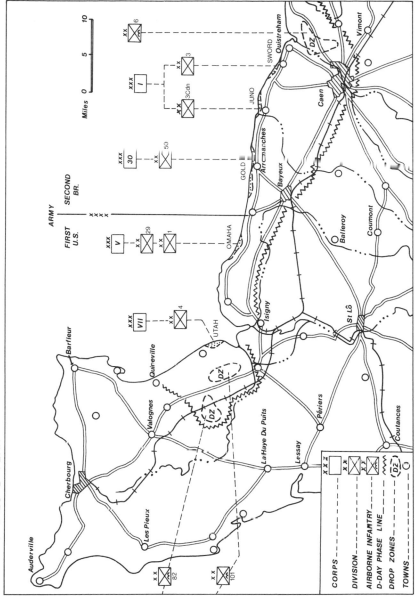

FINAL OVERLORD PLAN

he found, at last, other elements of his company, most of which had suffered heavily. Directed to go inland toward Colleville, he and his men spent the afternoon and early evening guarding approaches to the town, engaging in occasional firefights, until they were at last given reinforcements. They spent the night watchfully, only a few thousand yards inland from the beach. Of the 32 men the lieutenant had brought ashore, two were dead and ten wounded. For their bravery, five received Distinguished Service Crosses awarded personally by General Eisenhower.

This tiny segment of the D-day story is one of many that newsmen and combat historians, like myself, got from others. Although we were involved, because we shared some of the discomforts and a few of the dangers (indeed, some were killed or wounded), our D-day stories are composites of the experiences of others. Field Marshal Wavell named an anthology of his favorite poems *Other Men's Flowers*. We who collected interviews might call them "Other Men's Memories." One man's story cannot tell the whole, but it can give a sampling of a battle that many men—airmen, sailors, and soldiers—helped make.

The stories of other units that fought their way ashore and then inland show that many of them were less successful than the one I have described. Although by midnight all regiments of the 1st Division, two regiments of the 29th division, and the 2d and 5th Rangers had landed on Omaha Beach, the position was precarious.

The factors responsible for D-day difficulties are many: the launching of small boats too far from shore; the heavy seas; landings on the wrong beaches; concentration of men in front of exits; the foundering of all but five out of 32 DD tanks that were launched toward Omaha Beach from ships five or six miles out (most of those sent in by ship arrived); the loss by capsizing of nearly all howitzers in one 105-mm battery; abnormally high casualties among junior officers; delays in opening the beach exits; the tendency of some men in the first waves to crouch behind the first seawall they reached, exposing themselves to artillery fire and the danger of drowning in the incoming tide; the lack of sufficient gaps in underwater and beach obstacles; the late decision to cancel the bombing of beach fortifications; and the unexpected presence of the 352d Division near the beach.

Amid all the gloomy summaries, there were many bright spots. On the 116th Infantry front, the assistant division commander, Brig. Gen. Norman D. Cota, and the regimental commander, Col. C. D. W. Canham, had set to work shortly after coming ashore around 0730 to organize the attack. Shortly afterwards, Colonel Canham was wounded, but he returned to the task after receiving first aid. According to the accounts of the sol-

diers, General Cota was everywhere that morning. His activities in rally-
ing the men and working to clear the exits from the beaches made him a
legendary figure. On the 16th Infantry's beaches, Col. George Taylor, the
regimental commander, said to his officers and men, "The only people on
the beach are the dead and those who are going to die—now let's get the
hell out of here." He and Canham were promoted to brigadier generals
for their D-day work, and a few months later Cota received command of
the 28th Division.

To the east and west of Omaha Beach, the battle had gone better. The
British 6th Airborne Division had landed in the early hours of 6 June to
seize bridgeheads east of the Orne River; along Sword, Juno, and Gold
beaches, troops of two British and one Canadian division of the 1 and 30
Corps landed with fewer difficulties than their American neighbors and
were pushing in by late morning toward Bayeux. They were helped by a
shorter landing trip for most of their tanks and the effective use of tank
flails, armored bulldozers, and other mechanical items that the Americans
had declined. Their losses, including the airbornes, came to some 3,600.
On Utah Beach, the battle also went well. Confused by the paratroops of
the 82d and 101st Airborne that had landed by glider and parachute on a
widely scattered front, the enemy in that area seemed unable to organize
a defense. Some pressure, therefore, was taken off the 4th Division, which
had landed by lucky error on fronts that were more lightly defended than
those where they were expected to put down. Stoutly supported by naval
gunfire, they moved swiftly inland with only some 200 casualties. The airborne suffered more heavily, sustaining approximately 2,500 casualties in
the two divisions.

For all its difficulties, the D-day performance was tremendously impressive. Some 5,000 naval ships and landing craft participated; bombers and
fighters made 11,000 sorties, dropping 12,000 tons of bombs; and approximately 125,000 men were put ashore. Heavy losses were inflicted
on the enemy units back of the beaches; the surprised enemy was now in
confusion. The Luftwaffe's activities had been held to almost nothing,
and there was a difference of opinion between the Commander-in-Chief
West, Field Marshal Gerd von Rundstedt, and his chief subordinate, Field
Marshal Erwin Rommel, as to the proper way to meet the invaders. Hitler
and his staff disagreed with the western commanders on future enemy intentions, withholding permission for the commitment of armored reserves and the use of troops from the Pas de Calais. Much remained to be
done before the Allies could establish the lodgment area, and there would
follow weeks of frustrating fighting in the hedgerows and narrow lanes of

Allied troops load in Britain to begin the cross-Channel invasion of Normandy.

Normandy until the way was opened for the breakout toward Paris. But the lodgment had been won, and the end seemed nearer at hand.

There were many D-days in World War II, but only one is understood when the term is mentioned. For the Western powers, at least, it represented the final focus of efforts to win a definite victory over the Axis in Europe. It was the decisive coming to grips with Germany that the Allies had been moving toward since the British withdrawal from the Continent and the fall of France. Concentrated in the mighty assault across the Channel from the ports of the United Kingdom were the power of the United States and the final surge of greatness of the British armed forces. It marked the finest hour of Anglo-American cooperation.

Just as there is only one D-day that comes to mind when the term is mentioned, there is one name above others that we associate with it—General of the Army Dwight D. Eisenhower. It is especially fitting that the Eisenhower Library was built near that leader's boyhood home and closer still to the chapel where he was laid to rest, a few weeks short of the twenty-fifth anniversary of the cross-Channel assault whose early plans he had sketched and whose armies he had directed.

Each man in Western Europe and the United States more than ten years of age in 1944 doubtless remembers where he was when the news first came of the landings, even as he can tell you where he first heard about Pearl Harbor or the death of John F. Kennedy. As far as my own memories of D-day are concerned, I cannot speak firsthand of the storming of the beaches or the fire and shells and moments of terror because I was off the Isle of Wight in a landing ship for tanks (LST) loaded with a company of the 175th Infantry and elements of combat engineers, scheduled for the afternoon follow-up on Omaha Beach. But the plans were disrupted, and we were told to wait across the Channel until the exits were fully cleared. As a result, it was not until evening that we crossed, getting our first sight of the beaches as the smoke and haze lifted the following morning. The infantry and engineers aboard our ship were taken off near noon, but a small party of us consisting of War Department observers, liaison officers, and the two combat historians covering Omaha Beach actions—Lt. William J. Fox and me, heavily laden with map cases, typewriters, and briefcases and armed only with pistols—were told to stay aboard ship until the following day.

My first knowledge of the fighting came from interviews with men who had been wounded in the early fighting and brought aboard our craft—one of dozens provided with hospital facilities for handling men evacuated from the beaches. Although my notes recall the words, my memories are stronger of wounded men being brought over the side and taken down to sick bay, some so badly wounded that they soon died. One I remember was a British airman whose foot was badly mangled, as he clenched his teeth to keep from crying out, he managed to ask that someone more seriously injured be treated first. I recall an artillery liaison officer shot through both hands which were now swathed in bandages, cursing himself for making the elementary mistake of climbing up a tree, where he was shot down before he had a chance to view the hedgerow country he had come to see. I also remember a Texan corporal with the combat engineers, suffering from a hole in his side; he was cheerful because the wound was bad enough to send him home to rejoin his wife and the baby he had never seen.

Recently, I thumbed through the few souvenirs I have of D-day. There are my slender notebooks, which I filled in the days after landing. I visited men in underground command posts or in foxholes to get their stories of that first long day, sometimes sitting under a lead shelter-half as I wrote, the water spilling down my helmet and washing out parts of a paragraph. There are bits of enemy and American propaganda dropped from planes, which I found in the hedgerows and the orchards: One is an American appeal, written in German, asking for an honorable surrender of the enemy; another is a fake American dollar bill that, when opened, contained an anti-Semitic attack, written in French, on Secretary Morgenthau and the "merciless Americans" who had launched the attack. There is a crumpled and dirty copy of Eisenhower's D-day message that was handed to every man engaged in the landings, and a firing plan showing ranges at various points on Omaha Beach, which I found southwest of Pointe du Hoc.

In a little notebook I carried with me is a sentimental souvenir I placed in it in 1944. As we went up the hill near Saint-Laurent, not far from the present American cemetery, I saw some poppies at the side of the road, some crushed by treads of tanks and all heavily covered with dust. But recalling the poems of the First World War, I picked a poppy and placed it in the notebook, where I recently found it intact. There are remnants of a script for a maneuver exercise, which I discovered in a bunker of a unit stationed near Isigny. Fishing it out of a pile of papers most gingerly, I feared every moment that it might be wired to explode. It was for a maneuver against an enemy landing in the area of Port-en-Bassin. Since the Germans wrote the script, it ended happily, with the Allied forces being thrown back into the sea after hard fighting.

There are many stories that recall the drama of D-day. But because the day itself has such tremendous interest, we forget all too quickly the long period of preparation that went before and the debt we owe to a number of men whose names are often forgotten when we speak of the great invasion. We should recall that D-day's achievements were the products of many minds: months of training; massive production of ships, planes, weapons, and equipment; skilled planning; the finding of competent leaders; and lessons learned from defeat and blood and death. It was the one moment of the war when the British and American leaders, the soldiers under their command, and the civilians who backed them with their labors and their understanding support came together for a brief period, subordinating personal and national interests and narrow ambitions to one great purpose, finding a unity and a dedication to which we can still turn with pride.

Let us turn our minds back to the day when the last British troops withdrew from the Continent, leaving from ports in Brittany and Normandy as the government of France went through its final agonies, and to the days when remnants of the defeated French forces rallied to General Charles de Gaulle in London. Despite the desperate situation, there was no doubt that the Allied forces would return. For months, the main energies of Britain would be devoted to defense of its shores and the skies overhead, but there was still a desire to plan. But when and how? An early outline sketched in this period started hopefully, "Having gotten ashore."

Those words, almost mocking in their nature, were not facetious but prophetic. They pointed up two problems that the Western Allies had not encountered in many years of fighting on the Continent: the lack of a hospitable landing place and the lack of proper landing craft. In the wars of the eighteenth and nineteenth centuries, the British had been able to find friendly ports for the entry of their troops, so that ordinary transports were enough for their purposes. Even when the great Napoleon had brought most of Europe under the Continental system, it had usually been possible to find a place in the Low Countries or in the Iberian peninsula for a landing place.

With the fall of France and the later extension of German power over that whole country, with Spain and Portugal neutral in the struggle, with Axis troops in firm control of most of western and central Europe and much of Russia, with German air power dominating the skies over Europe and raining destruction down on Britain, with German submarines endangering Allied ships in the Atlantic, the Mediterranean, and the Channel, it was clear that much had to be achieved before the Allies could attain the goal of getting ashore. Before a realistic plan could be drawn for invasion, an air offensive had to be started that could win the skies over the British Isles and Western Europe, cut off the movement of men and supplies to the invasion area, and reduce enemy resources to the point where they could be dealt with successfully. There also had to be landing craft that could carry ashore men and tanks and artillery. And there had to be solid support from the United States.

Not until the end of 1941, when the Japanese attack on Pearl Harbor triggered American entry into the war, was the last condition fulfilled And the requirements of the cross-Channel operation had to be measured against those of MacArthur and Nimitz, first in the Philippines and then in the southwest, south, and central Pacific; against the appeals of China and the desperate needs of Russia, caught up in a fight to the death on its own soil.

With all that remained ahead, it is interesting to note that early in 1942 the American commander and planners outlined the cross-Channel attack that was launched two years later. Brig. Gen. Dwight D. Eisenhower, newly brought to Washington by Gen. George C. Marshall and more recently made Chief of the War Plans Division, sketched the plan that reflected War Department thinking and won presidential backing for a return to the Continent.

Before we could go across the Channel, there were rivers to be bridged, seas to be crossed, islands to be seized, and landings to be made. Before the great goal could be attained came the landings in North Africa, the taking of Sicily, and landings in the south of Italy. Not until December 1943, when a supreme commander was actually selected to head the invasion and an approximate date of May 1944 given to Stalin, and not until General Montgomery was picked by the British to lead their forces and ordered to the United Kingdom to start final planning, did the cross-Channel attack move from the possible to the likely. The idea of grappling with the enemy on the Continent appealed to Churchill, but he dreaded the possibility of a bloodbath comparable to that which his generation had suffered in Flanders. "You are fighting the ghosts of the Somme," the prime minister's doctor said to Marshall. Churchill's dread was such that even into the final months, he seemed to hope for some miracle that would bring German collapse without an invasion. As late as March and April, he continued to say occasionally to American visitors, "I am hardening on this operation," as if even then it might be averted.

The Americans remained faithful to the concept. Never faltering in their devotion to the cross-Channel attack were two officials in Washington— Secretary of War Henry L. Stimson and General Marshall. Backing them were the U.S. Joint Chiefs of Staff and, for the most part, the president. Abroad, General Eisenhower, busy in North Africa and then in the Mediterranean—where he came to favor a later date for OVERLORD than he had at first suggested—remained loyal to his earlier proposal.

Yet it was Churchill who had helped pave the way for the return to France by appointing Admiral Lord Louis Mountbatten as head of Combined Operations Headquarters (COHQ) in October 1941. Mountbatten was told to prepare for raids along the whole of the enemy coastline from North Cape to the Bay of Biscay, but his main objective was to be the reinvasion of France. He was to develop appurtenances and devices to make the invasion possible, select and build up bases from which the assault could be made, create amphibious training centers, and select the place for attack. Although his attention would range far from the French coast in the months that followed, Churchill's directive had set into motion a planning group that would lay the groundwork for the later D-day landings—a fact that Churchill and the U.S. and British Chiefs of Staff recognized when they visited the Normandy beaches six days after the landing. They sent a message to Mountbatten, who was then in the South East Asia Command, that "much of the remarkable technique and therefore the success of the venture has its origin in developments effected by you and your staff of Combined Operations."[2]

Among his duties, Mountbatten acted as adviser to the Combined Commanders in considering a plan-in for a proposed return to the Continent, drawn up in early 1942. The Commander-in-Chief, Home Forces, General Sir Bernard Paget, the admiral commanding at Portsmouth, and the chiefs of the Fighter and Bomber Commands composed this group.

General Paget, an able officer, would later become commanding general of 21 Army Group, which he relinquished to Montgomery in late December 1943. He had little enthusiasm for the cross-Channel operation with which he was entrusted, and he was considered to be a defeatist. But he differed especially with Mountbatten and other planners in preferring the Pas de Calais for the landing area. There were paper arguments for his views: From Dover one could see the Calais shore and even shell it; air forces in southeast England could blanket the area; there would be a short turnaround for ships and landing craft; and the way to Germany was much shorter than from any beach further to the west. But Mountbatten reasoned differently. There were few ports in the area nearest the Pas de Calais, and troops brought from Wales and Cornwall would have a longer voyage to the attack area and would be subject to greater danger from the enemy. Again, the largest ports of the area, Calais and Boulogne, were not sufficient for developing the follow-on attack. Even more important, the Germans would expect an attack there and be prepared to meet it. Any advance in that area would expose its flank to German counterattack. It was in this period that the final attack area, the Bay of the Seine, was finally selected. Shortly afterwards, work began on port facilities from which the troops would sail. It would have been difficult in 1944 to change the landing area, even if Eisenhower had so desired.

The other important planning group that preceded Eisenhower's Supreme Headquarters was the staff known as COSSAC (Chief of Staff to the Supreme Allied Commander designate), which was set up early in 1943 to start planning a return to the Continent. The British Lt. Gen. Frederick E. Morgan and his American deputy, Maj. Gen. Ray W. Barker, were handicapped by the lack of a commander who could demand all that he needed to make a successful return to the Continent and by a restricted number of divisions on which to base the planning. As a result, COSSAC's plan was described by nearly all who saw it as insufficiently strong. Although the invasion front was later widened and a number of changes made in the overall plan, much excellent groundwork was laid by COSSAC and drawn on by later planners.

The important thing is that when the Supreme Headquarters was finally established, it succeeded to a rich harvest. Under way were experiments with and development of landing craft, artificial harbors, DD tanks, tank flails, PLUTO, and the like. Also in progress was the amassing of intelligence material that would be necessary for final planning.[3]

While the planning was in progress, the commander of 21 Army Group, General Paget, was sending his British troops through realistic training to a degree never before utilized in Britain. For this work, Paget was compared with Sir John Moore, who had helped prepare Wellington's army for its successes in the Napoleonic Wars. As Paget pointed out to me in a 1946 interview, this was not new to the Americans, who, he said, always spent more effort on their infantry than did the British. Realistic training of American troops had long been under way at the camps and in the maneuver areas in the United States. Then, as the buildup began in the United Kingdom in the fall of 1943, training centers were established for American troops. Amphibious training and exercises were speeded up after the appointment of General Omar Bradley as commander of the First Army.

Space does not permit me to cover the many developments that preceded D-day: the massive air offensive carried on for months to weaken the Germans and shut off the invasion area from enemy reinforcements; the great work of the Allied navies in bringing together warships, landing craft, and supply ships for the tremendous task of transporting the Allied force across the Channel and then supporting the troops as they went ashore; the gathering of intelligence material from hundreds of sources. For example, certain officials asked tourists who had visited beach resorts in Normandy and Brittany in happier times to send in their postcards and photographs and write out their observations about the beaches. Small parties were sent ashore at night to check out the depth of hard ground under the beaches to make certain that areas that appeared on medieval maps as marshy ground would actually bear the weight of heavy tanks. Some of this work was done as late as a few days before the landings, but much of it had been carried out much earlier. General Eisenhower, who was always generous in giving credit to others, made it clear that without all these efforts, the Allied forces could not have gone ashore as successfully as they did.

Although planning and training went forward, the whole affair was somewhat academic until a commander was selected for the invasion. In his frustration, General Morgan sometimes suspected that he was serving as a front for something that would not take place. As a result, when he was invited to the United States in October 1943 by Marshall (then regarded as the future supreme commander), the British officer asked President Roosevelt to name the commander of the cross-Channel attack immediately. Feeling that he could not let Marshall go at the moment,

Roosevelt temporized. It was not until the Cairo conference in December, after he had been pressed by Stalin for the name of the commander, that Roosevelt at last made his decision to name Eisenhower. Shortly afterwards, on the recommendation of Field Marshal Sir Alan Brooke, the prime minister placed Montgomery at the head of the British invasion forces. In turn, Eisenhower entrusted the British general with control of the Allied forces in the assault phases. Before he left North Africa for a brief trip to the United States, Eisenhower instructed Montgomery—who shared his views—to proceed to London and begin a fight to enlarge the invasion force.

While Eisenhower and Marshall were in Washington discussing future plans, Lt. Gen. Walter Bedell Smith (Eisenhower's Chief of Staff) and Montgomery outlined plans for strengthening the attack. With the confidence born of victories in North Africa and the Mediterranean, Montgomery stirred the COSSAC planners with calls for more of everything. His recommendations, which his Chief of Staff, Maj. Gen. Francis De-Guingand, thought were those "of any trained soldier," included more assault forces, a quicker buildup, a larger airlift, and an expanded invasion front. Realizing that many of the resources would have to come from the United States, the British commander insisted that Eisenhower take personal action, asking, "Will you hurl yourself into the contest and get us what we want?"[4]

I have read that Eisenhower was an amiable man, a pleasant man, a kind man, but that he was merely chairman of the board. I have read that all the plans and arrangements for D-day were actually made by Montgomery. However, the official Department of the Army histories, such as Gordon Harrison's *Cross-Channel Attack*, and my own *The Supreme Command*, based on Eisenhower's papers, showed that Eisenhower, particularly in the crucial decisions before D-day, was indeed the supreme commander. He exercised the authority of the man who had to bear the responsibility, and he had several important assets, the greatest of which was his strong link with Marshall. It was always clear that Marshall did not intend for this operation, on which he had set such great store for so long, to fail. And he did not intend for his protégé to fail. Another Eisenhower asset was the close personal relationship he had built with Churchill over a period of many months. A third was the fact that to a greater extent than any other American general or diplomat, he had gained the confidence of de Gaulle.

From the time that Eisenhower arrived in London in mid-January until the event of D-day, he was involved in getting what was needed for victory. In some cases, a long battle was required to convince the U.S. Joint

Chiefs of Staff or the American president; other cases involved achieving the acceptance of political decisions that were displeasing to the British War Cabinet and the prime minister; still other cases involved attempts to gain the cooperation of de Gaulle. Only an Allied commander-in-chief could have won from various governments what a British or American general could scarcely have asked from his own government. In the major political and military decisions of the period, Eisenhower made his authority felt.

Even before Eisenhower left the United States for London, Generals Montgomery and Smith had concluded that a landing in southern France (ANVIL), scheduled to coincide with the cross-Channel attack, should be canceled and the landing craft allocated to it sent to the Normandy area. Aware that the president and the Joint Chiefs of Staff were committed to the ANVIL operation, Eisenhower assured Washington that he would save the southern France attack if at all possible.

From the beginning, the British sensed that Eisenhower was the key to a shift in strategy. Despite growing doubts in London, Marshall still believed the operation to be feasible. But if Eisenhower thought that he must sacrifice ANVIL to make certain of OVERLORD, the U.S. Army Chief of Staff would listen. He wanted nothing to hamper the supreme commander's success. For the moment, the decision waited while resources and allotments were reassessed. By early March, Eisenhower recognized that he would need the ANVIL landing craft for OVERLORD, but he waited until all the returns were in. On 21 March, he informed the chief of staff that "ANVIL as we originally visualized is no longer a possibility."[5] The U.S. Joint Chiefs of Staff assented, provided the British would agree to an ANVIL operation later in the summer. After prolonged debates, on 18 April the Combined Chiefs of Staff accepted a compromise arrangement that left open the final decision on a delayed ANVIL operation.

The other decision required by the broadening of the invasion front was on the proposal that two airborne divisions be dropped in the Cotentin peninsula to help secure the new beach being added to the west. At once the commanding general of the tactical air expeditionary force, Air Chief Marshal Sir Trafford Leigh-Mallory, objected that he lacked the requisite airlift for the additional divisions; he feared heavy losses to glider forces because of unsatisfactory landing fields and possibly heavy antiaircraft fire. In view of pressure by Generals Montgomery and Bradley for the airborne drop, Eisenhower continued to advocate the plan that Leigh-Mallory persistently opposed until near the time for landing. At length, Leigh-Mallory declared that "at the most 30 percent of the glider loads will become effective for use against the enemy." Six days before the

General Eisenhower talks with replacements on their way to the battlefront in Normandy.

landings, the supreme commander shut off debate with a reminder that the airborne operation was essential to the success of the plan and "must go on." As a result, he added, "there is nothing for it but for you, the Army Commander and the Troop Carrier Commander to work out to the last detail every single thing that may diminish these hazards."[6] A week later, when it was clear that the landings had been achieved with much smaller losses than he had predicted, Leigh-Mallory conceded that Eisenhower had been right.

In the control and use of bombers before D-day and in the early phases of the battle for Normandy, Eisenhower showed himself in his most positive mood. Let no one claim, said Air Chief Marshal Sir Charles Portal later, that anyone pushed Eisenhower around.[7] He had in mind the heated debate over the supreme commander's control of the strategic air forces in the early phases of operations and the equally sharp arguments over the transportation bombing plan. In both these controversies, Eisenhower had the strong support of both Marshall and the Deputy Supreme Allied

Commander, Air Chief Marshal Tedder, but his own decision and arguments were emphasized.

The command dispute arose from the fear of the bomber chiefs that the long-range bombing program known as Operation POINTBLANK, which had been decided on at Casablanca and was yielding excellent returns, would be upset by a diversion to targets dictated by the interests of ground commanders. There was also the belief in some quarters that the bombers could decide the issue alone if the invasion could be temporarily postponed.

Eisenhower had discussed the matter of control of strategic air forces with Marshall in late December, pointing out the need to have men in command who were aware of the problems involved in air support of ground troops. "Otherwise," he declared, "a commander is forever fighting with those air officers who, regardless of the ground situation, want to send big bombers on missions that have nothing to do with the critical effort."[8] He brought up the matter personally a few days later in Washington, but Marshall needed no convincing. It was his initial view that Allied air superiority would make the invasion of northern France possible without overwhelming ground superiority, which had prompted him to back the cross-Channel operation so strongly.[9] Naturally, he was in favor of the maximum use of the bomber force to aid the Eisenhower forces in getting ashore and staying there. As a result, Marshall indicated that if he had been named supreme commander and had been denied what he required, he would have resigned the command.

Strongly backed by Marshall, Eisenhower insisted that he be given control over those bombing efforts essential to the cross-Channel battle, adding that if the British were for anything less than an all-out effort for the cross-Channel attack he would "simply have to go home." To remove British doubts about possible misuse of the bombers, he declared at the end of February that he would exercise such control through Air Chief Marshal Tedder. Impressed by the strong stand on principle being made by Marshall and Eisenhower, Air Chief Marshal Portal decided that some compromise must be devised.

The proposed formula indicated that when the plan for the air program in support of the cross-Channel assault had been approved by both Eisenhower and Portal, "the responsibility for supervision of air operations out of England of all the forces engaged in the program, including the U.S. Strategic Air Force and the British Bomber Command, together with any other air forces that might be made available, should pass to the Supreme Commander." The strategic air forces not used in support of Operation

OVERLORD would be committed in accordance with arrangements made by Eisenhower and Portal.[10]

This arrangement at once threatened to fall apart when the U.S. Joint Chiefs of Staff protested that it did not give Eisenhower "command" of the strategic air forces. The supreme commander, who had been inclined to accept the formula when first presented, now declared that in view of the question that had been raised, he must insist that there be no doubt over his authority and responsibility for controlling air operations of the bomber and tactical forces "during the critical period of OVERLORD." This point was settled on 7 April when the Combined Chiefs of Staff declared that the U.S. Strategic Air Force and British Bomber Command would "operate under the direction of the Supreme Commander, in conformity with agreements between him and the Chief of the Air Staff as approved by the Combined Chiefs of Staff."[11]

Equally stormy and drawn out was the debate over the transportation plan set forth by Leigh-Mallory's staff at the beginning of 1944; its intent was to reduce supplies carried by railway marshaling yards and repair facilities in key railway centers in Germany, Belgium, and France. The bomber chiefs objected at once to targets in Germany, saying that other targets such as oil or airplane plants were more remunerative. In addition, a strong political objection was raised by Churchill, Eden, and other members of the government. After the war, it was noted, the peoples of Eastern Europe and the Balkans would look toward the Soviet Union; Great Britain would have to depend on countries in the West for friendship. There was also the danger that heavy casualties inflicted on civilians in the attacks on railway centers would alienate them from the countries responsible for the losses—especially Britain.

Convinced that the plan was sound and necessary to the success of the invasion, Eisenhower gave it his strongest backing. Leaving to Tedder the task of fighting for the concept in meetings with the bomber chiefs, he worked on the prime minster and members of the War Cabinet. As the commander responsible for the assault, Eisenhower was impressed by the arguments of the transportation plan proponents. He fully agreed with Tedder's suggestion in late April that, although first priority should be given to POINTBLANK attacks deep into Germany to weaken the German air force, the remaining air effort should be used to delay and disorganize ground movement during and after the landings "so as to help the army get ashore and stay ashore." Since the first five or six weeks of OVERLORD were likely to be the most critical, Eisenhower argued, it was essential to ensure that the assault forces landed and held their ground. He insisted that it was "only necessary to show that there would be some reduction of German transportation, however small, to justify adopting this plan, provided there was no alternative available."[12]

When the prime minister continued to stress political objections, Eisenhower stood firm, saying, "I have stuck to my guns because there is no other way in which this tremendous air force can help us, during the preparatory period, to get ashore and stay there."[13] At last Churchill gave way, but he demanded that casualties be held below 10,000. He kept careful watch on reports of civilian losses in France, saying to Tedder, "I am afraid you are piling up an awful load of hate." He was mollified to an extent by General Smith's report that General Pierre Koenig, head of the French forces in the United Kingdom, had said, "We would take twice the anticipated loss to be rid of the Germans."[14]

The necessity of weighing preparations for D-day against political considerations that were disturbing to Great Britain was particularly marked in Eisenhower's efforts to ensure the security of his assault planning. Only a determined officer, able to gain the ear of the prime minister, could have turned the trick. This fact was illustrated in three episodes in the spring of 1944.

Reminded by members of his staff that visitors to beach areas and harbors were likely to imperil the secrecy of his operation, Eisenhower asked for an outright ban on civilians in restricted coastal areas during the critical days of final preparations. When the civil ministries objected, General Morgan, now Deputy Chief of Staff under Eisenhower, retorted, "If we fail, there won't be any more politics—and certainly no more Lend-Lease." But no final action was taken until Eisenhower warned the members of the War Cabinet: "It would go hard with our consciences if we were to feel, in later years, that by neglecting any security precaution we had compromised the success of these vital operations or needlessly squandered men's lives." Four days later the ban was imposed.[15]

This was followed by censorship of outgoing mail and a ban on leave for members of the armed forces outside the country. A more difficult step was the proposed censorship of diplomatic correspondence. The Foreign Office and War Cabinet were extremely dubious about the proposal. Again Eisenhower spoke of what might happen. This source of leakage, he declared on 9 April, represented "the gravest risk to the security of our operations and to the lives of our sailors, soldiers, and airmen." Eight days later the War Cabinet announced that foreign diplomatic representatives henceforth would not be permitted to receive or send uncensored communications and that their couriers would not be allowed to leave the United Kingdom. Only the United States and the USSR were exempt from this British decree.[16]

From Algiers, a furious de Gaulle ordered his representative in London, Koenig, to break off discussions then in progress with members of the Supreme Headquarters Allied Expeditionary Force (SHAEF) staff on questions relating to D-day. Fortunately, the tempest soon subsided when de Gaulle, who believed that matters would go well between Koenig and Eisenhower because of the latter's "friendly disposition toward France," permitted an arrangement to be worked out. An agreement was reached by which British and U.S. authorities would examine French messages before they were dispatched from London and would then permit them to be sent in code with Koenig's assurance that the original texts would not be changed.

The uproar over the diplomatic messages was but a foretaste of the protests that could be expected from de Gaulle in Algiers. Believing that the French National Committee's open support for the invasion was of great importance to Eisenhower, de Gaulle was determined to gain recognition for his committee as the government of France. This was an old and tiresome question that had long troubled Eisenhower but that he had been unable to solve. In Britain, the Foreign Office favored recognizing de Gaulle, but Roosevelt, never on friendly terms with the French general, firmly reminded Eisenhower that he could recognize no government of France until the people of that country had an opportunity to make a choice. He was willing for Eisenhower to discuss matters with the French committee on a military level but was resolutely opposed to any action politically. The situation, as Eisenhower reminded the Combined Chiefs of Staff near mid-May, was embarrassing and "potentially dangerous." He suggested a way out of their difficulty by inviting de Gaulle to London, where he could be briefed on the coming operation. Roosevelt agreed, provided that de Gaulle did not return to Algiers until the attack had been launched.[17]

As final plans were being made for the assault, Eisenhower and members of his staff concluded that it was essential to have de Gaulle issue an appeal to the French people to support Allied forces. At a very late hour, little more than 48 hours before the attack, the French general was flown to the United Kingdom and informed of the coming assault. Piqued by the lateness of his briefing, the irate leader reacted adversely when handed a statement that the SHAEF Psychology Warfare Division had prepared for him to read in support of Supreme Headquarters. He flatly refused to cooperate on the grounds that no mention was made of the French National Committee.

Through much of the night of 6 June, a number of conferences were held involving Foreign Secretary Eden; Sir Robert Bruce Lockhart of the

Political Warfare Executive; General R. A. McClure, SHAEF Psychological Warfare head; and de Gaulle. Bedell Smith was inclined to be blunt with de Gaulle and threaten to cut off grants of aid. Lockhart and McClure took the more diplomatic approach, reminding de Gaulle that his standing in France would be damaged if it were known that he was in London and did not add his voice to the representatives of other occupied countries. At last, in the early morning of 6 June, he agreed to make an appeal, but he made it on his own terms.

He did not speak when other representatives of occupied countries made their appeals. He did not call on Frenchmen to put themselves under Eisenhower's orders, as the prepared speech had done. Instead, he told them to follow the orders of the government of France (his committee) and its chiefs. And he got revenge on Roosevelt by pointedly omitting any mention of American efforts while graciously praising "old England's" contribution as the last bastion in the West.[18]

His eloquent speech touched the prime minister. Churchill, who was easily moved to tears, wept at the tribute. To disguise his feelings, he picked on one of his favorite targets, General Sir Hastings L. Ismay, who was standing nearby unmoved by the eloquence. Caustically, the prime minister demanded, "You great lump of lard, have you no finer feelings?"

Many of these developments were not then known to me and the other combat historians who were preparing for their own roles in the D-day invasion. Several of us had been briefed in Washington that spring and then flown to London in April in time to learn something of the invasion plans before the launching of the attack on 6 June.

Various signs signaled the approach of the assault. Nearly every day, regular traffic would be stopped in parts of London while great convoys of men and equipment moved eastward and to the south. The British were headed toward the old cities of Dover and Rye, while the Americans moved toward the fields and ports of Devon and Cornwall. Sometimes we talked to a pilot or a gunner. Tired, weary, but eager for a change from the excitement they had been experiencing, they would describe the work being done in preparation for the attack. Six missions in a row over Flak Corner on the "Milk Run" was the story of one gunner, who spelled out tales of recklessness, heroism, fatigue, and fear. He was sure that things were about to pop because the intensity of the attacks could not be maintained. As yet unbriefed as to the real area of the invasion, we tried to make deductions from the pattern of attacks and troop movements, only to make the same mistake the Germans did.

We learned much about the Allied forces in the briefings in London— the nature of the command organization, the logistic preparations, organization of various combat units, tables of organization, and the like—but we still did not know the area of attack or the precise development of the battle. Perhaps the most memorable thing that came from the session was the statement of the navy officer who summed up the report we could write in advance of D-day: "Confusion reigned on the beaches." This prophecy proved to be exact.

Not until we had made a brief visit to General Bradley's headquarters at Bristol—where our historical teams were split up for assignment—and Bill Fox and I had settled down at V Corps Headquarters at Norton Manor near Taunton in Somerset did we finally see the detailed plans. After being "BIGOTed,"[19] we were shown into a small room filled with paint buckets and brushes used to stencil boxes. In one corner was a wooden cabinet, and in it were the broad outlines of the high-level plan, sketches of 21 Army Group and First U.S. Army plans, the complete navy plan, and the detailed V Corps plan and annexes for Omaha Beach.

Feverishly we digested the material. We already knew that under Eisenhower was Montgomery's 21 Army Group with general direction of the Allied ground forces for the assault period, and that under him Bradley's First U.S. Army commanded the American effort in the fight. Now we learned of the dispositions on the respective beaches.

The area chosen looked unpromising on the map. The detailed, yard-by-yard descriptions of the beaches—once attractive to tourists—made them seem unlikely places on which to land, particularly in the V Corps area. The beaches, backed by cliffs, were rimmed by ledges from which antitank guns, mortars, and automatic weapons could bring murderous fire on the attackers. Air photos and reports from the French underground and from special landing parties that had been set ashore to conduct reconnaissance virtually pinpointed the defenses, the paths, the winding roads, the stone walls, the length of the beach, and the height of the shingle. More important, they revealed the location of almost every machine gun, the direction of fire, the rifle pits, the strands of wire, the communications trenches between bunkers, the tank ditches that cut off access to the exits from the beaches, and the underwater barriers. Gatelike C elements standing nine feet high, with slanting steel supports, topped by Teller mines; hedgehogs, ugly affairs made of crisscrossed steel beams from five to seven feet in height; log ramps and posts with jagged edges on which other mines were placed to rip and explode the small landing craft as they came in with troops—all protected the beaches from assault. This devilish collection of pitfalls, which the enemy had been installing at a rapid rate in recent weeks under Rommel's stern direction, seemed to grow more deadly each day. Because of the obstructions, it was necessary for the planners to arrange for the assault at low tide so that the first waves could go in while the barriers were exposed, thus avoiding the underwater terror, and the demolition teams could clear away the barriers before the later waves of craft and troops came in.

Naturally, the plans were extensive. Besides such matters as naval and air support and operational details, the massive appendices extended to civil government, supply, medical questions, and the like. One list detailed the amounts of cocoa, wheat, meat, and vegetables to be distributed to towns needing food. The quartermaster was given estimates of the quantities of uniforms, bandages, Purple Hearts, and even Bronze Stars he would be expected to provide. The medical section reassured us that there were no poisonous serpents in the area but failed to note that the region had a potent antidote against snakebite—an apple brandy called Calvados. We were even told where the Germans had their chief administrative offices, which local officials had been unduly friendly to the enemy, the location of possible pigeon lofts, and names of prostitutes in some localities who might be able to supply information about the Germans.

On Tuesday, 23 May, V Corps began its move from Norton Manor to the marshaling area in Cornwall. Our group was bound for Redruth, not far from Penzance near the southwestern tip of England. The morning was cold when we started, but slowly the chill was dispersed by the sun, and the day at last became one that made us happy to be in England now that spring was there. I remember the peaceful hills and valleys and the occasional breathless moment when we sat on a hilltop and saw a dozen roads in the valleys below jammed with thousands of vehicles, men, and equipment moving toward the south. I was reminded of Conan Doyle's *Sir Nigel*, in which the writer described a much earlier setting forth of men for battle in a chapter called "How the Comrades Journeyed Down the Old, Old Road." In his case, the men-at-arms traveled toward Dover rather than westward, but he had caught the picture of a crowded highway as he described "the throng which set the old road smoking in a haze of white dust from Winchester to the narrow sea."

The little towns, still filled with century-old quaintness, looked out of place as troops streamed through in flood tide to the Channel. There were half-concealed airfields, meadows that hid tanks and jeeps, and hedges filled with piles of shells. But we forgot the war momentarily when we passed a simple country house with a scrawled sign proclaiming, "Tea for Sale." The pleasant old lady poured tea in her parlor, where our fighting gear seemed somewhat out of place until we saw on the walls the photographs of her daughter, a WAAF in London, and her son, a lance corporal in India.

After a half-hour stop, we continued on our way, reaching at last the concentration area where members of our small party of liaison officers and historians were to be attached for rations and quarters to a company of the 175th Infantry Regiment of the 29th Division. Our camp was in a number of fields along a country lane, placed between small hills that hid us from the sea. Fox and I had been placed with this unit, as other colleagues had been placed with other companies, because our superiors wanted us to see how the men of a combat company slated for D-day landings lived, the type of briefings they received, and the spirit they had, so that we would know what we were talking about when it came time to write.

At this isolated camp, we felt for the first time the imminence of the invasion. Since we were to be briefed on the time and place of the attack, we were forbidden to leave the area without permission. Guards stood at regular intervals along the road to enforce that regulation, acting also as airplane watchers and carrying specially treated armbands that would indicate the presence of gas.

On Friday the soldiers were briefed. It was fascinating to watch the reactions of various groups as they saw silhouettes of the coasts showing how the beaches looked at one-half mile, two miles, and five miles out. In other cases, the men gathered around card tables or maps spread on the ground. They listened closely as the story of D-day was unfolded, still not clear as to the overall plan. They were told that under the full support of naval and air bombardment they would go in on beaches cleared of opposition. As the officers and men learned their specific missions, their faces showed the growing grins that one notes when a listener anticipates the ending of a well-known joke. "Jesus," one of them remarked, "now we can get started on the way home."

An outsider would not understand the enthusiasm of soldiers facing a deadly assault, but these men had participated in repeated exercises in the United States, marched up and down England, and practiced in assault training centers until it seemed that they would never strike at the target that had to be seized before they could turn back to the United States. So with no worry about the fact that the first day of battle might be the last of their lives, they hailed the announcement that they were going to Normandy.

There was little talk of the enemy; I saw no sign of hatred there. We spoke of this strange attitude, but no one worried. The soldiers were sure that when the shooting started and friends were killed, they would hate the enemy enough. "After all," said one artilleryman, "we don't see the men we kill anyway." There was not even great anxiety about the chance of getting hit. In an effort to keep down fears on this score, issues of *The Stars and Stripes* that were carefully distributed to the troops explained that shock kept the wounded from feeling much pain and that there were few cases in which the hurt persisted for long before unconsciousness or morphia gave relief. General Bradley, who proved to be an accurate prophet, struck out against wild estimates of casualties based on Tarawa percentages, which predicted losses of 50,000 in the first few hours.

The weather on our final Sunday in camp was extremely beautiful. The day was much like any other, until someone announced that there would be services in the mess hall. I half persuaded another chap to go, but he said that he would feel like a hypocrite by waiting until this late hour to go to church. Some twenty of us met in the tent, sitting on rude benches at wooden mess tables, while a young redheaded chaplain from Virginia led us in a group of songs that pointedly did not include "Onward Christian Soldiers" or "The Son of God Goes Forth to War." He preached simply on the text, "Suffer little children to come unto me." There was no threat of death nor talk of hate nor smell of battle in that tent, although his helmet, set before him on a table, served as a pulpit and we held our weapons close at hand while we prayed.

We were awakened at the usual time—0700—on 2 June and told to don our impregnated clothing as a protection against possible gas attack. Two hours later, after breakfasting, we started to a rendezvous point where we met a convoy. At noon we were fed at an improvised mess hall along the way. Two hours later we stopped and were fed again, as jokesters spoke of the condemned man eating a hearty meal. Occasionally we passed English homes, and the dwellers would come out to look curiously at the quiet groups of men going down to the sea. Now and then a mother would hold up her child to see the passing troops, as if she wanted him to be able to say when he was older that he had seen the soldiers march off to attack the distant shore.

Land's end for us was the edge of a small cove near Helston—an inlet that pirates or smugglers might have used, or a place where the Phoenicians might have anchored when they came 2,000 years ago to seek Cornish tin. The British had realized that an enemy intruder might seek out such a place for entry, and they had built machine-gun nests and barricades on the hills around. Now at last they could hope that soon these defenses would no longer be needed.

By early evening our party—a company of the 175th Infantry, attached engineer units, and our small party of "parasites"—had been loaded on our LST. Some two hours later we left the cove. As we sailed for Falmouth, we met some of the crew. It added nothing to our sense of well-being to find that most of them, like the LST, were on their first voyage. Many of them had been drafted only six months before. A few had been in Italy, but most of them were still so new that the skipper, after giving a nautical command, would immediately translate into layman's language.

On Sunday, 4 June, the weather was foul. Sometime during the day we learned that Eisenhower had postponed the invasion one day, and there was griping by the men who feared that they would have to go back to port. The plan had indicated that only 5, 6, and 7 June were satisfactory for the assault in the first half of the month.

The next morning at 0300, we started from Falmouth harbor, sailing slowly eastward. By 1500, there were 28 LSTs in sight in three parallel lanes, later expanding to five or more. Out on the horizon could be seen three or four destroyers, shedding confidence on us as they circled and turned to stay between us and unknown perils. Above were plane escorts, and we could see hundreds of planes or hear their motors as bombers flew to targets near the beaches. Two barrage balloons that floated above each LST gave a holiday appearance to the occasion. Behind us we towed a curious raft known as a Rhino ferry. Other vessels pulled along strange contraptions of concrete and steel that were to make up part of an artificial port. Everything was relatively quiet on shipboard. The sky was somewhat overcast, but the sea was relatively calm, and the sun came through now and then. The "abandon ship" drill was perfunctory, despite the sobering statement that the next alert we heard would be the real thing.

At noon, with our lunch, each man received General Eisenhower's order of the day. It was now certain that D-day was on. Later we were to learn of the dramatic meeting at which the decision was finally given.

For five months, Eisenhower had used a mixture of diplomacy, stubbornness, gentle words, and firm persuasion to gain the unity and support he needed from the disparate elements that would make up the Allied team for D-day. In all these he had the backing of one or more strong military leaders. But it was on 5 June, when he met for a second time with his chief advisers at Southwick House near Portsmouth to decide whether the invasion must again be postponed, that he faced one of his most crucial decisions of the war. Writing of it later, Eisenhower's chief of staff was struck by "the loneliness and isolation of a Commander at a time when such a momentous decision has to be taken, with full knowledge that failure or success rests on his judgment alone."[20]

At 2130 on the evening of 4 June, Eisenhower discussed with his advisers whether weather conditions, which had forced him to consent to a one-day postponement earlier that day, now showed sufficient improvement to authorize the assault for the sixth. Much depended on the observations of the weather officer, Capt. J. M. Stagg, of the SHAEF staff. One observer was convinced that Eisenhower's decision was aided in the final analysis by the fact that in the days preceding the D-day verdict, he had discussed the factors involved in weather predictions so that he not only had confidence in his meteorological adviser but also understood the elements himself.

The alternatives were not pleasant ones. Stagg reported that a new weather front gave some hope for improvement throughout 5 June and until the morning of the sixth. The skies were expected to clear sufficiently during the evening of the fifth for heavy bombers to operate during the night and in the early morning at H-hour, but it was not certain if favorable conditions would prevail during the assault stages.

Thus, there was some hope, but if the weather grew worse after the first waves had landed, what then? Caution favored delay. On the other hand, a second delay meant that ships would be returned to port and the men unloaded. The possibility that the enemy might spot the preparations would be increased. A second postponement might find even worse weather on the seventh, meaning that the operation would have to be postponed for two weeks. These delays reduced the period of good weather for fighting and increased the possibility that the V-weapons, now known to be readied for attack on British cities and harbors, might be in use (as indeed they were by that time). Worse still, a further wait would hurt troop morale. The men had been brought to a state of readiness. Another delay would make it hard to reach that pitch again.

All these points were in Eisenhower's mind as he pondered his decision. Looking around the room, he polled his advisers. Leigh-Mallory believed that from an air standpoint the attack would be "chancy," and Tedder agreed. General Montgomery, sticking to his view of the previous day, voted "go." The decision was now entirely in the supreme commander's hands. He pondered it briefly, dropped his head for a moment's thought, and decided, "We'll go."

A final review was slated for the early morning of 5 June. Despite the rain and wind that greeted Eisenhower at this final conference, the weather forecasters now thought that there might be a break of 36 hours. On the basis of this advice, Eisenhower held to his earlier decision, informing Washington, "Halcyon plus 5 [6 June] finally and definitely confirmed."

In fact, no other decision was possible, but it was important for the future of operations in Europe. Long afterward, one of Montgomery's aides said that the fact that Eisenhower took full responsibility for the decision

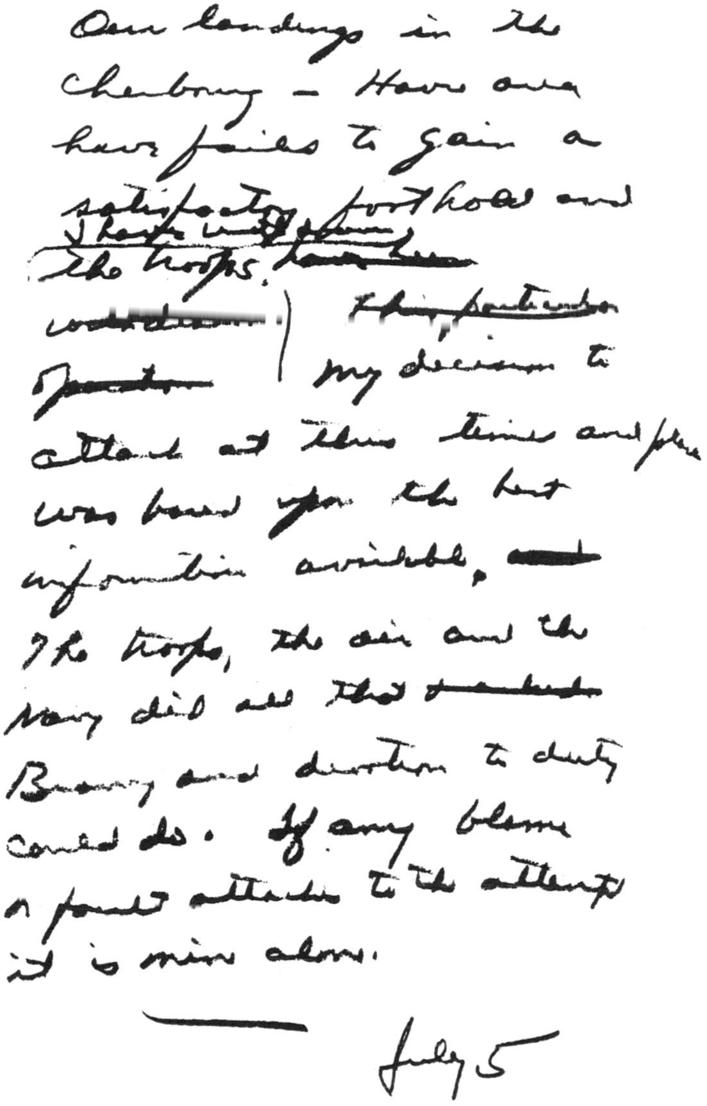

Our landings in the
Cherbourg – Havre area
have failed to gain a
satisfactory foothold and
~~I have withdrawn~~
~~the troops.~~ ~~have been~~
~~withdrawn~~) ~~This particular~~
~~operation~~ my decision to
attack at this time and place
was based upon the best
information available, ~~and~~
The troops, the air and the
Navy did all that ~~bravery and~~
Bravery and devotion to duty
could do. If any blame
or fault attaches to the attempt
it is mine alone.

——————

July 5

Between the decision to proceed and the invasion itself, Eisenhower drafted this statement blaming himself in the event of any failure.

to go was a prodigious contribution psychologically in that it took the weight of decision off others. The fact that he accepted the blame for any reverses that might come was indicated in a memorandum he wrote the day before the landings. Several days later, when the success of the assault was assured, he showed it to Commander Butcher. The key sentence read: "The troops, the air and the Navy did all that bravery and devotion to duty could do. If any blame or fault attaches to the attempt it is mine alone." Those words make it particularly fitting that we associate this Anglo-American action of D-day forever with the name of Eisenhower.

And it is important in this period of strained alliances, of misunderstandings, of the loosening of ties that once bound us tightly to friends in Western Europe that we recall the day in 1944 when a common effort and a common belief in the things we held most dear produced the D-day miracle. For it was with that rare unity forged in the years of peril and of fear and of defeat that victory was at last attained.

11. A Correspondent's View of D-day

Don Whitehead

The commemoration of D-day 1944 is unique not simply because we are reliving one of history's greatest days. Its uniqueness derives from the fact that seldom can a person in one generation—so soon after a given time—point to one day in his life and say with absolute certainty, as we can say: "On this day the history of the world was changed."

The history of the world was changed on D-day 1944. Had the cross-Channel invasion ended in failure, the consequences would have been immeasurable. The map of Western Europe, as well as large parts of the globe, would perhaps be different. Our own lives, and the lives of millions of others, would have been quite different from what they have been. The horizons of free people would have shrunk.

But D-day did not end in failure. In the larger sense, we are paying a tribute to the memory of a general who became president of the United States, Dwight D. Eisenhower. It was his responsibility to put together, and hold together, the forces that achieved the victory on the beaches that led to the defeat of Nazi tyranny. Had there been a failure on the beaches, the buck would have stopped with Eisenhower. He was the commander, and the final responsibility was his.

My purpose here, however, is not to pay tribute to Eisenhower but to provide a correspondent's view of D-day. But such a view of D-day cannot be adequately presented without an explanation of the press's relationship with the military and, most particularly, with Eisenhower. To gain perspective, we must go back to the campaigns in North Africa, Sicily, and Italy in 1942 and 1943. At that time, Eisenhower was gaining his first experience as a commander of Allied combat forces. He was learning the lessons of diplomacy in dealing for the first time with such strong men as Franklin D. Roosevelt and Winston Churchill. He was feeling his way through the mine fields of international politics. He was solving the problems of command with the British, with the unpredictable Patton, and with the great and restless 1st Infantry Division, whose men believed that they had earned home leave after taking the brunt of the heavy fighting in the Tunisian campaign.

And he was dealing for the first time with a large segment of the world's press—establishing the workable mechanisms through which the people at home could be informed while the security of the armies could be protected. At this time, the world's press knew little of Eisenhower. After all, only a few months before, while involved in training maneuvers in Louisiana, he had been identified in a photograph as "Lieutenant Colonel D. D. Ersenbeing."

To be frank, to many Allied army, navy, and air corps officers, the members of the press were an annoying and mysterious band of roving gypsies whose relationship to the military was confusing. We were parasitical creatures who slept, ate, and traveled with the fighting units or swarmed about headquarters. We carried no weapons, fired no shots, rated no salutes, were not subject to normal military discipline in dress and movements, and asked embarrassing questions. Perhaps the worst of it was that we acted like civilians. But even though we had civilian status, we were subject to certain military discipline once we were accredited by the War Department as correspondents. We were subject to court-martial for any violation of law, and we could be banished summarily from a theater of operations and sent home in disgrace for any serious breach of trust.

It is little wonder that many military men were confused. It didn't help much to explain that we had the rank of "simulated" army captains. I don't know who thought up that rank, nor do I know its history, but being a simulated captain was useful in many ways. It entitled us to PX privileges, to eat in officers' messes, to wear uniforms, to travel with proper orders on military transports, and, if captured by the enemy, to receive the same treatment accorded regular officers of equal rank. At times, Eisenhower would refer to us (and he must have suppressed a smile as he did it) as "quasi-staff officers." One correspondent commented, "When Ike says 'quasi'—I hope it isn't a lisp."

Our most cherished privilege was our extraordinary freedom to travel from unit to unit within a theater to gather news and question men and officers. Our dispatches were censored in the interest of security. At times we felt that the censorship was not related to security, but on the whole the censors were liberal in their handling of our stories.

We realized that the freedoms we had could be traced to Eisenhower's attitude toward the press. He recognized the importance of public opinion back home. His attitude became the attitude of his subordinates, and it filtered through the command. As for the men in combat, their reaction to the arrival of a correspondent was starkly simple: Any man who voluntarily joined a fighting unit had to be a damned fool.

In one important sense, Eisenhower was fortunate in the fact that he was dealing with a friendly press. This was a war in which the nation was unified in its purpose after Pearl Harbor. Fascism had to be defeated. At home, there were no banners of protest.

When the general was transferred to London to take command of the great cross-Channel operation known as OVERLORD, he followed the same policy in dealing with the press that he had followed in North Africa. By mid-May 1944 more than 500 reporters, radiomen, magazine writers, and photographers were gathered in London, accredited to Eisenhower's command. We knew that the invasion of the Continent was near, but I do not believe that any newsman knew the secrets of where and when. Most of us made no effort to find out. The burden of knowing would have been too great.

I arrived in London in late April. The first rumor I heard was that the invasion would be in Norway. The next fixed Pas de Calais as the spot. Still another was that we would land in Normandy. Some of the rumors were deliberately planted by our intelligence people. Others came from uncorked bottles in the pubs. But the barroom speculation was dampened considerably when the news got around that an American general had been sent home for talking too much and too accurately about the time and place of D-day.

Of the 530 newsmen accredited to the Supreme Headquarters, 28 were chosen to cover the assault phase of the D-day landing. We were told by public-relations officers to pack what gear we would need and to stand by for a call at any time. We also were told that once we landed with the assault forces, there would be no turning back to file a story from England. In short, we couldn't "chicken out." We had to remain with the units ashore.

Some of the correspondents were assigned to be with the infantry, some with the air corps, some with the navy, and some were to report the activities at Eisenhower's headquarters. Two were assigned to jump with the airborne troops. Others would have to remain in England until a beachhead had been established.

At 0930 on the morning of 29 May, I received a call from Col. Jack Redding of the public-relations office. We chatted for a minute or so and then he said casually, "I'd like for you to be at my office in an hour. You'd better pack a musette bag. You may be going out of town." There had already been a good many false alarms. Correspondents had been alerted, taken out of the city, and kept at remote bases for a few days. The comings and goings of correspondents had no pattern that would alert an enemy agent when our final move from London came.

I sensed that the call from Colonel Redding was no cover movement. I took a cab from Chelsea to Grosvenor Square, and when I entered Redding's office, I saw a good many of my friends from North Africa, Sicily, and Italy—most of them with two or more experiences in amphibious assault landings: Ernie Pyle, looking as though a strong breeze might blow him away; Jack Thompson of the *Chicago Tribune*, who had jumped with the paratroopers onto Sicily; Clark Lee of International News Service, who had been with MacArthur in the Philippines; and others.

We were issued impregnated clothing as a protection against possible gas attack, blankets, shovels with which to dig foxholes if needed, seasickness pills, medical kits, and boxes of K rations. Our bedding rolls and other gear were to precede us to the units we would join.

We spent that first cold, damp night in tents in an assembly area. The next morning we traveled by ones and twos to our final destination. My partner was Jack Thompson. We had no idea where we were going or to which unit we would be attached. Our jeep took us to Weymouth, near Portland, and when we arrived we knew that we had been attached to a unit that would be in the spearhead of the invasion. We were at the headquarters of the 1st Infantry Division.

We were then taken to the office of Maj. Gen. Clarence Huebner, commander of the Big Red One. This was his greeting:

> I want you to regard yourselves as members of this unit. You will have complete freedom of movement and I want you to get all the information you can. We are ready to help you [in] all possible [ways]. The people at home won't know what is happening unless you are given the information and I want them to know.
>
> You both know how to take care of yourselves. But if an unlucky shell should get you, we'll do all we can. If you're wounded, we'll take care of you. If you're killed, we'll bury you. So you have nothing to worry about.

I confess I was not as confident as General Huebner that I knew how to take care of myself. It is true that I had been reared in Harlan County, Kentucky, which was once known as "Bloody Harlan." But in the early coalmine wars of Harlan they did not have the size artillery I had seen employed on four previous assault landings and that I knew would be used in this one.

We boarded the Coast Guard transport *Samuel Chase* on Sunday, 4 June. I had been on the *Chase* before. During the Sicily invasion, she had served as the command ship for the 1st Infantry Division. Now she was the command ship for the 16th Infantry Regiment of the 1st Division, a regiment commanded by Col. George Taylor. We fully expected to sail that afternoon, but the storm that swept the Channel on Sunday forced the postponement of D-day from 5 June to 6 June. We remained sealed on the *Chase*, and not until we sailed the following afternoon did we know for certain that our destination was Normandy. In the hold of the *Chase* was a long table with a sponge rubber mock-up of a beach called Omaha. Regimental, battalion, and company commanders, platoon leaders, and officers in charge of sections were gathered there to study this miniature model of the beaches. Every house, outbuilding, ridge, tree, and hedgerow was reproduced as it had been seen by our aerial cameras. The men studied the model to fix in their minds the prominent landmarks, the terrain features, the roads, the towns, and the routes leading to their first day objectives. On the right of Omaha was Utah Beach, to be taken by the 4th Infantry Division. On the left before Caen were the British and Canadian beaches, Juno, Gold, and Sword.

Omaha—as viewed from the Channel—was divided into five sectors known as Fox Red, Fox Green, Easy Red, Easy Green, and Dog Red. The largest of these was Easy Red, roughly one mile in width. Low tide at Omaha would be at 0525 and sunrise at 0558. The first wave of infantry was to hit the beach at 0630—the first daylight landing to be attempted by the Americans.

Our assault group was known as Force O and was commanded by General Huebner. It was composed of the 16th and 29th Regimental Combat Teams of the 1st Infantry, the 115th and 116th Regimental Combat Teams of the 29th Infantry Division, the 2d and 5th Ranger Battalions, and attached units of artillery, totaling 34,142 men and 3,306 vehicles. The follow-up waves due in the afternoon included the 29th Regiment of the 1st Division and the 175th Regiment of the 29th Division. With their attached units, they numbered more than 25,000 men and 4,429 vehicles.

Once we were familiar with the assault plan, Colonel Taylor took Thompson and me to his quarters, where we asked him his estimate of the situation to be faced the next day. He said: "The first six hours will be the toughest. That is the period in which we will be the weakest. But we've got to open the door. Somebody has to lead the way—and if we fail . . . well . . . then the troops behind us will do the job. They'll just keep throwing stuff onto the beaches until something breaks. That is the plan."

I don't believe I have read or heard since a more concise and accurate summation of the Allied plan to crack the defenses to Hitler's fortress Europe. Stripped to the bare essentials, the months of planning and strategy added up to one sentence: "They'll just keep throwing stuff onto the beaches until something breaks." To an old infantryman like George Taylor, it was that simple.

It was interesting that Colonel Taylor, a regimental commander, and Gen. Bernard Montgomery—the commander of the invasion forces during the initial stages—should arrive at the same estimate as to the critical period of the invasion. On 15 May, Montgomery had briefed correspondents in the old St. Paul's schoolhouse in London and said: "Rommel is a disrupter. He will commit himself on the beaches. He will try to knock us back into the sea." In different words, Taylor was telling us the same thing.

On the morning of 6 June, we were up before dawn on the deck of the *Chase*. I carried my lightweight typewriter strapped to my back, encased in a raincoat for waterproofing. My other impedimenta included a blanket, a canteen of water, a couple of boxes of K rations, and a notebook and pencil. I was to go ashore in the landing craft with Brig. Gen. Willard Wyman, assistant division commander of the First, whose job it was to help organize the troops on the beach. His partner in this job was Brig. Gen. Norman Cota, assistant commander of the 29th Infantry Division.

First we heard the bombers. They came in waves overhead like a continuous rumbling of thunder. Then we saw the orange flashes of the bombs exploding on the shore. Unfortunately, the bombs fell behind the German beach defenses. We did not know it at the time, but only the day before, the Germans had moved the 352d Infantry Division into position on and immediately behind Omaha Beach for anti-invasion training maneuvers. Our intelligence had received news of this movement, but it came too late to relay to the spearhead elements sealed in their ships. Also in position was the 726th Regiment of the 716th Infantry Division.

When dawn came, there was a breathtaking sight of a vast array of ships standing off the coast of France. Never again will there be such an assembly of sea power—not in our nuclear age. They stretched as far as the eye could see in that murky dawn.

The Channel was still rough, the waves running as high as six feet. Landing craft were bobbing in the water, receiving their loads of infantry and then heading for the shore. My boat number was called over the ship's loudspeaker, and I climbed down the rope net into our craft. We were scheduled to land behind the first waves of the 116th Regiment—but scheduled landings that day were about as reliable as those at LaGuardia Airport today.

We headed for the beach, and I noticed that everyone in our boat appeared to be trembling violently. I knew that everyone was scared—but not that scared. And then I realized that the appearance of trembling was caused by the concussion from the big guns of the navy. The air vibrated from the sound.

We saw the DD tanks—the duplex-drive amphibious tanks girdled with inflated canvas doughnuts and having propellers—trying to wallow through those high seas. The 16th Regiment launched 32 of these tanks— a secret weapon to give the infantry added firepower going ashore. But the tanks were put into the Channel at H minus 50 minutes 6,000 yards from shore. Only two of the 32 made it ashore. The rough waters ripped the canvas doughnuts from the tanks and they were swamped, often along with their entire crews. The 32 tanks of the 116th Regiment were more fortunate. They were carried ashore. It was a terrible thing to see men from sunken tanks floating in the sea and not be able to stop and lift them to safety. But the juggernaut had been launched—it must not be delayed.

The tide was rising fast as we approached the long line of beach barriers built by Field Marshal Rommel to check the first thrust of the enemy. We could see the flat mines attached to the wooden posts and steel spikes of the barriers. Confusion was building up. It did not take a military man to realize that we were heading into chaos. Nothing was moving from the beach. Boats loaded with troops and guns were circling aimlessly. The navy men handling the boats could not find the gaps that they had been told would be blown in the barriers.

General Wyman ordered our boat to move along the obstacles on Omaha Beach. He wanted to see for himself the cause of this mess. The reasons soon became obvious: The German guns were pouring deadly fire onto the beach, and there was only limited access to the beach. Only two gaps had been blown through the barriers guarding the beach sectors assigned to the 116th Regiment. Four gaps had been blown on Easy Red. Three other partial gaps had been blown. But these were not enough, and a huge traffic jam had developed in the Channel.

The first and second waves of troops—scheduled to land at 0630 and 0700—had been thrown into disorder. Boats swung from their courses and drove through gaps wherever they could find them. This was possible because between 0700 and 0800 the tide rose eight feet in the Channel. But units landed far from their assigned sectors. Commanders were separated from their troops. Sections were fragmented. And those who landed were pinned to the beach by heavy machine gun, artillery, and mortar fire.

We rode the rising tide through one of the gaps and waded ashore at 0800. As far as I could see through the smoke of battle, troops were lying along a shelf of shale. Ahead of us stretched mined sand dunes to the bluffs where the Germans were sheltered in their trenches, bunkers, and

Soldiers wading through heavy surf during the initial assault on Omaha Beach.

blockhouses. There was no cover for the men on the beach. The Germans were looking down on them—and it was a shooting gallery.

There were many brave men on Omaha beach that day—Dutch Cota, Bill Wyman, George Taylor, and scores of men whose names were never imprinted on the honor roll of Omaha Beach. Under the guns of the enemy, they organized small units and established small islands of order in the chaos. In what seemed a formless, confused horde there gradually emerged a core of discipline. And even as the Germans believed that they were winning this battle on the beach, units of infantrymen were working their way through the mine fields and up the bluff.

I remember vividly Pvt. Vinton Dove of Washington, D.C. His name has remained with me to this day. He drove a bulldozer from a landing craft and began bulldozing a road from the beach as calmly as if he were grading a driveway at home. He sat there with only a sweatshirt to protect him from bullets and shell fragments.

The firepower of the navy was one of our salvations in those first few hours. I recall that we were about 200 yards west of a small draw on Easy Red marked on the maps as E-1 or Exit-1. A blockhouse had been built into the bluff above the dirt road that led inland. The German gunners

Medics treat wounded troops on Utah Beach during the afternoon of 6 June.

manning an 88-mm weapon had a clear field of fire to the west. They were firing at almost point-blank range at the landing craft and the troops trapped at the edge of the water.

A radio call for help went from an army navy beach team to a destroyer. We saw the destroyer come racing toward the beach and swing broadside, exposing itself to the fire of the batteries on the bluff. One shell from the destroyer tore a chunk of concrete from the side of the blockhouse. Another nicked the top. A third ripped off a corner. Then the fourth shell smashed into the gunport to silence the weapon. Always, in my mind, the knocking out of this gun was a major turning point of the battle in our sector. At 1330, General Wyman moved from the beach and set up his first sheltered command post in the knocked-out blockhouse, and this was where I wrote my first story of the landing. As I saw it, that was when the battle of the beach was won—seven hours after the first wave hit the beach.

It seems incredible to me that so many years have passed since that day. It has become a day to remember in the history of our nation—and in the legend of Dwight David Eisenhower. The legend of Eisenhower is a strange one. Often I think that the image we created of him through the years is far from the truth. I have a feeling that he was a far more complicated man than he seemed to be—a man who shaped events with such subtlety that he left others thinking that they were the architects of those events. And he was satisfied to leave it that way. But that line of thought is for the historians.

I was back in Normandy a short time ago. There are not many traces left of the invasion. The German bunkers are still implanted on and in the bluffs at vantage points along the beach. There is a little rusted wire, maybe a small part of a ship, a little bit of wood here and there, and perhaps a rusted rifle picked up out of the sand by a boy. But the signs of battle are gone. The French around Normandy are prosperous. The cattle are back in the fields. The big Norman horse has been replaced by tractors, and farmers have gone to mechanized farming. Bicycles that used to swarm the roads have all but disappeared. Now they all have small cars. Times have changed around Omaha Beach and that part of the world. Unless you had a landmark such as a bunker, you'd have a difficult time knowing where you were on that day and during that battle.

Above Omaha Beach today stands the American cemetery where many of those who fell on D-day are buried. It is a beautiful place. Among the white marble gravestones there is a lovely chapel. And on the chapel wall there is an inscription that says: "Think not only upon their passing. Remember the glory of their spirit." It was the spirit of free men fighting for the cause of freedom.

12. Deposited on Fortune's Far Shore: The 2d Battalion, 8th Infantry

Theodore A. Wilson

By 21 May 1944, the final contingents of BLT2—the Battalion Landing Team comprising the 2d Battalion, 8th Infantry, (2/8), and attached units were settling into one of the sausage-shaped U.S. Army marshaling areas in England, stretching from Buckfastleigh to Moreleigh and Halwell west of the small Devon resort of Torquay.[1] Along with other units of the 4th Infantry Division and its parent organization, VII Corps, the restless troops of the 2/8 knew that they would soon see combat (that the "sausage" enclosing them was under heavy guard both for security reasons and to deter deserters was a powerful confirmation of that reality), and they were generally aware that BLT2 had been designated the spearhead of the 4th Division's descent on Nazi-occupied Europe. Precisely where they were going and what would happen were still unclear to the great majority of the 976 men of the 2/8. When told that their destination was an inundated area, a Bronx shipping clerk-turned-soldier, Pvt. Lindley Higgins, insisted: "I know geography—it's got to be Holland."[2] Higgins later admitted being "dumb enough not to feel the slightest trepidation. . . . We really thought that we only had to step off that beach and all the krauts would put up their hands."[3] Their two weeks of incarceration was given to detailed briefings about the landing site and BLT2's mission in the assault and immediate postassault phase of the operation, completion of those innumerable details associated with preparing for battle, and dealing with the precombat jitters that were especially common in untested units. Their last meals—T-bone steaks and all the trimmings topped off by ice cream—only reinforced images of fatted calves and sacrificial lambs.

In fact, the 2/8 had been assigned a pivotal role in the gigantic, multidimensional operation that was OVERLORD. Among the several hundred U.S. Army infantry battalions in the European Theater of Operations, the 2/8 was being accorded the dubious distinction of leading the amphibious assault against the American northern invasion beach (designated Utah). Thus, along with its counterparts in the 1st and 29th Infantry Divisions destined for Omaha, it was one of that elite band of U.S. Army units that clawed their way ashore on D-day.

It is worth asking—50 years after that momentous event—not only for explanations of policy decisions at the highest level but also how it happened that this particular group of American youths entered battle at this juncture for an experience that forever defined and shaped those who survived the cauldron of Normandy. How did the men of the 2/8 come to be selected for this assignment? How did they find their way to that sprawling encampment outside Torquay? What did they bring to the challenges they were to confront? What produced the system of organization that assigned them to a company, battalion, regiment, and division that comprised x number of men, y types of weapons, and z equipment? What assumptions guided the process of training that was supposed to prepare them for this arduous mission? How was their training effected in the United States? In Britain? Who led the 2/8? How had its officers been selected? How qualified were they to command green troops in that most demanding of military operations, a seaborne assault against a heavily defended shore? And—that most difficult of questions—what made these young Americans willing to enter battle? Did they fight for abstractions such as country and the democratic way of life? For the unit of which they had become an integral element and to which they owed near-mystical loyalty? Because of discipline and self-confidence instilled by rigorous training and dedicated commanders? Or from a pervasive commitment to their buddies, the small group of intimates in whom an individual soldier placed implicit trust and to whom he owed a commitment not to fail? Last, how well did the 2/8 perform?

The 4th Infantry Division was in some ways typical of the U.S. component of the OVERLORD assault force, for it had been shaped by the turmoil of the effort to build ground forces during 1942–43. In comparison, the 29th Infantry Division had arrived in Britain in October 1942 and thus had avoided most of the difficulties resulting from the U.S. Army's frantic expansion. The 4th was also green, unlike the 29th's counterpart on Omaha Beach, the 1st Infantry Division, which had already seen combat in North Africa and Sicily. In addition, the 4th and its constituent regiments and battalions were, like most American units during World War II, given little time to prepare for the combat missions that came their way. Reflecting the view of Army Ground Forces (AGF) that properly trained units could perform any task, the important distinction between training for combat and for assaulting a defended shore was not adequately acknowledged in World War II. One result was that the soldiers of the 2/8 splashed through the surf off Utah weighed down by 70 pounds of clothing and equipment.[4]

The road to that sprawling preinvasion encampment outside Torquay began in a crowded officers' club at Fort Benning, Georgia, on 1 June 1940. "When France fell, there was not a division in the U.S. Army," confessed one contemporary account. "The first step in the military program was to organize the regiments, which themselves were scattered in many small posts, into divisions. . . . The new divisions were numbered one to nine, and thereby they succeeded to the history and the glory of their namesakes of 1918."[5] Having received official word of the "reactivation" of the 4th (Ivy) Division, a trio of officers "in civilian clothes, quietly talking in a corner," discussed how best to proceed with the daunting task of creating a modern infantry division that would be able to challenge the crack Wehrmacht units then blitzing their way across France. All they had to work with were a piece of paper, two tradition-cloaked but woefully understrength infantry regiments—the 8th and 22d—scattered over two states, the show troops of the Infantry School's 29th Regiment, cadres from the 6th, 17th, and 83d Field Artillery Battalions, and the "old" division's quartermaster, signal, reconnaissance, and headquarters troops.[6] Essentially, the 4th Division had to be built from scratch, for although the U.S. Army of 1940 was committed in principle to a triangular organization, it was still based on the ponderous square division of 1918.

The 4th's reorganization meshed with the perceived lessons from the Nazi blitz through France. "The Nazis had over 250 divisions," a contemporary account stated. "What was worse, the Nazis had a new kind of Army. Their blitzkrieg was as strange and terrible as an invasion from Mars. And we had yet to learn how to meet the blitz. We must create a vast force, great as the mighty Wehrmacht, out of our tiny army. And we must cut out a new pattern to build that Army while we were building it."[7] In August 1940, the 4th Division was selected "as an experimental unit for the development of tactics demonstrated by the German blitz," reflecting a mistaken notion that most German divisions possessed sufficient organic transport for all personnel. Lacking adequate vehicles (the division was still relying on ancient 1½-ton trucks during the Louisiana maneuvers of August—September 1941), the 4th Division was "motorized" in name only. Nevertheless, the War Department's mania for motorization led to its designation following the 1941 Carolina maneuvers as the 4th Motorized Division, a uniquely organized meld of infantry and armor. By spring 1942, the division boasted 2,300 vehicles, and the 8th Infantry was completely "mechanized." For nearly two years the troops affiliated with the "Rolling Fourth" masqueraded as mechanized infantry and were constantly used as tests or foils in maneuvers. An 8th Infantry officer later admitted: "We were never really trained tactically as motorized troops—except as mode of transportation. Actually, when I asked [what the term meant] nobody gave me a comprehensive answer."[8] This proved to be a doctrinal dead end, but only the shipping crisis of 1943, which drove home the logistic absurdities associated with the grandiose vision of hordes of armored and mechanized divisions flooding Europe, tolled the death knell for motorized divisions.[9]

Turbulence of all sorts was the lot of the 4th Division and its constituent units during the period from activation through the spring of 1943. Not until February 1941, when the 22d Infantry moved from Fort McClellan, Alabama, and the 8th Infantry came up to Benning from Fort Screven, were all the division's soldiers located in one place. The 12th Infantry replaced the 29th in fall of 1941, and the division moved to Camp Gordon, Georgia. The roll call of commanding generals—Brig. Gen. Walter E. Prosser from June to October 1940, Maj. Gen. Lloyd R. Fredendall from October 1940 to August 1941, Brig. Gen. Fred C. Wallace pro tem and then again—following Maj. Gen. Oscar W. Griswold—from September 1941 to June 1942, and finally, Brig. Gen. Raymond O. Barton—was one manifestation of turmoil. As well, the 4th Division counted seven assistant division commanders between 1940 and D-day; the longest tenure, that of Brig. Gen. Maxwell A. O'Brien, was twenty months.

Equally serious was the constant turnover of officers and enlisted personnel. As of June 1940, most of the 4th Division's officers were "regulars," West Point graduates and careerists who had stayed on after World War I, along with a sprinkling of reserve lieutenants. However, the army's insatiable demand for experienced officers to serve as training cadre for new units and the reality that modern war was a young man's game ensured that by summer 1942, only 28 of the 4th Division's officers were regular army. Junior grade slots were filled almost entirely by reserve and Officer Candidate School (OCS) graduates.[10]

When the great expansion began in 1940, the enlisted men in a regular army unit such as the 4th Division and its three line regiments were long-timers.[11] "These were men to whom the army was simply a job," noted a division chronicle. By one estimate, the division was made up of two-thirds regular army and one-third draftees by late 1942. On 1 January 1943, the 4th comprised 854 officers, 51 warrant officers, and 16,270 enlisted men; at year's end, the totals were 858 officers, 51 warrant officers, and 16,001 enlisted men. But over the course of the year, the entire complement of officers effectively turned over (448 new officers arriving and

417 departing, for a total of 865), and the division experienced a turnover of nearly half (7,232) of its complement of enlisted men.[12]

For the 4th's officers, "turbulence" was a fact throughout 1943 as individuals were promoted, transferred to serve in new units, or reassigned for incapacity or health and as waves of newly minted second lieutenants arrived from OCS at Fort Benning and elsewhere. Similar peaks and valleys afflicted the division's enlisted complement. One occurred in March, when a large consignment of "fillers" was received to replace those stripped out of the division when preparing for an abortive preparation for overseas movement (POM) in December 1942. Another took place during July–September, when some 650 enlisted men were sliced from the division's roster to bring it into conformity with the new "leaner and meaner" table of organization and equipment (TOE) for infantry divisions. Even more significant was the turnover of officers and enlisted men during the period immediately following the division's stay at Carrobello: 144 officers (one-sixth of the total) and 1,845 enlisted men (one-ninth) joined the 4th after it had trained for amphibious warfare.[13]

A significant factor in the constant personnel changes was concern about whether the quality of the men coming into the 4th Division and its constituent units was adequate for the tasks before them. Throughout 1942 and 1943, the AGF staff charged with training the millions of Americans drafted into the combat arms watched the average intellectual and physical qualifications of the men drop steadily. The best-qualified personnel were skimmed off by services—such as the Army Air Forces and the Army Service Forces—with a need for highly intelligent specialists; many other men who demonstrated aptitude for leadership were dispatched to OCS and often lost to the combat arms. In the spring of 1943, more than 100,000 of the brightest draftees were removed from the pool when the Army Specialized Training Program was created. As a result, AGF was getting "the dregs" in the opinion of AGF commander Lt. Gen. Leslie J. McNair. By late 1943, the typical infantry trainee was two inches shorter, fifteen to twenty pounds lighter, and significantly less able intellectually on the basis of scores on the Army General Classification Test. Were these men trainable? How would the much-maligned infantryman withstand the rigors of combat?[14]

From the vantage of the 8th Infantry, one of the most storied regiments in the entire U.S. Army, the mobilization saga embraced almost all the challenges faced by the 4th Division and the U.S. Army. The 8th Infantry had seen continuous service since it was first constituted by act of Congress on 5 July 1838. Originally raised to conduct operations against the Winnebago Indians in Wisconsin, the 8th saw action in Florida during the

Seminole War, served with great distinction in the Mexican War, fought in eleven major battles of the Civil War, raced up San Juan Hill alongside the Rough Riders, and served several tours in the Philippines. The 8th Infantry arrived in Europe too late to see action in World War I but performed occupation duties at Coblenz, Germany, from July 1919 to January 1923. Notably, the future commander of VII Corps, J. Lawton Collins, served with the 2/8 at Coblenz, and Maj. Raymond O. Barton (then commanding officer of the Machine Gun Battalion of the 8th and later of the 4th Division) had the honor of lowering the last American flag to fly on German soil for some 22 years.

During the interwar years, the 2/8 went to Fort Moultrie, South Carolina, and the 1/8 relocated to Fort Screven, Georgia. They were reunited during Col. George C. Marshall's tenure as the 8th Infantry's commander in 1933. Most officers who joined the 8th before the war nurtured fierce loyalty to the regiment. Many wartime additions acquired similar attachments.

By the time General Barton took divisional command, a substantial percentage of the senior leadership of the 8th Infantry was on board. Col. James Van Fleet took command of the 8th in 1941 and served until July 1944. Two of the regiment's battalion commanders were in their positions by mid-1942.

Training at the regimental and battalion level during these months meant chiefly repetition of small unit problems, qualification and familiarization courses in secondary weapons, and endless road marches and inspections. Though the 4th was on a list of seventeen divisions certified as "ready for combat" immediately after Pearl Harbor (and was ranked third in "excellence of training for normal operations" among infantry divisions), personnel changes and continued experimentation kept it at home.[15] Further disruptions to training occurred in the summer of 1942, when the division, then engaged in yet more full-scale maneuvers, was suddenly recalled to Camp Gordon to prepare for shipment overseas. That alert was the first of a number of false alarms, each linked to a projected major offensive.

In April 1943, the division was reassigned to Fort Dix, New Jersey. Though everyone believed that this was the first step toward the port of embarkation (POE), nothing happened. For the 2/8, Fort Dix was a time of unrelieved boredom and ongoing personnel changes. The move to Fort Dix witnessed belated attention to hand-to-hand combat skills and physical conditioning. Following the reorganization, the 2/8 and its sister units received some exposure to "combined arms" training through instruction about tanks, tank tactics, and practice in attacking a fortified area. As

Col. James Van Fleet, commander of the 8th Infantry Regiment, 4th Division, briefing senior army officers.

a result of the harsh judgments of AGF observers in North Africa and Sicily, such practical concerns as scouting and patrolling, administering first aid, and training in the use of foreign maps received emphasis.

A pivotal change took place on 4 August 1943. The War Department gods decreed that the 4th was to be "demotorized" and reorganized as the 4th Infantry Division. While the chain of command was sorting out the implications of reorganization, the division was sent to Camp Gordon

Johnston in Carrobello, Florida, for intensive training in amphibious operations. The move to Carrobello meant the temporary assignment of some officers and senior noncoms of the 2/8 for special courses while the battalion and its parent regiment were immersed in swimming instruction and other aspects of amphibious training. All told, soldiers of the 4th Infantry Division were at the amphibious training center for slightly less than six weeks.[16]

The division's history offers a favorable gloss:

> With the aid of Amphibious Engineers and under the guidance of expert instructors of the Amphibious Command, battalions, regiments, and the Division as a whole participated in amphibious exercises designed to promote familiarity with the equipment and techniques involved. Naval terminology, boat loadings, loading diagrams, landing procedures, and amphibious tactics were studied and practiced diligently. All possible realism was imparted to the problem and when the unit left Carrabello . . . officers and men alike felt that they were capable of adequately performing amphibious operations. A very splendid esprit existed in the Division, for, justly, individuals believed that they had acquitted themselves quite creditably at Carrobello.[17]

Notably, the December 1943 regular report to General Marshall regarding combat readiness confirmed that the 4th, having fulfilled all training requirements (and the only infantry division of the 23 still in the United States to have undergone amphibious training), had been earmarked for dispatch to Britain.[18] Thus, a checklist and circumstance rather than any expert assessment of the 4th's capabilities conspired to place the 2/8 on Utah Beach on 6 June 1944.

The next move was to a staging area for POM at Fort Jackson, South Carolina. Hard decisions as to "adjustment of personnel"—who was unfit for overseas service on physical or other grounds—had to be made. Still, the first departures of troops for Camp Kilmer, New Jersey, and POE on 3 January 1944 came as a shock to the great majority of the 2/8. Processing at Camp Kilmer (checks of gear and equipment, the voluminous paperwork, assessment by the Inspector General's office) required three days. After being ordered to remove all identifying insignia, the 2/8 made use of twelve-hour passes to enjoy the sights of Hoboken and Manhattan. Troops were kept under tight security—primarily to discourage desertion—until being transported to the Port of New York for embarkation. Early on 18 January, the 8th Infantry boarded the USS *Franconia*. In midmorning, in convoy with the *Capetown Castle* and *George Washington*, they put to sea. Those agonizing months of preparation were over. The 2/8 was on its way to war.

The trip across the Atlantic proved uneventful, though the nearly 1,000 soldiers of the 2/8, few of whom had ever been at sea and almost none of whom had dared the raging North Atlantic in midwinter, had little good to say about their ship, the food (those who were able to eat), or their hosts. Grimy and bored after the eleven-day voyage, the 2/8's troops perked up when the *Franconia* berthed in Liverpool harbor to the blare of a regimental band. But once the ritualistic speech of welcome had been delivered, these new arrivals, catching only glimpses of war-torn Liverpool, boarded trains and headed south through the blacked-out British countryside. Their destination was billets in Devon that had been prepared by a 4th Division advance party with the assistance of "old hands" from the 29th Infantry Division.[19]

For the first time since its activation in 1940, the elements of the 4th Division were separated. Britain was an armed camp, and the southwest—from which the U.S. assault divisions were to embark for Normandy—was almost filled by the 4th Division's arrival. This meant requisitioning housing in a number of towns scattered across south Devon. "Being spread over such distances, unit commanders were of necessity allowed greater latitude than ever before." General Barton's division command post was in Tiverton, and Colonel Van Fleet and the 8th Infantry (now designated Combat Team 8) were located some 40 miles southeast in the bustling village of Honiton. The 2/8 was assigned billets in Seaton, a small port on the south Devon coast west of Lyme Regis and fifteen miles from Honiton.[20]

The 2/8's troops were assigned to such varied billets as Warren's Holiday Camp and the Esplanade Hotel. A Seaton resident, blasé after five years, commented about the nervousness of these young Americans. During a desultory German air raid, one fired his rifle at the planes far overhead through the Esplanade Hotel's skylight! Seaton soon boasted a Red Cross "Donut Dugout," and there were American soldiers everywhere.[21]

Two days after their arrival, Barton and his staff met with First Army Commander General Omar Bradley at Supreme headquarters Allied Expeditionary Force (SHAEF) in London. They learned that the 4th Division was to lead the VII Corps assault on occupied France some three months hence. They learned that the VII Corps had only recently been added to OVERLORD. The original plan drafted the previous year by the Chief of Staff to the Supreme Allied Commander designate (COSSAC) projected an invasion of Normandy with an assault force of three divisions. The availability

THE 4th DIVISION PLAN

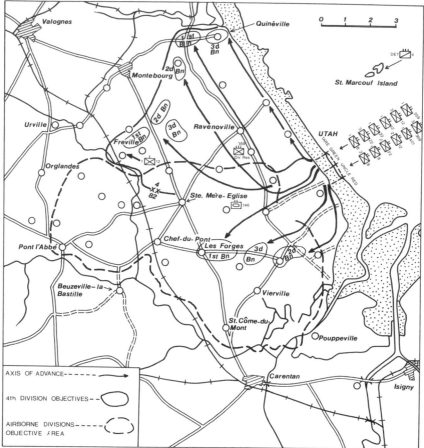

AXIS OF ADVANCE — — — — —

4th DIVISION OBJECTIVES — —

AIRBORNE DIVISIONS — — — — —
OBJECTIVE AREA

of landing craft had dictated a relatively modest assault on a narrow front. When shown the COSSAC plan, Eisenhower had argued for broadening the frontage of the attack and increasing the number of assault divisions. Once named to head SHAEF, he sent his deputy, General Bernard L. Montgomery, to London to review the invasion plan. Montgomery recommended that the early seizure of a major port such as Cherbourg be a priority and that the assault force comprise five infantry and three airborne divisions. The Combined Chiefs' promise to find the needed landing craft and transport aircraft led to VII Corps' inclusion in OVERLORD.[22]

Bradley explained that the VII Corps mission was deceptively simple.

VII Corps would land at the neck of the Cotentin peninsula in Normandy between Varremille and the Douve River's mouth alongside and to the northwest of V Corps, while the British and Canadian troops of the British XXX and I Corps attacked further along the Normandy coast. VII Corps was to clear the beaches, drive inland to link up with V Corps west of the Douve, and then push hard to capture Cherbourg. For the untried 4th Division, that meant preparing for both an assault against a defended shore and a campaign of rapid movement against an experienced and possibly numerically superior foe. Barton and his staff had much to consider during the trip down to Devon.[23] Drafting plans to deal with every aspect of the landings began at once.

Just as the widely scattered regiments of 4th were settling in, the 4th Division was visited by Eisenhower; his deputy, Air Marshal Sir Arthur Tedder; Bradley; and the just-appointed VII Corps Commander, Maj. Gen. J. Lawton Collins. Eisenhower's naval aide recorded that they visited the 4th Division, "one of the regular outfits," on 5 February. "Ike made five informal talks to officers and men during the day. In two of them and particularly the largest group, which was the 8th Infantry, assembled at Heathfield Camp at Honiton, he said he would see them all 'east of the Rhine' and would personally make certain they had champagne, 'even if I have to buy it myself.'" His private views probably accorded with those of his aide, who remarked, after looking over the 29th Division near Plymouth: "How good it will be in battle remains to be seen, as is true of any 'unblooded' division."[24]

Collins was more confident. Having been briefed about the invasion role of the 4th Division, whose commander he had known in Coblenz, Collins gave most of his attention to the Ivy troops during several visits in March and April. He concluded that Barton ("a first-class trainer, . . . not a brilliant man but . . . thoroughly versed in the tools of his trade") had done well. "The division was in splendid shape, sharp and eager to get under way." He was particularly impressed with the 8th Infantry and its commanding officer, Colonel Van Fleet, for whom he had great respect, and believed that Marshall had unfairly penalized because of an unfortunate mix-up about names. Bradley had said, "Well, Joe, he is in your Corps. Do something about it." Collins had replied, "If Van does as well on D day as I feel sure he will, I will recommend him at once to be a [brigadier general]." That promise was kept.[25]

Terrain dictated that unit training be limited chiefly to road marches and physical toughening. (This followed the pattern established by earlier arrivals. For example, the 29th Infantry Division regularly marched 200 miles a week.) The first week of February was given to lectures on the

British monetary system and appropriate behavior when off duty, film-strips on venereal disease, driver training, and preparations for Eisenhower's visit.[26] After that, road marches were the norm.

The centerpieces of the 2/8's time in Britain were its journey to Braunton, North Devon, to practice landing operations at the U.S. Army Assault Training Center, Woolacombe, and its subsequent participation in TIGER. As of 1 April 1944, the official record of the 2/8's training regime stated: "Training in the ETO has consisted of moving a composite combat team from its present location to Braunton Camp to participate in assault training at the U.S. Assault Training Center."[27] This interlude was apparently scheduled at the behest of Collins, who had observed the value of battalion-level combat exercises when he commanded the 25th Division in the Pacific. Fortunately, the amphibious training center at Woolacombe was available, and cadres were also sent up to Scotland to use a British artillery range on the River Clyde.[28] According to the divisional history, "the training at Braunton [in amphibious techniques, the reduction of hedgehog defenses, and the tactics of fortified localities] was well organized, intensive, interesting, and of immense practical value."[29] In reality, though, this course provided not much more than the opportunity to disembark from an actual landing craft onto a beach not unlike the tidal flats of Normandy. The troops did appreciate the effort to make the exercises as realistic as possible—calling supporting fire close to the battalion front and allowing incoming live fire. One officer noted that the exercises in Devon represented "the first time in our service we had enough ammunition to really get to know our weapons." Recalling the lavish supply of mortar rounds and smoke shells, he said, "that's where my mortar platoon became more expert—most of the men had never fired it."[30] There were a few training casualties, but the greatest risk came from road accidents.

Woolacombe's limitations led to the takeover of the stretch of Devon coast southwest of Dartmouth along Start Bay known as Slapton Sands. The beaches and terrain for several miles back from the shore closely approximated that across the Channel in Normandy. Several villages and surrounding farmsteads were evacuated, and low-lying land was flooded so that amphibious exercises, employing bombing and strafing runs and naval bombardment, could be held for units tagged for D-day.[31] Though the troops were unaware of their destination, they certainly realized what was to happen. The rehearsals now mimicked reality so closely—assembling in marshaling areas, being given mission briefings, loading on assigned landing craft, and sailing over a course that duplicated the length of a cross-channel voyage—that opening night was surely coming soon.

In late April, the most elaborate of these rehearsals, Exercise TIGER, fea-

4th Division troops coming ashore at Slapton Sands, the site for amphibious exercises such as TIGER.

tured Combat Team 8 and, in particular, its 2d Battalion, now designated Battalion Landing Team 2 and assigned the mission of spearheading the VII Corps assault on D-day. TIGER remains notorious because poor planning and worse communication allowed a flotilla of German E-boats to slip past the naval screening force and sink two landing ships for tanks (LSTs) carrying troops of the 4th Division and attached combat engineers. More than 700 soldiers died, far more than were killed in the initial phases of the 4th's battle in Normandy, though precise details—repressed because of the proximity of TIGER to the invasion—remain ambiguous and have fueled an ongoing controversy.[32]

Largely ignored in the hullabaloo about how many died and who was responsible were the negative judgments of those who observed TIGER. Eisenhower, Tedder, and Bradley, who watched from an infantry landing craft (LCI), were disturbed about a one-hour delay in H-hour for the exercise, manifest problems in naval-ground coordination, and confusion on the beach. Eisenhower's aide concluded: "I came away from the exercise feeling depressed. But frequently the poorest kind of exercise presages the best actual operation because the failures are noticed and corrected. I am concerned over the absence of toughness and alertness of young

American officers whom I saw on this trip. They seem to regard the war as one grand maneuver in which they are having a happy time. Many seem as green as growing corn. How will they act in battle and how will they look in three months' time?"[33] Such concerns were widely shared among the army's senior leaders, for rapid expansion had meant an unavoidable dilution of experienced officers who were schooled in rigid discipline and long accustomed to implicit obedience. How would these fuzzy-cheeked second lieutenants fresh from college and OCS perform? Would they be able to lead, and would their men—similarly young and seemingly unformed—respond?

After returning to Seaton, the 2/8 worked its way systematically down a preinvasion checklist. It received a flood of items for units undertaking amphibious operations: specially treated signal equipment, flamethrowers, a dozer blade to be attached to a Sherman tank once ashore, and cargo carriers designed to move through inundated terrain. "Much of this material was utterly new and surprising in appearance to the 8th Infantrymen," the regimental executive officer acknowledged. "Only after drawing it did they seem to fully grasp the vast scope of what lay in store for them."[34]

For the first time, Colonel Carleton MacNeely and the 2d Battalion's officers received precise information about their mission, now identified as Utah Beach on the western flank of the Allied assault on Normandy. Generally known, of course, were the dominant terrain features of the southern Cotentin peninsula: two rivers, the Douve and the Merderet, broadening into tidal flats and marshes near their mouths at Bancs du Grand Vey. The peninsula's east coast was marked by a several-mile-wide belt of low-lying land. Parallel to the beach was an inundated area that had been created by the Germans to block egress from the beaches. Passage through the inundation was limited to six causeways a mere foot above water level. Beyond the inundated area toward Sainte Mere-Eglise, the rising ground was dominated by small fields bordered by thick hedgerows.

The beach itself was smooth, formed of dense grey sand, and sloped gently toward dunes that stretched inland and rose ten feet or more. At its back was a masonry seawall from four to eight feet in height and extending some 10,000 yards between the Bancs du Grand Vey and Quineville.

Now revealed were treasures of the top-secret BIGOT. The Germans had been working frantically along the Cotentin coast since January 1944. Rows of defense obstacles—stakes, steel hedgehogs and tetrahydra, Belgian gates—were installed on the beach, and anchored to them were antitank and antipersonnel mines. Immediately behind the seawall were pillboxes, firing trenches, and underground shelters. Some strong points housed fixed and mobile field artillery pieces. The 2d Battalion's officers could take some comfort from the information that "distances between fixed defenses were greater on Utah Beach than Omaha Beach to the east," but that was because of the inundated areas.[35] Two miles inland were batteries of coast and field artillery at Crisbecq and Saint Martin de Varreville.

German units included the 709th Division, disposed along the east coast and manning the beach defenses. Elements of the 243d Division were in the vicinity of La Haye du Puits, some fifteen miles east of Utah. The 709th, known to contain a high percentage of non-German troops, and the 243d were static units, capable of rigid defense but not likely to launch aggressive attacks. At most, piecemeal counterattacks by four battalions and one battalion combat team were possible. Happily, no panzer units were sufficiently close to throw armor at the American assault troops.

While the briefings proceeded in the 2/8 "sausage," on 26 May SHAEF informed VII Corps of a potentially perilous change in the German order of battle (OB) in the Cotentin peninsula. Intelligence reports (most likely derived from ULTRA) stated that the German 91st Division had moved into the Carentan-Valognes area to the rear of the 709th Division. The 91st was first rate and comprised six infantry battalions and possibly one battalion of tanks. Its presence dictated that the assault force quickly secure a beachhead of sufficient depth to withstand strong pressure. It also made the drive toward Cherbourg more difficult.

Barton's operational order directed that the 4th Division would land in a column of regiments with the 8th Combat Team in the lead. In turn, Colonel Van Fleet informed his battalion commanders that—to no one's surprise—BLT2 would take the lead, landing at H-hour on Uncle Red Beach. It was to reduce beach defenses, turn south to the beach exit to seize causeway 1, move inland to capture Le Bout de la Ville, and secure the regiment's left flank. BLT1 was to land on Tare Red Beach to the right of Uncle Red, secure causeway 3, and open the way for the remaining elements of the 8th Regimental Combat Team to move ashore.[36]

On 21 May, BLT2 began the road movement toward its marshaling area west of Torquay. For the next two weeks it would be sealed into this artificial womb. Troops were issued charcoal-impregnated clothing, assault jackets, weapons, ammunition, and rations. While soldiers waterproofed vehicles, memorized the names of the others in their 30-man boat serial, wrote letters, grumbled, and gambled, BLT2's officers were receiving detailed briefings in a "war room" MacNeely had furnished with aerial photographs, map overlays, and a sponge rubber relief map. He reviewed terrain features and intelligence as to the German OB and then set out specific tasks for each component of his reinforced battalion. MacNeely insisted that "the briefing continue down through the chain of command until each soldier knew every detail that might influence his action as an individual or as a member of his group." The troops were informed that France was their destination and were given a sum of French invasion currency in exchange for their English pounds and shillings.[37] By the time they moved to the POE, one participant claimed, squads had selected particular ditches to be used while reducing a given strong point!

The transfer from BLT2's marshaling area to the *Barnet*, moored at its loading hards in Torquay, began early on 4 June. All of BLT2—the 976 officers and men of the 2/8, their 66 vehicles, and attached troops and equipment—were aboard *Barnet* by 1700. There they waited while the weather turned sour and Eisenhower consulted with his subordinates about what course of action to pursue. At 0855, 5 June, Barton received the go-ahead signal: "*Bayfield* moved at 0930. Operation is on." Then just fifteen minutes before sailing came confirmation that "D Day and H Hour fixed as follows: 6 June at 0630."[38] At 2100 *Barnet* began the tedious journey along the boat channel marked by minesweeper flotillas.

Shortly after 0200 on D-day, 6 June 1944, to a display of tracers searching for the incoming C-47s that carried the 82d and 101st paratroopers to drop zones inland from Utah, *Barnet* and other Force U transports dropped anchor some eleven miles off the Utah Beach. Loudspeakers blared. Sailors winched scores of 36–foot landing craft for vehicles and personnel (LCVPs) off decks into heavy seas. Bouncing and rolling, the landing craft struggled to hold position while the assault troops of BLT2 lined up far above on *Barnet*'s heaving decks. Soon the order came: "Now hear this—board your landing boats." The 600 men of Easy Company, commanded by Capt. Howard S. Lees, and Fox Company, commanded by Capt. Leonard T. Schroeder, Jr., climbed down cargo nets into their allotted twenty LCVPs. "Curses rang out as men lost their footing and dangled from the ladders from their arms alone, often kicking the man below. . . . A few feet below, the LCVPs heaved upward in the violent swells of the Channel and it was a perilous task to time the final leap into the bucking little boats. Many crashed onto the unyielding steel bottoms in tangled heaps."[39] Among the first group down the slippery netting was Brig. Gen. Theodore Roosevelt, Jr., who had wangled permission from Barton to accompany the first echelon of assault troops. Their buddies in G Company and the men of H Company, 3d Battalion, along with Colonel MacNeely and his staff, scheduled to follow after the first wave landed, next clambered into waiting LCVPs. As each craft was loaded, it pulled away and circled, surging through heavy seas, waiting for the signal to line up for the long run to the beaches. Clutching bulwarks and each other, the troops of E and F Companies were immediately drenched by frigid spray and waves washing over the crowded LCVPs. "Each man huddled in his tiny space in that little craft, feeling sick and more uncomfortable as the rough sea made the boat rise and fall with the surging waves," recalled Capt. George L. Mabry, Jr., the battalion operations officer (S-3).[40] *Newsweek* reporter Kenneth Crawford, accompanying the initial landing force, quoted a young soldier who was desperately seasick, his assault jacket stiff with vomit: "That guy Higgins ain't got nothin' to be proud of about inventin' this goddamned boat."[41] With H-hour fixed at 0630 and the trip inshore calculated at one hour and 45 minutes, the waiting seemed interminable. Many of BLT2's anxious troops wished themselves on dry land, preferring enemy fire to shivering and seasickness. At 0445—precisely on schedule—the first wave reached the line of departure, and the order came to head for the beaches. The 2d Battalion, 8th Infantry, was irrevocably committed to fortune's far shore.

At 0550, the lightening sky behind the line of crammed LCVPs erupted. Warships of the Task Force 125 bombardment group were firing on German shore batteries. Then came wave after wave of Ninth Air Force Marauders, dropping 250-pound bombs on seven beach objectives from Dunes de Varreville to Beau Gillot. (Subsequent investigations made clear that although naval gunfire had devastated German fixed defenses, the air attacks had done little damage, with most bombs exploding well behind the target area and only about one-third falling between high- and low-water lines.)[42]

When the LCVPs bearing E and F Companies were just 700 yards from the beaches, a rocket barrage (employing the oddly named Grasshopper) from seventeen specially modified LCTs screamed into the beach areas designated Tare Green and Uncle Red. A few rounds landed short, causing casualties among the bunched LCVPs. But none of the drifting clouds of smoke was the poison gas anticipated by many. When the LCVPs were 400 yards from shore, special smoke projectors were triggered to signal the naval bombardment force to lift their fire.

Return fire was light, mostly sporadic machine-gun bursts and German 88-mm guns shooting antipersonnel shells toward the incoming assault craft. An occasional splash erupted, and shrapnel caused several casualties among the huddled troops. Several sightings of enemy planes were reported, but no strafing or bombing interfered with the run to the beaches. Some 100 yards offshore, BLT2's LCVPs lowered their ramps amid tangles of wire and broken obstacles almost at 0630 on the dot, and the men of E and F Companies jumped into waist-deep water.[43] Wading that last 300 feet to the flat sandy shore of Normandy took longer than anticipated, for many soldiers—weighed down by waterlogged clothing and heavy loads—found the going hard. "Crossing the smooth beach was a slow and painful process. Troops having been chilled to the bone by cold channel water found it impossible to move faster than a slow walk."[44] For some, as well, concern that naval observers would not be able to distinguish the black smoke signals put up by their commanding officers from the black puffs of German airbursts dictated a cautious advance. Friendly fire was an ever-present if unspoken danger.

Enemy shelling picked up as the American soldiers moved across the beach to the shelter of the seawall. Nonetheless, the Utah landings went off with comparative ease and resulted in far fewer casualties than had been projected. The 8th Infantry's casualty totals for D-day were five killed, 60 wounded, and thirteen missing in action.[45] Nothing like the horrors experienced by men of the 1st and 29th Divisions on Omaha took place on Utah Beach.

The butcher's bill for the period H plus 30, the critical minutes for an amphibious landing, was only two killed. Morale shot up dizzyingly. "Goddam, we're on French soil," members of the right assault section of E Company yelled, waving their rifles.[46] The 4th Division historian's assessment was similarly blunt: "Opposition was slight. Apparently the German garrisons were completely cowed by the preparatory bombardment and most of the strongpoints gave up as soon as the troops closed on them. Apparently some of the forts did not even fire."[47]

In spite of the 24-hour delay and less-than-optimum conditions, to this point the meticulous VII Corps–4th Division plan had ticked along essentially as set forth by its drafters. But BLT2's entrance into battle brought inevitable confusion, unforeseen events, and accidental happenings, producing a sequence of unintended but mostly fortuitous consequences for the Americans on Utah. As one of Bradley's staff noted: "0730 and the reports are scanty. No one knows precisely what is happening for the battle is now in the hands of the junior commanders on the beach and it is not a corps or army battle but a company and battalion one."[48]

First came a worrisome delay in the arrival of the armor assigned to BLT2. The 32 duplex-drive (DD) tanks (sixteen allocated to Tare and sixteen to Uncle) of the 70th Tank Battalion were supposed to reach shore along with the first wave of troops, and the remainder of the 70th Tank Battalion, transported in LCTs, was to make landfall at 0645. The LCTs carrying BLT2's tanks immediately fell behind. One LCT with four DD tanks aboard hit a mine and sank as it was lowering its ramp. Because of the rough seas, the remaining DDs were taken much closer to shore. When finally launched, they were slowed by heavy seas and the gridlock offshore and on Uncle Red Beach. Most of BLT2's complement reached shore between H plus 15 and H plus 30. "Fortunately, the tanks were not needed for the assault on the first beach defenses," succinctly concluded the 4th Division's historian.[49] The tanks did not pass through the seawall until late morning, but they proved invaluable—avoiding many American casualties—in reducing concrete pillboxes and other German strong points from then on.[50]

Far more consequential was the discovery that the 2/8 had come ashore more than a mile from its assigned landing point. Instead of hitting Uncle Red beach opposite Exit 3, the men of E and F Companies had waded ashore astride Exit 2, nearly 2,000 yards to the south. How this happened was never fully explained, but some combination of factors—communication failures, a strong tidal current, the tremendous cloud of smoke and dust that obscured Utah when the first wave began its run, and, possibly, a natural flinching from the concentration of enemy fire ploughing the intended landing sites—was involved.[51] At the outset, command and control disintegrated when the Uncle Red secondary control vessel became fouled in a buoy and an hour later, 7,000 yards offshore, the primary control vessel for Uncle Red hit a mine and sank. Tare Green's backup then put back to sea to shepherd the amphibious tanks to the beach, leaving the LCVPs carrying the 2d Battalion assault troops to find their own way.

Brigadier Roosevelt's presence proved fortuitous. He quickly discovered that the first wave had landed far to the south. Roosevelt described his actions a few days later: "The moment I arrived at the beach I knew something was wrong, for there was a house by the seawall where none should have been were we in the right place. It was imperative that I should find out where we were in order to set the maneuver. I scrambled up on the dunes and was lucky in finding a windmill which I recognized. We'd been put ashore a mile too far to the south."[52] By the time Roosevelt returned to the beach, Colonel MacNeely, impatient to grasp his unit's reins, had disembarked, wading the last 200 yards along with the remaining elements of BLT2. Further reconnaissance determined that numerous "Minen" signs, indicating mine fields, lay back of the beach and that enemy artillery was concentrating on Exit 2. Not knowing how the 82d and 101st had fared, the threat of a German counterattack weighed heavily. Rather than move the elements already ashore up the beach to their original landing sites, Roosevelt decided to have these troops eliminate the remaining enemy fortifications in the beach area. Then the 2/8 was to move south along the coast to seize Exit 1, while the 1st of the 8th swung north to attack Exit 3.[53]

Most significant was the ability of junior leaders to adjust to the changed circumstances and obtain immediate responses from their men. As one observer stated: "Due to the change in landing position, the original detailed plans were worthless and all the assault elements had to attack positions nearest to them. These impromptu plans worked with complete success and little confusion. The two battalions of the 8th cleaned up the strongpoints on the actual landing beach and then diverged: the 1st to the north as far as La Percherie, the 2nd south to the Pouppeville road."[54] Typical of the uncertainty aboard the *Bayfield* was a message fired off to Barton at 12:00: "WHAT IS SITUATION OF THIRD BN 22 INF? WHAT ROADS HAVE BEEN SECURED? WHAT IS SITUATION OF PARATROOPS? HOW MUCH OF 4TH DIV IS ACROSS [INUNDATION]? WHAT WAVES ARE IN AND WHEN DID THEY COME?"[55] General statements and abstract language tend to sweep aside the innumerable individual and group responses that undergirded the 2/8's performance on and beyond Utah. Had they stayed put, waiting for direction from battalion or above, the intensifying German artillery fire might have wrought havoc among clustered troops and a worsening equipment pileup.

Overcoming initial confusion, F Company attacked the field fortification just south of the Exit 2 causeway. When its commanding officer, Captain Schroeder, was wounded, the company executive officer, 1st Lt. John A. Kulp of Columbus, Ohio, immediately assumed command.

Lt. John C. Rebarchek of Graceton, Minnesota, a Company E officer who became its commander when Captain Lees was wounded on 7 June, was on the right flank of the 2d Battalion front. "Rebarchek said he was confused for a little while after landing because he didn't know that he had landed too far to the south. He kept looking for the mud fort which was the first objective of his section. Then he looked for the old windmill. When he finally spotted it away off to the right he knew that he had landed in a different place than planned. He decided to give up taking the original objective and go straight in." When Rebarchek and his followers got across the dunes, artillery fire began to fall directly in front of them. Rebarchek went back to the beach to pick up the rest of his men, "and then led his section straight through the artillery barrage without losing a man. The company crossed the dune, then turned south, cutting across F Co. . . . The Lt. found a path, left by the Germans, through the minefield across the beach and behind the seawall, and the whole section marched right through the path."[56] One benefit of Company E's aggressiveness was the capture of numerous Goliaths, TNT-crammed mechanical tankettes dug into the dunes and intended to be maneuvered across the beach and exploded among the American troops as they emerged from the surf.[57]

Colonel MacNeely, who had talked with Brigadier Roosevelt, agreed that the men of the assault wave should continue to move inland. He eventually caught up with Rebarchek's band, got E and F Companies correctly aligned, and took charge of the march through the dunes to the road along the eastern edge of the inundated area.

Hitting the beach at H plus 5, just ahead of Colonel MacNeely splashing through hip-deep surf, the troops of G Company found the scene totally unlike the mental picture they had carried away from those briefings back in Devon. Following Capt. James W. Haley, they took cover against the seawall, which offered protection from German machine guns and a feeling of security. This soon proved to be a false security as casualties mounted from two German 88s firing through a gap in the seawall. G Company moved south toward Exit 1, hugging the seawall as small arms fire cracked overhead and whined off the concrete. Its objective was the closest intact objective, a German pillbox in the tiny hamlet of Beau Gillot. As G Company approached the strong point it began to attract artillery fire, and then its leading section stumbled into a mine field.

Captain Mabry, the 2/8's S-3, had come in with MacNeely's party. He walked south along the seawall, hoping to find G Company. "After advancing approximately 50 yards he saw seven enlisted men of Company G and was about to call to them when a terrific explosion occurred, killing three of the men and wounding the others. It was apparent that one of these unfortunate individuals had stepped on a mine which caused a number of additional mines to explode simultaneously." Realizing that more mines were probably scattered throughout the area, Mabry had advanced some 50 yards when small arms fire pinned him down. Mabry, a winner of the Congressional Medal of Honor, later described what happened next:

> From the crack of bullets passing inches above his head, he was able to locate the enemy dug in on a sand dune about 100 yards to his front. Making a hasty survey of his position, he could see mines that had been uncovered by strong winds and shifting sand. He now knew that he was in a mine field. A definite decision must be made and quickly! Would it be advantageous to try a withdrawal to the beach with the possibility of hitting a mine or should he continue the advance toward the enemy position. . . . Based upon previous training and remembering the necessity of contacting Company G, he elected to push through the mines and engage the enemy. The first rush forward directed at a shell hole was begun with good progress in spite of small arms fire; but,

8th Infantry troops taking a breather behind the seawall on Utah Beach.

upon the last leap for the inviting shell hole, his foot set off a mine. The explosion slammed him against the ground with a tremendous thud—no injuries from it—just shaken up a bit.

A lieutenant from F Company had seen Mabry and was working his way forward. Mabry "called a warning to watch for mines, but it could not be heard above the noise of battle. The lieutenant crumpled under the explosion of a mine. The S-3 sprang up and rushed toward the dug-in Germans, stopping once to deliver a few rounds of fire before closing in. The last rush of 25 yards carried him to the enemy foxholes. The first German encountered was quickly exterminated and immediately the remaining six surrendered." He turned his prisoners over to a G Company sergeant suffering from a hand wound, who marched them back to Uncle Red. This sergeant informed Mabry that G Company had been held up by the mine field and machine-gun fire, and thus he was some 200 yards in advance of friendly troops. "Since he had met with success thus far, he decided to push on and try to reach Causeway #1 as quickly as possible." He and three soldiers "crawled down ditches and along hedgerows," bypassing

pillboxes until coming under fire by the large pillbox guarding the Cause-
way/Exit 1 entrance. Mabry called back for reinforcements and a DD tank.
After a 30-minute wait, a platoon of G Company soldiers and two tanks
reached his position and brought the pillbox under fire. Its defenders surrendered after a sharp firefight, and 32 ambulatory prisoners and four seriously wounded Germans were dispatched to the collection point back
up the beach.[58] G Company continued south toward Pouppeville, located
across the inundated area.

Although to those involved it seemed like an eternity, these separate
actions occurred over a 2½-hour period following the initial landings.
Soon thereafter, all three companies of the 2d Battalion assembled at a
road junction northeast of Pouppeville. MacNeely pushed his soldiers
quickly toward Pouppeville, eager to link up with the 101st Airborne de-
fending the access routes to Causeways 1 and 2.

Once reunited with MacNeely, Mabry dragooned a nearby rifleman and
set out on a reconnaissance of the approaches to the important Exit 1
bridge. Crawling through a half-filled ditch to a point ten yards from the
bridge, the two-man patrol cut down two Germans discovered running
toward the causeway. Mabry was later informed that these Germans had
been setting demolition charges to destroy the bridge. Had they succeeded, the 4th Division's egress from Utah would have been seriously
impeded.

Instead, E Company, supported by F Company and several tanks, having been directed by MacNeely along the eastern side of the inundations,
began crossing Causeway 1 at 1030. The distinctive sound of Garand rifles and Browning machine guns confirmed that the 101st was already in
Pouppeville, and E Company troops pushed forward into the village.
Caught between E Company and troops of the 3d Battalion, 501st Parachute Infantry, only a few German defenders escaped, and 70 of them
were killed or captured. G Company crossed the causeway shortly thereafter.

E Company had already met several 101st paratroopers separated from
their units, but the most memorable encounter may have occurred when
an E Company scout, his rifle slung casually, ambled down the causeway
and, spying a group of weary 101st men, called, "Where's the war?" Sgt.
Thomas Bruff, who had fought all night alongside General Maxwell Taylor after landing eight miles from the drop zone, replied, "Anywhere from
here on back. Keep going, buddy, you'll find it."[59] The official linkup of
American airborne and seaborne forces occurred at 1105 when MacNeely
was welcomed to Pouppeville by Lt. Col. Julian Ewell, commander of the

3d Battalion, 501st Parachute Infantry and the 2d Battalion relieved the exhausted paratroopers.[60]

Elsewhere, elements of BLT1 pushed north from Tare Green to take Exit 3; the 3d Battalion, landing on Uncle Red as BLT2 moved west and south, attacked along Causeway 2. Thus, all three battalions of the 8th Infantry had reached shore by 0800. MacNeely and his troops, oblivious of these problems, pushed ahead to secure the battalion objectives for D-day. Advancing toward Le Bout de la Ville in a column with E Company in the lead, the battalion met up just east of Sainte Maire du Mont with elements of the 3d Battalion accompanied by Colonel Van Fleet. The soldiers of the two battalions, led by the 8th Infantry commander, brushed aside light opposition and took the rubble-choked village. Rebarchek recalled that the advance was a cakewalk. "At St. Marie du Mont," he noted, "the head of the company was held by machine gun fire from the church steeple, but tanks shot down the steeple. . . . From St. Marie du Mont the Company marched to la Bout de la Ville in a column of twos, right down the road!"[61] Reaching Le Bout de la Ville, just south of Les Forges, at about 1900, the battalion dug in for the night. The Utah beachhead was secure.

As the 2/8's men struggled out of grimy, mud-caked assault jackets and impregnated uniforms, broke open K rations, and sought to get comfortable in foxholes and beneath shelter halves, the more introspective among them sought to make sense of the preceding hours of frantic activity, constant fear, and uncertainty. Everyone knew that the battalion had been lucky. The 8th Infantry's unit report for D-day acknowledged: "The 1st Bn of 919 Regt occupied the beach defenses in our sector. They fell back as the attack progressed. Many mines on beach, none inland. Morale exceptionally low. Equipment and ammo abandoned."[62] First Army commander General Omar Bradley offered a succinct summation: "Utah was a piece of cake."[63] But BLT2 and its counterparts had conducted themselves well. The G-3 periodic report for 6 June summarized the efforts of the 8th Infantry: "Assaulted defenses on Utah Beach and broke through beach defenses. Advanced approximately 8000 yards inland to establish a beach head to cover the advance inland of remainder of 4th Division and VII Corps." Its combat efficiency was rated "superior" by Lt. Col. O. C. Troxel, 4th Division Assistant Chief of Staff (G-3).[64]

The "cakewalk" of D-day soon became a slugfest as German resistance stiffened in defense of the vital port of Cherbourg. The 2/8 took an active part in the strongly contested advance through Ecoqueneaville toward Sainte Mere-Eglise. A coordinated attack with the 505th Parachute Infantry of the 82d Airborne killed or captured some 300 Germans. Over the next two weeks, the 4th, joined first by the 90th and then by the 79th and 9th Division, experienced bitter fighting in the drive toward Cherbourg. VII Corps suffered a total of 22,000 casualties—2,800 killed, 5,700 missing, and 13,500 wounded—in the battle to clear the Cotentin peninsula.[65]

Pulled out of the line after its exertions on 6 to 8 June, the 2/8 rejoined its parent regiment on 19 June and went through flurries of difficult assaults and German counterattacks. The 8th Infantry suffered 330 killed and 978 wounded during the approach to Cherbourg from 9 to 25 June. The men of the 8th Infantry bore the stony-faced look of veterans when they marched into Cherbourg on 27 June. They had learned hard lessons—about themselves and about the adversary. They had discovered that their training had prepared them well to meet some of the demands of combat and poorly for other exigencies.

The tragedy of Omaha Beach and, too, the 2/8's experience on lightly defended Utah demonstrated how inadequately training had prepared these troops for the highly specialized mission dumped in their laps on 6 June 1944. The army's stubborn refusal to equip and train forces solely for amphibious assaults cost dearly.

The days given to carefully supervised briefings had proved valuable, but only because junior leaders exhibited resourcefulness and initiative. As Captain Mabry observed, Utah Beach demonstrated a "definite necessity" for capable small unit commanders, for the initial phase of the assault was in the hands of section leaders such as Lt. John Rebarchek.[66] What happened on D-day vindicated the OCS system, which had been established against bitter opposition four years before. Also vindicated, in a sense, were the qualities of the "typical" U.S. Army infantryman, the GI. Even if poorly coordinated, undersized, and less prepossessing intellectually than their peers in the Army Air Forces, Army Service Forces, or Army Specialized Training Program, soldiers of the 2/8 proved that when fit and imbued with loyalty to their buddies, unit identity, and confidence in their officers, they more than held their own against seasoned adversaries.[67]

13. Caught in the Middle: The French Population in Normandy

Arthur Layton Funk

As the cold winter of 1943–44 gave way to spring, everyone in occupied France knew that the Allies would sometime be landing on their shores. During the spring, signs began to multiply: increased bombardment, tighter security imposed by the Germans, and feverish construction of pillboxes and antitank devices along the Channel coast. A landing could happen anywhere, from Belgium to Spain, but the French people who lived closest to England along the 300-mile stretch from Calais to Cherbourg slept most uneasily. Although most wanted the invasion—indeed prayed for it—they hoped in their innermost hearts that it would strike elsewhere, sparing their own homes.

While all the inhabitants of Picardy and Normandy harbored such apprehension, only Gen. Dwight D. Eisenhower and the Allied staff knew that two Norman departments, Calvados and Manche, had been singled out to bear the brunt of the initial assault. No one, however, realized that for six arduous weeks the fair meadows and bocage countryside of lower Normandy would serve as a major battleground of World War II.

Normandy had for centuries epitomized the charm and prosperity of rural France. Before 1940, lower Normandy, which includes not only Calvados and Manche but also the Eure and Orne departments, contained about one million people, mostly farmers who tended the meadows and pastures that nourished almost as many horses and cows as human beings. With hourly rail service to Paris, the region's abundance supplied the metropolis with milk, cheese, and seafood; its quarries produced a justly renowned building stone; and iron foundries made significant contributions to industry and trade. From their orchards Normans crushed apples into cider for nonalcoholic tastes and distilled them into Calvados brandy for hardier palates.

In the first years of the occupation, the Germans did not make insupportable demands, and relations between inhabitant and conqueror tended to be "correct," following guidelines established by Marshal Philippe Pétain's Vichy government. The departmental prefects, professional administrators appointed by the central government, believed it to be their duty, regardless of personal feelings, to cope with a vexing situation as best they could.[1]

Most trying for the Normans were German requirements along the coast. At first, with Hitler's hopes of bringing Great Britain to heel, there was little need for shore defenses, but after the United States and Soviet Union brought a new perspective to the war, the German high command authorized the engineering experts of the Todt Organization to start construction of what came to be called the Atlantic Wall. The Germans took over a coastal strip several miles wide, evacuated the inhabitants, razed many buildings, conscripted labor, and began to build gun emplacements and pillboxes where an assault could be anticipated. In the Cotentin, the peninsula in the Manche department that contained the military and naval installations at Cherbourg, the Germans established a vast off-limits enclave. To safeguard their defenses, the occupiers either forbade fishing boats to operate or limited them to specified periods. Although such restrictions were not too onerous at first, by the end of 1943, as the threat of invasion loomed, the impositions became more and more taxing. Requiring workmen, the Germans made so many demands on local mayors that a labor shortage was created, forcing some business enterprises to shut down and many farms to lie fallow.[2]

The Normandy prefects did not officially order the inhabitants to evacuate, but a large number of people nevertheless left the province.[3] The many who remained were loath to abandon their farms so long as a living could be gained in the Paris market. Among those who stayed, hundreds of able-bodied young men went underground or joined the Maquis to avoid the STO (Service du Travail Obligatoire—conscripted work force). The Maquis, when armed, provided the military sting of the resistance. By early 1944, the population of lower Normandy had declined to less than a million, possibly 5,000 of whom had enlisted in the resistance, though not necessarily taking active roles. Most of the people, although uncommitted, detested the Germans; only a minority, those who were anti-Semitic and anti-Communist, collaborated with the occupiers and with their French auxiliaries.

Town dwellers without access to farm produce suffered more than those in the countryside. In lower Normandy, Caen was far and away the largest city, with a prewar population around 60,000. It was rivaled in size only by Cherbourg, which, as a military port and shipbuilding center, was not typical of this predominantly agricultural region. No other town in Manche or Calvados had more than 15,000 inhabitants, and after June 1944, the population of Caen fell to about 20,000. When the landings took place in June 1944, the Germans had about 200,000 troops in lower Normandy.

The spring of 1944 brought mounting hardships to the Normans. With the shortage of farmhands and continual bombing of the railways leading to Paris, the export of milk and cheese—an economic mainstay—declined drastically. Thousands of cows, if not commandeered, went unmilked. Although there was no shortage of cattle, meat was rationed as well as butter, salt, and other commodities. Prices went sky-high, and a black market, abetted by the occupying forces, flourished. The Germans, fearful of attack from the sky, had French workmen digging holes and erecting antiglider stakes that came to be known as "Rommel's asparagus." Bombing raids increased, and ever more frequently the air-raid alarms sent disconsolate residents scurrying into their cellars.[4]

Times were hard, but the Normans persevered, sometimes endeavoring to boost their morale by wit and humor. As an example, consider this announcement, ostensibly promulgated by the bishop of Bayeux in late 1943:[5]

> Because of current events, I regret to inform you that Christmas will not be celebrated this year. The stable has been requisitioned, the Holy Virgin and the infant Jesus have been evacuated and Saint Joseph is in a concentration camp; the shepherds have gone underground to escape the labor draft and have joined the Maquis; the sheep have been sent away to be consumed by the masters in Berlin; the Magi have passed into dissidence; the angels have been killed by anti-aircraft fire; the stars have been impounded by the Chief of State; the ass is in Rome; the cow in Berlin.

Such satirical barbs might have been circulated in various ways: posted on a public building, mimeographed, or even published in a clandestine newspaper. Many resistance groups, such as the one known as Combat, identified themselves with a newspaper of the same name. Resistance leaders often doubled as editors-in-chief. The press did much more than publish diatribes and cartoons: It kept the populace informed about the war's progress and served a political purpose, arousing citizens to oppose Vichy and, if Gaullist, to support Charles de Gaulle's French Committee of National Liberation as the French provisional government. Newspapers formed a basic element of the French resistance.[6]

Resistance organizations had proliferated throughout France. In Normandy the prominent ones included groups such as the Confrèrie Nôtre Dame, Libération-Nord, Ceux de la Résistance, and the OCM (Organisation Civile et Militaire). Made up of members of veteran associations along with administrative personnel (for example, the telephone and telegraph company—the PTT), the OCM was one of the more active and influential groups in Normandy. The Communist Party also played a significant role during the occupation but stood somewhat aloof from other units, focusing its efforts on its own resistance organization, the Front National.[7] Attempts to unify all the resistance movements into one organization supporting de Gaulle faltered after the death of Jean Moulin, "the unifier," in 1943. At the time of the Normandy landings, de Gaulle still had to overcome some bickering and rivalries within the ranks.

The resistance opposed the German occupation in various ways. For example, Frenchmen were able to obtain information about German movements and installations and send this information to England. They did this through a complex system that had been established in the early days of the war. We are speaking here not of British intelligence (SIS or M16), nor of foreign networks such as that organized by the Poles, but of French agents operating with de Gaulle's BCRA (Bureau Central de Renseignements et d'Action), cooperating with the British SOE (Special Operations Executive). One such network was the Confrèrie Nôtre Dame, organized by the colorful Rémy (Gilbert Renault-Roulier), who shuttled between France and England, bringing with him much useful intelligence. Another network, Alliance, which involved one of France's well-known heroines, Marie-Madeleine Fourcade, used so many agents with animal cover names it was nicknamed Noah's ark. One of the agents, Jean Sainteny, obtained in March 1944 a 50-foot-long map that identified every German fortification and mine field on the Norman coast. This was taken to London by a daring airlift operation in time for its use by the OVERLORD planners.[8]

The resistance also developed a significant political role that would affect France's liberation. In 1944, most of the resistance movements supported Charles de Gaulle, who was referring to himself as head of the French Provisional Government. Even the Communists gave de Gaulle grudging recognition, but they anticipated a power struggle between de Gaulle's French Committee of National Liberation in Algiers and the National Resistance Council, strongly influenced by Communists, in France. The more support de Gaulle gained from local resistance groups, the better he would be placed to assume power. De Gaulle had already undertaken to sponsor local liberation committees and had named prospective prefects for each department as well as regional prefects called Commissaires de la République. In the department of Calvados, for example, the secretary of the Departmental Committee of Liberation, Raymond Triboulet, was a strong Gaullist, and the commissioner-designate for Normandy had already been named.[9] Gaullist political preparations such as these promised to stand de Gaulle in good stead against the imposition of an Allied military government, which be believed might thwart his political aspirations.

The most dramatic aspect of resistance activity, at least in the public mind, related to sabotage and guerrilla fighting. Although resistance took many forms, most movements possessed a military organ. Gaullist groups such as the OCM supported the Armée Secrète (AS); Communists had their Francs-tireurs et Partisans (FTP); former members of the Armistice Army, disbanded in 1942, established the ORA (Organisation de Résistance de l'Armée).[10] All these were active in Normandy, and all received weapons parachuted to them by SOE, which had its own agents and missions to support sabotage and guerrilla fighting.[11]

Sabotage activities have been recounted in detail by French historians, who enumerate countless different kinds of sabotage: making factory equipment unworkable, damaging German war machines (such as by siphoning water into a tank's gasoline, removing powder from shells), obstructing roads (blowing bridges, placing obstacles in the highways, altering signposts), making the railway network unusable (derailing trains, blowing up locomotives, tampering with signals), cutting telephone and high tension wires.[12]

In 1944, de Gaulle tried to bring resistance military forces into closer cooperation with the Allies. He named General Pierre Koenig commander of the French Forces of the Interior (FFI). Koenig was a staunch Gaullist who had been in command of the first free French troops that fought alongside the British in North Africa. De Gaulle hoped that Koenig, with headquarters in London, would be able to work with Eisenhower's staff so that resistance military action could be coordinated with that of the Allied regulars.[13]

Formation of the FFI stimulated resistance military activity, but as the clandestine fighting units expanded, so did German efforts to penetrate and destroy them. The Gestapo, working with its French auxiliaries, succeeded only too frequently in recruiting traitors willing to identify members of the resistance. Sometimes personal animosity led a citizen to inform the authorities that a neighbor was keeping homing pigeons dropped by the British.[14] More serious was an agent who succeeded in penetrating an entire network, with consequent arrests, deportations, and executions. In 1942, incidents in Normandy brought about harsh reprisals. The resistance wrecked two trainloads of German soldiers, 30 of whom were killed. In retaliation, the Germans arrested 130 hostages and sent 80 to Auschwitz; only seven returned.[15] The infiltration work of a German Abwehr agent known as Raoul de Normandie led to the discovery and destruction of most of the hiding places where guerrillas had stored weapons and explosives.[16]

In spite of German diligence in identifying them, French leaders never ceased trying to bring the guerrillas under the FFI umbrella. All France was now divided into resistance areas; the M region covered Normandy and Brittany. Of most concern to OVERLORD were M-4, including the departments of Manche and Calvados, the landing areas, and the Eure department directly to the west; and M-1 to the south, which included the department of Orne. For coordination with London, Koenig's FFI headquarters had designated regional, subregional, and departmental delegates, who would transmit Allied commands to the respective FFI commanders in their areas. Before the landings, Valentin Abeille, codenamed FANTASSIN, was region M's military delegate, and his deputy, Charles Kammerer (ERIC), was the delegate for M-1 and M-4; a well-known resistance fighter, Marcel Girard (MOREAU), commanded the FFI in region M.

Informed about this FFI structure, the Germans made special efforts to destroy it. On 31 May, a week before D-day, they located Abeille and executed him, an act that influenced his deputy to flee to Paris, where he too was arrested. So many of Girard's staff officers were arrested before the landings that he himself went underground and left the area. All the FFI chiefs in the strategic Norman departments were arrested, executed, or rendered so helpless that by D-day, only the most rudimentary means of communication were left. Marcel Baudot, FFI chief in the Eure department, recounts that at this time he escaped from three traps and was scarcely able to maintain contact with his sector heads.

The Germans and their French auxiliaries not only rendered the FFI leadership impotent but also made devastating inroads against the long-standing movements: They decimated the OCM, practically destroyed the Alliance network, and filled the prisons to overflowing with suspected resisters. Nevertheless, although communication, direction, and coordination were greatly impaired, over a hundred independent Maquis groups, some of them helped by paratroopers from England, continued to harass, sabotage, and ambush the Boche.

On 6 June 1944, the Allies waded ashore along the Normandy coast. Hours before the actual landings, the resistance was brought into the game. To be sure, the top echelons of many networks had been shattered, but a fragmented command remained. Even though coordinated action could not be mounted, individual groups, when they were ordered, sprang to action. Five days before the landings, the resistance had received an alert code message transmitted over the BBC, and on 5 June came the action messages: "Les dés sont sur le tapis," and "Il fait chaud à Suez." Not only were there calls for a general uprising but also specific requests for sabotage of specific targets.[17]

One of the 5 June messages asked the Maquis to hinder movement toward the beachhead of the 275th Division, stationed 125 miles south of Saint-Lô. Among those who answered the call was Louis Blouet, whose own recollections are typical of the many who responded. He had formed an FTP group around Saint-Hilaire, a small town between Avranche and Mortain, in the southern part of the Manche department. On 6 June, he recalled, his group

> cut the St.-Hilaire-Fougères railway line as well as the national highway [N 177, now D 977] from St.-Hilaire to Juvigny-le-Tertre by felling an enormous tree across the road. During the night of 9/10 June this barrier caused a traffic jam of convoys moving to the front. When the convoy broke through in the morning it was neutralized by strafing from three RAF planes. Result: 100 killed, 27 trucks, 2 trailers, 2 guns and other vehicles destroyed.[18]

This sort of action was replicated in other areas. The 275th Division did not reach the front until 11 June. The Maquis had cut six out of seven strategic railway lines.[19] But what the resistance guerrillas could do was limited. Blouet went on to say:

> The impotence of the FTP came mostly from a lack of weapons. Parachute drops furnished some, but the distribution among the various Resistance groups was badly done. There did exist a fusion at the fighting level, but contacts were rare, and furthermore, the [Communist] FTP generated a kind of mistrust, in spite of the political diversity of their recruits. . . . After 5 July, a series of parachute drops brought in long-awaited weapons, explosives, and other material. Unfortunately it was too late for an effective use to be made. As a result of the drops, seven comrades of the group were arrested and shot.[20]

Actions such as those of Blouet's group developed all over Normandy. To the west, around Pont d'Audemer, some 40 miles east of Sword Beach, a legendary figure in the resistance, Robert Leblanc, led his Maquis Surcouf into action. For months he and others (such as Eugène Lefebvre, known as César) had been recruiting fighters, and by D-day they had registered about 2,000 enthusiasts in the Eure department south of the Seine River. All he needed was weapons. As he had contact with London, he expected the imminent landings to be augmented by massive parachute drops that would deluge his men with guns and ammunition. When the BBC messages came, he quickly gathered up 250 guerrillas, only 100 of whom carried arms. He assaulted the local Feldgendarmerie, and after a meeting with Marcel Baudot, the departmental FFI chief, embarked on an effort to cut telephone wires and block German traffic by felling trees across the roads. He was disturbed that no arms drops came his way and that he had little knowledge of what was happening at the beachhead.[21]

A hero of the bocage area between Caen, Saint-Lô, and Vire was Jean Renaud-Dandicolle, known widely as Captain Jean. Only twenty years old, he was one of those Frenchmen recruited to participate in the SUSSEX program. Dropped into Normandy in February 1944, he organized, along with André Le Nevez, the famous Maquis Saint Clair. With weapons and explosives parachuted from England, his group sabotaged German transport after the landings, and he was able to unify several Maquis groups for coordinated action. By regrettable chance, he, his radio operator, and a Canadian pilot were caught by a German patrol on 8 July. All three were executed.[22]

A month earlier, on 10 June, Koenig had ordered the FFI to cease further guerrilla activity. The announcement brought confusion into the field. Breaking off action was not an easy task. The Communist Front National defied Koenig's order and told the FTP to keep on fighting. The FFI regional and departmental commands, already decimated, had no alternative but to let the small Maquis bands such as Blouet's, Leblanc's, and a hundred others carry out what sabotage they could. Most of these operations have been tabulated and described in considerable detail by French historians, notably Jean Quellien, Raymond Ruffin, Jeanne Grall, and Marcel Baudot. Describing certain of the actions in Normandy, Baudot observed:[23]

> In Calvados, the FTP Maquis "William the Conqueror" of the Vire area, together with some SOE groups and FTP units around Lisieux and Orbec, were able, because of weapons drops in September 1943 and June 1944, to embark on intensive guerrilla activity. In the Manche, the FFI departmental chief Yves Gresselin controlled enough arms around Cherbourg to supply military units in the Cotentin, both FTP and OCM. The Seine-Inférieure Department [containing Le Havre and Rouen] . . . contained some fairly well equipped forces—2,000 members of *Libération Nord*'s free corps, 1,350 members of the ORA, 2,100 FTP and

more than 300 BOA [specialists in receiving aircraft]. To these should be added independent outfits such as the "Groupes Sappey de Méribel" at Le Havre, members of "Henri H" at Fécamp, and some 2,000 men in the Pays de Caux. But in May the Abwehr had arrested a large number of leaders, including the departmental chief, Alain Philipeau. No special orders had been given to this sector, not yet involved in the Normandy battle.

In July, with the beachhead consolidated and the breakout offensives getting under way, Koenig's staff, working with Eisenhower's Special Force Headquarters (SFHQ), developed plans that would significantly involve resistance groups. These plans, however, were not to come to fruition in Normandy but in Brittany, where an epic operation, combining special airborne forces (SAS), commando-type units such as the Jedburghs, regular army troops, and the Maquis, succeeded so admirably that it impelled Eisenhower to acknowledge the "inestimable value" of the FFI.[24]

While the Germans bitterly contested the landings at Gold and Omaha, they withdrew from the area between the two beaches, leaving the historic town of Bayeux, about seven miles from the shore, in Allied hands. General Bernard Montgomery parked his command post trailer a few miles to the east of Bayeux, and on 10 June he received Prime Minister Churchill, General George Marshall, and other top commanders. Churchill found it pleasant to observe the prosperity of the countryside: "The fields were full of lovely red and white cows basking or parading in the sunshine. The inhabitants seemed quite buoyant and well nourished and waved enthusiastically."[25]

On this same day in London, Charles de Gaulle was explaining his position at a news conference. He had been invited to England by Churchill to share in the D-day experience and to broadcast a message to the French people. De Gaulle knew full well that he was not immediately going to be recognized as head of a French provisional government, but he was shocked to learn that the invading troops brought with them French money that had been printed without his authorization. Furious, he forbade French liaison officers, in training for months under Supreme Headquarters Allied Expeditionary Force (SHAEF) auspices, to cooperate with Allied authorities in France.[26] De Gaulle was determined that civil affairs in France be controlled by his representatives, not by British or American officers serving as administrators of the Allied military government of occupied territory. France was an ally, not an occupied enemy country; by maintaining this principle, de Gaulle found strong support among the governments-in-exile and in the press. He insisted that he be permitted to visit the beachhead, as did Churchill. With some reluctance and much deliberation, SHAEF authorized the trip.

On 14 June, de Gaulle and his entourage disembarked from the French destroyer *La Combattante*, setting foot in his homeland for the first time in four years. Among those who accompanied him was François Coulet, an experienced administrator who had served as prefect in Corsica after the island's liberation in 1943. De Gaulle named Coulet Commissaire de la République for Normandy and told General Montgomery during a short courtesy visit that he planned to leave Coulet in France. The French leader then moved on to Bayeux. In his own words:[27]

At the sight of General de Gaulle the inhabitants stood in a kind of daze, then burst into bravos or else into tears. Rushing out of their houses, they followed after me, all in the grip of an extraordinary emotion. The children surrounded me. The women smiled and sobbed. The men shook my hands. We walked on together, all overwhelmed by comradeship, feeling national joy, pride, and hope rise again from the depths of the abyss. At the subprefecture, in the waiting room where the Marshal's portrait was still hanging an hour before, Rochat, the subprefect, put himself under my orders pending his relief by Raymond Triboulet. All those who held any office, wielded any power, or fulfilled any functions rushed up to greet me.

De Gaulle saw somewhat more of war-torn France than Churchill had. He and his retinue drove twenty miles west, across the ravaged countryside at Omaha Beach, to Isigny, "cruelly destroyed, where the corpses were still being carried out of the debris." When he returned to London, heartened by his reception in France, de Gaulle anticipated that his visit to the White House, proposed for early July, would pave the way for better relations with the Americans. A conversation with Roosevelt might, indeed, lead the president to accept de Gaulle as head of a provisional government.

The matter of de jure recognition, however, was preempted by an understanding between Eisenhower and Koenig reached on 23 June. The agreement gave Koenig the same authority as other Allied commanders and authorized him to confer with his government (i.e., de Gaulle) on questions involving French interests. De Gaulle found this de facto arrangement so satisfactory that he then permitted the liaison officers to carry out the functions for which they had been trained.[28]

The new French commissioner, François Coulet, lost no time in setting

up an office in Bayeux and obtaining acceptance of his Gaullist administration. His administrative seat should have been Rouen, but with most of
Normandy still under German occupation, he settled for the tiny liberated area that became an important symbol of de Gaulle's authority.
Coulet's choice of Triboulet as subprefect was a good one: Extremely energetic, he served on the departmental liberation committee and was well
known to the Norman populace. Coulet's tact and moderation and his efforts to obtain food and housing won him the support of the mayors and
local liberation committees and the backing of the OCM, the dominant resistance group in the area. A mild opposition was voiced by the bishop of
Bayeux, who wondered why a Protestant should have been given authority in a strongly Catholic region. "My God," Coulet expostulated, "this
war is not finished and the Wars of Religion are starting up again."[29]

The vital question was whether Coulet, representing a government not
recognized by the Allies, had precedence over SHAEF's civil affairs section. The Allied invasion currency proved to be a nasty obstacle not only
on grounds of principle—the right to issue money as a symbol of sovereignty—but also in terms of technicalities—how to establish a rate of exchange. The wily Normans used the controversial notes to pay their taxes
and debts, and in time, monetary specialists worked out the value. By the
end of June, a working arrangement had been reached: Both sides realized that cooperation brought better results than antagonism, and
Coulet's diplomatic approach smoothed out areas of possible friction.
That Coulet's headquarters lay within a British theater of operations probably helped, for Churchill had supported de Gaulle since 1940. Also, the
fact that Coulet was a Protestant did no harm. Coulet recalled that when
Montgomery, a devout Anglican, learned that the commissioner was not
Catholic, Anglo-French relations warmed up considerably.[30]

Coulet and the Normans did not at first develop comparable friendly relations with the Americans, many of whom seemed to consider France a
conquered enemy country. Moving inland from Utah Beach and Sainte
Mère-Eglise, the Americans first encountered French civilians in the Cotentin region, where for three weeks the fighting had been severe. Some
French peasants bitterly deplored the wreckage and pillaging; even
though they detested the Germans, they had not witnessed such destruction during the occupation.

This negative attitude gave some concern to SHAEF officers; worried
about their image, they pressed for a public opinion poll. SHAEF instructed PWD (Psychological Warfare Division) to survey attitudes in the
Cotentin area south of Cherbourg. With the support of Koenig, who obtained the cooperation of Coulet and French administrators, a SHAEF

French civilians search through the rubble in Montebourg, Normandy, sometime in late June 1944.

team recruited ten young French men and women, trained them, and had them interrogate about 1,000 French civilians. The questions related to conditions in France as well as attitudes toward American soldiers. The sampling showed that "the great majority of Normans were 'overjoyed,' given 'new hope' by the Allied landings. . . . To the majority of Normans the conduct of [the American] troops was satisfactory. They offered considerable unsolicited praise of the American soldiers, and the stories of their contacts with the troops are replete with accounts of agreeable and friendly relations for the most part."

About 20 percent of the respondents had some complaints, mostly that the soldiers drank too much and were not sufficiently disciplined; 4 percent complained about stealing and plundering and 3 percent criticized the way the soldiers behaved toward women, with 1 percent registering specific complaints of rape. Queried about conditions in general, only 2 percent complained about damaged homes; the principal concerns were the shortage of food (30 percent), anxiety about family and friends (10 percent), lack of material goods (9 percent), and travel restrictions (9 percent).[31]

Just south of the beachhead extended a strip, ten to fifteen miles wide, in which the struggle to take Caen and Saint-Lô raged on until the end of July. The French people who survived in this war-torn area—possibly 100,000—remembered the dreadful period as "a month in hell."[32] The rain of shells from the air and from mortars and howitzers of both Germans and Allies was incessant. At Saint-Lô, 5,000 tons of bombs fell into an area of four square miles. The fighting south of Bayeux left Tilly-sur-Seulles, which passed from one side to the other no less than 23 times, and Villers-Bocage nothing more than smoking desolation. The countryside became a wasteland.

Thousands of civilians fled not only voluntarily but under German orders. In anticipation of an Allied invasion, the occupying authorities had designated evacuation routes so that strategic arteries would not become clogged with refugees. In many instances the Germans ordered an entire village to be vacated. With no advance warning, the inhabitants gathered up what belongings they could and within hours took to the road on foot, on bicycles, or, when available, in horse-drawn carts. This was an organized exodus, with designated stopping points at which Red Cross and emergency team workers helped the refugees. Even then there were casualties. With German troops also using the roads, Allied strafing planes could not distinguish friend from foe. Months later many would return to their villages to find their homes in ruins.

Caen was especially hard hit. The initial D-day bombing destroyed the town's center, and incessant air attacks soon damaged all the larger buildings. A direct hit shattered the fourteenth-century bell tower of Saint-Pierre, tumbling the "king of Norman belfries" into the nave. All over town the flames defied efforts of firemen and volunteers to halt the awful destruction. By the end of June, the city had become no more than a mass of rubble covered with cinders.

Approximately 20,000 people remained in Caen. Where had they gone? Some hid in cellars, others fled. Around Caen are many quarries, such as that at Fleury, that contained open pits, galleries, and caves. Several thousand residents went to these quarries, surviving as best they could in the dark, damp passages, foraging in daytime for food.

Robert Aron recorded the reaction of a refugee emerging into the sunlight after weeks inside a cave: "I weep as I see the poppies and other wildflowers in the midst of golden wheat that no one will come to harvest. We had forgotten the flowers, the warm sun, the blue sky, the trees. We can hardly comprehend how nature can stay alive when so many of our friends and loved ones are dead."[33]

Others took refuge in what remained of the hospitals and churches.

About 2,000 people found shelter in the medieval church of Saint-Etienne, part of Caen's celebrated Romanesque Abbaye aux Hommes. The Norman historian Jean Quellien described the scene:

> Children run, shout, cry, play hide-and-seek among piles of suitcases and packages, in the presence of vacant-eyed old people resting quietly against the pillars. Here a young woman applies make-up, there some pinochle addicts play cards on the baptismal fonts. Entire families have set up their households in the apse chapels, using the confessionals for drying clothes. On the altars kitchen utensils share the space with sacred vessels. Only the choir has escaped the invasion, but the hubbub scarcely diminishes when the faithful are holding services.

Adjoining Saint-Etienne stood the premises of the Lycée Malherbe (later to become the city hall). It also took in refugees—about a thousand right after the landings and 5,000 more by the end of June. As Quellien noted:

> The Lycée became a veritable miniature town. There was a nursery as well as a morgue. The mayor's office was in one room, the prefect's in another; rooms served as a supply center, as a post office. A temporary social structure was established, quite different from what existed before. Money had lost much of its value and meaning. Rich and poor sat side by side in the outdoor dining area. *Fraternité* was no longer an idle word.[34]

In the same quarter stood the only hospital that had not been destroyed: Bon Sauveur. The accommodations here became completely filled, even though the space was urgently needed for the wounded, who kept coming in—some 2,000 between 6 June and mid-July. In three operating rooms, surgeons tended the wounded around the clock.

Three buildings, Saint-Etienne, the Lycée Malherbe, and the Bon Sauveur hospital, formed an enclave into which most of those remaining in the city had come. The Germans did not interfere, and a group of Frenchmen penetrated the front lines to ask the Allied authorities to respect the asylum area. The Allied command gave its word, and the enclave, marked prominently with Red Cross signs, was accepted as neutral ground.

Articles appeared in the Paris press bemoaning the fate of the starving population of Caen. But according to Quellien, the people were not badly nourished:[35]

> Credit is due the young people, mostly students, of the emergency squads; they volunteered to get food. They went out as scavengers,

found food and clothing, brought their booty back in garbage trucks and wheelbarrows. . . . Water was short as many mains had been broken, but there was wine and cider. They searched, even on the battlefield, for stray or wounded cattle, and herded them by the dozens back to the hospital, where one shed became the slaughterhouse. Every day the cooks from the Lycée, to everyone's amazement, would serve up thousands of steaks. Every morning, in spite of the shells, cows in the area would be milked, and dairies still produced butter and cheese.

Caen was finally liberated on 8 July, but Operation CHARNWOOD, the final assault, brought more grief to the citizens. Before the attack, Montgomery sent in waves of heavy bombers—450 in all—to soften the German defenses. But most of the bombs fell on Caen. Whole neighborhoods, hitherto lightly touched, were smashed into rubble; the university went up in flames—people picked up the charred pages of library books all over the countryside. As the Canadians came in, dazed citizens emerged from the smoke and ashes, disheartened by the destruction but excited by the flush of freedom. Five days later the first daily paper, the *Liberté de Normandie*, was being distributed on the city's torn-up streets.[36]

Only after Paris had been liberated, and the Germans pushed back across the Seine, could the Normans begin to assess the harrowing experiences they had undergone. Their sentiments were eloquently expressed by Henry Bourdeau, after he succeeded François Coulet as Commissaire de la République for Normandy:[37]

How much devastation, how much misery, and how much mourning. The terrible reckoning of a ruthless battle where the adversaries, intent on each other's destruction, at the same time destroy the finest buildings, the splendid countryside—even to the most peaceful hamlet, to the most tranquil farm. Cathedrals ruptured with gaping walls, spires demolished, abbeys razed: Saint-Lô, Montebourg, Caen, Lisieux, Argentan, Rânes, Vimoutiers, and incomparable Rouen. Old mansions in ruins, their ancient furnishings burned or pillaged: Falaise, Gacé, Vire. Towns completely gone with no more than empty space remaining: Villers-Bocage, Aunay-sur-Odon. Pastureland disembowelled by bombs, gutted by tanks, where carcasses of livestock lie rotting: Trun, Livarot, Bavent; forests of lopped-off trees filled with the odor of burned leaves—great dead forests: Cerisy, Andaines, Pont de l'Arche; ports with berths destroyed, anchorages empty: Rouen and Le Havre. And above all the misery of human beings, thousands killed in the terrible bom-

A young French girl makes an American flag.

bardments; tens of thousands homeless, weeping before their demolished hearths, living in caves or in houses that have no roofs.

No final assessment as to the number of civilians killed in lower Normandy (Calvados, Manche, Orne) is available, but the most reliable estimate—15,000—may be low. Caen lost about 2,000. To those actually
killed during the battle must be added those executed by the Germans
and those who died after deportation, possibly 1,500. The resistance in
all of Normandy accounted for another 2,700 killed.

The destruction of property was enormous—Saint-Lô and Caen were
practically obliterated. In Calvados, 26 towns, with a total population of
82,000, were more than 70 percent destroyed. In Normandy as a whole,
120,000 buildings were completely demolished, 270,000 were damaged,
and 118,000 acres of arable land had become temporarily unusable.

Before the war, lower Normandy had surpassed other provinces in the
abundance of agricultural production, especially wheat, oats, and barley,
along with cows, horses, and pork. The German occupation, with its innumerable requisitions, and two months of battle took their toll. Pork
production was hit most heavily, with about half the number of swine remaining in 1944. The area lost over 100,000 cows out of a million, and
dairy products declined by about 40 percent.

Other types of damage should not be overlooked. A large area of Calvados, estimated at 40,000 acres, had been flooded or mined by the Germans. Around the port of Le Havre, demolition crews detonated 520,000
mines between January 1945 and September 1946, at a cost of more than
200 crew members killed. Millions of bomb craters studded the fields.
Damaged generators put out only half the power they had produced before the war.[38]

Reconstruction, while appearing painfully slow to those living in temporary housing, gradually restored Normandy to its prewar prosperity. In
1950 there were more cows, more horses, more hogs, more grain in Normandy than there had been ten years earlier at the beginning of the occupation.

By 1970, Normandy had for the most part recovered from the terrible
damages of the war. Driving through the countryside, a traveler no longer
found signs of the frightful devastation: Lush meadows provided pastur-
age for well-fed cows and horses; the woodlands appeared intact, the
hedgerows bore no evidence of ruts from bulldozer tanks, and the previously demolished towns revealed few indications, except for monuments
and graves, of their earlier misfortunes. The discerning eye, however,

could notice tokens of rebuilding: The homogeneity of Norman stone suggested construction over a brief period, in contrast to the variety found in towns that had grown over several hundred years. Medieval churches, of which Normans are justifiably proud, appeared unscarred, but most had been restored. For example, a close scrutiny of the Abbatiale at Lessay, considered one of the most perfect of Romanesque buildings, reveals that it is a reproduction. The great timber beams of the covered market at Saint-Pierre-sur-Dives, burned to the ground in 1944, were hewed in the twentieth century, not the fourteenth.

A similar to Caen, which the war turned into a mass of rubble, today finds a gracious, pleasant city. Its famous Abbaye aux Hommes is more splendid than ever, its thoroughfares are bustling with shoppers, its drives are bordered with parks and gardens. What happened in Caen may be considered representative of the recovery process among other towns of lower Normandy. By the mid-1960s Caen—once more a thriving urban center—had grown to twice its prewar size.[39]

Reconstruction did not come easily. With their economic base badly destroyed, the hard-hit Norman towns had to await allocations from the central government's newly established Ministry of Reconstruction and City Planning. Two years after the war's end, Paris finally released the funds that would enable large-scale rebuilding to start.[40] Then the city fathers had to reach an important decision: Should they adopt a contemporary architectural style, constructing an entirely modern city of concrete, glass, and aluminum, or try to reestablish the city's 1940 appearance?

In Caen, the first postwar mayor, Yves Guillou, named a celebrated architect, Marc Brillaud de Laujardière, as director of planning, but not until April 1947 did the Municipal Council issue a directive to (1) take into account the town's historical heritage by integrating the public buildings that subsisted as the town expanded, and (2) remodel the destroyed sections by developing a workable structure for the downtown area, providing a modern traffic pattern, and choosing a concept for public architecture that incorporates green areas.

With these decisions, the town began to rebuild in the 1950s. The path was not an easy one: With 10,000 of 18,000 homes destroyed, many property owners faced diverse choices: architectural styles, kinds of utilities, methods of financing. As industry grew, some businessmen were disturbed at the amount of space given over to parks and greenways, but they supported the idea of an industrial park to be opened up in the northwest suburbs. The city nevertheless prospered: Steel foundries, closed since the war, resumed production in 1950; metallurgical products began to be shipped from Caen's small port, with an eightfold increase in traffic between 1946 and 1951. By 1954, the population of greater Caen had swollen to 91,000; by 1980, to 117,000.

During the mayoralties of Yves Guillou and his successor, Jean-Marie Louvel, the city gradually took on a new appearance. The venerable church of Saint-Pierre, at the town's center, received a rebuilt tower and nave. On the bluff to the north, site of the ancient citadel begun by William the Conqueror, the planners designed an entirely new and original concourse. The old citadel—or Château, as it is called locally—and the ramparts surrounding it had been so completely crowded by a mass of buildings that many citizens had not even known it was there. With the rubble cleared away, the Château emerged, surrounded by a park with restored walls and historic buildings. Farther to the north, completely modern buildings housed the University of Caen, which in postwar years rapidly expanded from 3,000 students to 13,000.

In 1965, a new municipal center was dedicated. After negotiations with Paris, the city transferred the church of the famous Abbaye aux Hommes to the French government. In return, the city obtained funds to convert the adjoining eighteenth-century monastery building, formerly used as a school, to a town hall. (The school was the Lycée Malherbe that had ministered to the homeless in 1944.) A spacious esplanade now provides an elegant setting for the abbey and the town's renovated administrative area.

In 1970, Senator Jean-Marie Girault became mayor. He and his colleagues had become distressingly aware that the new generation of young people knew nothing about the war: They had not suffered from Nazi brutality, nor had they witnessed firsthand the shame of occupation or the carnage of war. Girault and others conceived the idea of a museum that would be not simply a storehouse of Battle of Normandy artifacts but a memorial dedicated to peace. The concept became reality on 6 June 1988 when the $15 million Mémorial, an imposing white brick building, was dedicated. The museum is located in the northwest suburbs of Caen, on the site used by General Wilhelm Richter as his command post during the siege of Caen. The exhibits, panoramas, and films portray the ways in which liberty was lost after World War I and how it was regained in the Second World War. In the words of Mayor Girault: "It is our intention to arouse the consciousness of all the men and women, from whatever country, who visit the museum, so that they may realize that the tragedies surrounding liberty are as much a part of our contemporary world as they are of history, and that it is imperative that each individual person should renew his efforts on behalf of Peace, of Fraternity, and of Solidarity."[41]

The Mémorial at Caen is not the only museum in Normandy that helps visitors comprehend the vast drama that unfolded in this province during OVERLORD. But more than any of the others, it testifies to the distress and aspirations of the Norman people when, in 1944, caught in the middle, they suffered through their "month of hell."

Part Three

Assessments: Striking a Balance

14. Two Armies in Normandy: Weighing British and Canadian Military Performance

Raymond Callahan

The Anglo-Canadian force that waded ashore onto Gold, Juno, and Sword beaches that memorable sixth day of June 1944 were the advance units of what would grow into the last great field army imperial Britain would send into battle—the 21st Army Group. Over the next three months, British and Canadian divisions would fight a series of intense, bitter engagements to enlarge and break out from the footholds seized on D-day. Here I revisit those battles, now remembered only by aging veterans and specialist historians, because they remain controversial—and the controversy goes back almost literally to the day after the battles ended.[1] Although the campaign in Normandy produced an Allied triumph, questions have been raised ever since about both the generalship and the combat skills displayed by the British and Canadians during that Norman summer. Could Caen have been taken on the first day? Could the Falaise Gap have been closed more rapidly and completely? And—above all—could a more rapid tempo to Allied operations have led to a German collapse in 1944, with all that might have implied for the history of the next 40 years? That last massive question, a product of the rapidly fading Cold War, must await another time.

Discussions of British generalship in the conquest of northwest Europe have all too often begun and ended with Bernard Law Montgomery. Without denying his preeminence, it is important to keep in mind that in the Normandy fighting he had under him both British and Canadian army commanders—five corps commanders and seventeen divisional commanders. The focus on Montgomery has cast this very large group of senior officers into an undeserved shade. It is useful to remember just how large a force these men controlled. On D-day itself there was parity in the assault—four British and Canadian divisions and four American divisions. For the entire period 6 June–31 August (by which time American formations were flooding in), that parity remained remarkably close. Six American armored, two airborne, and fourteen infantry divisions took part in the Normandy fighting; the Anglo-Canadian contingent also numbered six armored divisions plus one airborne and ten infantry divisions. In addition, independent brigades in 21 Army Group held the equivalent of some five more armored divisions plus an infantry division. It was a remarkable performance for countries whose combined populations were less than half that of the United States and that had been at war 27 months longer. Winston Churchill pointed out in the second volume of his war memoirs that until July 1944, "British" units (which of course included dominion and empire formations as well as those of small allies, such as the heroic Polish armored division that fought in Normandy) outnumbered American units in contact with the enemy worldwide. It is a point that needs to be kept in mind when evaluating the British role in the war and its associated costs to British society.

Commentary regarding the combat performance of these formations has often been sharp. Recently Max Hastings offered a "tired army" thesis to explain such things as the disappointing performance in Normandy of the famed 7th Armoured Division: "Many of the [combat veterans], above all the old regular soldiers, were bitter that after fighting so hard for so long, they were now to be called upon once again to bear the brunt of the battle."[2] Canadian military historians have also been very critical of their (nonveteran) army's performance in Normandy. But collective fatigue, even if there was some satisfactory way to establish its existence and intensity, can explain only why certain units showed a lack of drive. Indeed, many British and virtually all Canadian formations in Normandy had seen no previous combat.

Although commanders' personalities (and quirks) may offer the key to certain episodes of the Normandy battle, and the collective experience of some units may provide insight into others, the whole is rather more than the sum of these parts. It may be more productive to look at the British and Canadian units that went to Normandy as products of institutions whose history—reaching back decades or centuries—conditioned battlefield performance as much as Montgomery's plans, the skills of his principal subordinates, or the prior battlefield experiences of some formations. (And, of course, we must never lose sight of the German army, whose qualities powerfully affected Anglo-Canadian performance).

A general's tools are, after all, the units he controls. Those units, in turn, are more than the sum of the men and equipment they carry on their organizational charts. Morale, leadership, training—all the intangibles that are so hard to quantify but that, time and again, decide battles and wars—have to be considered as well. Finally, an inescapable fact is that the circumstances and outlooks of societies differ. Attitudes and values brought into armies from the larger society survive, perhaps muted, to shape performance in ways that are difficult to measure but nonetheless crucial to how a given army functions. An analysis of British generalship has to begin with a brief look at the weapon those generals sought to wield and the forces that had shaped it.

The first of those forces was the fact that Britain was a small country waging a very big war. Ruthless use of its own assets (especially after Churchill took over) and the ability to draw on American factories allowed Britain to mount a war effort well in excess of its intrinsic strength. Churchill openly acknowledged this reality in the first chapter of *Their Finest Hour*, but it is still often overlooked (especially in the United States).[3] While American lend-lease aid could provide goods, it could not cure the most basic problem of all: not enough men. From their own manpower the British had to maintain the maximum possible industrial and agricultural output, man the Royal and merchant navies and the Royal Air Force (whose heavy bombers were at one point in 1940–41 seen as Britain's only real hope of victory), and provide an army. In the course of the Second World War, from a population of 48 million, the British army raised 48 divisions, and by 1944 British manpower was insufficient to keep even this small army up to strength. In comparison, from its 132 million people, the United States raised 90 divisions, while Germany (population 70 million) fielded 300 and the Soviet Union (population 170 million) 400. Even allowing for the fact that a division meant something different in each of these armies, the figures illustrate the poverty of Britain in what was—and still is—the most fundamental of all resources for war: people. The basic fact with which all British generals had to contend was that, if Napoleon was correct about God's partiality for big battalions, they did not have enough men to ensure His constant goodwill.

Demographics had held the British army to a size that made it the smallest of the major combatants. In addition, its generals had to deal with the legacies of Britain's military past, its social structure, and its industrial deficiencies. Together, these ensured that Britain would field not only a small army but one that was mentally ill prepared and materially ill equipped for the war to which it was committed in 1939.

From the early eighteenth century, when Britain emerged as a great power, until 1914, the Royal Navy had been the key element in national strategy. When British armies fought on the Continent, as they did under Marlborough, again during the Seven Years War, and under Wellington, they did so as part of a coalition. Often called into being by British diplomacy, financed invariably by British subsidies, these coalitions were the natural response of a wealthy maritime power with limited military resources to the problem of how to confront a powerful continental state.

The troops sent to Flanders, or Germany, or Spain (usually relatively small expeditionary forces, swelled by hired German troops) were a gage of Britain's commitment to the defeat of a common enemy. They were not, by themselves, expected to be the decisive force, nor were they.

This strategic approach began to change early in the twentieth century. The German threat to the European balance of power drew Britain inexorably toward a coalition with France and later Russia. Army reformers in England were simultaneously working to remedy the multitudinous weaknesses exposed by the Boer War. They argued for a national strategy that would place the army on an equal footing with the navy. Circumstances favored these changes. The Royal Navy had no impressive spokesman for its strategic vision, such as it was. The French wanted a visible commitment in the form of British soldiers on the ground in France. Gradually, the "continental commitment" was born.

In 1914–18 the British fielded the largest army in their history, 84 divisions (nearly double the 1939–45 total). Over 22 percent of the male population of the United Kingdom served in the army. In this war, the British Expeditionary Force played a central role on the most crucial front (for, unlike the situation in the Second World War, the Russian army could collapse without assuring German victory). After the grinding attrition of Verdun in 1916 and General Robert Nivelle's disastrous 1917 offensive temporarily wrecked the French army, the British Expeditionary Force carried the burden of the war on the Western Front, absorbed the hardest blows in the last great German drive in the spring of 1918, and drove relentlessly forward in attack from August until the armistice. The price for this continental commitment was very heavy. In numbers, nearly 50 percent of the 4.9 million wartime enlistments became casualties—700,000 dead; 1,600,000 wounded or sick. The trauma inflicted by the war on the larger society from which these 2.3 million men came is such a historical commonplace as to need no underlining.

This experience—atypical in terms of the British army's history—formed the backdrop to that army's performance in World War II. Every British army senior commander during 1939–45—all three incumbents of the Chief of the Imperial General Staff (CIGS) office and all those who became theater, army group, army, and corps commanders—were veterans of the First World War, as were a majority of the divisional commanders. Most had served on the Western Front; most had been wounded. Not a few had decorations attesting to great personal courage as a subaltern or battalion officer. The British army remembered World War I with good reason. There were also institutional reasons for remembering it well. In 1918, the British army had found a technique for advancing against the hitherto unbreakable German defenses on the Western Front. Careful planning, methodical and controlled advances, and lavish use of artillery employing carefully orchestrated fire plans were the keys that kept the British remorselessly advancing from August to the war's end. Those months tend to be overshadowed for us by the dreadful carnage of the Somme and Passchendaele, as well as by the knowledge that Germany collapsed in November. They were nonetheless a considerable achievement and one on which the British army pondered during the lean inter-war years.

The likelihood of another major continental commitment seemed slim during those years. The British government ruled out the dispatch of another expeditionary force to the Continent less than a year after the end of the war. That ruling was not changed until the spring of 1939. "Imperial policing" was the army's designated role during the interwar years—a reversion to its Victorian mission. An army committee formed to study the lessons of the Great War did not even issue its report until 1932. The British army between the wars may not have been quite as torpid as impatient reformers such as B. H. Liddell Hart later claimed, but it was certainly not looking forward, as was the German, to the re-creation of a mass army and to a continental war in which the internal combustion engine would avert the stalemate of 1914–18. The "big war" to which students and instructors at the Camberley staff college turned their attention in those years was based on the (victorious) second half of 1918. All the senior British commanders of World War II were inheritors not only of the memories of the trenches and the trauma they had inflicted but also of a concept for the next war that built on the lesson that careful, methodical preparation and rigid control brought victory. All this was reinforced by the type of army British society gave its generals

The stereotypical British army officer of popular imagination is a combination of Hollywood and the undeniable fact that the ineffable Crimean War trinity of Lords Raglan, Lucan, and Cardigan had been allowed to fumble an army to near destruction. By the time of the World War II, however, untrammeled aristocratic incompetence was no longer a factor. The titled landowning class was heavily outnumbered by men whose parents came from the professional and middle classes (Alexander was the second son of an earl, but Montgomery's father was a clergyman and William Slim's a not very successful small businessman; Archibald Wavell and Claude Auchinleck were sons of army officers). Other long-standing problems remained, however. The cult of gentlemanly amateurism, so widespread in British society, had not passed the army by. One extremely capable graduate of the Army Staff College at Camberley (who ended his career a lieutenant general) later recalled that, during his time there in the early 1930s, the commandant placed great emphasis on his assessments of students' on their participation in the college foxhunt.[4] Such attitudes grew out of the cult of the horse (a trait the British army shared with its American cousins). They retarded modernization, although perhaps not quite as much as has been alleged; inadequate resources and, above all, a mission oriented away from Europe probably did as much. From such attitudes also grew the favored persona of many British officers, described by two shrewd British historians as "self-deprecation combined with an ineffable sense of superiority."[5] It proved to be an attitude that alternately baffled and infuriated foreigners. Combined with an outlook that found thrusting professionalism (like Montgomery's) a trifle vulgar was a parochialism born of one of the few aspects of the British army generally admired by foreign observers: the regimental system.

Embedded deeply in the army's history and psyche, regimental loyalties undoubtedly fostered unit cohesion and that redoubtable endurance for which the British soldier was famed. The regimental system promoted other things as well. One bright soldier whose career began in the early 1930s remarked in his memoirs: "I . . . always thought of myself as being in The Black Watch, rather than in the army."[6] Regimental parochialism helped foster the tendency of different arms to fight separate wars, a trait seen at its worst in the Western Desert Force, 8th Army, in 1941–42. Combined arms tactics, at which the Germans excelled, did not come easily to an army that had not been trained for them before the war and whose officers, in any case, felt almost subconsciously that they were part of a federation of quasi-autonomous groups rather than a unitary service.

The power of the regimental system may explain something else about the British army in World War II. What differentiated one regiment from another was not merely the date it had been raised or the names of the engagements on its battle flags but minutiae of dress and custom. All these were useful in bonding men to the extended family of the unit, but they also accustomed the British army to cherishing individual quirks and oddities. This may explain the otherwise hard-to-account-for fact that this very conservative organization spawned more unorthodox and irregular formations than any other combatant power. Neither the revolutionary Soviets nor the American champions of individualism could begin to match the British with regard to numbers and variety of special-purpose units. Whether this was a fruitful use of Britain's limited and shrinking pool of military manpower is another question entirely.

Officers are not the whole of an army. What an army is and does is determined by what sort of soldiers those officers command. Just as the cult of gentlemanly amateurism pervaded those classes from which Britain drew its leadership and affected the type of leader the army had, so the nature and culture of the British working class determined what that army's other ranks were like and were capable of doing.

The gap that had yawned between officers and other ranks before 1914 may have narrowed slightly by 1939, but not by very much. The British officer corps, mostly middle class in background and saddled with attitudes by the landed aristocracy out of the public schools (to use an appropriately equine metaphor), derived from what could be characterized as almost a different nation from the other ranks, who came overwhelmingly, from the British industrial working class. That class, whose culture and attitudes had been shaped by the experience of the first industrial revolution, lived in a remarkably homogeneous and self-contained world, one in which solidarity and pride kept company with poor education, inadequate housing, and minimal health care. These people enjoyed little social mobility. Their general situation, although less bleak than before 1914 thanks to a generation of cautious social legislation that had mitigated many of the harsher features of working-class life, was still a depressing one. Corelli Barnett, surveying the condition to which more than a century of laissez-faire had reduced the British working class by 1939, characterized the result as the creation of a body of "coolies."[7] He also pointed out that British workers were worse trained for work in an advanced technological society than either German or American workers. (And war, as waged by Western industrial nations, was and is very much an advanced technological activity.) In particular, the British working class lacked the sense of initiative that education and self-confidence can foster. They were conditioned to accept the leadership of the sort of people who made up the officer corps of the British army. That acceptance was not necessarily the cheerful "good master and happy servant" stereotype popularized by romantic dramas of the English countryside or servant's hall or by the idealized picture in many officers' memoirs. But it was acceptance nonetheless.

Putting together the characteristics of officers and other ranks, one gets a picture of an army that could be dour and stubborn in defense and dogged in attack but that lacked many of the skills needed in modern maneuver warfare. This should not be exaggerated. The British army had officers who took their profession every bit as seriously as any German (or American), even if being too obvious about it was just "not done." Not all British privates were "coolies" in outlook and abilities. These things are not absolutes but tendencies. One other factor, however, that was close to an absolute and that strongly affected British army performance was the poor quality of much of the material with which British designers and manufacturers supplied that fighting force.

Britain had a number of technological breakthroughs and produced some excellent weapons during World War II. Most of these successes, however, benefited services other than the army. Although the infantry-man's basic Lee-Enfield rifle was sturdy enough and the Royal Artillery's 25–pounder field gun was a fine weapon, the story of British tank development is a dismal one, particularly for the nation that originated armored warfare. To some extent, this was due to the neglect of tank design and procurement by the British army during the interwar years, when a continental commitment had been ruled out by the government. But it was also due at least as much to the poor state of design and production in the British motor industry. By the end of the war the British, in their Churchill and Cromwell tanks, had reasonably successful models, but two-thirds of the tanks in Montgomery's 21st Army Group divisions in 1944–45 were American-made Shermans (and neither Churchill, Cromwell, nor Sherman tanks could face the German Tiger). The story was similar where other vehicles were concerned. The British had a motorized army in 1939, which put them in a category by themselves (and probably saved them at Dunkirk), but the quality of British trucks, especially, left a great deal to be desired. The mobility of the British army owed a great deal to the North American motor industry. Over the course of the war, the British imported one vehicle for every one they manufactured. (And much of what was made at home was mechanically inferior. In the pursuit after the Normandy breakout, the logistic support of the 21st Army Group was seriously compromised by the fact that 1,500 newly delivered British trucks turned out to have defective pistons.) Even in small things the British army was victimized by the failings of its industrial base. One of the minor mysteries of the war is why British industry could not produce a gasoline container at least as good as the German "jerrican," an item gratefully used whenever it could be procured.

What does all this add up to? Britain went to war with an army whose size could never equal that of any of the major continental powers and that, in a long war, would have trouble replacing its casualties. It was an army, moreover, that had not been oriented toward warfare on a continental scale for nearly twenty years and that had virtually ceased to hold large-scale maneuvers during much of that period. Its equipment was, initially, in short supply; if it was British made, it would be unimpressive throughout the war. But the British army's greatest weakness was probably neither its size nor its material, but its approach.

British doctrine for large-unit action was based on the final hard-earned

Churchill tanks in action on D-day.

victories at the end of the First World War. If permitted to fight that sort of battle—careful, methodical, rigidly controlled—the British army would give a good account of itself. This was not the kind of battle it fought, however, until the war was half over and Soviet and American participation had made victory virtually certain. Until then, its lack of skill in maneuver warfare and nearly complete innocence of the combined arms concept resulted in a series of defeats, often at the hands of embarrassingly outnumbered opponents. Many of its problems could never be completely overcome. Nothing could remedy the fact that Britain possessed only a limited manpower base. British industrial failings were also beyond quick remedy. The nature of the other ranks, grounded in the social history of the country for over a century, was also a given.

What then could be changed? Ideas about how to fight—doctrine— were an obvious candidate. These ideas did change, particularly in the second half of the war, with the emergence of new commanders as well as the provision of more (and sometimes better) equipment. But armies are among those institutions most resistant to change. Many of the characteristics of the British officer corps, noted above, were also too deeply ingrained to be changed quickly, even under the stress of war and even at the behest of an autocrat such as Montgomery. Effective doctrinal change means retraining an officer corps—an impossible task in the midst of war. So British generals, in the war's victorious final stages, still had to work with the army bequeathed to them by its own, and the nation's, history. Only with an assessment of how well they did this is it possible to make some reasonable verdict about British generalship in Normandy (and, indeed, in the war as a whole).

The Canadians had a less complicated history—military and social—than the British, but the past gripped them firmly as well. Canada had never known a standing army. After the withdrawal of the British army from North America, Canada's real defense from its only likely assailant, the United States, lay in good Anglo-American relations. Despite the essential indefensibility of the dominion, Canada had a long-standing militia organization (with a minuscule active service cadre), whose geographically scattered units were built around a regimental system that had become as parochial as the British and as firmly embedded in local social structures and politics as had the National Guard in the United States. Canada had only one experience in its national history of large-scale combat on land. The Canadian corps that fought on the Western Front in World War I left behind not only a formidable combat record but an intellectual legacy as well. Just as with the British army, the lessons of 1914–18 and, above all, the techniques of 1918 set the framework within which Canadian professional soldiers thought about any future war. The close links between the exiguous Canadian military establishment and the War Office reinforced this trend.

Perhaps the most powerful reinforcement of the tendency to read World War I lessons into preparation for future war was the man who became the dominant influence in Canadian military affairs in the 1930s, Maj. Gen. A. G. L. McNaughton. Like Alan Brooke in Britain, McNaughton was a gunner with extensive Western Front experience. The Canadian army that began to grow from its militia base in 1939 suffered from the parochial mentality and constricted professional opportunities that were inherent in its history. It suffered as well from the belief, embodied in McNaughton, that modern war, like engineering, was a matter of mastering and then applying certain technical skills. The Canadians ultimately built up a five-division army overseas by 1944. Two of those divisions, one infantry and one armored, moved from the United Kingdom to the Mediterranean in 1943 and did not return to northwest Europe until nearly the end of the war. The other three—one armored and two infantry—remained in Britain and were committed to the eventual cross-Channel attack. These formations had been training, in some cases for years, but much of that training was characterized (on the basis of results in Normandy) as "casual and haphazard" by Canada's official historian.[8] A more recent critique pointed out that much of the Canadian training centered on the "battle drill" concept developed in Britain in 1940 and stopped well short of the battalion-, brigade-, or division-level command skills that would be needed in Normandy. Although exchanges of personnel brought some combat experience back from the Mediterranean, the fact remains that on the eve of D-day, the Canadian divisions in Britain had no combat experience except for 3d Canadian Division's day at Dieppe (hardly an encouragement to boldness). Most British and all Canadian units of 21st Army Group had in common a lack of combat experience as they approached D-day, an attribute they shared with most American formations. But the British and Canadians faced another much more intractable problem, one to which the Americans were substantially immune: shortage of men.[9]

The British army was, of course, based on a conscription system applied to a wider segment of the population than any other major combatant, but it faced a manpower crisis even before 6 June. The War Office had warned Montgomery before D-day that it could replace his anticipated casualties only until the end of June. After that date, the British formations in 21st Army Group would begin to shrink. The Canadians faced a similar problem. Their population base was much smaller than that of Britain. Furthermore, Ottawa's use of that manpower reflected none of the ruthless efficiency that characterized the Churchill administration. Voluntary enlistment for overseas service was the norm in Canada. Legislation providing for conscription (with farmers and factory workers largely exempt) was passed in 1940, but with the proviso that no conscript could be sent overseas involuntarily. In 1942, a national referendum gave the government the power to order conscripts overseas, but that power was not invoked until November 1944 (perhaps one reason being that Quebec had voted heavily no in the 1942 referendum). Meanwhile, the stream of voluntary enlistments in Canada was drying up. On the eve of D-day, the Canadian army units scheduled to deploy in Normandy included both whole British formations and a considerable number of British personnel attached to Canadian formations. If the Canadians were not already confronting a manpower crisis, one was clearly in sight.

One of the most fateful (and least examined) decisions of the war was the choice of deployment areas in Britain for the swelling British, Canadian, and American armies based there. From their concentration areas in western England (which had been determined by available port capacity), an American landing on the western beaches in Normandy was the logical—and logistically correct—decision. It had, however, the effect of committing the British and Canadian units to those beaches closest to open country and approaches to Paris that were sure to be heavily defended by the Germans. As it happened, the formations least able to absorb heavy casualties landed where Montgomery's operational design was most likely to involve precisely that result. It is hard to show that manpower problems by themselves determined any single battlefield decision during the Normandy fighting. The difficulty of replacing heavy losses was, however, one of those factors that were always present in the minds of British and Canadian commanders and that form the background to any assessment of Anglo-Canadian performance in Normandy.[10]

British and Canadian armies had one other factor in common: Both were trained according to the same doctrine. That doctrine, born of World War I, had gone through a great many changes since 1940. The British army and its associated dominion formations had gone to war in 1939 with an unresolved argument about the role of mechanized mobility embedded in its thinking. The combination of guns and infantry that had won the battle of the last hundred days in 1918 remained the backbone of the British approach to war on land. Tanks figured in the picture, of course; they would support the infantry as they had in 1918. However, there was a competing vision—that of the "apostles of mobility"—that emphasized speed, maneuverability, deep penetration, and dislocation of the enemy's command and control system as the road to a quick, decisive victory. The first eighteen months of the war appeared to vindicate their views. Taken together, the German victory in Poland, their even more spectacular success in France, and then Sir Richard O'Connor's dramatic blitz in the Western Desert at the end of 1940 seemed to demonstrate the soundness of the arguments made by the advocates of independently acting armored formations. In a sense, the history of British doctrine over the next four years is the story of the attempt to replace this misperception with a more balanced combined arms approach to battle.

The sixteen months of desert fighting against Rommel that ended with the defeat of the Desert Fox by Auchinleck at the first battle of Alamein in July 1942 (the decisive battle of the desert war) demonstrated all the weaknesses in the structure and equipment of British and dominion armies, not to mention the fallacies in their approach to battle. (It also induced in British armored formations a caution that would remain with them for the rest of the war.) Montgomery's arrival marked an important turning point, not so much in the desert war—Auchinleck had already deprived Rommel of his one slender chance of victory—but in the British army's method of fighting. Beneath the arrogance, insensitivity, and abrasiveness that made Montgomery so disliked during his lifetime and so controversial in retrospect was a hard core of dedicated and intelligent professionalism. One of Montgomery's favorite words was "balance." British tactics had become unbalanced in the desert, with almost fatal results. Montgomery's signature, from his first battle at Alam Halfa on, was tight control by the army commander and the utilization of all his army's assets, including tactical air power. At Alamein, it was Montgomery's infantry and gunners who crumbled Rommel's forces. The performance of his armor was less impressive both during the battle and in the pursuit. Although there are a variety of reasons for this circumstance—not the least of which were the flaws in Montgomery's own design for the initial phase of the battle—Alam Halfa and second Alamein set a pattern that would become standard: the restoration of infantry and artillery to the central role on the battlefield, the integration of tactical air power into the battle plan, and an end to the virtual independence of the armored formations.

The war was also changing by late 1942. Forced on the defensive, German tactics became a modernized version of the elaborate defensive schemes seen on the Western Front in 1917–18, with larger and more heavily armed and armored tanks thickening the defensive carapace through which attackers had to grind their way. Montgomery's strategy was in some ways simply the Western Front tactic of attrition updated technologically and managed intelligently. Montgomery relied on guns, air power, and whatever he could get from his own armor to spare his infantry as much as possible. He had, of course, no choice; Britain's inadequate supply of manpower, not to mention national psychology, made any other approach unworkable. Montgomery saw this clearly. Planning the invasion, he kept eight armored brigades with some 1,400 tanks, as well as six brigades of artillery (700 guns) and six Royal Engineer groups, under army group command. He thus had available the firepower of some half dozen additional divisions. When Montgomery's infantry set out to crumble the enemy, they would not fail for lack of fire support.[11]

The new technique was supported by changes in the organization and training of the army in Britain (many of which Montgomery had a hand in before leaving for Egypt). Artillery control was recentralized, and the ability to bring down devastating support fires was perfected; ground-air cooperation, in the face of high-level RAF indifference, was brought to a high pitch of efficiency. The web of radio links that functioned as the nervous system of the Western Allies' industrialized, high-tech approach to battle was vastly improved. By the eve of the landings in Normandy, it was plain that victory over the German army in the west was much more

Generals Eisenhower and Montgomery confer during their Channel crossing to the Normandy beachhead.

likely to resemble 1918 than the slashing tank assaults of 1939–41. Much of the technology and technique for an updated version of 1918 were in place. In Montgomery, the Anglo-Canadian armies had a commander who was a careful craftsman of controlled attrition. The question remained whether Anglo-Canadian manpower resources were equal to the stress of attrition (however cautiously done) and whether the skills of Montgomery's subordinates were equal to the demands that defeating a still formidable German army would place on them, whatever the weight of material with which they were supported. If lavish firepower could not help the infantry take their objectives without great loss, lack of infantry reserves would soon present Montgomery and his commanders with an intractable problem.

At this point, Montgomery's plans and intentions need to be looked at briefly. The first task, of course, was to get ashore. To make the securing of the lodgment certain, he had insisted on broadening the front and increasing the weight of the initial assault. Indeed, the fears of possible D-day carnage on the beaches—felt from Churchill down to the subaltern level—may have induced a measure of caution that, when added to all the other factors already mentioned, made the initial Anglo-Canadian operations in Normandy sufficiently slow that the Germans were able to prevent Montgomery from taking Caen, as planned, on the first day. Montgomery, of course, later claimed that this was comparatively unimportant next to the objective of drawing in and wearing down German armor. Suspicion must linger, however, that Montgomery hoped that attrition might lead to breakthrough on his army group's front.

In any case, failure to reach Caen denied him the ability to break out into the open country beyond, which was much coveted by the Allied air commanders who were desperate for airfield sites in the bridgehead. Failure to get those airfield sites would figure notably in the indictment that the senior Allied airman, Air Chief Marshal Sir Arthur Tedder, would draw up against Montgomery over the next few weeks. Nonetheless, the first objective—a solid beachhead—was attained at a cost of some 3,000 casualties out of 75,000 men in the three assaulting divisions (two British, one Canadian), whose collective D-day experience was less traumatic than that of the Americans at Omaha Beach. Within that figure, however, lurked another, more ominous, one. A fresh, full-strength British infantry battalion, 1st South Lancashires, suffered casualties amounting to thirteen officers and 96 others in knocking out a single German coastal strong point. One comment on this small action seems particularly apposite: "soldiers learn quickly and the lesson most deeply ingrained in veterans is caution."[12]

The rest of June and early July saw continuous fighting as the bridgehead slowly expanded. Montgomery's overall design to pull German armor into the battle against the Anglo-Canadian advance and "write it down," thus facilitating an American breakout at the western end of the lodgment, was made easier by the obvious fact that an Allied breakout from the eastern end of the beachhead was the most dangerous possibility the Germans faced. Rommel had to commit his armored formations in the British-Canadian area to enable his depleted infantry to hold on there. The relentless hammering by the Allied ground and air assault was inflicting massive losses on the Germans. Just before he was wounded on 17 July, Rommel reported that, since D-day, he had suffered 100,000 casualties, with replacements covering barely 5 percent of that number. Anglo-Canadian casualties, however, especially in infantry units, were also alarmingly high. Until the end of June, replacements covered these losses, but as fighting intensified throughout July and losses mounted, the situation worsened. In Operation EPSOM (25–29 June), 8 British Corps seized a bridgehead across the Orne River in an attrition battle as intense as anything in 1916–17. Infantry losses were over 50 percent. "Wastage" on this scale could not be covered. Montgomery was on the horns of a dilemma. Maintaining the pressure on the Germans was necessary not only in terms of his operational design but seemed increasingly important to the maintenance of his personal position as well. By early July, uneasiness about the stalemate in Normandy was widespread in the press, among American commanders, and, most ominously, at Supreme Headquarters Allied Expeditionary Force (SHAEF) and at Ten Downing Street. To continue the crumbling process, gain ground south of Caen, and perhaps reach the longed-for open country, Montgomery mounted GOODWOOD, an operation that provides a good case study of British combat effectiveness.

The solution to the problem of how to attack and possibly break out of the beachhead was—or at least seemed to be—clear. "The generals, from Montgomery onwards, together with his corps and army commanders, perceived that all their plans depended on protecting their infantry by one means or another until they were close enough to the enemy to use their own weapons," Shelford Bidwell and Dominic Graham noted.[13] Since it was clear that the tactics of combined tank-infantry attack had not yet been mastered by some British formations, the solution was to use firepower—from the air, from artillery, and from a mass of armor—to break through the German crust. In fact, it was not Montgomery but Lt. Gen. Miles Dempsey, the commander of British Second Army (and a former student of Montgomery's at Camberley), who developed the concept for GOODWOOD.[14] Three armored divisions were to deploy in the crowded Allied bridgehead on the east bank of the Orne River and then strike south, preceded by a massive bomb carpet laid by some 1,600 heavy and 400 medium bombers.

Montgomery had clearly revised his expectations for the performance of British armor since he had formed an armored corps before second Alamein. In fact, in January 1944, he had stated that he would not employ such a corps in Europe. The passage of time had changed none of the fundamental problems, observable in the desert fighting, that had led to Montgomery's disenchantment. Brig. James Hargest, a New Zealander with vivid memories of the desert, wrote after observing the fighting in Normandy, that British armor was "badly led and fought." He attributed this to the "cavalry mentality" of many armored regiments: "Because there is no work for cavalry, the Cavalry Regiments were given tanks. The officers are trained in armor not because they like armor, but because they are cavalrymen. They are in armor because they like horses in other units."[15]

Dempsey persuaded Montgomery to use the sort of armored punch that had failed to break through initially at Alamein—and to use it in the same way, deploying a huge mass of vehicles through a congested front held by another corps. Why did Montgomery accept Dempsey's idea? No definitive answer seems possible, but he may have decided that it would certainly continue the crumbling process and just possibly do more. Montgomery was more flexible than he would ever, in retrospect, admit.

Another curious aspect of GOODWOOD is the corps commander chosen to conduct the attack. Lt. Gen. Sir Richard O'Connor of 8 British Corps, an infantryman by background, had planned and directed Operation COMPASS, the one authentic British blitzkrieg of the war, which destroyed the Italian forces in North Africa in the winter of 1940–41. His reward was to precipitate the arrival of Rommel in the theater and to be captured during the first German offensive in the spring of 1941. Escaping at the time of the Italian armistice, after two and a half years as a POW, O'Connor reached Allied lines in December 1943. Six months later he was a corps commander in Normandy. Whether this was a wise decision on the part of Brooke (who complained constantly in his diaries about the quality of candidates for high command) and Montgomery (who was related to O'Connor by marriage) is questionable. O'Connor was not the same man he had been in 1941—nor was it the same war. Dempsey told O'Connor not to worry about anything but getting his armored and motorized infantry units to their objectives, the ridge line south of Caen. But O'Connor's grip on the battle is hard to discern. His three divisional commanders were an ill-assorted trio. Maj. Gen. G. P. B. ("Pip") Roberts of the 11th Armoured Division may have been Britain's best tank commander. Maj. Gen. A. H. S. Adair of the Guards Armoured Division, however, had never commanded an armored unit in combat; Maj. Gen. G. W. E. J. Erskine's 7th Armoured, the legendary "Desert Rats," had already turned in a series of disappointing performances. Launched on 18 July to the accompaniment of a crashing fanfare of bombing—7,700 tons—and a very optimistic communiqué from Montgomery, GOODWOOD added 35 square miles to the beachhead but stalled in front of a screen of German antitank guns and dug-in armor. As at Alamein, infantry were needed to clear the way, but this time they were not available. British tank losses were considerable (11th Armoured alone lost over 126 on 18 July) but easily replaceable; personnel losses were low—the three armored divisions together suffered only 521 casualties that day. An associated 2 Canadian Corps attack, Operation ATLANTIC, produced infantry casualties of 76 percent due to inexperience and poor cooperation between infantry and supporting armor—whose casualties were 7 percent.

GOODWOOD raises in concentrated form the key questions about British combat performance in Normandy: the quality of Montgomery's subordinates and of the planning process, and the vicious circle that sought to spare the infantry (itself subject to higher than necessary casualties due to poor combined arms training) by substituting firepower, which, in its armored form, could not penetrate the German defenses without infantry. All this not only stultified GOODWOOD but nearly produced a very high-ranking casualty: The disappointment caused by yet another failure led Tedder to hint broadly that Eisenhower would find British support for a move to replace Montgomery.

In fact, Montgomery was more secure than he seemed. Brooke still supported his longtime protégé. More important, whatever occasional irritation Churchill may have felt with Montgomery, he understood that "Monty" symbolized victory to an increasingly weary Britain, especially to the part of it in uniform. Moreover, the Normandy campaign was at last entering its decisive phase. Bradley had taken Saint-Lô the day GOOD-WOOD began. On 25 July, Operation COBRA shattered the German front, and American armor began to break through the dislocated German defenses and push deep into their rear. An envelopment of the whole German position in Normandy glimmered on the horizon.

Montgomery now pushed the Anglo-Canadian forces hard against a German front that was at last beginning to give ground. The urgency of the situation—and perhaps Montgomery's eagerness to vindicate himself to assorted critics in his last days as Allied ground commander—produced a number of command changes. Under Lt. Gen. G. C. Bucknall, 30 British Corps had not earned a distinguished record on the beachhead. Now, pressed by Montgomery, Dempsey ordered Bucknall to "get on or get out" and within 24 hours removed him.[16] His replacement was Brian Horrocks, another former Montgomery student at Camberley, whose performance during MARKET GARDEN in the autumn would be as problematic as O'Connor's in GOODWOOD. At the same time, Dempsey made a clean sweep of 7th Armoured's headquarters: Erskine went, as did his chief staff officer, artillery commander, and the commanding officer of the division's armored brigade. The problem was not so easily resolved, however. Weaknesses in technique and the institutional problems noted by Hargest may have been compounded by lackluster leadership, but they were too deep-rooted to be solved simply by changing commanders (even if a large pool of talented senior officers had been available). The fundamental problem of declining infantry strength was beyond any solution. Within a month of COBRA, Montgomery would be forced to break up the first of his divisions to provide the replacements the War Office could no longer find.

As American armor curled around the German western flank in early August and Hitler's abortive counteroffensive at Mortain thrust German armor deeper into a rapidly developing sack, Montgomery launched a series of operations south from Caen toward Falaise, the point at which the mouth of the sack could be drawn shut. The spearhead of these operations was the second of his armies, Lt. Gen. G. D. H. Crerar's First Canadian Army. If the formations of the Second British army had problems rooted in demography and the social history of the British army, the Canadians had to face difficulties that were the product of how their army had grown and then trained during its long wait in Britain.

The British army grew fifteenfold from its prewar base; Canadian expansion was fiftyfold. Although there had been Canadian troops in Britain since 1940, their training, as noted above, had important gaps. Training above the individual level in one Canadian division had been substantially neglected as late as March 1944. Montgomery admired the quality of Canadian soldiers and junior officers, although he had some reservations about their senior commanders. Lt. Gen. Guy Simonds of 2 Canadian Corps was an exception. Montgomery almost certainly would have preferred the young and dynamic Simonds to Crerar as Canadian army commander.[17] But Simonds's corps, while launching the subsidiary ATLANTIC operation in support of GOODWOOD, had suffered a tactical disaster, as noted above. Tank-infantry cooperation was poor; one infantry battalion collapsed into disorder; another, stranded without adequate support, was decimated. The disparity in infantry and armored casualties previously noted tells the story of a poorly coordinated attack better than any narrative.

By the time the drive down the Falaise road began, First Canadian Army had just become operational, but with only a single corps—Simonds's 2 Canadian Corps. The Falaise operations indicated that Simonds and Crerar were even more willing than Montgomery and Dempsey to sack commanders. The commander of the 4th Canadian Armored Division, two of the nine brigadiers in Simonds's corps, as well as the commanding officers of two armored regiments and five infantry battalions lost their jobs. Simonds may have been ruthless with his subordinates, but he also displayed an intense —and Montgomeryesque—desire to economize on blood through the use of firepower. Operation TOTALIZE, launched on 8 August by Simonds, featured a GOODWOOD-style preliminary air strike, then an armored advance with infantry following in improvised armored personnel carriers. The attack rolled forward into a massive dust cloud and some badly shaken defenders but, like GOODWOOD (or second Alamein, for that matter), failed to achieve the breakthrough hoped for. It was a week before the Canadians took Falaise, ringing down the curtain on the Normandy fighting.

What, in a half-century's retrospect, can we make of it all? Reflecting on British military performance in Norway in the spring of 1940, General Sir David Fraser commented that "British training appeared, even at its best, to have produced an army over-deliberate, slow, reactive."[18] Had anything changed by 1944? One could argue that the traits Fraser listed had proved remarkably durable, a testimonial to how deeply ingrained institutional habits can become. Indeed, they seem to have affixed themselves as well to a second army drawn from an entirely different society. But there is another side to the story.

This chapter has focused on the problems faced by British and Canadian units, but it is important to remember that—despite all difficulties stemming from demography, history, training, equipment, and leadership—British and Canadian formations fought their way forward in the face of bitter resistance and casualty levels occasionally reaching Western Front proportions. The 12th SS Panzer Division that faced the Canadians on the Falaise road—like its opponents, new to combat—is often cited as an example of the German army's fighting power. So it was. But it would be wrong not to recognize the courage and determination of the British and Canadian troops who were committed, as their initiation into combat, to the technically more difficult task of repeatedly attacking the formidable defense they faced. One historian has recently advanced the thesis that discussions of the quality of Allied soldiers and commanders are, in a sense, beside the point. Allied material superiority was so great that its simple application would bring a victory wrought by "brute force."[19] Without denying the element of truth in this thesis, it is perhaps time to recognize that the unvoiced assumption in many critiques of Allied operations—that it was somehow unfair to defeat the Germans by anything other than man-to-man infantry combat—is a decidedly curious way to assess World War II. As Churchill wrote in the autumn of 1941: "he is an unwise man who thinks there is any *certain* method of winning this war, or indeed any other war between equals in strength. The only plan is to persevere."[20] Once the tactical arabesques of 1939–41 were no longer possible, the only choice Allied (or German) commanders had was to fight within the parameters their strength, technology, and doctrinal beliefs allowed. Perseverance might have been the watchword of the Anglo-Canadian armies in Normandy. Perhaps the last word about the lavish use of material to achieve victory belongs to the greatest British army commander since Wellington, Field Marshal Sir William Slim. He is said to have replied to criticism of the margin of superiority he accumulated in his first battle as an army commander by remarking that the use of a pile driver to crack a walnut did not matter as long as one had the pile driver and was indifferent to the subsequent appearance of the walnut.

The British and Canadian (and American) soldiers who fought in Normandy were the product of national and institutional histories that gave them certain great strengths and some not inconsiderable weaknesses. Given that mix, it is hard to argue that, however much this or that individual action might have been better handled, the British and Canadian armies in Normandy could reasonably have been expected to do much better than they did. Most major wars turn into contests of attrition. World War II in Europe was no exception. Certainly, some Anglo-Canadian operations in Normandy can be critiqued for faulty design, execution, or both. But to demand, as some critics do, a radically different level of performance is to demand a different history leading up to that performance. As Field Marshal Lord Kitchener told Churchill during the previous war of attrition against Germany, Britain had to make war as it could, not as it would like to—nor, he might have added if he had followed the ongoing war of words about Normandy, as subsequent writers might wish it had.

15. Assessing American Military Leadership: Two Postinvasion Corps Commanders

Robert H. Berlin

Assessing American military leadership in post–D-day operations from the perspective of 50 years should be a relatively easy task for historians. Unlike the situation with the presently emerging examination of American military leadership in the Gulf War, the documents are available and unclassified, there is ample secondary literature covering many significant aspects of the campaign, and the major military leaders themselves, for the most part, are dead and unable to champion their claims.[1] Yet the debate goes on. How well prepared were American high-level military commanders for the demands of modern war and for leading large units in sustained, coordinated operations against a determined foe? To answer the question, one needs to look at events long before D-day, to the preparation of military leaders, and at those after the invasion, to the actions of commanders in France and Germany that secured the initial D-day success.

Although American high-level commanders at army level and above (Omar N. Bradley and George S. Patton, for example) have secured their reputations, the actual battles were fought by lower-level commanders who also merit attention.[2] Of particular interest are corps commanders who executed the broad plans of their superiors and carried out the actual operations planned at higher headquarters. A total of 34 U.S. Army general officers commanded 22 U.S. Army corps in World War II.[3] Twenty-one corps commanders served in the European Theater of Operations (ETO), and two American corps participated in the D-day landings: VII Corps, commanded by General J. Lawton Collins, and V Corps, led by Maj. Gen. Leonard T. Gerow. Though Collins in retirement documented his own contributions by writing a fascinating autobiography, neither of the D-day corps commanders has to date been the subject of a full-blown biography.[4] Nor, with very few exceptions, do we have studies of those senior officers who succeeded to division and corps command in the weeks and months after 6 June 1944.

For many years, assessments of American military performance in the

European theater tended to take the accomplishments of senior commanders as a given, emphasizing such other factors as the seemingly inexhaustible torrent of munitions available to the U.S. Army and a deeply flawed conception of war. As Russell Weigley observed, "In the end, the American army rumbled to victory because it had enough material resources to spare that it could exhaust the enemy's resources even without adequately focusing its own power for a decisive, head-on battle of annihilation, or exploiting its mobility in behalf of a consistent strategy of indirect approach."[5] Nevertheless, the overall performance of the U.S. Army's senior battlefield commanders, taking into account the emergence of "superstars" such as Patton and Bradley from almost total obscurity prior to 1941, continued to earn comparatively high marks.

Noted World War II historian Martin Blumenson raised some troubling concerns about America's World War II leaders in Europe. Blumenson, editor of *The Patton Papers* and biographer of Mark Clark, questions whether U.S. high-level military leaders were well prepared by education and experience to face the challenges of war in their time. Blumenson asserts that the commanders' record of accomplishment was "essentially bland and plodding." He claims that "far too many officers failed to realize that the time-and-space factors prevalent in World War I were now outmoded and irrelevant." And Blumenson asks, how good were our military leaders in World War II? Were they exceptional or merely adequate? Could we have won with almost any other group in command?[6]

These are relevant and troubling questions for historians of World War II. Although it may be surprising that they are still being asked 50 years after the events in question, time and distance from events should not detract from finding objective answers. At General Dwight D. Eisenhower's request, on 1 December 1944 Bradley submitted a ranking of 32 senior American commanders in the ETO. If one strikes off staff, services, and Army Air Forces generals, two relatively obscure corps commanders— Manton S. Eddy and Edward H. Brooks—occupy median places on Bradley's list.[7] On statistical and other grounds, an examination of the careers of two lesser-known World War II corps commanders who led post–D-day operations can illumine questions about U.S. Army World War II leadership. Generals Edward H. Brooks and Manton S. Eddy are not names commonly associated with American World War II leadership, though each played a significant role in achieving Allied victory in Europe. Assessing their development as officers and their military achievements provides a keyhole view of how the small interwar army produced the leadership that defeated the Germans.

What were the attributes of a successful corps commander and high-level World War II combat leader? First, to be selected for corps command, success as a division commander, particularly in combat, was a vital requirement. Particularly after Normandy, and for younger commanders such as Brooks and Eddy, proven battlefield leadership of a division was a necessity.

General George C. Marshall, the Army Chief of Staff, who had a direct role in and responsibility for selecting many of the corps commanders, emphasized that "vital qualifications for a general officer are leadership, force and vigor." In a December 1942 memorandum to General Lesley J. McNair, commander of Army Ground Forces, Marshall emphasized that "ordinary training, experience, and education cannot compensate for these and the officers who possess them must be singled out and advanced regardless of other considerations."[8] Marshall sought capable, forceful leaders who were chosen based on ability rather than seniority.

General Matthew B. Ridgway, who successfully commanded at both the division and corps levels during World War II, described in his memoirs the characteristics of the World War II U.S Army corps commander:

> He is responsible for a large sector of a battle area, and all he must worry about in that zone is fighting. He must be a man of great flexibility of mind, for he may be fighting six divisions one day and one division the next as the high commanders transfer divisions to and from his corps. He must be a man of tremendous physical stamina, too, for his battle zone may cover a front of one hundred miles or more, with a depth of fifty to sixty miles, and by plane and jeep he must cover this area, day and night, anticipating where the hardest fighting is to come, and being there in person, ready to help his division commanders in any way he can.[9]

Determining how and to what extent two corps commanders acquired, developed, and displayed the necessary attributes will help unravel the "mystery," as Blumenson terms it, of the miracle by which the U.S. Army produced its World War II leadership.

Brooks and Eddy are worthy of study for several reasons. Although they were quite different in personality, demeanor, appearance, and outlook, they were contemporaries whose careers paralleled each other, including their precommissioning education, World War I combat experience, interwar professional education, instructor duties, World War II commands, and postwar service. They entered active duty within nine months of each other—Eddy in late November 1916 and Brooks in August 1917—and they retired within one month of each other in 1953.

Above all, they served their country. Yet history has not been kind to either. Brooks is mentioned only in division and corps histories, while Eddy's claim to fame in terms of historical memory is his relief of Maj. Gen. John S. ("P" for Professor) Wood, commander of the Fourth Armored Division, in December 1944, a subject of lasting controversy. They were "supporting actors" in the historical drama of World War II.

Certainly Eddy and Brooks were not born leaders, even if such persons exist. Neither one came from military families nor did they attend the Military Academy. Manton Sprague Eddy was born in Chicago, Illinois, on 16 May 1892. He never lost the midwestern twang in his speech and always called Chicago his home, though he was seldom there. He graduated from the Shattuck School, a military preparatory school, in Faribault, Minnesota, in 1913. Instead of going to Princeton with his younger brother, who became a successful Chicago business executive, he entered the army in November 1916, commissioned as a second lieutenant of infantry.[10] He was promptly promoted to first lieutenant and went to the First Provisional Officers Course of the Army Service Schools at Fort Leavenworth in March 1917. His instructor noted that Eddy "gives promise of being a very good officer."[11] Similar comments appear in his other early officer efficiency reports. His first duty posting was to Eagle Pass, Texas, for Mexican border service. From there, Eddy went to the 39th Infantry at Syracuse, New York, in May 1917. He moved with the 39th to Camp Greene, North Carolina, and on 30 April 1918 Captain Eddy sailed as part of the 4th Infantry Division to France.[12]

Edward Hale Brooks was born 25 April 1893 in Concord, New Hampshire. By virtue of his name and upbringing, Brooks inherited staunch New England values. His father came from Maine and his mother, of English birth, came from Nova Scotia. Brooks, known to his family and friends as Ted, was an outdoorsman who liked riding and fishing. He earned a B.S. degree in civil engineering from Norwich University in 1916. While there, he was a member of the 1st Vermont Cavalry, the Corps of Cadets. Upon graduation he worked as an engineer for a year with the Koppers Company in Pittsburgh, Pennsylvania. Commissioned a second lieutenant of cavalry in August 1917, Brooks was promoted the same day to first lieutenant. He attended the Army Service School at Fort Leavenworth and joined the 76th Field Artillery at Camp Shelby, Mississippi. He moved with his regiment to New Jersey in March 1918 and took command of a detachment of the 3d Field Artillery Brigade. In April he too sailed for France.[13]

Eddy and Brooks arrived in France with some military schooling and less than two years of duty experience. They both participated in the major campaigns of the American Expeditionary Force. During the Aisne-Marne offensive, Eddy commanded a machine-gun company of the 7th Infantry Brigade of the 39th Infantry, 4th Infantry Division. He was wounded in action during the offensive on 5 August 1918, though not evacuated for a day; he remained on duty and continued to give directions for the action of his company. Returning for duty in late October and having been recommended for promotion to the temporary grade of major, he was assigned to command of the 11th Machine Gun Battalion on 1 November 1918. According to his regimental commander, "He conducted the Battalion with energy and ability during the final stages of the Meuse-Argonne offensive, though his battalion was in reserve." He led the battalion on the march of the army of occupation into Germany. His commander noted that Eddy led his unit with "energy and marked skill."[14]

In France, Captain Brooks served with the 76th Field Artillery, 3d Field Artillery Brigade, 3d Division. He participated in the Marne, Saint-Mihiel, and Meuse-Argonne campaigns. His personnel file contains some specific documentation concerning the cancellation of his award of a Silver Star for extraordinary heroism—and its upgrading to a Distinguished Service Cross. On 5 October 1918, while Eddy was recovering from his wounds, Brooks was near brigade headquarters on the north slope of Montefaucon when five ammunition trucks came over a hill and came under heavy artillery fire, killing some of the truck drivers. The fire was high explosive mixed with gas. Amid exploding trucks, heavy fire, and flying splinters, the unwounded drivers abandoned the trucks and took cover. Two burning trucks continued to draw fire.

According to the brigade commander, Col. William. M. Cruikshank, "Capt. Brooks, instead of seeking shelter, as he might well have done, called for volunteers to help remove the loaded trucks from the vicinity of the burning ones and from their exposure to hostile fire." He added that Brooks and his men performed an "act of especial bravery under heavy hostile fire and outside of the sphere of their usual duty."[15] This act, according to the colonel, resulted in the saving and delivering of valuable ammunition and possibly saved the lives of others in the area—including Colonel Cruikshank. Clearly, Brooks was a cool and confident man under fire. His heroism would be repeated in World War II.

Eddy and Brooks saw the face of battle in World War I. They proved that they could successfully lead men under fire. Eddy's wound and rise to battalion command and Brooks's artillery service and heroism influenced their knowledge of war, though their combat time equaled only six months. They both returned to the United States experienced, dedicated, professional soldiers.

They also returned with an understanding of war based on rifle, machine-gun, and artillery tactics—a type of warfare that would not occur in World War II. They experienced leadership that relied on the telephone, the usefulness of the horse for transport, and the ponderous movement of large military organizations.[16] In size, organization, and purpose, the units they were to command in World War II were far removed from their World War I counterparts, and neither Eddy nor Brooks had any experience of armored warfare, though they probably witnessed tanks in battle. However, given that both men were to command large armored forces in World War II, their World War I experiences provided limited tactical or operational vision for the future.

At the conclusion of hostilities, Brooks promptly married on 29 November 1918. His marriage to Beatrice lasted 60 years and brought forth a son and daughter as well as four grandchildren and six great-grandchildren. Eddy married Mamie Peabody Buttolph in 1921. They had one daughter.[17]

During the interwar period, both officers spent considerable time in the formal study of the profession of arms as either students or teachers. Between 1919 and 1941, both Eddy and Brooks had twelve years in tours at military schools. They also spent considerable time in grade during the interwar period. Eddy reverted to his permanent rank of captain and was not promoted to major until 1935, while Brooks did not make major until 1938. Following the armistice, Eddy returned with the 39th Infantry to the United States in August 1919. After commanding a company at Camp Dodge, Iowa, he attended the infantry school at Fort Benning and graduated from the company officers' course in June 1921. His officer efficiency report (OER) judged him, along with his colleagues, as "an average officer of good presence, manners and personality."[18] The rater, the school's assistant commandant, knew him only slightly. Eddy was found deficient in "hippology" (the study of the horse) and in light mortar. However, he must have done well enough, since his next assignment kept him at Fort Benning for three years as a test officer in the Department of Experiment of the infantry Board.

He then commanded a company in the demonstration regiment of the infantry school at Fort Benning for one year. Eddy stayed in Georgia for four more years as professor of military science and tactics at Riverside Military Academy in Gainesville. His rater, the colonel in charge of ROTC in the 4th Corps area, wrote of Eddy in 1926: "A well trained young officer of forceful character. Quiet, thorough and willing worker. Gets results. Uses common sense in his dealings with others. Loyal to the Service and deeply interested in his profession."[19]

In September 1929, Eddy returned to Fort Benning as a student in the infantry school advanced course. He achieved an excellent academic rating, and his reporting officer, the infantry school assistant commandant, Lt. Col. George C. Marshall, described him as a "superior type. A natural leader."[20] From the advanced course, Eddy traveled to Hawaii where he commanded an infantry battalion for six months and served on the staff of the G-3 at Fort Shafter for eighteen months until June 1932. His commanders consistently judged him to be an outstanding officer—balanced, earnest, and easy to get along with.

Brooks's career from the armistice to 1932 was equally instructive. Brooks returned from France with the 3d Field Artillery Brigade to Camp Pike, Arkansas, where he was regimental and brigade adjutant. His OER for this period reveals that Brooks promptly found himself caught up in the trivialities of a peacetime army. His rating officer judged him below average in initiative and noted that he had ordered Brooks to audit the 10th Field Artillery noncommissioned officers' club accounts, suspecting a shortage. Brooks, according to the reporting officer, "reported to me that everything was O.K. It now develops that the Club is some $200.00 short which he should have detected had he done as I told him to instead of taking somebody's word for it."[21]

Fortunately for Brooks, he soon left for the field artillery basic course at Fort Sill. He graduated in June 1922; his class standing was fifth of 81; he stood third in tactics. After commanding the headquarters battery at the school, he joined the faculty of the field artillery school for four years from 1922 to 1926 as instructor of gunnery and football coach. His efficiency report for this period noted that Brooks is "a very bright, intelligent officer; conscientious; a rapid worker with excellent results; this officer has an exceptionally fine mind."[22]

In September 1926, Brooks left Sill for a two-year tour commanding a battery in the 24th Field Artillery in the Philippines. One of his raters during this tour, Maj. S. LeRoy Irwin, also a World War II corps commander, wrote of Brooks, he is "an officer possessing a very brilliant mind, and thinks very rapidly. Pays great attention to detail."[23] From September 1928 to June 1932, Brooks commanded a battery of the 18th Field Artillery stationed at the cavalry school at Fort Riley. Brooks did well at Fort Riley and enjoyed the opportunity for frequent horseback riding and football; he played with the field artillery team in 1931 in their successful 39 to 6 victory over the previously undefeated cavalry team. Brooks, however, was tired of Riley and, like most interwar officers, was concerned about his future in the army. Accordingly, he sought to no avail to attend the field artillery advanced course. Brooks's future prospects brightened, however, when he learned from a friend with the chief of artillery's office that he was one of the branch's best "direct to Leavenworth" prospects.[24]

The paths of Eddy and Brooks finally intersected when they both came to Fort Leavenworth—Eddy from Hawaii and Brooks from nearby Junction City, Kansas—as students in the two-year course at the Command and General Staff School (CGSS). We can only speculate how well they knew each other. There were 118 graduates in their class, so surely they came into contact. At Leavenworth they worked tactical problems at the division and corps levels. The school's function was, according to the commandant, Maj Gen Stuart Heintzelman, "not to disseminate dogma, but to teach its students to think." Some, including George C. Marshall, criticized the school's rigid instruction methods, emphasis on detailed written operations orders, and use of "too perfect" maps and unrealistically optimistic assumptions on troop strengths.[25] Still, their two years at Leavenworth gave these intelligent officers a perspective on larger unit operations—units they would be commanding in less than a decade.

Academically, Brooks exceeded Eddy, standing thirteenth to Eddy's forty-ninth and having five superior blocks checked on his OER to Eddy's consistent excellent. Brooks was judged "keen, dependable, assured, analytical" on his report; Eddy was viewed as "energetic, dependable, methodical and sound." These observations by the director of the first-year course, while mandated by the reporting process, appear to be valid.[26]

Brooks and Eddy both spent the summer of 1933 between the first- and second-year courses with the Civilian Conservation Corps (CCC). Eddy served as district quartermaster for the Missouri CCC district, and Brooks was a company officer with the CCC at Big Falls, Minnesota. His commander observed that Brooks was "intelligent and resourceful . . . quick to seize an opportunity and turn it into practical results."[27] Historians have noted pros and cons of the CCC experience for the army. Some comment that the mobilization preparation and training of thousands of young men was a positive and relevant experience; others, such as Russell Weigley, observe that the "diversion from military tasks probably more than erased any advantage."[28] In the case of Major Eddy and Captain Brooks, the time away from study at Leavenworth was probably both a pleasant diversion and a useful experience.

For Eddy and Brooks, the CCC diversion kept them from classrooms for only a short period. Brooks went from Leavenworth to Cambridge, Massachusetts, as an assistant professor of military science at Harvard University. Duty at Harvard made use of Brooks's obvious intellect while bringing him back to New England for the first time since graduation from Norwich. Brooks did well at Harvard. His June 1936 OER credited him as an "exceptional able officer." The report's praise was so glowing that it brought the following retort from the endorsing officer, who wrote that although "Major Brooks is a superior officer . . . I consider this report somewhat exaggerated, although he did perform in a superior manner his duties as asst. chief of staff G-4, HQ I Corps, during First Army Maneuvers (12–31 August 1935)." This was signed by Maj. Gen. Fox Conner, who then commanded the First Corps area. Conner, of course, was Dwight D. Eisenhower's mentor in Panama in the early 1920s and was his great promoter.[29]

Brooks was promoted to major on 1 August 1935; he had been a captain for fifteen years. After two years at Harvard, he attended the Army War College in Washington, graduating in 1937. Once again he earned respect for his excellent performance. His OER noted his even disposition, thorough and accurate work, openmindedness, and ability to "view problems from all angles while producing practical ideas."[30] Clearly, Brooks had equal measures of intelligence and common sense. Though recommended for duty with the general staff, Brooks headed back to Leavenworth for two years' duty as an instructor from 1937 to 1939. His first year on the faculty overlapped Eddy's final year of a four-year stint from July 1934 to June 1938.

Eddy's work during his second year at the CGSS merited a negative entry on his academic efficiency report, judging him unfavorably for general staff duty; he had not done well on his corps staff and logistics courses but was still chosen for the school faculty. Eddy was a loyal and active member of the faculty who enjoyed his posting and displayed a good sense of humor.

As to the content of his instruction, Eddy himself noted some years later how faulty it had been. In 1935, Major Eddy gave the opening lecture on corps operations. In his lecture, he stated, "the corps is a large and unwieldy unit. The transmission of orders down through all echelons is a slow and tedious process." Eddy went on about the slow process of assembling and moving a corps. That process resembled the World War I experience, and that is what Eddy taught at CGSS. Eddy later claimed that as an instructor of corps operations, he and his fellow instructors "tried to keep abreast of modern developments and tried to project our teachings based on those developments as far into the future as possible."[31] Yet, in less than ten years, Eddy would be commanding a frequently rapidly moving corps that changed directions in a matter of hours. Use of the radio, motorization, and mechanization changed warfare. Eddy, along with many others, did not figure this out in advance of World War II. Although he knew much about tactical procedures and the five-paragraph field order, he knew little if anything of the ideas of the interwar British military theorists J. F. C. Fuller and Basil H. Liddell Hart, who foresaw many changes in warfare.

From Leavenworth, Eddy moved to staff and command duties as his awareness of the possibility of having to apply academic lessons on the battlefield increased. Promoted to lieutenant colonel in 1938, he served until 1940 as a regimental executive officer with the 10th Infantry in Kentucky; a year of hard work as a general staff G-2 in Third Corps area headquarters in Baltimore followed. In October 1941, he participated in the North Carolina maneuvers. From December 1941 to March 1942, Eddy commanded an infantry regiment in training at Fort Dix and Camp Claiborne. Promoted to colonel in October 1941, he was a brigadier general when he left his regimental command to serve five months as assistant division commander of the 9th Infantry Division training at Fort Bragg. He took command of the 9th Division in June 1942, and in December he moved with it to North Africa.[32]

Brooks took command of the 11th Armored Division in July 1942, keeping pace with Eddy. Following his stint as Leavenworth instructor, Brooks was chief of the statistics branch of the general staff in Washington. While in this assignment, General Marshall assigned Brooks to escort a ten-member congressional delegation to observe the Louisiana maneuvers in May 1940. These were the first corps-level maneuvers in U.S. history. The delegation included the chairman of the House Subcommittee on Military Appropriations, and Marshall wanted the congressmen to see new weapons and vehicles, "with a view to the restoration of some items . . . recently slashed by the House Committee." Marshall also wanted to give them a "definite idea of what an Army corps really is."[33]

The secretary of the general staff, Lt. Col. Orlando Ward, Brooks's rater for his Washington assignment, noted that Brooks was an outstanding soldier by reason of background, ability, education, and character and recommended him for high command.[34] His ability for battle command was readily apparent. Brooks was promoted to lieutenant colonel in 1940 and skipped the grade of colonel to become a brigadier general on 15 December 1941. From September 1941 to June 1942, Brooks served as artillery officer for the armored force at Fort Knox. His commander, Maj. Gen. Jacob L. Devers, ranked Brooks number one of the 102 general officers known to him of that grade.[35]

Brooks's command of the 11th Armored Division lasted twenty months. He trained with the division in the Louisiana maneuver area, in Texas, and at the desert training area in California. Here the paths of Eddy and Brooks diverge. While Brooks trained an armored force, he remained in the United States until taking command of the 2d Armored Division in the European Theater of Operations in March 1944. By then, Eddy had led the 9th Infantry Division in the campaigns of North Africa and Sicily during 1943.

In North Africa, Major General Eddy served under Patton, who noted his "great force, loyalty and enthusiasm." Of all general officers of Eddy's grade known to him, Patton ranked Eddy 17 of 183 in January 1943 and 15 of 153 in June 1943. Eddy did not fare so well with his next commander, Lt. Gen. Omar Bradley, who ranked him seventy-ninth of 124 in September 1943. Yet Eddy proved himself in North Africa, winning the Legion of Merit for his actions in Tunisia, where he led the division "against strongly fortified positions held by two divisions." He was cited for his courage, tactics, and grasp of the situation. General Eisenhower made a special handwritten note on Eddy's December 1943 OER, acknowledging Eddy as a good division commander in Tunisia.[36] Eddy's excellent leadership of the division continued in Sicily, where he kept the division on the move, leading to the capture of Bizerte. As the Allies prepared for the invasion of Europe, Eddy was a proven division commander who had earned the respect of Patton, Bradley, Eisenhower, and Marshall. Eddy's leadership of the division against battle-hardened German forces largely involved relatively slow, difficult ground combat and mastery of division-level infantry and artillery tactics.

From January to June 1944, Eddy served under Maj. Gen. J. Lawton Collins, who judged him an "exceptionally able and aggressive division commander . . . who always operates with his front-line troops." Collins ranked him fifteenth of 150 major generals known to him and noted that Eddy was "susceptible of development to Corps Command."[37] Eddy led the 9th Infantry Division to France in July 1944 to fight in the Cherbourg campaign and in the hedgerows of Normandy. The war correspondent Ernie Pyle described Eddy in an article as "sort of old shoe and easy to talk with—we think he is a mightily good general."[38] General Collins agreed, observing in August 1944 that Eddy was "one of the finest front line division commanders in the Army . . . with plenty of both mental and physical courage."[39] One reason for Eddy's success was his reliance on a competent staff who ran his command post while he assisted units engaged in combat. Eddy's brave and aggressive leadership of the 9th Division in France merited award of the Distinguished Service Cross.

When in March 1944 the army activated the headquarters of the Third Army with Patton as the commander, Patton chose a loyal colleague, Maj. Gen. Hugh J. Gaffey, commander of the 2d Armored Division, as his chief of staff. Brooks now became commander of the 2d Armored. After train-

Eisenhower and Bradley during a jeep tour of the front lines shortly after the invasion.

ing the division in England, he led them into France on 9 June. The 2d Armored, called "hell on wheels," was a heavy division with two tank regiments and one Infantry regiment; these were often supplemented by an additional infantry regiment and artillery battalions. As the division historian noted, "In effect, the division commander wielded a small corps."[40] Serving under General Collins in VII Corps, Brooks led the division in the Operation COBRA breakout attack. After the breakout, Brooks led the division across the Seine and Somme rivers and into Belgium. In August 1944, Eisenhower rated Brooks "among the first 10% of the combat division commanders" he knew.[41]

Brooks's absolute courage earned him a Silver Star and a cluster while in command of the division. The 2d Armored's efforts to block German attempts to split the First and Third U.S. Armies at their narrowest junction in France led to Brooks's first Silver Star. In Belgium in September 1944, Brooks gained his second Silver Star award when he stopped with his staff and the commander of his reserve regiment to watch one of the division's combat commands pass by. As soon as they had departed, a German column came barreling down the street. Brooks deployed his force of ten officers and men, including his two aides, at a crossroads to delay the German column with small arms fire. Brooks himself fired one round from his armored car's .50 caliber before it jammed. Brooks turned his armored car and jeep around, escaping over plowed fields and farm paths to catch the combat command. His efforts succeeded, and tanks bottled up the Germans, leading to their destruction. Seldom in World War II did division commanders actually take part in the fighting. Evidently, Brooks's "intelligence and resourcefulness," repeatedly noted in his OERs, stood him and his staff in good stead in September 1944.[42]

Eddy and Brooks were well prepared for corps command. They each had 28 years of commissioned service, extensive professional education, leadership experience at all levels, combat service, and proven success as division commanders. Clearly, they possessed the necessary attributes of leadership, force, flexibility of mind, vigor, and physical stamina as outlined by Marshall and Ridgway. No miracle produced these World War II leaders. Rather, the steady pattern of officer career development combined with the pyramidal process by which the U.S. Army selects its leaders enabled Brooks and Eddy to be prepared for and to reach corps command.

Eddy took command of XII Corps, serving under Patton in the Third Army, in August 1944. The former commander of XII Corps, Gilbert R. Cook, asked to be relieved due to ill health. Eddy remained in command until right before the end of the war; he was relieved due to high blood pressure in May 1945. In a talk on corps command after the war, Eddy offered some insights into his methods. He demanded three essentials, as he dubbed them: time to think, time to sleep, and time to get up to see a subordinate unit. Eddy placed this responsibility on his chief of staff, whom he wanted to be a "little bit smarter than he was" and someone he had complete confidence in. This man, Brig. Gen. Ralph J. Canine, served Eddy and the corps ably, freeing Eddy to spend time with his division commanders.[43]

Eddy was concerned about his health, which I suspect he realized was beginning to suffer from the strains of war. He required his sleep and insisted on good food prepared by a chef who was with his headquarters.

His nine months in command of XII Corps brought Eddy into daily contact with Patton. Though Eddy suspected that Patton had a secret source of information on which he based his decisions, he did not know of ULTRA's existence and often found Patton's demands puzzling. Patton and Eddy also had different personalities, which required accommodation on Eddy's part. Upon taking command of XII Corps, Eddy moved from the rigidity of fighting in Normandy to a fluid situation. He noted that the corps' right flank was unprotected and asked Patton how much he had to worry about this. Patton replied, "Eddy, that depends how nervous you are by nature." Eddy kept a daily diary as corps commander, which is most informative. Eddy observed on 2 September 1944, "it seems strange to me that we should be sitting here due to lack of fuel when all the other armies are forging ahead. . . . I am convinced that if we should obtain the necessary fuel this war might be over in a few weeks."[44]

Eddy led the corps through the difficult Lorraine campaign. Here he relieved Maj. Gen. John S. Wood and created lasting controversy. Eddy's assumption of command hurt Wood, who was a West Point graduate, armor officer, and senior to Eddy.[45] These differences made Wood envious, and he repeatedly asserted his superior knowledge of armor operations. Wood was relieved of command of 4th Armored Division for the following reasons: First, he disobeyed Eddy's orders; second, he was, in Eddy's own words, "a temperamental subordinate as a division commander."[46] Eddy claimed after the war that he "had two such babies that" he "tolerated entirely too long."[47] Third, Wood was "emotionally drained" and unable to accept losses; and fourth, Wood was physically exhausted. According to Omar Bradley's diary, "P. Wood tried to prove he could live as the enlisted men did." The entire chain of command agreed that Wood had to be relieved.[48]

There are two recent studies of the affair. One champions Wood as "probably more able than Eddy";[49] the other criticizes Eddy for "a distinct absence of synchronization within the XII Corps."[50] Clearly, Eddy's intent differed from Wood's, and Wood was partly to blame for any lack of synchronization. Wood was inconsistent, while Eddy's proven tactical concepts brought results and success. Though unglamorous by some standards, they brought XII Corps across the Rhine and into Germany. Indeed, Eddy crossed the river with Patton and observed one of the most famous acts of urination in military history. Eddy cautioned the photographer to make no prints of the picture and to give him the negatives.[51]

Brooks left the 2d Armored Division in September 1944 to command V Corps for one month. In October 1944 he took command of VI Corps, which he successfully led until the conclusion of the war in Europe. He led the corps against the Siegfried line. Brooks was caught up in the Battle of the Bulge. Organizing a flexible defense, he moved his forces around and successfully stopped repeated German counterattacks. Then VI Corps moved into Germany, captured Heidelberg, and drove across the Danube to the Italian border.[52] Brooks provided steady, reliable, unsensational leadership. He neither sought nor received much publicity. Hence he remains unknown.

Personal tragedy struck Brooks at the end of the war in Europe. His only son, Capt. Edward H. Brooks, Jr., a graduate of the Military Academy class of 1943, was killed on a routine air flight in Belgium on 22 September 1945. He had commanded a bombardment squadron.[53] Brooks, who had given tirelessly of himself, was required to give more.

Having been successful commanders in the European Theater of Operations, Brooks and Eddy continued in high positions following the war. Brooks held various positions at headquarters in Atlanta, commanded the U.S. Army Caribbean in Panama for a year in 1948, was assistant chief of staff for personnel, and ended his career a lieutenant general commanding the Second Army at Fort Meade in April 1953. He died at age 85 in a Concord, New Hampshire, nursing home.[54]

After the war, Eddy spent seven months in the hospital and on sick leave. An operation cured his blood circulation problems, and he resumed an active career. Promoted to lieutenant general in 1948, Eddy was chief of information in the office of the chief of staff and then commandant of the Command and General Staff College, where he changed both the curriculum and the teaching methodology. In 1949, Eddy served as president of a review board on the army officer educational system known as the Eddy Board. He commanded the Seventh Army in Europe in 1951–52 and ended his career in March 1953 as commander in chief of the U.S. Army in Europe. He retired to Columbus, Georgia, where he was a businessman. Eddy died in April 1962.[55]

In his *Summary of the Art of War*, Antoine-Henri Jomini, the Napoleonic military writer, observed: "If the skill of a general is one of the surest elements of victory, it will readily be seen that the judicious selection of generals is one of the most delicate points in the science of government and one of the most essential parts of the military policy of a state. Unfortunately, this choice is influenced by so many petty passions that chance, rank, age, favor, party spirit or jealousy will have as much to do with it as the public interest and justice."[56] A glance at the voluminous exchanges to be found in the Marshall, Eisenhower, and Bradley papers about promotion (or relief) of individual officers confirms that all of those factors were present in the pattern of command appointments in the ETO. On the whole, however, this system, though skewed by the West Point mystique and personal preferences, worked surprisingly well. Indeed, the advancement of Eddy and Brooks, two outsiders, to corps command demonstrates the effectiveness of the American way of selecting World War II commanders. There was no mystery or miracle behind the elevation and success of these two well-prepared, competent officers. They served ably and well in peace and in war. Their leadership contributed to the success of the Normandy invasion and helped the Allies win World War II.

16. Dwight D. Eisenhower: Architect of Victory

Mark A. Stoler

Dwight D. Eisenhower's specific role in the Allied successes at Normandy has long been hotly debated. Whereas supporters see "Ike" as one of history's great commanders and the true architect of Allied victory, detractors tend to view him as a barely competent and largely ceremonial "chairman of the board" under whose genial smile the true architects of victory—primarily British—labored. As Chief of the Imperial General Staff General Sir Alan Brooke contemptuously concluded, Eisenhower was a "charming personality and a good coordinator" but "no real commander."[1]

Although often heated, this debate has usually possessed an air of unreality because of the limited temporal and geographic frameworks in which it has been conducted. Focusing on England and northern France in the spring and summer of 1944, these frameworks virtually ignore all that had occurred globally in the years preceding the war. Yet OVERLORD did not take place in a vacuum. It was the culmination of two years of occurrences and planning on a global scale.

Eisenhower was deeply involved in many of these events and much of this planning. His successful command over Allied forces in their pre-OVERLORD campaigns of 1942–43 in North Africa, Sicily, and Italy is well known and requires little additional commentary. What is not as well known is that prior to these commands, and more than two years before D-day, he produced both the global strategic conception and the first draft plan for OVERLORD. He then fought aggressively for their acceptance in Washington and became their chief proponent in London during the late spring and summer of 1942. Although this effort failed and cross-Channel operations were postponed for nearly two years, Eisenhower's conception remained the guiding principle of U.S. strategic planning throughout 1942–44. And although circumstances made the final OVERLORD plan quite different from the one he had originally prepared in March 1942, its essence in terms of approach as well as rationale remained what he had written and fought for in the eight months after Pearl Harbor. Eisenhower was thus in many ways the true architect of victory long before he assumed command of OVERLORD itself, and any assessment of his role in the success of that operation must begin with this relatively forgotten period of his World War II service.

A few days after the Japanese attack on Pearl Harbor, Army Chief of Staff General George C. Marshall brought Eisenhower to Washington to serve as assistant chief of the Army General Staff's War Plans Division. Within a few months he would be promoted to chief of this crucial staff agency and its even more important successor, the Operations Division (OPD).[2] In that role, Eisenhower served as Marshall's chief strategic planner in the first half of 1942 and was the individual most responsible for the U.S. cross-Channel proposal that emerged at that time.

As the army's chief strategist, Eisenhower inherited both a preexisting global strategy and an immediate military crisis. Unfortunately, the two stood in direct conflict. The global strategy, as approved earlier in the first American-British Conversations (ABC-1) and revised RAINBOW 5 plans, called for Anglo-American offensive operations against Germany in the European theater in the event of U.S. entry into the war, with efforts in the Far East limited to defensive operations.[3] But these plans had been approved in early 1941 and had not anticipated either the destruction of the U.S. fleet at Pearl Harbor in December or the ensuing massive Japanese offensive throughout Southeast Asia and the Pacific. Consequently, Eisenhower had to focus his early efforts on trying to stop the Japanese onslaught, save the beleaguered Philippine garrison, and establish a firm base in Australia—all while giving lip service to the Europe-first approach, which the British and American Combined Chiefs of Staff were at that moment reaffirming at the ARCADIA conference in Washington.[4]

As part of that reaffirmation, British Prime Minister Winston S. Churchill and U.S. President Franklin D. Roosevelt had approved the sending of American troops to Northern Ireland to release additional British forces for combat (Operation MAGNET) and the launching of a combined Anglo-American invasion of French North Africa later in the year (Operation GYMNAST).[5] Assigned to and totally immersed in the immediate Far Eastern crisis, Eisenhower in early January condemned both these operations as diversionary "expeditions, directed by politicians," which interfered with the reinforcement of Australia. The Far East, he insisted, was "critical," and "no other side shows should be undertaken until air and ground are in a satisfactory state."[6]

By late January, however, the collapse of Allied defenses in the Philippines and Malaya forced Eisenhower to realize the futility of his reinforcement efforts and that, in actuality, they were merely additional diversionary "side shows" and an unwise dispersion of scarce American shipping and resources.[7] Consequently, he began to formulate a new global strategic concept, one that was more in line with ABC-1 and RAINBOW 5. It was by no means an easy task. "The struggle to secure the adoption by all concerned of a common concept of strategical objectives is wearing me down," he admitted in the privacy of his diary on 22 January. "Everybody is too much engaged with small things of his own—or with some vague idea of larger political activity to realize what we are doing—rather *not* doing."[8]

What the Allies were not doing—concentrating forces for decisive offensive operations in the European theater—was clear to Eisenhower. Neither MAGNET nor GYMNAST constituted such a decisive operation. To the contrary, they diverted resources from it. "We've got to go to Europe and fight," he wrote on 22 January, "and we've got to quit wasting resources all over the world—and still worse—wasting time. If we're to keep Russia in, save the Middle East, India and Burma; we've got to begin slugging with air at West Europe; to be followed by a land attack as soon as possible."[9]

Although this notation contained most of the basic concepts behind the cross-Channel plan, it would take Eisenhower and his staff another month to sort out their priorities and present a clear proposal. The virtual disintegration of Allied defensive efforts in the South Pacific and Southeast Asia acted as a constant spur. In one sense, it also simplified their task, since Japanese conquests quickly removed many areas from the list to be defended and negated the primary rationale for those defensive stands: denying Japan the resources of Southeast Asia. Burma thus left the list of areas capable of being defended in late January. By 19 February, reinforcements for the entire southwest Pacific had been downgraded to second priority.[10]

In late February, Eisenhower forwarded to Marshall a major strategic proposal. Somewhat misleadingly entitled in its final form "Strategic Conceptions and Their Application to Southwest Pacific," the proposal actually called for a reorientation of American effort away from that area in order to focus on the European theater and launch offensive operations from England as soon as possible. Eisenhower admitted that such a proposal appeared to violate the military axiom of attacking and destroying first the weaker portion of a divided enemy, but he argued that Japan's conquests, geographical position, and distance from its enemies actually made Japan relatively stronger, "given the force that can now be brought and maintained against her," than Germany. "This is particularly true," he carefully noted in regard to what would be his consistent preoccupation, "as long as Russia is in the war."[11]

Given Allied failure to prevent the Japanese from conquering the resources of Southeast Asia, Eisenhower boldly argued that defense of the
entire southwest Pacific had become merely a "desirable" as opposed to a
"necessary" objective, as was the defense of Alaska, Burma, South America south of Natal, Australia, air and naval bases west of Hawaii, and West
African bases and air routes. Indeed, assuming that the continental United
States, Hawaii, the Caribbean, and South America north of Natal were safe
from major attack, only three goals were truly "necessary": maintenance
of England and the North Atlantic sea lanes; retention of the Soviet Union
"as an active enemy against Germany", and prevention of a German-Japa
nese junction in the India–Middle East region. Despite their geographic
distance from each other, the three were closely related, since complete
failure to accomplish any one of them would lead to failure in the other
two. And at that moment the second aim, keeping the Soviet Union in the
war, was the most problematic and required "immediate and direct
action."[12]

The key issue, Eisenhower clearly recognized, was that the Red Army
was successfully tying down the bulk of the Wehrmacht and would have
to continue to do so if the Allies hoped to defeat Germany. The Soviet Union thus could not be allowed to reach such a precarious military situation
by the summer that it would be willing to "accept a negotiated peace, no
matter how unfavorable to herself, in preference to a continuation of the
war." Avoiding such a scenario, Eisenhower insisted, required lend-lease
aid and "the early initiation of operations that will draw off from the Russian front sizable portions of the German Army, both air and ground."
These operations, he further asserted, were political as well as military in
nature, for they had to be sufficient to convince the highly suspicious Soviets that Britain and the United States were *willing* as well as able to provide meaningful assistance. As he emphasized, *"such an operation must
be so conceived, and so presented to the Russians, that they will recognize the importance of the support rendered."*[13]

Only concentration of all available forces in the United Kingdom for
cross-Channel operations as soon as possible fulfilled these requirements.
Indeed, as Eisenhower had clearly realized as early as 19 February, the
logic behind such operations was to a certain extent circular: They were
necessary to keep the Soviets in the war, and they could be launched successfully only if the Soviets stayed in the war.[14] He thus recommended on
28 February the mandatory tasks of maintaining a maximum flow of lend-
lease supplies to the Soviet Union and immediately developing, in conjunction with the British, "a definite plan for operations against Northwest Europe" capable of engaging an "increasing portion" of the German

air force by May and the German army by late summer. The only other mandatory tasks would be to keep the shipping lanes open to Britain, which would occur as a byproduct of concentrating forces in England, and to defend the India–Middle East theater, a task for which England should bear primary responsibility.[15]

Eisenhower's reasoning was by no means original. Throughout the late summer and fall of 1941, U.S. Army assessments had emphasized the importance of maintaining Soviet resistance and had warned that failure to do so would leave Germany in control of virtually all of Eurasia and "practically invulnerable" against any Anglo-American operations.[16] As early as August 1941, one officer in the Intelligence Division (G-2) of the General Staff had concluded that lend-lease aid in and of itself would be insufficient to keep the Soviet Union in the war. Its military collapse could be avoided, Col. Edwin Schwien argued, only by the immediate creation of a new front in northern France to divert German forces from the east and to serve as an eventual base for decisive offensive operations on the Continent. Creation of such a front, he bluntly argued, constituted "the only possible method of approach to an ultimate victory of the democracies."[17]

Far from coincidentally, such warnings and conclusions echoed those being offered by the Soviet press, foreign office, and Stalin himself. As early as 3 September 1941, the Soviet leader had warned Churchill that only a "second front" in the Balkans or France capable of drawing 30 to 40 German divisions from the Eastern Front could prevent Soviet defeat, a warning echoed again and again in ensuing months.[18] Within these warnings was the clear implication that Moscow viewed failure to provide such a second front as a deliberate betrayal rather than a military exigency, one that would justify a separate peace. On 12 February 1942, U.S. Army Intelligence warned of the "distinct possibility" of such a peace due to Soviet suspicions and argued that the threat could be minimized by more aid and by decisive military action to convince the Soviets of American "desire" as well as ability "to fight a war vigorously and victoriously."[19] Eisenhower's proposal called for just such action, thereby clearly illustrating his understanding of the political as well as the military aspects of global strategy.

Eisenhower's proposal also fit in perfectly with the U.S. Army's traditional "direct" strategy of confrontation and annihilation, as well as its year-old assault on the "indirect" British approach in the Mediterranean. As early as November 1940, U.S. military strategists had maintained that victory over Germany would ultimately require a major land offensive in Europe, and by the fall of 1941 they were calling for a 215-division army to accomplish this task. Air and naval forces, they warned in a thinly veiled assault on British strategy, "seldom, if ever, win important wars. It should be recognized as an almost invariable rule that only land armies can finally win wars."[20]

Eisenhower was also far from alone in his February call for cross-Channel operations. His proposal clearly verbalized the thoughts of many within the War Department at that time, including Secretary of War Henry L. Stimson, Army Air Forces Chief General Henry H. Arnold, numerous members of the army general staff, and, most important, Chief of Staff Marshall (who was in many ways the originator of and driving force behind the cross-Channel concept). Eisenhower, however, put these thoughts into a coherent, tightly reasoned, and comprehensive memorandum that the army chief could use to win naval, presidential, and British approval.[21]

Such approval would not be easily attained. Although continuing to pay lip service to the Germany-first approach, the navy was far from willing to abandon the entire Pacific west and south of Hawaii in the aftermath of Pearl Harbor. To the contrary, its new chief, Admiral Ernest J. King, was at that very moment requesting additional army and air forces to garrison numerous Pacific islands, a request that Eisenhower opposed and that may have catalyzed him into writing his February proposal.[22] King remained unimpressed, informing the president on 5 March of his continued preference for Pacific operations and reminding him that the United States could not allow Japan to overrun the "white man's countries" of Australia and New Zealand "because of the repercussions among the non-white races of the world."[23]

Nor were Roosevelt or the British prepared to accept Eisenhower's proposed direct confrontation with German armies in France or the casualties that would ensue. Although such a confrontation fit in perfectly with the U.S. Army's traditional direct strategy of annihilation, it stood as the antithesis of the British indirect approach, which Churchill championed and Roosevelt seemed to support via GYMNAST.[24]

By early March, however, Allied defeats and dispersion had forced the indefinite postponement of GYMNAST, and Roosevelt was searching for an alternative 1942 offensive in the European theater to focus public attention on that part of the world rather than the Pacific.[25] Supported by Marshall and Eisenhower, the president combined this search with a far-reaching proposal to Churchill on 9 March that the United States assume primary responsibility for the Pacific theater and Britain for the Middle and Far East, with combined responsibility for the European-Atlantic theater and "definite plans for the establishment of a new front on the European continent" during the summer.[26] Simultaneously, army planners, realizing that the navy would never agree to complete abandonment of the southwest Pacific, began to modify their cross-Channel proposals to allow for reinforcement of that area "in accordance with current commitments." The Joint Chiefs of Staff agreed on 16 March. On the following day, Churchill agreed to Roosevelt's proposed division of areas of responsibility, thereby giving the Joint Chiefs control over those reinforcements.[27]

Eisenhower himself had noted in his 28 February memorandum that "a desire to concentrate in one direction must not wholly remove protection in another," and in a key 25 March memorandum to Marshall he addressed this issue directly in regard to the southwest Pacific.[28] Whereas all tasks beyond the mandatory retention of England, the Soviet Union, and the Middle East remained only highly desirable, some of them were so important as to warrant diversion of "at least a small proportion of our strength to their accomplishment. Foremost among these is probably the support of Australia and New Zealand and the lines of communication thereto." The main task for 1942, however, remained a major attack against Germany through Western Europe. Summarizing and clarifying points he had made on 28 February, Eisenhower now asserted that such an operation would place minimum strain upon U.S. shipping by using the shortest sea routes, simultaneously protect lines of communication to England, and assist the Soviet Union by diverting German forces. Equally important, it would follow "the direct approach to the seat of German power"; make use of a preexisting large forward base in England with extensive airfields, from which a large air force vital to success could operate; employ offensively a large portion of British combat power; and attack the main Axis enemy "while he is engaged on many fronts." Indeed, so vital, obvious, and pressing was such an operation that Eisenhower recommended a complete reversal of U.S. global strategy should the plan not be adopted, whereby the Americans would "turn our backs upon the Eastern Atlantic and go, full out, as quickly as possible, against Japan!"[29]

Supported by presidential adviser Harry Hopkins, Marshall used these arguments to win presidential approval of Eisenhower's proposals at a luncheon meeting that same day, 25 March. Roosevelt also ordered his advisers to formalize the plan so that they could deliver it directly to Churchill in London rather than go through the existing military bureaucracy, and Marshall immediately gave the task to Eisenhower and his Operations Division. Two days later the OPD planners presented Eisenhower with their conclusions, which he and his assistant, General Thomas Handy, carefully reviewed and submitted on 1 April to Marshall, who in turn revised it and presented it to Roosevelt.[30]

Entitled "Operations in Western Europe" and commonly known as the Marshall Memorandum, the final document called for the immediate concentration of all available Anglo-American forces in Britain for a spring 1943 cross-Channel assault between Le Havre and Boulogne consisting of 48 divisions (30 American and 18 British) and supported by 5,800 aircraft, with the possibility of landing five divisions in a very limited September 1942 operation should Germany become "critically weakened" in Western Europe or the Soviet situation become "desperate." The opening paragraphs of the memorandum neatly summarized all the reasons Eisenhower had given in the preceding month for such a strategic approach. Through England and France lay "our shortest route to the heart of Germany" and the only area in which the Allies could obtain massive air superiority while employing the bulk of their ground forces in conjunction with those of the Soviets. Furthermore, a successful cross-Channel attack would "afford the maximum possible support to Russia, whose continued participation in the war is essential to the defeat of Germany." Immediate preparation for such an attack would provide a "unique opportunity to establish an active sector on this front this summer" through air operations and raids that would help the Soviets, satisfy public opinion, create veterans, and heighten troop morale.[31]

Strongly supported by Hopkins, Marshall won naval and presidential approval of Eisenhower's memorandum at the 1 April White House meeting, along with a presidential order that he and Hopkins depart immediately for London to win British approval. Roosevelt then informed Churchill of the forthcoming visit and proposal, carefully noting its importance for both the Soviets and public opinion and concluding that, even if full success in the operation was not obtained, "the *big* objective will be." After a series of meetings with the American envoys, Churchill replied that London was "in entire agreement in principle with all you propose."[32]

Formal approval and codenames were thus given to Eisenhower's proposals in the form of three related operations: the immediate concentration in England of all available Anglo-American forces (BOLERO) in preparation for a massive cross-Channel assault in the spring of 1943 (ROUNDUP), with the possibility of an emergency operation in the fall of 1942 with whatever forces were then available should Germany suddenly weaken or the Eastern Front become critical (SLEDGEHAMMER). In the latter situation, permanent success should not be expected. Since continued Soviet participation in the war was essential to victory, such an operation would be "considered a sacrifice for the common good" because it would divert German forces from the Eastern Front.[33]

Throughout the spring, Eisenhower remained too busy to savor the success involved in this approval of his proposals. Indeed, so intense was his schedule that when his father died on 10 March, all he could do was send a telegram, quit work on the following evening at the "early" hour of 7:30 p.m., and "shut off all business and visitors for thirty minutes" on 12 March, the day of the burial, "to have that much time, by myself, to think of him." Continued Allied defeats and requests for additional dispersions did nothing to improve his disposition. The London conference did, however, and by 20 April he was cautiously optimistic that "at long last, and after months of struggle . . . we are all definitely committed to one concept of fighting! If we can agree on major purposes and objectives," he predicted, "our efforts will begin to fall in line and we won't just be thrashing around in the dark."[34]

Within a few months, however, Anglo-American agreement to Eisenhower's "major purposes and objectives" was to collapse, and cross-Channel operations would be postponed for two years. The key reason was disagreement over the 1942 SLEDGEHAMMER operation. Everyone could agree to focus Allied forces in England for cross-Channel operations a year away, but the agreement to save the Soviet Union by means of a 1942 sacrifice operation was an agreement in principle only and masked serious differences. They soon surfaced.

The operation had been labeled a "sacrifice" as a result of continued shortages and dispersions, most notably in the southwest Pacific. Upon agreeing in March that this area could not be completely abandoned, Eisenhower and the entire army staff had backed away from his original insistence in February on a 1942 cross-Channel operation under any circumstances because the U.S. forces necessary to ensure its success simply would not be available in England. Indeed, a joint army-navy study pointed out in March that as a result of other shipping commitments there might be no American ground forces in England for an assault "at the time deemed essential from strategic considerations"—that is, 1942. Its solution was to state that Britain would have to provide the forces for such an operation and that if London refused to do so Washington should reevaluate the entire Germany-first approach and consider concentration in the Pacific instead.[35]

In his 25 March memorandum, Eisenhower did not go this far. He and the rest of the OPD agreed that such a strategic shift would indeed be in order if Britain did not agree to the principle of immediate concentration

for a cross-Channel attack as soon as possible, but now they did not mention any specific 1942 target date. Nor did they do so in their final 1 April
memorandum, which labeled the operation an "emergency" measure
and "sacrifice in the common good" to prevent a Soviet collapse. They
also made clear that no more than three and a half U.S. divisions could be
available for it by 15 September and concluded that available landing craft
could sustain no more than five divisions total.[36]

The British clearly recognized the problems with SLEDGEHAMMER but
voiced no objections to this or any other component of Eisenhower's
proposal for fear of driving the Americans to the Pacific and further alien-
ating a public that was demanding immediate action. Indeed, Brooke bitterly noted in his diary that political factors had forced him to agree to
proposals in which he had little or no faith. Adamantly opposed to any
1942 landing and far from convinced that a 1943 operation could succeed, he labeled Eisenhower's entire proposal nothing more than "castles
in the air" and a political ploy. Given the lack of any consideration regarding what to do after the landings had taken place, he concluded that Marshall (and implicitly Eisenhower) was a strategic fool in supporting it.
Many of his associates agreed, with one later labeling the entire memorandum "fantastic" and "almost childish in its simplicity."[37]

Political factors precluded open disagreement. Furthermore, agreement
to the BOLERO buildup and a 1943 ROUNDUP would bind the United States
to the Germany-first approach, while agreement to SLEDGEHAMMER in principle could speed the buildup but leave options open for the future. Churchill, his chiefs of staff, and the War Cabinet thus approved the Eisen-
hower-Marshall memorandum in its entirety but almost immediately set
about negating the 1942 section.

Yet the 1942 operation was the one that mattered most to Roosevelt.
With public opinion highly critical of his handling of the war and still
geared toward revenge in the Pacific, he desperately needed the 1942
cross-Channel operation for domestic reasons. He also needed it for diplomatic reasons—both to keep the Soviets in the war and to use as a substitute for the treaty they were demanding (and he opposed), recognizing
their 1939–40 territorial conquests in Eastern Europe. On 28 May, Churchill provided him with an alternative by resurrecting the old GYMNAST
plan for the invasion of French North Africa.[38]

Marshall was well aware of British objections to SLEDGEHAMMER as well
as mounting logistic problems throughout April and May. Despite London's official agreement in principle to SLEDGEHAMMER, he warned the War
Department on 13 April that British acceptance would have to be "considerably and consistently bolstered by firmness," a firmness that he and

Eisenhower attempted to show over the next two months by focusing on cross-Channel operations and limiting dispersions elsewhere—especially in the Pacific, where Roosevelt as well as the navy were pressing for reinforcements.[39] The effort was only partially successful, and by mid-May the BOLERO buildup and planning were in serious trouble. Consequently, Marshall sent Eisenhower to England on 21 May to examine the situation, and in early June he warned Roosevelt not to promise the Soviets any specific operation in 1942—a warning that Roosevelt ignored in his meetings with visiting Soviet Foreign Minister Vyacheslav Molotov.[40]

Marshall's warning was partially the result of Eisenhower's pessimistic conclusions upon his return from England. "Our own people are able but do not understand what we want done," Eisenhower noted on 5 June. "It is necessary to get punch behind the job or we'll never be ready by spring, 1943, to attack. We must get going!"[41]

As part of the effort to focus on BOLERO, Eisenhower had recommended on 11–12 May the establishment of a specific European Theater of Operations (ETO) in England and the appointment of a theater commander. Now he pressed Marshall for immediate action on these matters to save BOLERO.[42] Marshall agreed with Eisenhower's general conclusions but not with his specific recommendation for the officer to command the ETO. He appointed Eisenhower himself to this critical position.

Ironically, Eisenhower had, in effect, written his own job description prior to the appointment. He had informed Marshall that the commander of the ETO had to be able to exercise "absolute unity of command" so as to organize, train, and prepare for operations all U.S. ground, naval, and air forces in conjunction with British forces. He also had to "enjoy the fullest confidence of the Chief of Staff" to accomplish his tasks and be able to "fit perfectly into the final organization" in "any one of several possible roles"—from actual theater commander to deputy commander or chief of staff to the commander, should Roosevelt decide to place Marshall in charge of the final operation.

While in England a few weeks later, Eisenhower discussed command arrangements with the British. He emphasized the need for a single supreme commander rather than a committee and the need to assure total unity of command. Unbeknownst to him, Marshall had already concluded that Eisenhower himself possessed the necessary characteristics and had sent Eisenhower and a few associates to England partially "so the British could have a look at them." When their reaction was positive, Marshall acted.[43]

As Eisenhower prepared to depart for London, Churchill and his military advisers arrived in the United States to argue that SLEDGEHAMMER could not sustain itself and would be so small as to be incapable of diverting any German forces from the Eastern Front. Fearful of the course of events then transpiring in the Middle East, the British Chiefs of Staff were equally critical of GYMNAST. They recommended doing nothing in 1942 except to continue the BOLERO buildup while arranging to reinforce the Suez region, if necessary. This the Americans could and did agree to, especially after the unexpected and disastrous fall of Tobruk. Churchill and Roosevelt both demanded action in 1942, however, and on 24 June, in what the official British military history labeled the "Day of Dupes," they repudiated the Combined Chiefs of Staff's conclusions to the contrary. Two weeks later the British formally rejected SLEDGEHAMMER and pressed, instead, for GYMNAST. "This has all along been in harmony with your ideas," Churchill told Roosevelt on 8 July. "In fact it is your commanding idea. Here is the true second front of 1942."[44]

Despite his shift from OPD to command of the ETO in England, Eisenhower now reentered the debate. An incensed U.S. Joint Chiefs of Staff had concluded that GYMNAST would not aid the Soviets and would so disperse Allied forces as to make impossible the launching of both ROUNDUP in 1943 and SLEDGEHAMMER in 1942. In line with Eisenhower's original reasoning, they suggested to Roosevelt a U.S. shift to the Pacific should Churchill persist. The president angrily rejected this proposal and ordered Marshall, King, and Hopkins to go to London and reach agreement on *some* 1942 offensive operation in the European theater. Still hoping to salvage SLEDGEHAMMER, Marshall now ordered Eisenhower to have available a "searching analysis" of the operation on his arrival, thereby bringing Eisenhower back into the center of the debate.[45]

The plan devised by Eisenhower and his staff differed from the original SLEDGEHAMMER project by proposing a permanent landing and shifting the location westward to the port of Cherbourg. After the war, Eisenhower conceded that launching this operation would have been a mistake. In July 1942, however, he concluded in a series of memoranda for Marshall that it was far preferable to GYMNAST and should be launched—even though he originally estimated the chances of successfully landing the invasion force at only one in two and of maintaining the beachhead at one in five—because the "prize" of keeping "8,000,000 Russians in the war" justified the risk. The Red Army was in serious trouble and might well require this front to survive in 1942. Without continued Soviet participation in the war, neither ROUNDUP in 1943 nor eventual victory over Germany would be possible.[46]

The GYMNAST alternative, Eisenhower argued, would not help the Soviets and would so disperse Anglo-American forces as to negate the possibil-

Key SHAEF figures during a break in one of their marathon meetings: (left to right, seated) Air Chief Marshal Sir Arthur Tedder, General Eisenhower, General Montgomery; (standing) General Omar Bradley, Admiral Bertram Ramsay, Air Chief Marshal Trafford Leigh-Mallory, General Walter Bedell Smith.

ity of launching ROUNDUP in 1943. It thus made sense only as a limited, defensive alternative to cross-Channel operations, to be undertaken only if London and Washington concluded that the Red Army was "certain to be defeated." In such a situation, Eisenhower concluded, the Germany-first approach should itself be overturned.[47]

In reply to the British contention that SLEDGEHAMMER would not be large enough to divert any German forces from the east, Eisenhower once again emphasized the psychological effect of the operation on the Soviets and argued that this alone would make it worthwhile. He also argued that the operation would have a similar psychological effect on the English and the Americans. "We have sat up nights on the problem involved and have tried to open our eyes clearly to see all the difficulties and not to be blinded by a mere passion for doing something," he wrote on 22 July. "However, this last factor alone is worth something. The British and American armies and the British and American people need to have the feeling that they are attempting something positive. We must not degenerate into a passive and mental [*sic*] attitude."[48]

Marshall made use of Eisenhower's memoranda and reasoning in his conversations with the British, but to no avail. "Poor old Ike is terribly fed-up with our refusal" to launch SLEDGEHAMMER, one British officer noted on 22 July.[49] On that date, which Eisenhower believed might go down as the "blackest day in history," Roosevelt was informed of the deadlock and ordered his envoys to reach agreement on *some* 1942 operation against the Germans, preferably in North Africa, as soon as possible. GYMNAST, now rechristened TORCH, was the result, with American command of the operation to seal the bargain and perhaps ease bitter U.S. feelings over losing the debate.[50]

As Eisenhower biographer Stephen Ambrose aptly noted, everything Eisenhower had worked on for the preceding six months was now "in the ashcan, and it was time to start all over." The new start would be as an active theater commander rather than a planner, however, for Marshall selected Eisenhower to command TORCH.[51]

As TORCH commander, Eisenhower dropped out of the Allied strategic debate. His conception, however, remained the focal point of both U.S. strategic plans and Anglo-Soviet-American strategic disagreements. While Allied forces under his command successfully landed in Morocco and Algeria in November 1942 and then joined with the British Eighth Army to trap and force the surrender of substantial Axis forces in Tunisia by May 1943, the Combined Chiefs of Staff argued bitterly over whether to pursue his cross-Channel plan or Britain's Mediterranean strategy for 1943. London won this debate, for—as Eisenhower and his planners had predicted—TORCH so dispersed Allied forces as to preclude sufficient concentration in England to launch ROUNDUP in 1943. It also provided the U.S. Navy with additional ammunition to demand further dispersion in the Pacific, which in turn made a 1943 cross-Channel attack even less likely. As early as January 1943 it was apparent that no cross Channel attack could be launched that year unless Germany was severely weakened or the Allies virtually shut down their offensives in North Africa and the Pacific. This they were unwilling to do in light of their triumphs in these theaters as well as the fact that they still did not control the skies over the English Channel or the Atlantic sea lanes.

Consequently, the Combined Chiefs agreed at the 1943 Casablanca, Washington, and Quebec conferences to continue in the Mediterranean, with the invasion of Sicily and Italy under Eisenhower's overall command as the primary objectives after North Africa had been cleared of Axis forces. In return, the Americans obtained from their British colleagues a definitive commitment to a cross-Channel assault in 1944, to be preceded by major naval and air offensives to win control of the Atlantic and the skies over Western Europe. They also obtained the establishment of a combined cross-Channel planning staff under a chief of staff and an agreement that planned Mediterranean operations would be subordinated to this Channel crossing.[52] By the summer of 1943, General Sir Frederick Morgan, the Chief of Staff to the Supreme Allied Commander designate and his staff (COSSAC) had produced a draft plan for cross-Channel operations that received formal Anglo-American approval at the August QUADRANT conference in Quebec. Churchill's efforts to postpone the operation in order to reap additional benefits in the Mediterranean were stymied at the November Big Three summit conference in Tehran, where Roosevelt and Stalin simply outvoted him and insisted that the operation be launched as scheduled in May 1944.[53]

COSSAC's cross-Channel plans were in many ways quite different from those Eisenhower had drawn up in 1942. The proposed location was now the Normandy beaches around Caen rather than the Le Havre–Boulogne area or the Cherbourg peninsula, as Eisenhower had proposed in 1942, with the landings connected rather than dispersed, as in the original plans. The operation was also smaller than Eisenhower had originally suggested. Continuing dispersions and landing craft shortages made clear that even in 1944 the cross-Channel attack could not be as large as conceived in the original ROUNDUP plan (48 divisions), though it would be larger than the proposed SLEDGEHAMMER operation. Appropriately code-named ROUNDHAMMER and then renamed OVERLORD, the draft plan of July 1943 called for a cross-Channel assault and landing of 26 to 30 divisions.[54]

The rationale and place of the operation in overall Allied strategy appeared to be as different from Eisenhower's original conception as the location and size. Whereas in 1942 it had been designed as a massive, direct thrust replacing virtually all other operations, it was now simply to be the foremost of multiple operations around the globe. Furthermore, whereas in 1942 it had been designed to save the Soviets by diverting German forces from the east, in 1943–44 such a rescue was no longer necessary. To the contrary, cross-Channel operations were now perceived as a supplement to the massive Soviet offensives of 1943–44—and indeed they required the continuation of those offensives to divert German forces from the invasion beaches.[55]

Despite these differences, COSSAC's OVERLORD plan still bore the marks of its principal and original architect. Twenty-six to 30 divisions might not be as large a force as the 48 originally envisaged, but it still constituted a massive, direct assault as Eisenhower had suggested—by far the largest Anglo-American operation of the war and the largest amphibious operation in history. It was also officially listed as the primary Anglo-American operation of 1944, with all other operations strictly limited, subordinated to it, and designed to aid it by diverting German forces from the Normandy beaches. Although avoiding Soviet collapse was no longer a key motivating factor, avoiding a separate Russo-German peace was, for Stalin continued to view the operation as the sine qua non of wartime as well as postwar collaboration. Indeed, Big Three conflict over further postponement of the operation in 1943 and the resulting separate peace rumors played a major role in the final Allied agreement to OVERLORD and to the creation of the supplemental RANKIN plans to occupy Western and Central Europe as soon as possible should Germany weaken or collapse before OVERLORD could be launched. Also spurring London and Washington was fear of the consequences of a unilateral Soviet victory over the Germans.[56]

The critical importance of the operation in Allied relations also played a major role in the surprise announcement that Eisenhower was to be its commander. At Tehran, Stalin had asked who would command OVERLORD. When informed by Roosevelt that no decision had yet been made, he bluntly concluded that "in that case nothing will come of Operation OVERLORD," for without a responsible commander the proposed invasion was "just so much talk."[57] Such comments forced Roosevelt to make a decision he had been avoiding for months. Marshall was, of course, the favored candidate, with Eisenhower replacing him as Army Chief of Staff. Throughout the fall, however, objections had been raised to such an arrangement on the grounds that Marshall was indispensable in Washington and that theater command would, in effect, be a demotion for him. Eisenhower was the logical alternative because of past experience and successes in coalition commands, the trust Marshall and Roosevelt had in him, and the fact that he had originated the OVERLORD plan two years earlier.[58]

One of the most important issues the new OVERLORD commander had to confront in early 1944 was whether and how to modify the invasion plans he had inherited. Facing severe logistic limitations, COSSAC had originally proposed a landing by only three infantry divisions and part of an airborne division—fewer forces than had been used to invade Sicily. Newly appointed ground commander General Sir Bernard Montgomery insisted that this was woefully insufficient and in January pressed for additional assault forces on an expanded front. His was neither a unique nor an original stipulation. Churchill, Marshall, Hopkins, Eisenhower's chief of staff, Walter Bedell Smith, and the Combined Chiefs of Staff had called for a strengthening of the assault in the summer and fall of 1943. So had Eisenhower, who informed Marshall on 8 February 1944 that it was he who had originally requested Montgomery to study the COSSAC plan in detail and "seek . . . intensification of effort to increase the troop lift in OVERLORD, which I told him in my opinion was necessary." Eisenhower was thus one of the originators and driving forces behind the call for a larger assault and one of the strongest supporters of Montgomery's resulting recommendation that the invasion force be expanded from three to five infantry divisions and from part of one to parts of three airborne divisions over an extended 50-mile front.[59]

Numerous additional landing craft would be needed for such an expanded assault. Although postponing the invasion from May to June enabled Eisenhower to obtain an extra month's production, a deficit still remained. The British suggested obtaining the additional craft by canceling the planned simultaneous invasion of southern France (Operation ANVIL), but the U.S. Joint Chiefs of Staff, fearing another British attempt to launch additional Mediterranean operations with the forces to be made available, refused to agree.

Eisenhower found himself in the middle of this quarrel, desiring the ANVIL landing craft on the one hand but insisting on the other that the southern France invasion was necessary for a successful OVERLORD and that the two operations constituted "one whole." On 21 March 1944, he helped negotiate a temporary compromise by supporting postponement of ANVIL so that OVERLORD could obtain additional landing craft. He insisted that ANVIL was a necessary complement to a successful OVERLORD, however, even if launched after the Normandy assault and on a smaller scale than originally anticipated, to provide his forces with desperately needed port facilities. The British continued to disagree and after D-day pressed for cancellation and alternative operations in the Mediterranean. In effect, this constituted the last chapter in the ongoing Anglo-American debate over Mediterranean versus cross-Channel operations, with Eisenhower demanding the return of Mediterranean forces to support operations in northern France. London eventually acceded to launching ANVIL on 15 August, but only under American pressure so intense as to engender cries of blackmail. Churchill may well have renamed the operation DRAGOON to represent his feelings of being dragooned into it.[60]

Although the most important, this was by no means the only modification of or debate over OVERLORD-related plans to concern Eisenhower in the first half of 1944. Numerous issues and disputes, ranging from bombing targets before the invasion to whether or not to proceed on 6 June in light of the weather, required his intervention and placed his personal stamp on the operation. In all these controversies Eisenhower exhibited the personal characteristics that had proved so effective in his previous commands—most notably his desire and ability to create a working multilateral staff and his capacity as a military diplomat. Although not directly concerned with his role as military architect, these characteristics deserve some mention in this chapter.

As early as the ARCADIA conference in 1941–42, Eisenhower had championed the concept of both Allied and interservice unity of command, and his ability to create workable, unified staffs had been a hallmark of his generalship in 1942 and 1943. It remained so in 1944. This was no mean feat. Interservice rivalries and disputes were particularly intense within the U.S. armed forces, with cooperation the historical exception. The same held true historically for interallied relations in general and Anglo-American relations in particular. Eisenhower's strong efforts to minimize such tensions were so effective that they became legendary. "He only called me the son of a bitch, sir," a British officer on his North African staff had pleaded in an effort to save an American counterpart with whom he had argued and whom Eisenhower had consequently ordered home, "and all of us have now learnt this is a colloquial expression which is sometimes used almost as a term of endearment, and should not be taken too seriously." Eisenhower replied, "I am informed that he called you a British son of a bitch. That is quite different. My ruling stands."[61]

Making a unified command work required enormous diplomatic tact— not only with officers of different services and different nationalities but also with their civilian superiors. Here Eisenhower once again excelled. Indeed, his ability to deal with such headstrong personalities as Winston Churchill and Franklin Roosevelt in the civil sphere, as well as Bernard Montgomery and George S. Patton in the military, has become legendary. The fact that many of the civilians with whom he dealt considered themselves brilliant military strategists did not make his task any easier (he once quipped that there were two professions in which the amateur excelled the professional: military strategy and prostitution).[62] And whereas their military abilities remain questionable, his diplomatic skills in dealing with them do not.

Was Eisenhower, then, the true architect of victory? Nothing in his original 1942 plans foresaw the actual shape of the decisive campaigns of 1944–45; nor did anything in the COSSAC plans of 1943 or his revisions

A somber Eisenhower studies a map of the invasion area.

of those plans in 1944.[63] Nevertheless, the evidence presented here points overwhelmingly to an affirmative response to the question.

In terms of the architectural metaphor, Eisenhower was clearly responsible in early 1942 for developing the general ideas of Marshall and the army general staff into a strategic concept and a set of original "blueprints" for the OVERLORD operation, which became the key to Allied victory in Europe,[64] and for insisting on its central place in Allied strategy. He also played a major role in obtaining the approval of the "customers," in this case Roosevelt and Churchill, and of such vital "subcontractors" as the U.S. Navy and the British Chiefs of Staff. From April though July he played a pivotal role by keeping the project viable, minimizing dispersions to other projects, pressing for the appointment of an actual "construction manager," and defining that individual's characteristics. Indeed, his boss General Marshall sent him to the "construction site" in England to check on progress in May and June and, after his negative assessment, assigned him to be that manager as a means of keeping the plans alive. Then in July, Marshall had Eisenhower revise the blueprints in one final effort to retain the plan as the focal point of Allied strategy in 1942.

After the failure of this effort, Eisenhower was assigned to other projects in North Africa, Sicily, and Italy while Marshall and his staff fought for a modified version of his original blueprints for 1943 and 1944. Although they were unable to halt the other projects, they did succeed in forcing reconcentration on Eisenhower's original project for 1944. Meanwhile, Eisenhower's direction of those other projects in 1942–43 enabled him to obtain the experiences and exhibit the characteristics necessary to implement successfully a modified version of the original plan. When it became clear that Marshall could not be spared from Washington for this task, Eisenhower became the logical choice. Soon after his appointment he also played the role of architectural overseer and modifier of the plan. Key subcontractors further modified it as they proceeded, and they bore a major responsibility for the successful completion of the project—but always under the watchful and approving eye of the original architect, who had appointed many of them. By this time, Eisenhower had become the "chairman of the board" as well as the construction manager charged with ensuring completion on time and within budget.

One role did not negate the others. To the contrary, they were mutually reinforcing. Who was better qualified to serve as chairman of the board, construction manager, and overseer of the modification and implementation of plans than the architect who had originally written those plans— and the commander's job description—more than two years earlier?

17. D-day: Analysis of Costs and Benefits

Gerhard L. Weinberg

When we look back on the events of D-day and the campaign that followed, a number of images immediately appear before our eyes, even if no pictures are projected onto a screen. We see in our imagination the vast fleets approaching the shore, men scrambling into the water from landing craft as the gates open or the ramps are lowered, parachutists jumping into the unknown, defensive fire—at first sporadic, then picking up—long siegelike warfare reminiscent of the trenches of World War I, Cherbourg surrendering and Caen obliterated, more and more French communities shattered by bombs and artillery, the carnage of the German forces trying to escape the Falaise Gap, the dash across France, the liberation of Paris, the failure of MARKET GARDEN and the grinding campaign of the late fall, the German Ardennes offensive and death in the snow, the bridge at Remagen, the rush into Germany, the ruined towns of Germany with white—or more likely gray—sheets hanging out of the windows, ghastly scenes in the camps as Allied troops enter as liberators, the endless miles of German soldiers trudging to POW camps on one side of the road as Allied tanks and trucks roll forward on the other.

These mental images present some glimpses of the costs: death at Omaha Beach and parachutists hanging in the trees, destroyed towns and the gaunt looks of men too long under fire, crashed gliders and a storm-wrecked Mulberry harbor. If we visit the battlefields today, we see much reconstruction from the physical damage of war, but not too far away are the rows of crosses and stars of David in the cemeteries. A reasonably accurate compilation arrives at a total of over 850,000 Allied military casualties, a figure that does not include the sick or the tens of thousands of civilian casualties.[1] German casualties were substantially higher, even if we exclude the enormous numbers of prisoners taken by the Allies in the last weeks of the fighting. A German estimate of 250,000 military casualties, compared to 170,000 Allied casualties, up to 22 August 1944 seems to provide a reasonable benchmark for the campaign as a whole.[2] If the human costs were high, the material ones were enormous. The 1944 joke, that the barrage balloons alone kept the British Isles from sinking under the weight of supplies stocked in preparation for the invasion, may serve as a reminder of the vast expenditure of money and material resources that went into the invasion and its follow-up operations.

Was it worth it? To answer this question demands consideration of the alternatives. After all, the Allies did not land in Normandy because they thought the scenery beautiful or the people charming, and the Germans did not try to hold on in Western Europe because they had always wanted to see Paris. The Allies were trying to defeat Germany the quickest and least costly way possible, while the Germans were hoping to hold on until either victory in battle or a split in the hostile alliance they themselves had created provided the opportunity to continue that demographic revolution on which they had set their hearts, to which they had harnessed their power, and which they were carrying forward with grim determination even as the fighting raged on. Thus, alternatives to an invasion of northwest Europe in the summer of 1944 for the Western Allies would appear to comprise two basic types: geographical and chronological. Anglo-American leaders could have made their major push elsewhere, or they could have attacked in the same place but at another time.

The geographic alternatives to northwest France were Italy, the Balkans, or a combination of these two. An assault on Norway, though repeatedly considered during the war, was quite correctly thought of as an operation for significant but local advantages, even by its advocates, and was never believed to be a substitute for a major invasion of Europe. Even if completely successful, such an operation would have left the Germans in full control of Central and Western Europe. The campaign in Italy, of course, had already been in progress for almost a year by the time of D-day. Why not massively reinforce the Italian front and perhaps supplement operations there with a major landing in Greece and/or on the coast of Yugoslavia? At various times, some in the British leadership made suggestions along these lines, though always with the claim that an invasion of northwest Europe at "some time in the future" would not thereby be precluded. In practice, however, that future time most likely would not have arrived before the Red Army overran all of Western as well as Central Europe or, alternatively, the first atomic bombs fell on Germany in August 1945.

The reasons that the geographical alternative would have led to indefinite postponement of any cross-Channel invasion were twofold. In the first place, the logistic support needed for the sorts of operations and the size of forces called for by such a strategy would have made any invasion of northwest Europe impossible before the summer of 1945 or, more likely, the summer of 1946. Even the small-scale British operation in Greece in the winter of 1944–45 absorbed vast numbers of soldiers and great quantities of logistic support. In his diary, Field Marshal Alan Brooke repeatedly lamented these diversions, but he at no time acknowledged how precisely this experience, limited though it was, proved the correctness of General George Marshall's assertion that any added operation in the Mediterranean would act like a suction pump on the resources of the Allies and thereby preclude effective action elsewhere. And in Greece the British were not fighting any Germans, for the Wehrmacht had already left.

A second reason that any larger operations in the central and eastern Mediterranean would have precluded an invasion in the west was the nature of the terrain Allied troops were certain to encounter. The suggestion, occasionally voiced during the war, that any such operation would quickly bring the forces of the Western Allies into Eastern and Central Europe was based on the entirely erroneous assumption that the area is as flat as the maps on which these thrusts were happily projected. Just because Joseph Stalin was an accomplished liar, one ought not automatically to assume that everything he ever said was false. His statement at the Moscow conference on 27 October 1943 that a campaign in Italy would eventually run into the Alps can be confirmed by a look at any map.[3] In view of the trouble the Allied armies had pushing the Germans back in the mountainous terrain of Italy, there is no reason to assume that they would have found the even more difficult terrain of the Balkans any easier. The minimal openings in this forbidding landscape, like the often-mentioned Ljubljana gap, were unpromising avenues for the unfolding of Allied military power.

It has become something of an axiom among both historians and the public that the Italians could not or would not fight. These assertions ought to be examined carefully. James Sadkovich has done so for several engagements of World War II,[4] but the stereotype of Italian buffoonery persists. The point that begs to be made here relates to World War I and to the fact that a great deal of fighting took place in the very areas Allied troops would have been obliged to traverse while moving from Italy into Central Europe. Anyone who has ever taken a good look at the Dolomite Alps from the air, on the ground, or by taking the train from Vienna to Venice is likely to acquire a new view of Italian military effectiveness. Going up those steep slopes against an enemy entrenched in the higher elevations was an awesome task for any army; that the Italians got as far as they did in the Isonzo battles testified to their bravery and persistence, even if they never reached their ultimate goal.

The terrain had in no way changed between the wars. On the contrary, a good case can be made for the assertion that the high rate of fire of modern weapons made a World War II army even more dependent on logistic support than a World War I force, so that the limitations of steep terrain and poor, narrow roads would have imposed even greater obstacles on the Allied armies than on the earlier Italian army. The reality of 1943–45 was that the "soft underbelly of Europe" might be slightly more difficult for the Germans to reinforce than any front in the west, as Brooke always argued; but as the beaches at Gela, Salerno, and Anzio, to say nothing of the mountains of Italy, showed all too dramatically, the Germans could always send in enough forces to combine with difficult terrain in holding the Allies to minute advances when they could advance at all.

A further point is that it would have been impossible for the Allies to permanently conceal from the Germans that their main effort was in the south, not the northwest, of Europe. Obviously, German recognition of such an emphasis by the Western Allies would have encouraged them to redeploy units from the west to the southeastern theater. Such a reallocation would, of course, have made fighting over the poor terrain even more difficult for the Allies—and in an area that could not have been reached by fighters and fighter-bombers from the highly developed system of air bases in the United Kingdom. A massive campaign in the south might have brought the Western Allies to the Alps and into Albania and Bulgaria as well as Greece, but hardly much further. I will return to this point later; suffice it to say that Italy and southeast Europe simply offered no prospect of making a truly major contribution to the defeat of Germany. From a purely military point of view, it certainly would have made no sense for the Western Allies to employ the bulk of their forces in terrain most suited for defense, least suited for any rapid offensive drives, and hardest both to protect from the air and to supply. Maximizing disadvantages and minimizing whatever advantages one does have hardly constitutes military brilliance.

If no other place made sense, what about another time? What about an invasion in the west earlier or later than June 1944? In his 1980 book, Walter S. Dunn, Jr., argued in great detail that an invasion in the west was not only possible in 1943 but would have been both easier militarily and more politically desirable.[5] There are a number of difficulties with this argument. Moving the Allied victory over the submarines from the summer of 1943 forward to 1942 may provide a brilliant basis for arguing that there was no shipping problem and no submarine menace in 1943, but it in no way alters the sad reality that the Allies did not turn the tide in the war against the U-boats until May 1943 and that ship construction did not exceed total losses until the fall of 1943.[6] A shortage of shipping constituted a stranglehold on the strategy of the Allies; this is a major factor in all World War II situations that has all too frequently been disregarded.

Furthermore, there is something weird about the argument advanced by Dunn that the German units in the west were weak in 1943—because of the losses incurred in Tunisia, Sicily, and Italy—and would therefore have been overwhelmed easily by the Allies, under a set of assumptions that required that those prior battles should never and would never have been fought.[7] Those who suggest alternative courses of action for specific operations or choices in World War II all too often assume that everything else would have gone exactly the way it did, when the different course advocated necessarily implies changes in any number of other developments.

The Allies originally did hope to land in the west in 1943. They did not give up on this possibility until their loss of the race for Tunisia in late November 1942 showed them that a major campaign in North Africa was still ahead in 1943, and that this in turn would preclude the transfer of sufficient forces to England for a cross-Channel attack in 1943 before the weather turned too bad. Although Sir Arthur Bryant later excised the relevant portions of Brooke's diary, the fact is that until the events in North Africa determined otherwise, the Chief of the Imperial General Staff, as did Churchill and the Americans, hoped that an invasion in Western Europe would be possible in 1943.[8]

When the Germans and Italians, as a result of the unwillingness of Vichy French forces to assist the Allies, won the race for Tunisia, the options for the Western powers were limited. Given the complicated situation in French North Africa, there was never any possibility of simply leaving a force sufficient to contain the armies of Rommel, von Arnim, and Messe in Tunisia while shifting resources and units to England for a summer 1943 invasion of France. The only option was to drive the German-Italian forces out of Africa entirely, and that was going to take time. The real question was, what to do thereafter?

It is conceivable that not invading Sicily and the mainland of Italy in 1943 would have made it possible to move D-day up a month or so, but at enormous political and military cost for the Allies. What would the Soviet Union have thought? The political cost would have been the great risk of a separate peace on the Eastern Front had the Allies halted all serious fighting against the Germans for twelve months. Once the Germans recognized that the Allies were through campaigning in the Mediterranean, why would they not move additional units to meet an invasion of France, thus greatly increasing the risks of the invasion—risks that, as we will see, were much higher than generally thought? Whatever may or may not be said about the campaigns in Sicily and Italy in 1943–44, they certainly obliged the Germans to devote more forces to the Mediterranean theater than they intended, imposed substantial losses on those forces, increased the number of Allied units with substantial combat experience, and provided air bases of great significance for air attacks on portions of German-controlled Europe that were otherwise practically inaccessible at the time.

The other temporal alternative for the Normandy invasion would have been to attack later than June, a possibility that Brooke preferred in order to push greater operations in Italy, and one that General Eisenhower was obliged to contemplate if the weather in early June was too bad for an invasion attempt. Had the weather precluded an early June crossing, the timing and tide conditions would clearly have left no choice but to wait; however, the disadvantages were obvious, and Eisenhower knew what most of them were at the time. Leaks would not have been an issue had the invasion originally been scheduled for a later date, so this point, which surely weighed heavily on Eisenhower once the troops had been briefed for an early June landing, need not be considered here.

What does have to be looked at is a set of other factors. First, the speculation that a later invasion would have been easier because of a greater weakening of German military strength by the fighting on the Eastern Front ignores the prior decision of the Allies to try to coordinate the timing of their respective attacks on the Germans from east and west. Had the invasion in the west not been scheduled for May or June, the Soviets might have decided to wait with a major offensive themselves. Nor was the offensive launched by the Allies in Italy on 12 May 1944 likely to have any effect of further weakening German strength in France. Everything that was known then and everything known now about German force al locations makes clear that no additional German units were going to be transferred from the west to the Italian front in the summer of 1944, regardless of what happened on the latter front. Quite the contrary, the Germans in 1944 were strengthening, not weakening, their defenses in the west, and a postponed invasion would have run into heavier, not lighter, resistance. There is, in addition, another side to the issue of weather: The longer the Allies waited, the shorter the good campaign weather in the west and the sooner storms in the Channel could be expected to interfere with the building up of any bridgehead.

Indeed, the weather proved to be one of the two factors that argued most strenuously for an invasion in early June. That date had two enormous advantages—one that was in part fortuitous, and one that was in part the result of careful Allied planning. The partially fortuitous event was a very short opening in the weather. The prior Allied success in sweeping the Germans out of both the waters of the North Atlantic and the skies over it enabled them to see its approach and to act on that knowledge—while the Germans had no idea of its coming. As a result, the success of the invasion was greatly favored by its attaining of tactical as well as strategic surprise; the Germans simply assumed that in the terrible weather no invasion would be attempted. They therefore believed that they had a wonderful opportunity to arrange a conference of commanders who were obviously not needed at their own headquarters; the rest, as well as their minimal sea and air reconnaissance forces, could take a few days off.

The other argument for an invasion at the earliest possible date is related to the success of the great deception operation, FORTITUDE.[9] The carefully designed Allied effort to deceive the Germans into thinking that the Normandy landing was a diversion and that the main invasion would come in the Pas de Calais area proved to be as important for the success of the invasion as the Allies had anticipated; but, of course, no one could be certain beforehand how long it would work. We know today that the Germans were misled by this deception well into late July—even longer than the Allies had hoped for—and that the notional or imaginary divisions fabricated in the course of the deception were still mucking up German intelligence estimates in August.[10] A point that cannot be stressed too heavily is that Eisenhower simply could not count on the indefinite maintenance of the deception; every day that passed was another day when some slip or mischance could blow the whole scheme, with terrible implications for Allied efforts. Here was another factor that argued for launching the invasion at the earliest possible date.

These two points—the fortunate break in the weather (which the Germans had been prevented from learning about) and the extraordinary success of the deception operation (which convinced the Germans to believe information that was false)—bring us to a major issue concerning the invasion that has not always been given the attention it deserves: the enormous risk in the whole enterprise. In retrospect, the success of the landing is often seen as a foregone conclusion; the image created is one of great bravery but little doubt. German postwar scholars have at times referred to the great caution of the Western Allies and their reluctance to move at all unless assured of overwhelming odds in their favor.[11] Such assertions, frankly speaking, amount to a lot of nonsense.

The element of risk in the invasion should be seen from two perspectives: German hopes and Allied fears. At the time, the Germans not only hoped but seriously expected to defeat any invasion attempt in the west and believed themselves to be in an excellent position to accomplish this goal. They anticipated such a victory with considerable confidence and even pleasure because, among other reasons, they planned to follow it up with a massive transfer of forces to the Eastern Front for a resumption of their earlier string of victories there. They assumed, entirely correctly, that any second invasion attempt would take the Allies a long time to prepare, that the general time frame for such a renewed assault would be fairly easily predictable, and that they would therefore have plenty of time to rebuild their forces in the west in anticipation of a second D-day. The Germans hoped to take advantage of their interior lines, shifting units from front to front somewhat as they had in World War I.

What gave the Germans confidence? First, it must be remembered that on three prior occasions the Germans had come close to throwing an Allied landing force back into the sea: at Gela in Sicily, at Salerno, and at Anzio. In the case of Anzio, they at one point actually thought that they had smashed the beachhead. Having come so close three times, they anticipated doing better when challenged close to their main center of power, a center where their own forces in the initial stages were likely to be substantially larger than any invading army, and where their 1942 success at Dieppe appeared to offer a marvelous precedent. There were, however, serious concerns on the German side, particularly about the weakness of the German air force and qualitative and quantitative deficiencies of manpower in German combat units. There was also much argument about the best way of conducting operations against an Allied landing, but there is simply no evidence that the Germans believed the prospect to be hopeless—quite the contrary. In a portion of Europe that they had controlled for four years, the Germans awaited an invasion with some awareness of the dangers ahead but with considerable confidence.

Substantially reinforcing the German hopes of rebuffing any assault was the knowledge that two of the new V-weapons—so often delayed by development problems and the impact of the Allied bomber offensive— were finally to become available. The expectations that the Germans attached to those weapons proved to be exaggerated, but that, of course, could not have been known at the time. Furthermore, the Germans also believed, with some justification, that new developments in U-boat warfare, upon which they had been feverishly working for some time, would assist in weakening any Allied invasion force by depriving it of reinforcements and supplies. They anticipated that the new submarines, which did not have to surface to recharge their batteries and could move underwater much faster than the convoys, would turn the tide in the battle of the Atlantic once more in Germany's favor. Such a success would leave any Allied landing force that did establish itself ashore in a terrible predicament.

The other side of this equation was the very real concern of the Western Allies that the invasion might fail. Their leaders, for obvious reasons, did not advertise these worries at the time, and they have tended to vanish in the afterglow of victory, but they were most certainly present beforehand. The Allies were well aware of the size of the force with which they intended to assault the Germans: Even after the increase on which General Montgomery had insisted and in which all the others concurred, eight divisions would undertake an invasion against an area held by well over 50, possibly as many as 60, German divisions. It was obvious at the time, though often overlooked since, that in the initial weeks of operations the Germans would enjoy a vast superiority in numbers of men, tanks, and guns. The critical point was whether the Allies could get ashore and then build up their forces quickly while simultaneously restraining the Germans from concentrating their superior strength against the beachhead. This objective was to be attained by a combination of deception—keeping a large proportion of German units tied up elsewhere in anticipation of a landing the Allies did not intend to make—and disruption of the transportation system by bombing and sabotage, to slow down the rate of German reinforcement.[12] These projects both ended up working, but there were no money-back (or lives back) guarantees associated with them. The evidence is solid that the American air commanders were exceedingly skeptical about the success of the enterprise;[13] many of the British commanders had their doubts. Churchill himself came around to full support of the whole landing operation only in early May 1944.[14]

The text of Eisenhower's draft announcement in case the invasion failed has been known since its publication by his naval aide in 1946.[15] It has also long been known that the famous picture of Eisenhower with the paratroopers the night before D-day reflects his concern over having to put aside his advisers' written objections to the American airborne operation because of anticipated excessive casualties. The possibility of a disaster was not discussed very much at the time, but it had to be in the back of all the Allied leaders' minds. When President Roosevelt decided to appoint Eisenhower rather than Marshall to lead the invasion, the close calls in Sicily and Salerno were in the recent past. The Sicily landing was one of the few times when Roosevelt personally went to the map room during the war to get the most up-to-date reports on a military operation; in the early stages of the Salerno landing, Brooke was concerned that it had failed.[16]

The appointment of Eisenhower to command the invasion should be

SHAEF commander Eisenhower conducting the man who was to have taken his job, General George C. Marshall (to Eisenhower's right), on a tour of American positions in Normandy.

seen at least in part as a measure that would leave open the possibility of designating Marshall to head up a second cross-Channel assault if the first one did not work.[17] The gathering of the Combined Chiefs of Staff in England in June 1944 ought to be viewed as part of the same conceivable scenario. Everyone wanted the invasion to be successful, would do what they could to make it so, and put on a serious, optimistic exterior. But there was, in the background, recognition of the enormous risk, the possibility of failure, and the need to consider the option of a second try.

Precisely because they thought it so unlikely that they could contribute in a major way to any second attempt, the British leaders, including Churchill, were hesitant. Their army had been driven off the Continent three times already: from Norway, from the west, and from Greece. If the cross-Channel invasion failed, only minimal contingents of British soldiers would be available for a second try. The financial resources of the United Kingdom had been exhausted long since, and the material resources were no longer adequate for the equipment of the nation's armed forces; only American aid and Commonwealth participation were keeping Britain in the war. Now the human resources were also running out: Even before the liberation of Paris, a British division had to be broken up to provide replacements for others. The British army was shrinking, not growing; in the background, for those in charge, were not only the terrible memories of Ypres, the Somme, and Passchendaele but the more recent mass surrenders at Singapore and Tobruk.

The Americans had gambled on creating fewer divisions than their original program had once called for, but the possibilities of reversing that decision or of shifting existing men and material to the ground forces and to Europe were still open. It must be remembered that the first time a whole American army was engaged in the Pacific theater in one operation at one time—something that had occurred in Sicily in July 1943—did not take place until the Leyte landings of October 1944. By that time, three whole Allied army groups were already deployed in the ground fighting in the west. (The first engagement of even one army group in the Pacific was not expected to take place until the spring of 1946, and then with an army from the European theater [First Army] included in it.) Therefore, from the American perspective, a June 1944 landing looked like a great risk that was worth taking. If it should fail, there would just have to be another try, and the necessary human and material resources could and would be made available.

This weighing of risks necessarily raises the question of what precisely was at stake, both as seen at the time and as viewed in retrospect. A most important consideration as of the spring of 1944 as well as from today's perspective is the issue of costs. The record of wars over the preceding hundred years shows all too clearly that human and material costs go up, not down, as a conflict is prolonged. The second year is worse than the first, the third is worse than the second, and so on. In the very final days there may be a quick collapse of resistance and hence a reduction in casualties, but up to that point, the record is clear: Casualties and destruction increase the longer a war lasts. Allowing the Germans more time to consolidate their hold on Europe, mobilize their resources, exploit the occupied area, develop new weapons, and strengthen their defenses against amphibious assault was sure to raise, not lower, the ultimate cost in lives and treasure regardless of the specific strategy adopted.

The Americans' push for a direct thrust as opposed to peripheral operations was in part a recognition of the fact that an escalation in sacrifices accompanies the passage of time. One need only contemplate the possibility of the atomic bomb's being available a year earlier to end the war in Europe in August or September 1944 instead of May 1945 to get a sense of the millions of lives saved and cities preserved; or, alternatively, to think of a further period of struggle in Europe, ended by the explosions of August 1945 after hundreds of thousands of additional deaths and further enormous destruction.

In addition to their belief in the speediest possible attainment of victory, the Americans and British clearly recognized the political and psychological importance of the Western Allies making a substantial contribution to the fighting. The Soviet Union was carrying the overwhelming majority of the burden. Was it really in America and Britain's interest to have that situation continue to the end of hostilities in Europe? There was, on the one hand, the danger of exhaustion or defeat of the Soviet ally; on the other hand was the possibility that the Soviet Union would practically win the war by itself. Neither offered an inviting prospect. If Germany defeated the Red Army, the burden that would have to be carried by American and British forces was certain to increase enormously; surely it made more sense to fight the Germans under circumstances in which the Soviet Union carried a substantial share. The horrendous price that the latter was paying for the stupidity of Stalin's earlier policy of helping the Germans drive the Allies off the Continent in the north, west, and southeast, only to find the Soviet Union having to fight the Germans off in the east, showed just how much wiser it was to participate in a joint effort than to be by one's self.

But what if it all went the other way? What if the Red Army defeated the Germans single-handedly? Would it be in the interest of Britain and the United States to face a postwar Europe with the Red Army in control from the Pyrenees to the Black Sea? Could they expect the Soviets to draw back to the lines the British had proposed in the European Advisory Commission (EAC) in 1943 if they had, in effect, been left to fight the overwhelming bulk of the German army by themselves? Would it, in the meantime, have been helpful for Britain to have endured the whole onslaught of the V-1s and V-2s from nearby German launching sites all through 1944 and the first half of 1945? In this connection, it must be remembered that the Western Allies had considerable knowledge about those weapons *before* they began to fall on the United Kingdom. They also knew a great deal about the German plans for a renewed offensive with their new and greatly improved submarines. Was it not in their interest to seize or neutralize the bases on the French Atlantic coast from which such an offensive would be mounted most effectively?

These considerations affected Great Britain as well as the United States. Would an already weakened Britain not have been even more exhausted had there been no cross-Channel invasion? However grim the road from Normandy to the Baltic—to borrow the title of Montgomery's memoirs—

was that course of action not preferable to being battered from the air and at sea until the Red Army displaced the Wehrmacht on the far shore? Was OVERLORD essential even if, in the interim, the Allied armies in Italy had, under British overall command, finally reached the Alps? To phrase the question is to answer it; whatever the reservations and doubts entertained in London, there was always a belief in the need for an invasion at some point in time. That commitment, even though in a minimal form, had been nurtured even during the dark days when Britain stood alone.[18]

As for the United States, the situation looked then and looks in retrospect to be one of compelling logic, of inevitable action. If the United States expected to play a major role in the postwar world, a role that might enable it not merely to assert its continued independence but also to adopt policies to preclude a third world war, it could do so only by actually getting into Central Europe. One of the most important byproducts of the German decision to call for an armistice in 1918 rather than to fight on had been the ending of World War I under circumstances that were very different from those that the Allies had anticipated. The expectation then had been that the war would run at least into 1919 and possibly into 1920, with the United States providing a large proportion of the needed troops: The American buildup was geared to an 80- or 100-division force on the Western Front on 1 July 1919. Had those expectations been fulfilled, the U.S. role at the peace conference, as compared with that of Britain and France, would have been far greater. America's influence diminished when the war ended so much sooner than expected, at a time when the American contribution was substantial but far smaller than had been anticipated. Nor had the armies of the Allies, including the American one, reached Central Europe when the fighting ended in November 1918.

In World War II, because there was no way to supply any American army in Italy with the pogo sticks needed to hop the Alps, it had to batter its way into Central Europe across France. The British had needed the army of Wellington at Waterloo, not only the navy of Nelson, to ensure that Britain had a major role in the establishment of the settlement at the end of the Napoleonic Wars. If the United States were to have a significant share in the organization of the post–World War II order, it could not be done from bases in Iceland, escort carriers in the North Atlantic, or a presence in the Mediterranean. It had to come from the establishment of a significant presence in the middle of the continent of Europe, and to this end there was no other route than the one taken on D-day. No one could predict just how great that American share would end up being, but it was clear to President Roosevelt, Secretary Stimson, and U.S. military leaders that a major invasion in the west, whatever the costs and whatever the details, was the best road to a secure future.

Once the basic issue of costs has been faced, significant details remain to be considered. I now turn to matters that are minor only by comparison to the issue of victory or defeat. Issues that appear to have sufficiently broad implications to require at least a brief discussion within the framework of a general review of D-day and the subsequent campaign include the following: performance of top-level personnel on both sides, the role of Hitler in the direction of Germany's effort, the argument over ANVIL-DRAGOON, the issue of the broad versus the narrow front, the various disputes over bombing policy, and the question of Berlin and the related topic of occupation zones.

As one looks back today on the leading figures on the Allied side, only one appointment is hard to understand. In view of the difficulties that so many in the command structure had with Air Chief Marshal Sir Trafford Leigh-Mallory, it is baffling why he was selected to head the air component of the invasion force. Leigh-Mallory's death in a crash en route to a new post in Southeast Asia precluded his writing any memoirs, and the materials from his headquarters in the Public Record Office do not provide much in the way of clues to his problems, so this may be an unfair assessment. Nonetheless, the issues associated with this rigid, prickly individual remain something of a puzzle.[19]

There was never any chance that Montgomery would retain an overall ground command. It was a terrible mistake in judgment on the part of several of the British leaders to keep flogging this dead horse and encouraging Montgomery to believe that it could be resurrected. As Sir Michael Howard pointed out in a thoughtful paper, Montgomery was well adapted to the special problems of Britain's World War II army, but he was not the man to command a large Allied campaign.[20] On the American side, Patton was repeatedly rescued from the effects of his follies by Eisenhower, but that made the picturesque commander all the more eager to prove himself. It seems to me that he did so. The most striking demonstration is his breakthrough to Bastogne during the Battle of the Bulge; had Montgomery devoted energy to a drive from the north to meet Patton rather than making silly comments about the battle, the German spearheads might have been cut off instead of being pushed back.

On the German side, the personnel question that is most striking on even a cursory examination is the plethora of high-level commanders. Just as the German navy in World War II always seemed to have a vast excess of admirals and headquarters over available surface ships, the German military bureaucracy in the occupied west had grown, and continued to grow, beyond all conceivable utility. It is, of course, easy to understand the preference of field marshals, generals, and staff officers for cushy berths in France—especially in Paris—over assignments on the more dangerous and less comfortable Eastern Front. Precisely to cope with this problem, the Germans established a special command, that of General Walter von Unruh, dubbed General Heldenklau, or "hero kidnapper," by German soldiers. I have no explanation for the failure of von Unruh to carry out his assignment in the west. A 75 percent reduction in German headquarters in France would have immeasurably increased the effectiveness of the German forces and the difficulties of the Allied forces in the 1944 campaign. A dramatically smaller command apparatus could have reacted more effectively against Allied moves and made better use of Germany's limited manpower.

Much has been made—especially in the memoirs of Hitler's former generals—of the Führer's defects as a military commander. This is a vastly more complicated subject than the postwar self-exculpations of those who shortly before had been happily vying for medals, promotions, and bribes from him might lead one to expect. Whether a more mobile defense in Normandy would really have been better for German prospects, for example, is difficult to assess, especially in view of the late but effective development of Allied close air support operations. Although an argument can be made for the superior firepower and armor of the German Mark V and VI tanks, two aspects of armor operations on a looser front must be kept in mind: The Sherman tank, whatever its deficiencies in other respects, had a far more reliable engine than any German tank; and the Germans were running short of fuel. Both considerations make it doubtful that a more elastic German defensive posture would have been substantially more effective than the linear scheme adopted at Hitler's insistence.

The basic strategy of holding on to the ports for as long as possible and then wrecking them as completely as possible—Hitler's personal decision—certainly proved to be correct from the German perspective. The order to withdraw the two German armies threatened with being cut off in southwest France by the junction of Allied forces from the Normandy and Riviera landings was given reluctantly but in time for the bulk of the troops to avoid entrapment. Hitler still planned to win the war; there is not much evidence that his generals would have done better had they been kept on a longer leash. Certainly, they were as much misled by the deception operation and by the inability to read the weather as their Führer.

Reference to the Riviera landing brings up the argument over Operation ANVIL-DRAGOON, certainly one of the bitterest Anglo-American differences during the campaign in the west. Given the centrality of that campaign to the whole Allied effort and the serious logistic problems it faced, it seems that one must now come down on Eisenhower's side. Barring his insistence, it is certainly conceivable that Roosevelt and Marshall might have deferred to Churchill's opposition to an invasion of southern France. The prime minister, however, undermined his own argument by offering substitutes that could only look preposterous to the Americans. If one weighs the possibilities of a greater effort in Italy against the importance of the Mediterranean ports for the main front against Germany in the west, the balance clearly endorses Eisenhower's judgment.

Two further aspects of this question need to be drawn into the picture. Had there been no landing in southern France, the advance of the Allies from Normandy would have forced a withdrawal of the two German armies in southwest France anyway; these forces either would have been moved into Italy to slow down Field Marshal Alexander's drive or would have confronted a smaller Allied force in the west in the winter of 1944–45 on the old German-French border (or they could have been divided between the two fronts). None of these prospects looks wonderful in retrospect. A second point is related to the role of the French forces in the war. Arthur Funk pointed out that Eisenhower was one of the few higher Allied leaders who managed to develop a reasonable working relationship with Charles de Gaulle—no mean accomplishment. It surely made sense to assign the bulk of the reconstituted French army, and not just a token armored division, the task of liberating France instead of keeping them in the Italian campaign. Such a commitment of French forces, however, could be made most effectively in the south of France, directly across the Mediterranean from their major training and supply base in North Africa. There were, as is well known, major incidents of friction about Strasbourg, Stuttgart, and a small piece of territory in the alpine border area between France and Italy, but there is no reason to assume that there would have been fewer clashes under other deployment arrangements. The only thing these uproars tell is how completely some historians have misread President Truman when they emphasize his rough treatment of Soviet Foreign Commissar Molotov during the latter's visit to Washington—a treatment that was positively sweet and gentle by comparison with Truman's reaction to French conduct.

A fourth issue is the argument over the wide versus narrow front for the advance to and across the Rhine into Germany. Here again, one must endorse Eisenhower's judgment. Nothing in the record of Montgomery, by that time designated Field Marshal, justifies the belief that he could have brought the war to a quick end by a drive across the Low Countries and northern Germany to Berlin. Ignoring the possible responses of the Germans to such a narrow-front thrust, there is nothing in Montgomery's own record—when he had both the upper hand at the front and an opportunity to move rapidly—to suggest that such a procedure promised the results some have postulated. When he landed in southern Italy, Montgomery authorized his troops to sit tight—while the Salerno bridgehead was in dire straits and newspaper correspondents were driving north without hindrance. He forbade the American Ninth Army, the very army he always wanted kept under his control, to try to bounce the Rhine the way the American First and Third Armies did. During the last days of the war, he was still thinking of staging a repeat on the Elbe River of the set-piece crossing of the Rhine; only insistent prodding by both Churchill and Eisenhower could get Montgomery moving as rapidly as the situation at the front warranted. Numerous additional examples could be cited; whatever Montgomery's talents, mounting rapid thrusts was not one of them.

Could a narrow-front thrust by Patton have ended the war in 1944? The American Third Army was actually closer to the Rhine than Montgomery's armies, and on Patton's route the river was narrower and not divided into a series of separate waterways. The risks, however, compared with those of the invasion itself were much too high. With most of the ports in shambles or still in German hands, dependence on the beaches for logistic support of a massive thrust into Germany looked foolhardy then and looks equally—if not more—foolhardy now. The only avenue to an end of the war in 1944 lay on the other side: a recognition by the Germans— as the Italians, Finns, Romanians, Bulgarians, and Hungarians had seen earlier and the Japanese would see later—that fighting until the bitter end only makes the end more bitter.

The controversies associated with bombing policy are considerably more difficult to comment on. Once the Allied victory over the German air force in the early months of 1944 had cleared the way for an invasion and confirmed Allied control of the air over Western and much of Central Europe, the Allies probably had numerous alternatives available. The near-sainthood status acquired by Sir Arthur Harris in British eyes probably made it impossible for the Chief of the Air Staff to control him. If the enormous resources of Bomber Command were to be fully harnessed to an integrated Allied war effort, Churchill would have had to intervene in matters of bombing policy even more directly than he did. Surely the man who had allowed Sir Hugh Dowding, the winner of the Battle of Britain,

One manifestation of the application of strategic bombing in northwest Europe.

to be retired as his reward for gaining the most important British victory of the war could have found a way to handle this situation had he been so inclined. One must conclude that either Churchill was not so inclined or his military advisers failed to impress him as to the significance of the issue. A larger and more continuous commitment of Bomber Command to the bridge cutting, transportation, or oil bombing plan would have contributed more to quick victory than the continuation of area bombing. Bombing technology and expertise, which had earlier dictated such an approach, had greatly improved by the summer of 1944.[21]

The last issue that needs to be looked at is the interrelated questions of Berlin and the zonal division of Germany. The perspective of most people about this matter may have changed with the unification of Germany, but as with so many other questions, policy toward a defeated Germany must be examined partly in terms of what circumstances looked like when the decisions were originally made. President Roosevelt had repeatedly stated his preference for having the Americans reach Berlin first; but once the British had sold the Soviets on their proposal for the zonal division of Germany—a division that left a four-power-controlled Berlin deep inside the Soviet zone of occupation—that question was, in effect, one for the Germans rather than the Americans to answer. The German decision in the fall of 1944 to throw their last major reserves against the Americans in what they called the Ardennes offensive and the Western Allies came to call the Battle of the Bulge meant that the winter fighting would bring the Red Army within 50 miles of Berlin at a time when the Western Allies had not yet reached the German portion of the Rhine. Those circumstances and the resistance the Germans still put up meant that it simply made no sense for the Americans, who still expected a long and bloody campaign in the Pacific in which they wanted Soviet assistance, to pay a price for the capture of even more of the future Soviet zone of occupation than they were already likely to take. From today's perspective, one may be tempted to ask the rhetorical question whether it made any difference that the largest city in East Germany, Leipzig, had been cleared by American troops and then turned over to the Red Army. Leipzig was the city in which the biggest demonstrations took place in 1989. Is there anyone who thinks that the presence of American GIs there 44 years earlier had anything to do with Leipzigers' fervor for unification?

The zonal conception that President Roosevelt originally drafted in 1943 while en route to the Cairo conference, featuring a huge American zone reaching to Berlin,[22] would certainly not have been acceptable to the Soviet Union in 1943 when the Western Allies had not yet landed in the west. Whether a postponement of drawing the lines in the EAC (as the president clearly would have preferred) could have produced a division into zones whose borders were somewhere between the lines of the British proposal and those of the Roosevelt map is something we will never know. The possibility cannot be excluded, however; here, as in so many other places, the picture Churchill painted of himself in his memoirs—a picture all too often reflected in discussions of the war—was the exact opposite of the contemporary reality. It was the British who, in view of their diminishing power, wanted early agreements with the Soviet Union even at the cost of great concessions; the United States opposed such concessions in the expectation of slow but steadily unfolding American strength. Nothing in the record suggests that when Churchill changed his mind on this subject in the spring of 1945 Roosevelt would have followed a policy any different from that adopted by President Truman: The deal had been done, and the zonal borders stood.

In any case, if the Western Allies had not launched the invasion essentially when they did, we would hardly be examining such a question at this time. The question instead, at the very least, would have been whether the Soviet leadership would have been willing to permit any role at all for the United States and Great Britain in the control of a Germany overrun by the Red Army. Without D-day, the world would look very different indeed. What if the Western Allies had liberated Albania and occupied Bulgaria while the Soviet Union had come to control the human and material resources of all of Germany and most if not all of Western Europe?

As it is, the Western powers, although doing far less of the fighting than the Soviets, ended up with the most important and productive part of Europe. We will never know whether there could have emerged a Soviet school of revisionists, blaming Stalin for his foolishness in being bamboozled by Roosevelt into calling for an invasion in the west when any sensible Soviet leader would have invited the Western Allies to try their hands (or rather their feet) at mountain climbing in the Balkans while the tank armies of the Soviet Union roared through the richest part of the Continent.

Interestingly, the passage of time makes the significance of the invasion as the basis for major postwar developments all the more, not the less, apparent. If one asks a similar question about other major operations of World War II, one would, in my judgment, come up with a different answer. If the Anzio landing had never taken place, if General MacArthur had not insisted on a massive campaign in the central and southern Philippines, if we had left the Japanese sitting and freezing on Attu and Kiska, would the world look substantially different today? The answer in these cases is almost certainly no. It is entirely true that in size, complexity, and cost, none of these operations can compare with OVERLORD, but the point is still of interest. The case of D-day offers one example of image—of popular perceptions on both sides of the war at the time as well as those in the public memory afterwards—corresponding broadly with reality. The Normandy invasion was an event in the greatest conflict in the history of humankind that was indeed of enormous importance and to which, in spite of the great cost, there was no realistic alternative.

Notes

Introduction

1. Eisenhower Foundation, *D-Day: The Normandy Invasion in Retrospect* (Lawrence, University Press of Kansas, 1971).
2. A serious limitation of many of the earliest-published volumes was their almost total reliance on the records of the U.S. Army. In addition, the definition of their task—to concentrate on the actions of the U.S. Army and its constituent units—focused attention on organizational history and drastically restricted the interplay of personalities.
3. For a succinct discussion of Winston Churchill's enduring achievement in imposing his version of the history of World War II on succeeding generations, see Theodore A. Wilson, *The First Summit: Roosevelt and Churchill at Placentia Bay, 1941*, rev. ed. (Lawrence: University Press of Kansas, 1991), x–xii.
4. For example, see Omar N. Bradley and Clay Blair, *A General's Life* (New York: Simon & Schuster, 1983); J. Lawton Collins, *Lightning Joe* (Baton Rouge: Louisiana State University Press, 1979); and Sir Brian Horrocks, *Corps Commander* (London: Magnum, 1979).
5. A fascinating diary of this sort is John Colville, *The Fringes of Power: 10 Downing Street Diaries, 1939–1955* (New York: W. W. Norton, 1985).
6. See Forrest C. Pogue, *George C. Marshall*, 4 vols. (New York: Viking Press, 1963–86), and Randolph S. Churchill and Martin Gilbert, *Winston S. Churchill*, 8 vols. (Boston: Houghton Mifflin, 1966–1990). An example of the "personal conflict" genre is Nigel Hamilton, *Master of the Battlefield: Monty's War Years, 1942–1944* (New York: McGraw-Hill, 1983). Also see the magisterial biographies of General Eisenhower by Stephen E. Ambrose, *Eisenhower: Soldier, General of the Army, President-Elect, 1890–1952* (New York: Simon & Schuster, 1983); and David Eisenhower, *Eisenhower at War, 1943–1945* (New York: Random House, 1986).
7. A sampling of these works include Terry Copp and Bill McAndrew, *Battle Exhaustion: Soldiers and Psychiatrists in the Canadian Army, 1939–1945* (Montreal: McGill/Queen's University Press, 1990); John A. English, *The Canadian Army and the Normandy Campaign: A Study of Failure in High Command* (New York: Praeger, 1991); J. L. Granatstein, *Bloody Victory: Canadians and the D-Day Campaign, 1944* (Toronto: Lester and Orpen Dennys, 1984); and Reginald H. Roy, *1944: The Canadians in Normandy* (Toronto: Macmillan, 1984).
8. Russell F. Weigley, *Eisenhower's Lieutenants: The Campaign of France and Germany, 1944–1945* (Bloomington: Indiana University Press, 1981); Carlo D'Este, *Decision in Normandy* (New York: Dutton, 1983); Max Hastings, *Overlord: D-Day and the Battle for Normandy* (New York: Simon & Schuster, 1984); English, *The Canadian Army*.
9. Stephen E. Ambrose, *Band of Brothers: E Company, 506th Regiment, 101st Airborne From Normandy to Hitler's Eagle's Nest* (New York: Simon & Schuster, 1992); Stephen E. Ambrose, *Pegasus Bridge, June 6, 1944* (New York, Simon &

Schuster, 1985); Joseph Balkowski, *Beyond the Beachhead: The 29th Division in Normandy* (Harrisburg, Pa.: Stackpole Books, 1989).

Chapter 1. Wilmot Revisited: Myth and Reality in Anglo-American Strategy for the Second Front

1. Chester Wilmot, *The Struggle for Europe* (London: Collins, 1952), 11.

2. Ibid., 12.

3. Various aspects of the development of the cross-Channel concept and Anglo-American debate over it may be pursued in a number of official and unofficial accounts of World War II. On the British side are the United Kingdom Military Series, History of the Second World War, edited by Sir James Butler, especially J. R. M. Butler, *Grand Strategy*, 7 vols., vol. 2 (London: HMSO, 1957); J. M. A. Gwyer and J. R. M. Butler, *Grand Strategy*, vol. 3 (London: HMSO, 1964); Michael Howard, *Grand Strategy*, vol. 4 (London: HMSO, 1972); and John Ehrman, *Grand Strategy*, vols. 5 and 6 (London: HMSO, 1956). The memoirs of Sir Winston Churchill and Sir Frederick Morgan and the diaries of Sir Alan Brooke (Lord Alanbrooke) are also useful and provocative. On the American side the story can be traced in the series United States Army in World War II: Mark Watson, *Chief of Staff: Prewar Plans and Preparations* (Washington, D.C.: GPO, 1950); Gordon A. Harrison, *Cross-Channel Attack* (Washington, D.C.: GPO, 1951); Forrest C. Pogue, *The Supreme Command* (Washington, D.C.: GPO, 1954); Maurice Matloff and Edwin M. Snell, *Strategic Planning for Coalition Warfare, 1941–1942* (Washington, D.C.: GPO, 1953); Maurice Matloff, *Strategic Planning for Coalition Warfare, 1943–1944* (Washington, D.C.: GPO, 1959); Richard M. Leighton and Robert W. Coakley, *Global Logistics and Strategy, 1940–1943* (Washington, D.C.: GPO, 1956); and Robert W. Coakley and Richard M. Leighton, *Global Logistics and Strategy, 1943–1945* (Washington, D.C.: GPO, 1968). The memoirs of Admirals Leahy and King and Generals Arnold and Eisenhower are helpful, as is the Forrest C. Pogue, *George C. Marshall*, 4 vols. (New York: Viking Press, 1963–1986). Henry L. Stimson and McGeorge Bundy, *On Active Service in Peace and War* (New York: Harper Brothers, 1948); Robert E. Sherwood, *Roosevelt and Hopkins*, rev. ed. (New York: Harper Brothers, 1950); and Herbert Feis, *Churchill, Roosevelt, Stalin* (Princeton, N.J.: Princeton University Press, 1957) are also illuminating.

4. Quoted in Matloff, *Strategic Planning 1943–1944*, 11.

5. For discussion of American prewar strategic planning, see Watson, *Chief of Staff*, ch. 4; Matloff and Snell, *Strategic Planning 1941–1942*, chs. 1–3; and Maurice Matloff, "Prewar Military Plans and Preparations, 1939–1941," *United States Naval Institute Proceeding* 79 (Jul 1953): 741–48.

6. Notation by Eisenhower, 22 Jan 1942 entry, item 3, Operations Division (OPD) History Unit File. Quoted in Matloff, *Strategic Planning 1943–1944*, 12.

7. Notations by Eisenhower, 20 Apr 1942 entry, item 3, OPD History Unit File. Quoted in Matloff, *Strategic Planning 1943–1944*, 13.

8. For the development of the BOLERO plan and the decision for TORCH, see Matloff and Snell, *Strategic Planning 1941–1942*, chs. 8, 12, 13; Sherwood, *Roosevelt and Hopkins*, chs. 23, 25; Stimson and Bundy, *On Active Service*, ch. 17; and Winston S. Churchill, *The Hinge of Fate* (Boston: Houghton Mifflin, 1950), bk. 1, chs. 18, 22, and bk. 2, ch. 2.

9. For an analysis of this last phase of the debate, see Maurice Matloff, "The AN-VIL Decision: Crossroads of Strategy," in K. R. Greenfield (ed.), *Command Decisions* (Washington, D.C.: GPO, 1960), 383–400.

10. Wilmot, *Struggle for Europe*, 128, 338.

11. Ibid., 109.

12. Ibid., 448.

13. Ibid., 128.

14. For a detailed description of the organization and functions of Marshall's wartime planning staff, see Ray S. Cline, *Washington Command Post: The Operations Division, United States Army in World War II* (Washington, D.C.: GPO, 1951).

15. Quoted in Matloff, *Strategic Planning 1943–1944*, 523. For an analysis of American politico-military relations with the Soviet Union in the war against Germany, see Maurice Matloff, "The Soviet Union and the War in the West," *United States Naval Institute Proceedings* 82 (Mar 1956): 261–71.

16. Wilmot, *Struggle for Europe*, 130.

17. Matloff, *Strategic Planning 1943–1944*, 342.

18. For a more extensive analysis of Roosevelt's role as war leader, see Maurice Matloff, "Franklin Delano Roosevelt as War Leader," in Harry L. Coles (ed.), *Total War and Cold War* (Columbus: Ohio State University Press, 1962), 42–65.

19. Michael Howard, *The Mediterranean Strategy in the Second World War* (New York: Praeger, 1968), 69–70.

20. Wilmot, *Struggle for Europe*, 636; Hanson Baldwin, *Great Mistakes of the War* (New York: Harper and Brothers, 1950).

21. Ehrman, *Grand Strategy*, 5:393–94.

22. Wilmot, *Struggle for Europe*, 717.

Chapter 2. Biffing: The Saga of the Second Front

1. Churchill to Ismay, 8 Aug 1943, in Winston S. Churchill, *The Second World War*, 6 vols. (London: Cassell, 1948–54), 5: 583. If these examples appear fanciful, it is well to recall the proposed Operation ARMPIT (a thrust through Istria toward Vienna)—"a codename Churchill surely would have changed had the plan been approved." Warren F. Kimball, *Churchill and Roosevelt*, 3 vols. (Princeton, N.J.: Princeton University Press, 1984), 3: 225.

2. Churchill to Roosevelt, 6 Jul 1942, in Kimball, *Churchill and Roosevelt*, 1: 519. "One-Third BOLERO" was a Rooseveltian coinage. "Semi-Gymnast" seems to have been a misreading of "Super-Gymnast."

3. Roosevelt to Churchill, 8 Jul 1942, in ibid., 523.

4. Churchill to Hollis, 15 Jul 1942, in Churchill, *Second World War*, 5: 394. Ismay called it "somewhat bombastic." *The Memoirs of General Lord Ismay* (London: Heinemann, 1960), 248.

5. See J. R. M. Butler, *Grand Strategy*, vol. 3, pt. 2 (London: HMSO, 1964), 568–69, summarizing JP(41)823(O), "Operations on the Continent in the Final Phase," 9 Dec 1941. A copy of this plan was given to Marshall by Dill on 16 Mar 1942. ABC 381 BOLERO (3–16–42) sec. 1, Record Group (RG) 165, National Archives (NA), Washington, D.C.

6. See, e.g., Brooke diary, 1 Nov 1943, in Arthur Bryant, *Triumph in the West* (London: Collins, 1959), 59; Dill and Portal at CCS 56th and 58th meetings, 14

and 16 Jan 1943, Cabinet File (CAB) 99/24, Public Record Office (PRO), Kew, England.

7. Churchill, *Second World War*, 5: 67. Cf. Lt. Gen. Sir Frederick Morgan (COSSAC): "I was finding it harder and harder to laugh at the voice of certain of the people as recorded in whitewash on many a blank wall adjuring me to 'open the Second Front now.' I felt a pity that open publication was never permitted of the advice of our leading wit, 'Let's hear less nonsense from the friends of Joe.' " *Overture to* OVERLORD (London: Hodder and Stoughton, 1950), 38–39.

8. War Ministry (WM)(42)73, 11 Jun 1942, CAB 65/30, PRO. The aide-mémoire given to Molotov, with the key phrase suitably emphasized, is in Churchill, *Second World War*, 4: 305. Cf. Martin Gilbert, *Road to Victory: Winston S. Churchill 1941–1945* (London: Heinemann, 1986), 110–14, 119–21; Ivan Maisky, *Memoirs of a Soviet Ambassador* (London: Hutchinson, 1967), 282.

9. Churchill to Roosevelt, 8 Jul 1942, in Kimball, *Churchill and Roosevelt*, 1: 520–21. Amplified in COS to JSM, 8 Jul 1943, CAB 105/54, PRO.

10. War Cabinet Paper (WP)(42)373, 23 Aug 1942, CAB 66/28, PRO. Paraphrased in Churchill, *Second World War*, 5: 429–35; quoted in Gilbert, *Road to Victory*, 173–82.

11. Quoted in Harry C. Butcher, *My Three Years with Eisenhower* (London: Heinemann, 1946), 24. See also Dykes diary, 22 Jul 1942, in Alex Danchev, *Establishing the Anglo-American Alliance* (London: Brassey's, 1990), 178. Cf. Eisenhower to Ismay, 3 Dec 1960: "Many of our people, looking backward, still believe that we would have been better off had we undertaken that operation in late 1942 in view of the fact that Hitler was so busy on the Eastern Front. I do not share this view and have often publicly stated that I think the alternative, 'TORCH,' provided us with many later advantages, not the least of which was the training opportunity, through which both sides learned how Allied commands could and should work effectively." Quoted in Carlo D'Este, *Decision in Normandy* (London: Pan, 1984), 27.

12. Dykes diary, 22 Jul 1942, in Danchev, *Establishing the Alliance*, 179.

13. Brooke diary, 15 Apr 1942, in Arthur Bryant, *The Turn of the Tide* (London: Collins, 1957), 358.

14. See Forrest C. Pogue, *George C. Marshall*, 4 vols. (New York: Viking, 1963–87), 2: 345–49. Cf. Pogue notes, 28 Sep 1956, in Larry I. Bland (ed.), *George C. Marshall Interviews and Reminiscences for Forrest C. Pogue* (Lexington, Va.: George C. Marshall Research Foundation, 1991), 580–81.

15. Cf. the analyses in David Reynolds et al. (eds.) *Allies at War* (New York: St. Martin's Press, forthcoming).

16. See Brian Bond, "Alanbrooke and Britain's Mediterranean Strategy," in Lawrence Freedman et al. (eds.), *War, Strategy and International Politics* (Oxford: Clarendon, 1992), 175–93; Alex Danchev, "Britain: The Indirect Strategy," in Reynolds, *Allies at War*; Tuvia Ben-Moshe, "Winston Churchill and the 'Second Front': A Reappraisal," *Journal of Modern History* 62, 3 (1990): 503–37.

17. "So convincingly did the Prime Minister speak that King, as he remarked afterward, kept his hand on his watch." E. J. King and W. M. Whitehill, *Fleet Admiral King* (London: Eyre & Spottiswoode, 1953), 216. For glimpses of his sensitivity on this subject, see Churchill, *Second World War*, 5: 226–27, 542–43.

18. Dill to War Cabinet, 31 Dec 1942, Prime Minister's Papers (PREM) 3/499/7, PRO.

19. "Churchill took a special interest in the codenaming of the main operation

and with a dramatic flourish christened it 'OVERLORD.'" W. G. F. Jackson, *OVERLORD* (London: Davis-Poynter, 1978), 89.

20. The dichotomy of "opportunistic" and "determinist" is axiomatic for most writers on the Second Front, though many refuse both the thought and the vocabulary. For an unusually explicit treatment, see Trumbull Higgins, "The Anglo-American Historians' War in the Mediterranean," *Military Affairs* 34, 3 (1970): 84–88. The elaboration of "contingent" and the "exogenous-endogenous" formulation offered here are, as far as I know, my own.

21. The so-called Marshall memorandum, "Operations in Western Europe" (Apr 1942) shows this breakdown, including nine armored divisions. In Butler, *Grand Strategy*, 3(2): 675–81; extracted in Churchill, *Second World War*, 4: 281–82. At his meeting with Stalin, Churchill spoke of 27 American and 21 British divisions, adding, "Nearly half of this force would be armoured." WP(42)375, 29 Aug 1942, CAB 66/28, PRO.

22. "Note by the Minister of Defence," 3 Dec 1942, in Churchill, *Second World War*, 5: 588; "Cross-Channel Operations," Annex III to COS(42)466(O)(Final), "American-British Strategy in 1943," 31 Dec 1942, in Michael Howard, *Grand Strategy*, vol. 4 (London: HMSO, 1972), 612–13.

23. CCS 94, "Operations in 1942–43," 24 Jul 1942, in Howard, *Grand Strategy*, 4: xxiii–xxiv.

24. CCS 135, "Basic Strategic Concept for 1943," 26 Dec 1942, in ibid., 614–16.

25. COS(42)466(O)(Final), "American-British Strategy in 1943," 31 Dec 1942, in ibid., 612. "He himself had been against a campaign in Northern France in 1942 and 1943," Churchill told the dominion prime ministers in May 1944. "We had not then had experience of large-scale land operations, and the time was not ripe." Prime Minister's Meeting (PMM)(44)2nd, 1 May 1944, CAB 99/28, PRO.

26. F. M. Cornford, *Microcosmographia Academica* (Cambridge: Bowes and Bowes, 1938), 32. See Alex Danchev, "The Franks Report: A Chronicle of Unripe Time," in Alex Danchev (ed.), *International Perspectives on the Falklands Conflict* (London: Macmillan, 1990), 127–52. The medlar is a small fruit tree.

27. COS(42)345(O)(Final), "American-British Strategy," 30 Oct 1942, PREM 3/499/6, PRO. In a later version, "a sudden crack in German military power."

28. COS(42)466(O)(Final), "American-British Strategy in 1943," 31 Dec 1942, in Howard, *Grand Strategy*, 4: 602–13. Legal language peppered the Anglo-American strategic debate. The British, for example, were prone to rail against "*lawyers' agreements* made in all good faith months before, and persisted in without regard to the ever-changing fortunes of war." Churchill to Eden, 26 Oct 1943, quoted in Gilbert, *Road to Victory*, 541 (emphasis added).

29. Brooke to Dill (canceled draft), 16 Dec 1942, War Office (WO) 193/146, PRO. In the British paper for the Casablanca conference, the American divisional total was down to nine, "with perhaps a further three . . . collecting in the United Kingdom." COS(42)466(O)(Final), "American-British Strategy in 1943," 31 Dec 1942, in Howard, *Grand Strategy*, 4: 604.

30. Alan Brooke, "Notes for My Memoirs," quoted in Bryant, *Turn of the Tide*, 530. Cf. his diary, 30 Nov and 11 Dec 1942, in ibid., 528–29, 534–35.

31. CCS 170/2, "Symbol," 23 Jan 1943, and CCS 242/6, "TRIDENT," 25 May 1943, in Howard, *Grand Strategy*, 4: 625–31, 660–67.

32. Walter Scott Dunn, Jr., *Second Front Now* (University: University of Alabama, 1980); John Grigg, *1943* (London: Eyre Methuen, 1980), and "Looking Back at 1943," *Encounter* (Feb–Mar 1981): 88–93.

33. Russell F. Weigley, "The Political and Strategic Dimensions of Military Effectiveness," in Allan R. Millett and Williamson Murray (eds.), *Military Effectiveness*, vol. 3 (Boston: Allen & Unwin, 1988), 361–62. Cf. Stephen E. Ambrose, *Eisenhower*, vol. 1 (New York: Simon & Schuster, 1983), 181–82.

34. Churchill to COS, 2 Jan 1944, in Gilbert, *Road to Victory*, 633.

35. F. H. Hinsley et al., *British Intelligence in the Second World War*, 4 vols. (London: HMSO, 1979–90), 3(2): 9.

36. Strictly, Marshall spoke of "a democracy," meaning the United States. The remark has been given currency by Maurice Matloff, who quotes it in *Strategic Planning for Coalition Warfare 1943–44* (Washington, D.C.: GPO, 1959), 5; "Wilmot Revisited: Myth and Reality in Anglo-American Strategy for the Second Front," in Eisenhower Foundation, *D-Day: The Normandy Invasion in Retrospect* (Lawrence: University Press of Kansas, 1971), 119; and "Allied Strategy in Europe, 1939–1945," in Peter Paret (ed.), *Makers of Modern Strategy* (Oxford: Clarendon, 1986), 681.

37. See Morgan, *Overture to* OVERLORD.

38. See D'Este, *Decision in Normandy*; for the authorized version, see Nigel Hamilton, *Monty*, vol. 2 (London: Hamish Hamilton, 1983).

39. Later to include three airborne divisions and three armored brigades. These eight divisions would be built up to 24 by D plus 30 and to 30–plus by D plus 60.

40. Churchill, *Second World War*, 5: 69–70. The original document is COS(43)416(O), 30 Jul 1943, CAB 80/72, PRO.

41. Hinsley, *British Intelligence*, 3(2): 7–8.

42. Richard M. Leighton, "OVERLORD versus the Mediterranean at the Cairo-Tehran Conference 1943," in Kent R. Greenfield (ed.), *Command Decisions* (Washington, D.C.: GPO, 1960), 207. Elsewhere, he remarks that "the theory that the British planned to undertake 'OVERLORD' only against negligible opposition is unproved." "OVERLORD Revisited: An Interpretation of American Strategy in the European War, 1942–1944," *American Historical Review* 68 (1964): 937.

43. Churchill, *Second World War*, 5: 329; see also 331.

44. For recent reassessments, see Tuvia Ben-Moshe, *Churchill: Strategy and History* (Boulder, Colo.: Lynne Rienner, 1991); and John Charmley, *Churchill: The End of Glory* (London: Hodder and Stoughton, 1993). The former is the weightier. Cf. Noel Annan, "How Wrong Was Churchill?" *New York Review of Books*, 8 Apr 1993.

45. McCloy to Gilbert, 26 Apr 1982, quoted in Gilbert, *Road to Victory*, 760; Eisenhower to Ismay, 3 Dec 1960, quoted in D'Este, *Decision in Normandy*, 29; Morgan, *Overture to* OVERLORD, 38. Cf. Churchill, *Second World War*, 5: 514. A hecatomb was a great public sacrifice, properly of 100 oxen.

46. John Keegan, "Churchill's Strategy," in Robert Blake and William Roger Louis (eds.), *Churchill* (Oxford: Clarendon, 1993), 328.

47. Elisabeth Bowen, *The Heat of the Day* (London: Penguin, 1962), 92–93. First published in Britain in 1949, it was not published in the United States until 1968.

48. Pogue notes, 5 Oct 1956, in Bland, *Marshall Interviews*, 600.

49. Bowen, *Heat of the Day*, 178.

50. Churchill to COS, 19 Jul 1943, in Gilbert, *Road to Victory*, 445. Churchill was especially worried about relative reinforcement rates during the period D plus 30 to D plus 60. See Churchill to Eden and Roosevelt, 20 and 23 Oct 1943, in

Churchill, *Second World War*, 5: 254–55, 277–79. The other operation, interestingly, was JUPITER.

51. Portal interview by Forrest C. Pogue, 7 Feb 1947, quoted in D'Este, *Decision in Normandy*, 30.

52. This was Churchill's characterization after Yalta. Colville diary, 24 Feb 1945, in John Colville, *The Fringes of Power*, vol. 2 (London: Sceptre, 1987), 204. The anthropomorphism varied: After Tehran it was a donkey, a bear, and a buffalo. Lady Asquith interview by Kenneth Harris in *The Listener*, 17 Aug 1967.

53. First plenary meeting, 28 Nov 1943, CAB 99/25, PRO. Churchillian chauvinism is a theme developed in Michael Howard's influential distillation, *The Mediterranean Strategy in the Second World War* (London: Weidenfeld and Nicolson, 1968). It has not been much explored, however, in contradistinction to the grossly overworked theme of Churchillian imperialism.

54. Pogue notes, 5 Oct 1956, in Bland, *Marshall Interviews*, 589.

55. Churchill to Grigg and Brooke, 6 Nov 1943, and to Clementine, 6 Apr 1945, in Gilbert, *Road to Victory*, 548, 1283.

56. Jacob to Marder, n.d. [1966], Roskill Papers, 7/219, Churchill College, Cambridge.

57. Churchill, *Second World War*, 5: 332 (emphasis added).

58. Pogue notes, 28 Sep 1956, in Bland, *Marshall Interviews*, 580; Evelyn Waugh, *Men at Arms* (London: Penguin, 1964), 140. The opposition between Machiavelli and Ritchie-Hook was suggested to me by Timothy Garton Ash. See "In the Churchill Museum," *New York Review of Books*, 7 May 1987.

59. Churchill to Smuts, 11 Sep 1943, in Churchill, *Second World War*, 5: 116.

60. JSM to COS, 11 Jun 1944, quoted in Gilbert, *Road to Victory*, 805; Oliver Franks, *Britain and the Tide of World Affairs* (Oxford: Oxford University Press, 1955), 35.

61. All four, 16–20 Dec 1941, are in Kimball, *Churchill and Roosevelt*, 1: 294–308.

62. On the sources and interpretation of this pronouncement, see Alex Danchev, "Haig Revisited," *RUSI Journal* 135, 2 (1990): 71–74. Maurice Matloff noted that "the impact of the First World War on national approaches to coalition strategy in the Second World War needs more emphasis." "Allied Strategy in Europe," 696.

63. "1943," in Kimball, *Churchill and Roosevelt*, 1: 302–3.

64. The COS response, "Note on the sequence of events in the offensive against Germany," 20 Dec 1941, and Churchill's spirited rejoinder of 21 Dec 1941 are in PREM 3/499/2, PRO. See also Gilbert, *Road to Victory*, 20–22.

65. Churchill to Stalin, 24 Nov 1942, repeated to Roosevelt, 2 Dec 1942, in Kimball, *Churchill and Roosevelt*, 2: 51.

66. Warren F. Kimball, "Wheel Within a Wheel: Churchill, Roosevelt and the Special Relationship," in Blake and Louis, *Churchill*, 547.

67. Churchill to COS, 21 Dec 1941, PREM 3/499/2, PRO.

Chapter 3. Constraining OVERLORD: Civilian Logistics, TORCH, and the Second Front

1. James Huston, *The Sinews of War: Army Logistics, 1775–1953* (Washington, D.C.: Office of the Chief of Military History [OCMH], 1966), vii–viii; and

Richard Leighton and Robert Coakley, *Global Logistics and Strategy*, 2 vols., *1940–1943* and *1943–1945* (Washington, D.C.: OCMH, 1955 and 1968), 1: 3–15.

2. Roland G. Ruppenthal, "Logistic Planning for OVERLORD in Retrospect," in Eisenhower Foundation, *D-Day: The Normandy Invasion in Retrospect* (Lawrence: University Press of Kansas, 1971), 87–103; see also Ruppenthal, *Logistical Support of the Armies* (Washington, D.C.: OCMH, 1953), 178ff.

3. The historiography of Allied grand strategy and logistics is extensive. In the Department of the Army's green books series, The United States Army in World War II, see especially Maurice Matloff and Edwin M. Snell, *Strategic Planning for Coalition Warfare 1941–1942* (Washington, D.C.: OCMH, 1953); Gordon A. Harrison, *Cross-Channel Attack* (Washington, D.C.: OCMH, 1951); Kent Roberts Greenfield (ed.), *Command Decisions* (Washington, D.C.: OCMH, 1960); and Leighton and Coakley, *Global Logistics*. In the British series History of the Second World War, among the seven official volumes on grand strategy, see especially Michael Howard, *Grand Strategy*, vol. 4 (London: HMSO, 1972). See also Mark Stoler, *The Politics of the Second Front* (Westport, Conn.: Greenwood Press, 1977); Forrest Pogue, *George C. Marshall: Ordeal and Hope* and *Organizer of Victory* (New York: Viking, 1965 and 1973); Winston Churchill, *The Second World War* (Boston: Houghton Mifflin, 1948–53); and Arthur Bryant's compilation of British Chief of the Imperial General Staff Sir Alan Brooke's diaries, *The Turn of the Tide* and *Triumph in the West* (Garden City, N.Y.: Doubleday, 1957 and 1959).

4. Leighton and Coakley, *Global Logistics*; Ruppenthal, *Logistical Support*; Richard Leighton, "U.S. Merchant Shipping and the British Import Crisis," in Greenfield, *Command Decisions*, 199–223. Leighton and Coakley admirably detailed the "chronic, pervasive competition for resources" in relation to ground warfare logistics.

5. Harrison, *Cross-Channel Attack*, 8. See Eisenhower's 28 Feb 1942 appreciation of British civilian logistic needs as a primary argument for a cross-Channel emphasis: "no matter where we fight, the North Atlantic shipping routes must be guarded and kept relatively free of the enemy, so that England will not starve. A tremendous commerce traverses these routes monthly. Maximum safety of these lines of communication is a 'must' in our military effort, no matter what else we attempt to do." Alfred Chandler (ed.), *Papers of Dwight David Eisenhower*, 13 vols. (Baltimore: Johns Hopkins University Press, 1970), 1: 149–50. Military logistic considerations led to disregard for British import needs. See Jean Edward Smith, *Lucius Clay* (New York: Henry Holt, 1990), for the army approach to procurement and assessment of civilian needs.

6. See army officers' Anglophobia in Albert C. Wedemeyer, *Wedemeyer Reports!* (New York: Henry Holt, 1958), and civilian disgust at army attitudes toward Britons and civilians in Robert Paul Browder and Thomas G. Smith, *Independent: A Biography of Lewis W. Douglas* (New York: Knopf, 1986).

7. The official and most recent British account of merchant shipping management remains C. B. Behrens, *Merchant Shipping and the Demands of War* (London and Nendeln, Liechtenstein: HMSO and Kraus Reprints, 1978; 1st ed. 1955), which largely ignored the relationship between civilian logistics and grand strategy. See my multiarchival reassessments of Anglo-American wartime logistics diplomacy in Kevin Smith, "The Causes and Consequences of Dependence: British Merchant Shipping and Anglo-American Relations, 1940–1943" (Ph.D. dissertation, Yale University, 1990), and "Logistics Diplomacy at Casablanca: The Anglo-American Failure to Integrate Shipping and Military Strategy," *Diplomacy & Statecraft* 2 (Nov 1991): 226–52.

8. See Correlli Barnett, *The Audit of War: The Illusion and Reality of Britain as a Great Nation* (London: Macmillan, 1986); Brian Hogwood, *Government and Shipbuilding: The Politics of Industrial Change* (Westmead, Great Britain: Saxon House, 1979); Leslie Jones, *Shipbuilding in Britain: Mainly Between the Two World Wars* (Cardiff: University of Wales Press, 1957); J. R. Parkinson, *The Economics of Shipbuilding in the United Kingdom* (Cambridge: Cambridge University Press, 1960). For further discussion of industrial, managerial, and geopolitical impediments to increasing British merchant shipping capacity, see my unpublished paper, "The Onset of Dependence: British Shipbuilding and Anglo-American Shipping Relations in 1941," and "Causes and Consequences," 8–198.

9. Smith, "Causes and Consequences," 199–258; Behrens, *Merchant Shipping*, 91 103, Central Statistical Office (Britain) *Statistical Digest of the War* (London: HMSO, 1951), tables 152, 155, 156, 158; S. McKee Rosen, *The Combined Boards of the Second World War: An Experiment in International Administration* (New York: Columbia University Press, 1951), 108–30; Ministry of Transport (MT) File 65/28, "Estimate . . . for 1943," app. B, Public Record Office (PRO); Cabinet (CAB) File 123/86, Lionel Robbins note on War Cabinet Paper (WP) (42) 497, 12 Nov 1942, and J. M. Flemming memorandum, "Shipping Position," 29 Dec 1942, PRO; MT 59/2206, Salter to Churchill, 9 and 14 Jan 1942; MT 59/1937, F. H. Keenlyside to F. A. Griffiths, 30 Jan 1942; MT 59/2210, Salter to Leathers, 6 Apr and 22 May 1942; Churchill to Roosevelt 36 and Roosevelt to Churchill 113, 4 and 8 Mar 1942, in Warren F. Kimball, ed., *Churchill and Roosevelt: The Complete Correspondence*, 3 vols. (Princeton, N.J.: Princeton University Press, 1984), 1: 379–80, 390–93.

10. Smith, "Causes and Consequences," 231–58; MT 62/37, WP (42)157, 9 Apr 1942; MT 59/694, Minute by Minister of War Transport Frederick Leathers, 3 Jun 1942, Minute by Sir Cyril Hurcomb, Director-General of the Ministry of War Transport (MWT), 1 Oct 1942; Prime Minister's Papers (PREM) File 3/383/6&7, LP (42) 39th meeting, 26 Jun 1942, PRO; CAB 123/86, Robbins to Anderson, 20 Jul 1942.

11. Smith, "Causes and Consequences," 231–58, 464–94; W. K. Hancock and M. M. Gowing, *British War Economy* (London: HMSO, 1949), 417–35; R. J. Hammond, *Food: The Growth of Policy* (London: HMSO, 1951), 243–45; R. J. Hammond, *Food: Studies in Administration and Control* (London: HMSO, 1962), 254–57; MT 59/2206, Salter memorandum, 22 Jun 1942; CAB 86/3, AUB (43) 1, 5 Jan 1943.

12. PREM 3/383/6&7, LP (42) 39th meeting, 26 Jun 1942; Cherwell to Churchill, 17 Jul 1942.

13. PREM 3/383/6&7, WP (42) 311, 21 Jul 1942; Churchill to Roosevelt 123, 27 Jul 1942, in Kimball, *Churchill and Roosevelt*, 1: 541–42.

14. For further discussion of the Marshall memorandum and early Allied planning, see Stoler, *Politics*, 40–51; Ruppenthal, *Logistical Support*, 55–57; Matloff and Snell, *Strategic Planning*, 183–89; Leighton and Coakley, *Global Logistics*, 1: 360–62; Harrison, *Cross-Channel Attack*, 13–19; Larry I. Bland and Sharon Ritenour Stevens (eds.), *The Papers of George Catlett Marshall*, 3 vols. (Baltimore: Johns Hopkins University Press, 1991), 3: 157–59.

15. Churchill to Roosevelt 69 and 70, 15 and 17 Apr 1942, in Kimball, *Churchill and Roosevelt*, 1: 452–54, 458–59; Bryant, *Turn of the Tide*, 286–88; CAB 69/4, Defense Committee (Operations) (42) 11th meeting, 14 Apr 1942.

16. Eisenhower memo for Marshall, 23 Jul 1942 and CCS 94, Operations in 1942/3, 24 Jul 1942, cited in Harrison, *Cross-Channel Attack*, 30. Dwight D.

Eisenhower, *Crusade in Europe* (Garden City, N.Y.: Doubleday, 1948), 71; Robert Sherwood, *Roosevelt and Hopkins* (New York: Harper, 1948), 605–11; Pogue, *Marshall: Ordeal and Hope*, 313–32, 340–47; Bryant, *Turn of the Tide*, 320–29, 340–45; Matloff and Snell, *Strategic Planning*, 233–44, 266–67, 273–83; Leighton and Coakley, *Global Logistics*, 1: 383–87; Harrison, *Cross-Channel Attack*, 9–32; Bland and Stevens, *Marshall Papers*, 3: 242–46, 269–70, 277–78; Stoler, *Politics*, 52–63; Ruppenthal, *Logistical Support*, 88–90.

17. Bryant, *Turn of the Tide*, 450–51, 501, 528–29; Matloff and Snell, *Strategic Planning*, 236–38; MT 62/68, Salter to Hurcomb, 29 Oct 1942; MT 59/2210, BILGE 1301, Salter to Leathers and Hurcomb, 4 Nov 1942.

18. PREM 3/383/6&7, WP (42) 311, 21 Jul 1942; Matloff and Snell, *Strategic Planning*, 266; Leighton and Coakley, *Global Logistics*, 1: 455; Harrison, *Cross-Channel Attack*, 29–32; MT 62/59, Churchill minute to Leathers, 22 Jul 1942.

19. Bryant, *Turn of the Tide*, 450–51, 501, 528–29; Harrison, *Cross-Channel Attack*, 21, 32ff, 95–97. Eisenhower, the most Anglophilic of senior army officers, recoiled at Churchill's astonishment that TORCH eliminated a 1943 ROUNDUP, perceiving dilettantism as Machiavellian maneuvering: "Either the original TORCH decision was made without a clear realization of all its possible adverse consequences upon the military situation of the Allies and upon projects that are considered of primary importance in the successful prosecution of the war, or these considerations were ignored in the anxiety to influence the TORCH decision." Eisenhower to Marshall, 21 Sep 1942, in Chandler, *Eisenhower Papers*, 2: 570–72.

20. Bryant, *Turn of the Tide*, 398–403; Pogue, *Marshall: Ordeal and Hope*, 349; Leighton and Coakley, *Global Logistics*, 1: 417–35; Eisenhower to Harry Butcher, 2 Sep 1942, to Handy, 7 Sep 1942, and to Somervell, 9 and 13 Sep 1942, in Chandler, *Eisenhower Papers*, 2: 524–27, 546, 549, 558–59.

21. Harrison, *Cross-Channel Attack*, 60–62; Ruppenthal, *Logistical Support*, 90; MT 40/60, SABLO (Combined Shipping Adjustment Board, London, to CSAB, Washington) 98, 5 Dec 1942; MT 65/28, "Estimate . . . for 1943," app. B.

22. Smith, "Causes and Consequences," 355–62; Leighton and Coakley, *Global Logistics*, 1: 417–87; MT 40/60, EPS (42)72(M), 24 Aug 1942, B. F. Picknett minute, 29 Dec 1942, B. E. Bellamy minutes, 14 Jan and 22 Apr 1943, Ralph Metcalfe minute, 25 Jan 1943, and H. G. McDavid minute, 27 Jan 1943; MT 62/68, Salter to Douglas, 26 Oct 1942, Salter to Hurcomb, 29 Oct 1942; MT 59/586, S. W. Hill minute, 2 Jan 1943; MT 40/61, Picknett minute, 17 Feb 1943.

23. Smith, "Causes and Consequences," 362–67; PREM 3/383/9, Cherwell memorandum, 8 Jan 1943; Central Statistical Officer, *Statistical Digest*, table 161; MT 59/595, Shipping Committee (SC) (42) 72, 14 Oct 1942, "The Shipping Implications of the Minimum Indian Ocean Area Program from North America and the United Kingdom"; MT 62/73, Hurcomb minute, 4 Jan 1943 and Prime Minister's Personal Minutes M.640/2 and M.642/2 to Leathers and Secretary of State for War P. J. Grigg, 26 Dec 1942; Board of Trade (BT) File 87/101, Prime Minister's Personal Minute M.641/2 to Lyttleton, 26 Dec 1942, PRO.

24. Smith, "Causes and Consequences," 303–23; Douglas and W. Averell Harriman to Roosevelt, 2 Aug 1942, Hopkins Folder, Douglas Papers (DP), Record Group (RG) 248, National Archives (NA), Washington, D.C.; MT 59/2210, Salter to Leathers, 6 Apr and 22 May 1942; "Memorandum to the President and the Vice-President on the Wartime Transportation Situation," 25 Apr 1942, cited in Rosen, *Combined Boards*, 108; Douglas letter to Harriman in Apr 1942 and letter to Wil-

liam Mathews, 5 Nov 1942, cited in Browder and Smith, *Independent*, 167, 171, 186; PREM 3/384/2, JSM 775, 3 Mar 1943, Dill to COS.

25. Smith, "Causes and Consequences," 259–82; MT 59/694, BILGE 2311, Leathers to Salter, 31 Oct 1942; Churchill to Roosevelt via Lyttelton, 31 Oct 1942, and Roosevelt to Churchill via Lyttelton, 30 Nov 1942, cited in Kimball, *Churchill and Roosevelt*, 1: 648–50, 2: 44–45; MT 62/68, BILGE 1356, Salter to Leathers, 22 Nov 1942; CAB 66/31, WP (42) 568, 9 Dec 1942; MT 59/2210, BILGE 1301, Salter to Leathers, 4 Nov 1942 and Salter letter to Leathers, 2 Jan 1943; MT 65/28, "Estimate . . . for 1943," app. B.

26. Smith, "Logistics Diplomacy," 229–31; MT 59/2210, Salter to Leathers, 2 Jan 1943; Deane to Marshall, King, and Arnold, 26 Dec 1942, File CCS 400 (11–30-10), RG 218, NA; Roosevelt to Marshall, 8 Jan 1943 (enclosing Roosevelt to Churchill, 30 Nov 1942), and Gen. Joseph McNarney (acting Chief of Staff in Marshall's absence) to Roosevelt, 9 Jan 1943.

27. Smith, "Causes and Consequences," 303–23; Smith "Logistics Diplomacy," 228–31; Browder and Smith, *Independent*, 177, 188; Leighton and Coakley do not connect this struggle with Douglas's catastrophic absence from Casablanca. *Global Logistics*, 616–23. Douglas meeting with Somervell, 18 Mar 1942, Control of Transportation Folder; Roosevelt-Douglas conference, 18 Dec 1942, Minutes of JCS/WSA meeting, 28 Dec 1942, and phone conversation with Wayne Coy, 9 Jan 1943, WSA Directive 12–18–42 Folder; Douglas to McCloy, 21 Dec 1942, December 1942 Reading File; all in DP, RG 248, NA; Douglas to Oscar Cox, 29 Dec 1942, Douglas File, Oscar Cox Papers, Franklin D. Roosevelt Library (FDRL), Hyde Park, N.Y.

28. Smith, "Logistics Diplomacy," 234–37; Harrison, *Cross-Channel Attack*, 129; MT 62/86, Report on Casablanca conference by B. F. Picknett of Sea Transport Department, (hereafter cited as Picknett's Report), Enclosure 71: Operation BOLERO; CCS 55th meeting, 14 Jan 43, CCS 155/1, 20 Jan 1943, *Foreign Relations of the United States [FRUS]: The Conferences at Washington, 1941–1942, and Casablanca, 1943* (Washington, D.C.: GPO, 1968), 774. Ruppenthal's brief discussion of the Casablanca conference does not describe the U.S. demands for British personnel and cargo shipping assistance. *Logistical Support*, 114–32.

29. Smith, "Logistics Diplomacy," 234–41. British archives are remarkably silent about Leathers's motivations. MT 62/83, TRIDENT Report; MT 62/75, Keenlyside's Report, diary for 18 Jan 1943; MT 62/86, Picknett's Report, Enclosures 64 and 71; Salter memorandum to Douglas, 25 Feb 1943, Allocations General Folder, DP, RG 248, NA. Leighton and Coakley argued that Leathers was surely "puzzled" by the bureaucratic intrigue that caused Somervell's ignorance (*Global Logistics*, 1: 681), yet neither that intrigue nor Somervell's ignorance should have surprised him, for Salter had kept him well informed (MT 59/2210, Salter to Leathers, 2 Jan 1943). Leathers knew why Somervell's assumptions did not correspond with his own—and was reluctant to enlighten him.

30. PREM 3/384/2, JSM 764, 27 Feb 1943, COS (W) 511, 7 Mar 1943.

31. Smith, "Logistics Diplomacy," 241–46; MT 59/19, Gross to Douglas, 27 Feb 1943; HQ ASF (Army Service Forces) File Shipping 1941–1943, Gross's comment of 10 Mar 1943 on Douglas's 9 Mar cable to Harriman, and CCS 183/2, Enclosure A, RG 160, NA; U.S. Army ABC (American British Conversations) 560 (2–26–43) sec. 1–A, Gross memorandum to Marshall, 17 Mar 1943, RG 165, NA; MT 65/151, Washington CCS minutes, 12 Mar 1943. While Americans complained that BOLERO had become a residuary legatee of Allied strategy—getting only scraps

from the table—Cherwell grumbled that British imports were the logistic residuary legatee. PREM 3/384/3, WP (43)100, 9 Mar 1943.

32. Smith, "Logistics Diplomacy," 246–47; Central Statistical Office, *Statistical Digest*, table 161; Huston, *Sinews of War*, 435–37; Douglas to Hopkins, 13 Apr 1943, File 540, Hopkins Papers (HP), FDRL; Douglas/Hopkins conference, 19 Mar 1943, Hopkins Folder, Douglas Conference with Eden, Roosevelt, and Hopkins, 30 Mar 1943, Allocations General Folder, and Douglas to Harriman, 27 and 30 Mar 1943, January–March Reading File, all in DP, RG 248, NA; MT 62/89, Washington to Foreign Office 1497, Eden to Churchill and Roosevelt to Churchill 266, 30 Mar 1943, RG 165, ABC 560 (2–26–43) 1–A, JCS 251, 6 Apr 1943, JCS 73d meeting, 9 Apr 1943, and JCS letter to President, 10 Apr 1943.

33. Ruppenthal, *Logistical Support*, 129; Harrison, *Cross-Channel Attack*, 63; Pogue, *Marshall: Organizer of Victory*, 208.

34. Pogue, *Marshall: Organizer of Victory*, 211–12; Stoler, *Politics*, 92–96; Leighton and Coakley, *Global Logistics*, 2: 82; Bryant, *Turn of the Tide*, 512.

35. Smith, "Causes and Consequences," 412–40; MT 62/83, Annex II, app. A, Keenlyside to Jacob, 17 May 1943; CAB 66/38, WP (43)258; MT 65/145, TRANS 128, Washington to London, 27 May 1943; Stoler, *Politics*, 80ff; Douglas notes of "Meetings of American and British Shipping Experts, May 22, 1943, Beginning at 4 P. M.," cited in *FRUS: The Conferences at Washington and Quebec, 1943* (Washington, D.C.: GPO, 1970), 176, 270; Leighton and Coakley, *Global Logistics*, 2: 85, table 10.

36. Smith, "Causes and Consequences," 464–94; Ruppenthal, *Logistical Support*, 135–36.

37. Ruppenthal, *Logistical Support*, 121, 133, 138, 231, 235.

38. Harrison, *Cross-Channel Attack*, 9–10, 90–97; Pogue, *Marshall: Organizer of Victory*, 241–50; Ruppenthal, *Logistical Support*, 131; MT 65/145, Bellamy, "Allocation of Cargo Shipping for Mediterranean Operations," 13 Oct 1943, paras. 4–5, BILGE 2698, Maclay to Nicholson, 14 Oct 1943; WACOP 2, Schneider to Nicholson, 14 Oct 1943; MT 59/632, McDavid to Principal Sea Transport Officer, Middle East, 291011B, 29 Jul 1943; Appreciation of McDavid's 36 of 19 Aug 1943; Nicholson draft for Rogers, 19 Aug 1943; Hynard and Nicholson (London) to Metcalfe and Rogers (Quebec) 211208A, 21 Aug 1943; NASAB 595, MWT Representative, Algiers, to London, 29 Sep 1943, BILGE 3487 and 3506 (London to Washington), 2 and 6 Oct 1943, BILGE 2660 and 2765 (Washington to London) 5 and 27 Oct 1943; "Developments in the Immediate Tonnage Situation," 18 Aug 1943; compare with MT 65/167, "Notes on Dry Cargo Tonnage Prospects," 4 Aug 1943, paras. 7 and 13; CAB 102/802, Garrard, "American Shipping Assistance: Problems of Flexibility and Score Keeping"; MT 62/84, QUADRANT Statistical Report, app. C, pt. II; Douglas to Leathers, 18 Oct 1943, Post-war Shipping File, HP, FDRL.

39. Ruppenthal, *Logistical Support*, 121; MT 62/87, SEXTANT General Report, 1–2, Leathers' Addendum, 5 Jan 1944, and pt. II, Programs, 2; SEXTANT Report on Allocation of Tonnage Aspects, sec. 3: Allocations; MT 62/88, FROZEN 123 and 174, Leathers to Hurcomb, 24 and 27 Nov 1943; GRAND 223, Hurcomb to Leathers, 25 Nov 1943; MT 65/164, J. H. Gunlake, "Statistical Aspects of SEXTANT Conference"; CAB 123/86, Flemming note on WP (44)37, 20 Jan 1944.

40. Ruppenthal, *Logistical Support*, 239; Eisenhower to Churchill and Marshall, 20 and 23 May 1944, in Chandler, *Eisenhower Papers*, 3: 1877, 1885.

41. Leighton, "OVERLORD versus the Mediterranean at the Cairo-Tehran Confer-

ences," and Matloff, "The ANVIL Decision: Crossroads of Strategy," in Greenfield, *Command Decisions*, 257–85, 383–400.

42. Eisenhower noted: "The fighting in the Pacific is absorbing far too much of our limited resources in landing craft during this critical phase of the European war." See memorandum for diary, 7 Feb 1944, as well as Eisenhower to W. B. Smith, 5 Jan 1944; to CCS and COS, 23 Jan 1944; to Marshall, 8 and 22 Feb and 20 and 21 Mar 1944; to COS, 18 Feb 1944; to Montgomery, 21 Feb 1944; and to JCS, 9 Mar 1944, in Chandler, *Eisenhower Papers*, 3: 1652–53, 1673–76, 1712–15, 1732–34, 1743–45, 1763–64, 1775–79. See also Pogue, *Marshall: Organizer of Victory*, 328–43; Ruppenthal, *Logistical Support*, 184.

Chapter 4. ULTRA, FORTITUDE, and D-day Planning: The Missing Dimension

The author gratefully acknowledges the gentle hand of T. A. Wilson. The opinions presented in this chapter do not represent those of the Air War College, the Air University, the U.S. Air Force, or the Department of Defense; they are those of the author alone.

1. Consensus on a definition of ULTRA among military historians remains elusive. As Michael Howard observed, "The term ULTRA, which has become current as a name for intelligence obtained by interception and decryption of enemy radio communications, was not in general use during the war except as a caveat attached to document classified as MOST (later TOP) SECRET. . . . Signals intelligence (Sigint) was the phrase in most general use." Michael Howard, *British Intelligence in the Second World War* (London: HMSO, 1990), 5: 13n.

2. This definition is taken from L. Bell, *The Second World War: A Guide to Documents in the Public Records Office* (London: HMSO, 1972), 203.

3. Winston Churchill, *The Second World War*, 6 vols. (Boston: Houghton Mifflin, 1948–53). See Raymond A. Callahan, *Churchill: Retreat from Empire* (Wilmington, Del.: Scholarly Resources, 1984), and Theodore A. Wilson, *The First Summit: Roosevelt and Churchill at Placentia Bay, 1941*, rev. ed. (Lawrence: University Press of Kansas, 1991).

4. J. H. Plumb, "The Historian," in A. J. P. Taylor et al., *Churchill's Four Faces and the Man* (London: Macmillan, 1969), 86.

5. There are 78 volumes in this distinguished series, edited by Kent Roberts Greenfield and his successors and published over the past several decades by the Office of the Chief of Military History, U.S. Army, and its successor, the Center of Military History. For more information, see Richard D. Adamczyk and Morris J. MacGregor (comp.), *U.S. Army in World War II: Readers Guide* (Washington, D.C.: Center of Military History, 1992).

6. Maurice Matloff, *Strategic Planning for Coalition Warfare, 1943–1944* (Washington, D.C.: Office of the Chief of Military History [OCMH], 1959); Forrest C. Pogue, *The Supreme Command* (Washington, D.C.: OCMH, 1954); and Gordon A. Harrison, *Cross-Channel Attack* (Washington, D.C.: OCMH, 1951). The official U.S. Air Force histories follow this trend. See Wesley Frank Craven and James Lea Cate (eds.), *The Army Air Forces in World War II*, vol. 3, *Europe: ARGUMENT to V-E Day, January 1944 to May 1945* (Chicago: University of Chicago Press, 1951), in particular John F. Fagg, "The Plan for OVERLORD," 67–83.

7. J. R. M. Butler (ed.), *History of the Second World War: United Kingdom Military Series*, 6 vol. (London: HMSO, 1965–72).

8. Michael Howard, *Grand Strategy*, vol. 4, *August 1942–September 1943* (London: HMSO, 1972); John Ehrman, *Grand Strategy*, vol. 5, *August 1943–September 1944* (London: HMSO, 1956); and L. F. Ellis, *Victory in the West*, vol. 1, *The Battle of Normandy* (London: HMSO, 1962).

9. F. H. Hinsley et al., *British Intelligence in the Second World War*, 5 vols. (London: HMSO, 1979–90).

10. Matloff, *Strategic Planning*, 363.

11. Pogue, *Supreme Command*, 106.

12. Harrison, *Cross-Channel Attack*, 56.

13. Dwight D. Eisenhower, *Crusade in Europe* (Garden City, N.Y.: Doubleday, 1949), 231.

14. Harry C. Butcher, *My Three Years with Eisenhower* (New York: Simon & Schuster, 1946), 522.

15. Steven E. Ambrose, *The Supreme Commander: The War Years of General Dwight D. Eisenhower* (Garden City, N.Y.: Doubleday, 1969), 339–409. See also Joseph P. Hobbs, *Dear General: Eisenhower's Wartime Letters to Marshall* (Baltimore: Johns Hopkins University Press, 1971), 134–64.

16. Forrest C. Pogue, *George C. Marshall: Organizer of Victory, 1943–1945* (New York: Viking, 1973), 370–90.

17. For example, see Cornelius Ryan, *The Longest Day: June 6, 1944* (New York: Simon & Schuster, 1959).

18. Eisenhower Foundation, *D-Day: The Normandy Invasion in Retrospect* (Lawrence: University Press of Kansas, 1971).

19. Ibid., 15, 121.

20. Ehrman, *Grand Strategy*, 183, 315–16.

21. Ellis, *Victory in the West*, 25, 103–4

22. Winston S. Churchill, *Closing the Ring* (Boston: Houghton Mifflin, 1951), 404, 596.

23. Kenneth Strong, *Intelligence at the Top: The Recollections of an Intelligence Officer* (Garden City, N.Y.: Doubleday, 1969), 192; and John Kennedy, *The Business of War* (New York: William Morrow, 1958), 319–30.

24. Arthur Bryant, *Triumph in the West: A History of the War Years Based on the Diaries of Sir Alanbrooke* (Garden City, N.Y.: Doubleday, 1959), 68; and Alan Moorehead, *Montgomery: A Biography* (London: H. Hamilton, 1946).

25. Chester Wilmot, *The Struggle for Europe* (New York: Harper Brothers, 1952), 200.

26. J. C. Masterman, *The Double-Cross System in the War of 1939 to 1945* (New Haven, Conn.: Yale University Press, 1972).

27. For a summary of Masterman's routine career, see Lord Blake and C. S. Nicholls, *The Dictionary of National Biography, 1970–1980* (Oxford: Oxford University Press, 1986), 551–52.

28. Masterman, *Double-Cross*, 159.

29. *Time Literary Supplement* (hereafter *TLS*), 18 Feb 1972, 171.

30. Alexander S. Cochran, " 'MAGIC', 'ULTRA,' and the Second World War: Literature, Sources, and Outlook," *Military Affairs* (Apr 1982): 88–92.

31. F. W. Winterbotham, *The ULTRA Secret* (New York: Harper & Row, 1974).

32. Cochran interviews with Pogue, Matloff, Howard, and MacDonald.

33. David Hunt, *TLS*, 13 Dec 1974, 1425.

34. *New Statesman*, 15 Nov 1974, 703.

35. Anthony Cave-Brown, *Bodyguard of Lies* (New York: Harper & Row, 1975).

36. Ibid., 409–43.

37. *TLS*, 26 Apr 1976, 641–43.

38. *New York Times Book Reviews*, 9 Nov 1975, 3.

39. Roger Spiller, "Some Implications of Ultra," *Military Affairs* (Apr 1976), 49.

40. Harold C. Deutsch, "Clients of Ultra: The American Captains," *Parameters* 15 (Summer 1985): 55–62, "The Historical Impact of Ultra on World War II," ibid. 7 (1977): 16–23, and "The Influence of Ultra on World War II," ibid., 8 (Dec 1978): 2–15.

41. Cave-Brown, *Bodyguard of Lies*, 867–72.

42. Ibid., 823.

43. William Stevenson, *A Man Called Intrepid: The Secret War* (New York: Harcourt Brace Jovanovich, 1976).

44. Alexander S. Cochran, *Magic Diplomatic Summaries* (New York: Garland, 1982), vii–ix.

45. Carl Boyd, *Hitler's Japanese Confidant: General Oshima Hiroshi and Magic Intelligence, 1941–1945* (Lawrence: University Press of Kansas, 1992).

46. For instance, "Reports by U.S. Army ultra Representative with Army Field Commands in the European Theater of Operations, May 1945," "Reports Received by U.S. War Department on Use of ultra in the European Theater, World War II," SRH-037; and "Synthesis of Experiences in the Use of ultra Intelligence by U.S. Army Field Commands in the European Theater of Operations," SRH 006; all in Record Group (RG) 457, National Archives (NA).

47. DEFE 3, "Intelligence from Enemy Radio Communications," Public Records Office (PRO), United Kingdom.

48. See David Syrett, "The Secret War and the Historians," *Armed Forces and Society* (Winter 1983): 293–328. See also Diane T. Putney, *Ultra and the Army Air Forces in World War II: An Interview with Associate Justice of the U.S. Supreme Court Lewis F. Powell, Jr.* (Washington, D.C.: Office of Air Force History, 1987), 107–10.

49. For instance, see Peter J. Calvocoressi, *Top Secret Ultra* (New York: Ballantine Books, 1981); Ewen Montagu, *Beyond Top Secret Ultra* (New York: Coward, McCann & Geoghegan, 1978); and Gordon Welchman, *The Hut 6 Story* (New York: McGraw-Hill, 1982).

50. For instance, Jozef Garlinski, *The Enigma War: The Inside Story of the German Enigma Codes and How the Allies Broke Them* (New York: Charles Scribner's Sons, 1979); and R. V. Jones, *The Wizard War: British Scientific Intelligence, 1939–1945* (New York: Coward, McCann & Geoghegan, 1978).

51. Ralph Bennett, *Ultra in the West: The Normandy Campaign, 1944–45* (New York: Charles Scribner's Sons, 1979); Ronald Lewin, *Ultra Goes to War: The First Account of World War II's Greatest Secret Based on Official Documents* (London: Hutchinson, 1978).

52. Bennett, *Ultra in the West*, 37–59.

53. Interview, Cochran with Lewin, May 1979.

54. Lewin, *Ultra Goes to War*, 349–87.

55. For instance, "Magic, Ultra, and the Second World War: New Insights from New Sources," American Historical Association meeting, Chicago, 29 Dec 1986. See also David Kahn, "International Conference on Ultra," *Military Affairs* (Apr 1979): 97–98, and "The Ultra Conference," *Cryptologia* (Jan 1979): 1–8.

56. Charles B. MacDonald, *Mighty Endeavor: The American War in Europe,*

rev. ed. (New York: William Morrow, 1988), 578. Interestingly, however, he warned that "some have suggested that . . . the entire history of the war would have to be rewritten. That is hardly the case." Ibid., 571.

57. Steven E. Ambrose, *Ike's Spies: Eisenhower and the Espionage Establishment* (Garden City, N.Y.: Doubleday, 1981), 73–94.

58. David Fraser, *Alanbrooke* (New York: Atheneum, 1982), 280.

59. John Keegan, *Six Armies in Normandy: From D-Day to the Liberation of Paris, June 6th–August 25th 1944* (New York: Viking, 1982), 150.

60. Carlo D'Este, *Decision in Normandy* (New York: Dutton, 1983), 484.

61. Russell F. Weigley, *Eisenhower's Lieutenants: The Campaign of France and Germany, 1944–1945* (Bloomington: Indiana University Press, 1981), 54.

62. Max Hastings, OVERLORD: *D-Day and the Battle for Normandy* (New York: Simon & Schuster, 1984), 24–25, 237.

63. Most of these records are in RG 457, NA. The best effort here is Thomas Parrish, *The ULTRA Americans: The U.S. Role in Breaking the Nazi Codes* (New York: Stein and Day, 1986).

64. The ULTRA intercepts are found in DEFE 3, "Intelligence from Enemy Radio Communications," PRO.

65. References to ULTRA by other codewords can be found in the War Office Files WO 109, the Admiralty Files ADM 199 and 223, and the Air Ministry Files AIR 8 and 9. References to BONIFACE and other ULTRA codewords in Churchill records are in PREM 4. All records are at the PRO.

66. David A. T. Stafford, "ULTRA and the British Official Histories: A Documentary Note," *Military Affairs* (Feb 1978): 29–31.

67. F. H. Hinsley with E. E. Thomas, C. F. G. Ransom, and R. C. Knight, *British Intelligence in the Second World War: Its Influence on Strategy and Operations,* vol. 1 (London: HMSO, 1979).

68. Ibid., vii–x. This caveat was to appear in all the subsequent volumes.

69. F. H. Hinsley with E. E. Thomas, C. F. G. Ransom, and R. C. Knight, *British Intelligence in the Second World War: Its Influence on Strategy and Operations,* vol. 2 (New York: Cambridge University Press, 1981) and vol. 3, pt. 1 (New York: Cambridge University Press, 1984).

70. Hinsley, *British Intelligence,* 1487–95, 528–48.

71. Brian Loring Villa, *Unauthorized Action: Mountbatten and the Dieppe Raid* (New York: Oxford University Press, 1989).

72. Ibid., 7.

73. Hinsley, *British Intelligence,* 3(1): 46.

74. F. H. Hinsley, *British Intelligence in the Second World War: Its Influence on Strategy and Operations,* vol. 3, pt. 2 (London: HMSO, 1988).

75. Ibid., 48.

76. JIC (44) 232 (O), 3 Jun 1994, as cited in ibid., 63.

77. David Kahn, *Hitler's Spies: German Military Intelligence in World War II* (New York: Macmillan, 1978), 501–20. See also Klaus-Jurgen Muller, "German Perspective on Allied Deception Operations in the Second World War," in Michael E. Handel (ed.), *Strategic and Operational Deception in the Second World War* (London: Frank Cass, 1987).

78. Hinsley et al., *British Intelligence,* 3(2): 80.

79. Ibid., 84.

80. Michael Howard, *British Intelligence in the Second World War,* vol. 5, *Strategic Deception* (London: HMSO, 1990).

81. Ibid., 105.

82. Ibid., 21.
83. Ibid., 121.
84. Ibid., 128.
85. F. H. Hinsley and C. A. G. Simkins, *British Intelligence in the Second World War,* vol. 4, *Security and Counter-Intelligence* (New York: Cambridge University Press, 1990). For OVERLORD preparations, see 247–60.
86. Howard, *British Intelligence,* 5: 129.
87. For an example here, see Eisenhower's letter on ULTRA as quoted in Cave-Brown, *Bodyguard of Lies,* 815.
88. Pogue, "Deception and Security Plans" and "Situation Estimates and Deception Policies," RG 380.01, Cover and Deception, Center of Military History, Washington, D.C. In 1985, the Center's Research and Analysis Branch produced an unclassified study for the internal use of the Army staff that discussed FORTI-TUDE in more detail than before.
89. Thomas Faybonic et. al., *United States Army Air Force Intelligence Operations in World War II* (Washington, D.C.: Office of Air Force History, forthcoming).
90. The conference proceedings are in Handel, ed., *Strategic and Operational Deception Planning in the Second World War,* special issue of *Intelligence and National Security* 2, 3 (July 1987). The unpublished paper on FORTITUDE is T. L. Cubbage, "The Success of Operation FORTITUDE: Hesketh's History of Strategic Deception."

Chapter 5. Technology at D-day: Allied Weapons Old and New

For the researcher wishing to go further, the chapters in Gerald S. Jordan, *British Military History* (New York: Garland, 1986), and in Robin Higham and Donald J. Mrozek, *A Guide to the Sources of U.S. Military History,* suppl. 3 (Hamden, Conn.: Archon Books, 1993), and its antecedents, as well as Dennis E. Showalter, *German Military History* (New York: Garland, 1984), provide a path, as does Keith W. Bird's *German Naval History* (New York: Garland, 1985).For the general introduction to the subject and identification of characters and equipment, see *The D-Day Encyclopedia* (New York: Scribners, 1993).There is some material on the technical developments in the Dwight D. Eisenhower Presidential Library at Abilene, Kans., notably an inside account of the meteorological section, Maj. Gen. Harold R. Bull Papers, Box 3, undated memo of 1960 vintage, "Behind the Scenes with the 'Overlord' Weathermen," which complements Scot J. M. Stagg's *Forecast for Overlord: 6 June 1944* (New York: Norton, 1972). The largest mass of papers is to be found in the many classes of documents in the Public Record Office (PRO) in London. Almost all the World War II files were declassified in 1972. For their organization, see L. Bell, *The Second World War: A Guide to the Documents in the Public Records Office* (London: HMSO, 1972), supplemented by mimeographed guides to departmental deposits. Two difficulties exist for the historian of technology. The first is that each government department in World War II created about 2 million files (file folders) during the six years of the conflict, and the second is that those charged with screening them before their consignment to the PRO had little interest in technology. Some writers, such as Correlli Barnett in his *Engage the Enemy More Closely: The Royal Navy in the Second World War* (New York: Norton, 1991), give an idea of what exists at command level, but there is still a vast amount of material that is either only just coming to light as historians ask for it or has long been destroyed as not of operational interest. Company histories do exist in some cases; many archives are closed, companies being notably tight-fisted in this area. The Militärgeschichtelich Forschungsamt in Freiburg is producing detailed volumes of German military history, but the records of the Luftwaffe were largely lost in transit from Berlin at the end of the war.

A number of volumes provide more insights into than details of technical and technological developments in regard to D-day in the course of telling a wider story: Martin van Creveld, *Supplying War: Logistics from Wallenstein to Patton* (New York: Cambridge University Press, 1977); Martin Blumenson's chapter in Noble Frankland and Christopher Dowling (eds.), *Decisive Battles of the 20th Century: Land, Sea, Air* (New York: David McKay, 1976); Capt. Eric Bush, *Gallipoli* (New York: St. Martin's Press, 1975); Brig. Shelford Bidwell, *Gunners at War: A Tactical Study of the Royal Artillery in the Twentieth Century* (London: Arms & Armour, 1970); Lee Kennett, *G.I.: The American Soldier in World War II* (New York: Scribner's, 1987); Omer Bartov, *Hitler's Army: Soldiers, Nazis, and War in the Third Reich* (New York: Oxford University Press, 1992); and James J. Sadkovich, *Re-evaluating Major Naval Combatants of World War II* (Westport, Conn.: Greenwood Press, 1990). Bush's *Gallipoli* is especially useful, since he was present at that 1915 affair and also at all the amphibious operations in Europe during 1940–44, including D-day.

Special technical aspects are discussed in F. H. Hinsley et al., *British Intelligence in the Second World War*, vol. 3, pts. 1 and 2 (London: Cambridge University Press, 1984, 1988); and Lyman B. Kirkpatrick, Jr., *Captains Without Eyes: Intelligence Failures in World War II*, reprint. (Boulder, Colo.: Westview, 1987). Kirkpatrick is especially cogent on Dieppe.

There are a number of accounts of the invasion that pay some attention to the technical side of D-day. One of the clearest overall because of its excellent maps and illustrations is that by the head of Field Marshal Montgomery's planning staff from 1943 to 1945, Maj. Gen. David Belchem, *Victory in Normandy* (London: Chatto and Windus, 1980). Max Hastings, *Overlord: D-Day and the Battle for Normandy* (New York: Simon & Schuster, 1984), provides personal views of various activities. See also John Keegan's face-of-battle approach in *Six Armies in Normandy from D-Day to the Liberation of Paris* (New York: Penguin, 1983).

The German West Wall is exposed in Keith Mallory and Arvid Ottar, *The Architecture of War* (New York: Pantheon, 1973). Guy Hartcup provides a short critical assessment in *Code Name Mulberry: The Planning, Building, and Operation of the Normandy Harbours* (New York: Hippocrene, 1977). The evolution of tanks is covered in a number of books: A. J. Smithers, *Rude Mechanicals: An Account of Tank Maturity during the Second World War* (London: Leo Cooper, 1987), Kenneth Macksey and John Batchelor, *Tank: A History of the Armoured Fighting Vehicle* (New York: Scribner's, 1970); G. MacLeod Ross, *The Business of Tanks, 1933–1945* (Ilfracombe, United Kingdom: Stockwell, 1976). Peter Chamberlain and Chris Ellis, *Pictorial History of Tanks of the World, 1915–1945* (Harrisburg, Pa.: Stackpole, 1972) is helpful for the evolution of the variants used in Normandy. More on British tank development, as well as that of other weapons, is contained in the official M. M. Postan, D. Hay, and J. D. Scott, *The Design and Development of Weapons* (London: HMSO, 1964). Information on American armored fighting vehicles is found in Christopher F. Foss, *Armoured Fighting Vehicles in Profile*, vol. 4, *American AFV's of World War II* (New York: Doubleday, 1972). The most important opponent of Allied tanks was Field Marshal Erwin Rommel, who is portrayed in Admiral Friedrich Ruge's *Rommel in Normandy* (San Rafael, Calif.: Presidio, 1979); and Col. Samuel W. Mitcham, Jr., *Rommel's Last Battle, The Desert Fox in Normandy* (New York: Stein and Day, 1983). Artillery is covered by Ian V. Hogg in *British and American Artillery in World War II* and in the companion volume, *German Artillery in World War II* (both New York: Hippocrene, 1978 and 1975, respectively), and in John Batchelor and Ian Hogg, *Artillery* (New York: Scribner's 1972). There is also a recent official history of the U.S. field artillery by Boyd Dastrup. On the most ubiquitous vehicle, see J. G. Jeudy and N. Taraine, *Jeep* (New York: Vilo, 1981).

On the naval side, there are a variety of helpful guides, mostly concentrating on ships. Alan Raven and John Roberts, *British Battleships of World War II: The Development and Technical History of the Royal Navy's Battleships and Battlecruisers from 1911 to 1946* (Annapolis, Md.: Naval Institute Press, 1976), includes the case histories of those present on D-day. Ian Buxton, in *Big Gun Monitors: The History of the Design, Construction, and Operation of the Royal Navy's Monitors* (Annapolis, Md.: Naval Institute Press, 1978), tells the story of these coastal bombardment ships, two of which served off Normandy. Alan Raven and John Roberts, *British Cruisers of World War II* (Annapolis, Md.: Naval Institute Press, 1980), is an invaluable guide that rivals Norman Friedmann's series on U.S. Navy warships. Edgar J. Marsh, *British Destroyers, 1892–1953* (London: Seeley, Service & Co., 1966), is a mine of technical information on these invaluable vessels.

Two volumes on photo reconnaissance are Andrew J. Brookes, *Photo Reconnaissance: The Operational History* (Shepperton, United Kingdom: Ian Allan, 1975), which is a concise overall history; and Col. Roy M. Stanley II, *World War II Photointelligence* (New York: Scribner's, 1981), which is a highly detailed technical volume and provides a fine introduction to the subject. A related subject is covered in Charles Cruickshank, *Deception in World War II* (New York: Oxford University Press, 1979).

There is no single-volume history of the U.S. Army Air Forces in World War II to match John Terraine, *A Time for Courage (The Right of the Line in the UK)* (New York: Macmillan, 1985), the story of the RAF over Europe. On the American side, the comprehensive story of the development of material is found in Ray Wagner, *American Combat Planes*, 3d enlarged ed. (New York: Doubleday, 1982). This may be supplemented with Gordon Swanborough and Ray M. Bowers, *United States Military Aircraft since 1908* (London: Putnam, 1971). For the British, see Owen Thetford, *Aircraft of the Royal Air Force since 1918* (London: Putnam, 1988). J. R. Smith and Antony Kay, *German Aircraft of the Second World War* (London: Putnam, 1972), is a more concise and usable version of William Green's encyclopedic *Warplanes of the Third Reich* (New York: Doubleday, 1970), which explains much about why the German air force was where it was equipment-wise in 1944, as does Richard Overy, *The Air War, 1939–1945* (New York: Stein and Day, 1985).

Vincent Orange's recent *Coningham: A Biography of Air Marshal Sir Arthur Coningham* (London: Methuen, 1990) and Bill Newton Dunn's *Big Wing: The Biography of Air Chief Marshal Sir Trafford Leigh-Mallory* (Shrewsbury: Airlife, 1992) both shed light on the air commanders, while W. A. Jacobs, "The Battle for France," in Benjamin Franklin Cooling (ed.), *Case Studies in the Development of Air Support* (Washington, D.C.: Office of Air Force History, 1990), tells how this technical material was employed.

Alfred Price's *Aircraft versus Submarine* (London: William Kimber, 1973) helps explain why the Allies held the upper hand in 1944. Stuart Macrae's *Winston Churchill's Toyshop: The Invention and Making of England's Secret Weapons* (New York: Walker, 1971) provides insight into the British scientific mind.

Ronald W. Clark, *War Winners* (London: Sidgwick & Jaclson, 1979), has a well-illustrated section on D-day. More information can be located in Brian J. Ford, *Allied Secret Weapons: The War of Science* (New York: Ballantine, 1971); Brian Johnson's special volume, *The Secret War* (London: BBC, 1978), which includes material on the development of the V-1 and V-2; and R. V. Jones, *The Wizard War: British Scientific Intelligence, 1939–1945* (New York: Coward, McCann & Geoghegan, 1978). Lastly, there are the controversial memoirs of Sir Solly (later Lord) Zuckerman, *From Apes to Warlords* (New York: Harper & Row, 1978), the man who advised Air Chief Marshal Tedder.

Many of the memoirs and other works cited in the other chapters of this book also provide insights into contemporary and hindsight attitudes about the success or failure of technology at D-day.

Chapter 6. The Navies and NEPTUNE

1. For the naval way of thinking about war and the intrusion of amphibious operations, see Russell F. Weigley, *The American Way of War* (Bloomington: Indiana University Press, 1977), 254–64. For initial planning and preparations for opening a second front, see Gordon A. Harrison, *Cross-Channel Attack* (Washington, D.C.: Office of the Chief of Military History, 1951), 62.

2. Samuel Eliot Morison, *History of United States Naval Operations in World War II*, vol. 11: *The Invasion of France and Germany 1944–45* (Boston: Little, Brown, 1968), 15. This is the semiofficial U.S. naval history. The official British naval history is Stephen W. Roskill, *The War at Sea 1939–1945*. NEPTUNE is covered in chs. 14 and 15 of vol. 3, *The Offensive*, pt. 2, *1 Jun 1944–14 August 1945* (London: HMSO, 1961).

3. Frederick Morgan, *Overture to OVERLORD* (Garden City, N.Y.: Doubleday, 1950), 148–49.

4. They were navy Captains L. A. Thackrey and Gordon Hutchins. Morison, *History of U.S. Naval Operations*, 18–19; see also Harrison, *Cross-Channel Attack*, 53.

5. Harrison, *Cross-Channel Attack*, 64–65, 180–81. For Admiral King's suspicions, see, for example, Mark A. Stoler, *The Politics of the Second Front* (Westport, Conn.: Greenwood Press, 1977), 55, 102, 106. For a discussion of the problems of unifying the various services of different countries for a single operation, see Alfred D. Chandler, Jr. (ed.), *The Papers of Dwight David Eisenhower: The War Years*, 5 vols. (Baltimore: Johns Hopkins University Press, 1970), 1: xx–xxvii.

6. Morgan, *Overture to OVERLORD*, 139–40; Harrison, *Cross-Channel Attack*, 57; Philip Ziegler, *Mountbatten* (New York: Knopf, 1985), 213–14; Correlli Barnett, *Engage the Enemy More Closely: The Royal Navy in the Second World War* (New York: W. W. Norton, 1991), 756–57; Brian B. Schofield, *Operation Neptune* (Annapolis, Md.: Naval Institute Press, 1974), 30. Barnett makes extensive use of the papers of Admiral Ramsay at Churchill College, Cambridge. Schofield remains the best study of Operation NEPTUNE. Vice Adm. Schofield was at Southwick House during the runup to D-day.

7. Harrison, *Cross-Channel Attack*, 99–105.

8. Ibid., 127.

9. Barnett, *Engage the Enemy*, 753–54; Schofield, *Operation Neptune*, 28; Morison, *History of U.S. Naval Operations*, 24, 63–64; George M. Elsey, "Naval Aspects of Normandy in Retrospect," in Eisenhower Foundation, *D-Day: The Normandy Invasion in Retrospect* (Lawrence: University Press of Kansas, 1971), 174. Elsey was a well-placed observer of the American naval side of D-day, and he has valuable insights into the thinking of senior U.S. Navy officers.

10. For landing craft, see Schofield, *Operation Neptune*, 31–32; Morison, *History of U.S. Naval Operations*, 27–28, 56–58; Elsey, "Naval Aspects," 175–76; Walter Scott Dunn, Jr., *Second Front Now 1943* (University: University of Alabama Press, 1980), 58–63. One may admire Dunn's research without accepting his conclusion that an invasion of northwest Europe could have been successful in 1943.

There is a tendency for the issue of allocation of assault craft to be seen in national terms. The British were sure that the U.S. Navy in the Pacific was prodigal in the use of landing vessels, while the Americans pointed the finger at Churchill's pet Anzio operation as one that devoured landing craft that should have been available for OVERLORD. For the expectations of the planners, which generated the increased demand for landing craft, see F. H. Hinsley et al., *British Intelligence in the Second World War* (New York: Cambridge University Press, 1988), 3(2): 38.

11. Even the U.S. Navy's official chronicler, Morison, felt that King was tardy in addressing this need. Morison, *History of U.S. Naval Operations*, 55–56. The delay seems to have been inspired by Kirk reporting to King that the British were retaining a greater force, including three modern battleships, in the Home Fleet at Scapa Flow than required to cope with the then operational German force of one heavy and two light cruisers. Elsey, "Naval Aspects," 175. Kirk's complaint has some merit, but there are certain obscenities no admiral will tolerate; among them appears to be the use of modern, fast battleships in gunfire support of amphibious landings. The Admiralty also intended these ships to go to the British Pacific Fleet and was doubtless reluctant to risk them in shallow waters liable to mining. British Naval Intelligence appears to have presented the Admiralty with a worst-case scenario, which may have influenced the British decision to hold so much strength at Scapa Flow. For this, see Hinsley et al., *British Intelligence*, 3(2): 95, 95n. In the event, Ramsay got three battleships, three cruisers, and 31 destroyers from the U.S. Navy. Ramsay himself displayed considerable caution, holding back in reserve on D-day his two most powerful units, the *Nelson* and the *Rodney*. See Roskill, *War at Sea*, 3(2): 62. All military officers are indoctrinated to hold a force in reserve for emergencies and to cope with the unforeseen. Still, in retrospect, the weight of these two ships' eighteen 16-inch guns would have been very welcome on D-day.

12. Morgan, *Overture to OVERLORD*, 269.

13. Barnett, *Engage the Enemy*, 781–82, 791; Schofield, *Operation Neptune*, 42, 45; Roskill, *War at Sea*, 3(2): 19, 22–23.

14. Barnett, *Engage the Enemy*, 759; Morison, *History of U.S. Naval Operations*, 25–26.

15. Barnett, *Engage the Enemy*, 762.

16. Morgan, *Overture to OVERLORD*, 267. For the Mulberries, see Chapter 5 in this volume.

17. Schofield, *Operation Neptune*, 52; Barnett, *Engage the Enemy*, 792. This resilient officer survived the experience of having HMS *Repulse* sunk out from under him by Japanese aircraft in Dec. 1941.

18. Morison, *History of U.S. Naval Operations*, 26.

19. Schofield, *Operation Neptune*, 52–53; see also Barnett, *Engage the Enemy*, 793.

20. Elsey, "Naval Aspects," 292; Barnett, *Engage the Enemy*, 779–80, 796–97.

21. Friedrich Ruge, *Rommel in Normandy*, trans. Ursula R. Moessner (San Rafael, Calif.: Presidio, 1979), has an extensive discussion of the German mining effort. Rommel is quoted on p. 15. See also Harrison, *Cross-Channel Attack*, 250, 253, 264.

22. Hinsley et al., *British Intelligence*, 3(2): 165–67.

23. Quoted in Barnett, *Engage the Enemy*, 776. See also Harrison, *Cross-Channel Attack*, 177, 180–90. At low tide, an average beach width of about 300 yards would exist; however, the erection of obstacles started at the high-tide line and had only reached the eight-foot mark above low water in May 1944. Thus the landings did not have to be at absolute low tide. A spring tide on the invasion beaches took about three hours to rise from low water to high water; a three-hour stand of high water followed before receding. On 6 Jun off the Normandy coast, the full moon set and the sun rose at almost exactly 6:00 a.m. High water on the beaches was between 9:45 and 12:45 that day.

24. Morison, *History of U.S. Naval Operations*, 32–33; Schofield, *Operation Neptune*, 58; Barnett, *Engage the Enemy*, 799–800; Roskill, *War at Sea*, 3(2): 40n; Hinsley et al., *British Intelligence*, 3(2): 39, 88. A suspected reef off Juno dictated its late time; landing craft needed sufficient water to clear it. All H-hours are British double summer time (Zone B, or -2). Worth noting is a meeting on 4 Jun 1944 of Admiral Kirk with Generals Bradley (U.S. First Army), Collins (U.S. VII Corps), and Royce (U.S. Ninth Air Force), where the parties agreed that if D-day were postponed beyond 6 Jun, they would accept the difficulties of landing as late as 8 or 9 Jun rather than wait until 18–20 June. J. Lawton Collins, *Lightning Joe: An Autobiography* (Baton Rouge: Louisiana State University Press, 1979), 195–96.

25. Elsey, "Naval Aspects," 177; Barnett, *Engage the Enemy*, 798. For the circumstances attending the TIGER tragedy, see Chapter 12 in this volume.

26. Morison, *History of U.S. Naval Operations*, 72; Schofield, *Operation Neptune*, 59; Elsey, "Naval Aspects," 178–79.

27. Schofield, *Operation Neptune*, 64, 72–73; Morison, *History of U.S. Naval Operations*, 80–83.

28. The paragraphs that follow on minesweeping draw heavily on Peter Elliott, *Allied Minesweeping in World War 2* (Annapolis, Md.: Naval Institute Press, 1979), 107–13. According to Elliott, some 306 minesweepers participated in NEPTUNE, a higher figure than normally given. He carried out extensive research on the subject, and his figures appear authoritative.

29. This number excludes the 1,900 landing craft that were carried across the Channel in the larger assault and landing ships. Barnett, *Engage the Enemy*, 810.

30. Barnett, *Engage the Enemy*, 784–85; Morison, *History of U.S. Naval Operations*, 84; Schofield, *Operation Neptune*, 75; Roskill, *War at Sea*, 3(2): 29. Between D-day and D plus 1, the dan buoys were replaced with large ocean light buoys. The channels running south from Position Z were collectively referred to as the Spout.

31. Quoted in Barnett, *Engage the Enemy*, 785. See also Schofield, *Operation Neptune*, 43–44.

32. Barnett, *Engage the Enemy*, 811; Morison, *History of U.S. Naval Operations*, 77.

33. Barnett, *Engage the Enemy*, 812; Morison, *History of U.S. Naval Operations*, 87; Hinsley et al., *British Intelligence*, 3(2): 128.

34. Morison, *History of U.S. Naval Operations*, 88.

35. Elliott, *Allied Minesweeping*, 114–16. Hinsley et al., *British Intelligence*, 3(2): 62, 92, 151n, observed that although the laying of the mine field over the Cardonnet bank was reported by ULTRA on 1 May, Admiral Kirk, an ULTRA recipient, appears not to have taken note of it. The authors speculated that Kirk may have been misled by the last intelligence assessment before D-day of enemy minelaying in the Bay of the Seine, which did not refer to this field. Whoever must accept responsibility, it was a costly oversight.

36. Hinsley et al., *British Intelligence*, 3(2): 130.

37. See Barnett, *Engage the Enemy*, 814–16; Elsey, "Naval Aspects," 190, 194; Harrison, *Cross-Channel Attack*, 194.

38. The description of Utah landings is drawn largely from Morison, *History of U.S. Naval Operations*, 93–102, 108; Barnett, *Engage the Enemy*, 813; Schofield, *Operation Neptune*, 79–82; and Historical Division, War Department, *Utah Beach to Cherbourg* (Washington, D.C.: GPO, 1948), 43–50.

39. Collins's memory of the circumstances was slightly different when he wrote his memoirs 35 years later, but the essential point was his need to overcome the admiral's hesitation. See Collins, *Lightning Joe*, 201.

40. Morison, *History of U.S. Naval Operations*, 119.

41. The description of the Omaha landing is drawn from Morison, *History of U.S. Naval Operations*, 114–41, 147–51; Schofield, *Operation Neptune*, 82–83, 86–89; Barnett, *Engage the Enemy*, 817–18; Elsey, "Naval Aspects," 181–83, 186; and Historical Division, War Department, *Omaha Beachhead* (Washington, D.C.: GPO, 1945; reprint 1989). Of nearly 200 landing craft carrying the two initial assault regimental combat teams (RCTs), at least ten swamped before reaching the surf line. *Omaha Beachhead*, 38.

42. Morison, *History of U.S. Naval Operations*, 148.

43. The Gold Beach account is based on Schofield, *Operation Neptune*, 89–92; and Barnett, *Engage the Enemy*, 821.

44. For the Juno Beach landings, see Schofield, *Operation Neptune*, 94–95; and Barnett, *Engage the Enemy*, 821–22.

45. The description of the Sword landing is drawn largely from Schofield, *Operation Neptune*, 97–102; and Barnett, *Engage the Enemy*, 823–27.

46. For a somewhat different assessment of the reasons for the failure to capture Caen, see Hinsley et al., *British Intelligence*, 3(2): 132, 134–35, 146.

47. For the mine problem, see Elliott, *Allied Minesweeping*, 118–22; Morison, *History of U.S. Naval Operations*, 172–73; Schofield, *Operation Neptune*, 103–7; Barnett, *Engage the Enemy*, 827, 830; and Hinsley et al., *British Intelligence*, 3(2): 165–67. Inside the ten-fathom line, large warships and merchant vessels were not safe at any speed. Elliott, *Allied Minesweeping*, 118.

48. Elliott, *Allied Minesweeping*, 122.

49. Morison, *History of U.S. Naval Operations*, 170–71.

50. Schofield, *Operation Neptune*, 108–10. There are tables showing the achievement of the *schnellboote* and their losses during the first two weeks of NEPTUNE in Hinsley et al., *British Intelligence*, 3(2): 860–61 (app. 16, tables 4 and 5).

51. Morison, *History of U.S. Naval Operations*, 192. There is a description of the characteristics and capabilities of the Marder in Roskill, *War at Sea*, 3(2): 454.

52. For a vivid description of their experiences, see Herbert A. Werner, *Iron*

Coffins (New York: Bantam Books, 1969), ch. 21. Werner commanded one of the nonsnorkel boats.

53. For the U-boat effort, see Barnett, *Engage the Enemy*, 831–32; Schofield, *Operation Neptune*, 111; and Roskill, *War at Sea*, 3(2): 57–58, 67–68. British naval intelligence considerably overestimated the scale of effort the U-boat command could mount. Hinsley et al., *British Intelligence*, 3(2): 96–99.

54. For the follow-up phase, see Schofield, *Operation Neptune*, 112, 116–17; Morison, *History of U.S. Naval Operations*, 163–66, 187; and Barnett, *Engage the Enemy*, 828–29.

55. Quoted in Morison, *History of U.S. Naval Operations*, 165; and Barnett, *Engage the Enemy*, 828.

56. Schofield, *Operation Neptune*, 113–14, 118–19.

57. For the storm, see Morison, *History of U.S. Naval Operations*, 176–77, 188; Harrison, *Cross-Channel Attack*, 423, 426; Barnett, *Engage the Enemy*, 835; and Schofield, *Operation Neptune*, 122–23. About 600 beached craft could be repaired and refloated.

58. Roskill, *War at Sea*, 3(2): 66; and Elsey, "Naval Aspects," 193–94.

59. Roskill, *War at Sea*, 3(2): 66; Barnett, *Engage the Enemy*, 837. Ramsay would not survive the war, dying in a plane crash on 2 Jan 1945.

60. On the significance of the element of surprise in the success of NEPTUNE, see Hinsley et al., *British Intelligence*, 3(2): 42, 126. Allied intelligence seems to have missed the movement of the German 352d Infantry Division, a field-grade unit, into positions along Omaha Beach. See Ruge, *Rommel in Normandy*, 92; Harrison, *Cross-Channel Attack*, 254, 257, 319; Hinsley et al., *British Intelligence*, 3(2): 72–73, 842–43; and Ralph Bennett, ULTRA *in the West: The Normandy Campaign 1944–45* (New York: Charles Scribner's Sons, 1980), 43–46. One reason for the problems on D-day was the late expansion of the landing effort from three to five divisions, essential though that was. Captain Roskill has some wise words on the importance of naming an overall commander early enough to cast an adequate plan from the start. *War at Sea*, 3(2): 9. Unfortunately, this is easier said than done.

Chapter 7. German Naval Operations on D-Day

1. Both are included in Gordon A. Harrison, *Cross-Channel Attack*, (Washington, D.C.: GPO, 1951), 459–67. The quoted portion appears on p. 460.

2. Raeder made an inspection of my force in Jun 1939. In a conversation afterward, I complained about not having been able to go on a vacation the preceding fall because of the Czechoslovakian crisis. He assured me that in the fall of 1939 everything would be quiet. I knew him well; he would not have deceived me. He could have said nothing, but when he told me that, he believed it himself.

3. Incidentally, from the point of view of naval construction, it would have been possible to build the fast underwater types XXI and XXIII much earlier. All the elements for them existed before the war.

4. I was in Italy in 1943. Early that spring, we received the first planes with radar. They proved excellent for protecting supply ships going to Tunisia. There were enough men in Tunisia, but the losses of supplies at sea were terrible and, of

course, decisive. But when I asked for the radar planes for the next operation a few days later, I was told that they had been expended for a bombing attack on Tripoli. It was entirely futile.

5. In 1940–41, I had instituted two close-combat schools. This kind of training proved valuable in a number of scraps in the Channel as well as in the British raid on Saint-Nazaire, where the British commandos could not overcome the men of the local minesweeping flotilla.

6. The *Räumboat* was an inshore minesweeper.

7. In the winter of 1941–42, I took part in several operations, when a formation of 24 of these R-boats laid mine fields in the middle of the Channel—by night, of course.

8. Incidentally, most pictures of the so-called Atlantic Wall were taken either there or at the submarine bases along the Bay of Biscay.

9. That was one of the reasons for instituting the close-combat schools, and that's where knowledge of history proved very valuable.

10. I talked to the man in charge on the day before D-day, and he told me that they had practically every single station going again. I think that the mass of targets seemed too incredible to the observers, so the possibility that this kind of disturbance was the enemy was discounted.

11. I thanked the British after the war.

12. You see, there was OB WEST, but Navy Group West was only slightly under the command of Rundstedt and mostly under Admiral Theodore Krancke and Oberkommando der Kriegsmarine. The same arrangement applied to the air force.

13. In 1957 or 1958, the Norwegian Defense College class visited Bonn for the first time. The Norwegian ambassador gave a party in their honor. I was invited and soon steered toward three Norwegian naval officers who were present. Somehow, they seemed to be out of sorts. Eventually, they told me that all three of them had been on *Svenner*. They did not mind so much being sunk by the German boats, but why had the German commander attacked their harmless destroyer and not the bigger ships immediately behind them? Fortunately, I was able to produce the German commanding officer, Captain Hoffman, a former petty officer and an excellent man with a great sense of humor. The same night, over quite a few glasses of beer, they refought that action. He finally convinced them that he too would have preferred the battleships, but he had not made them out with his poor radar, and there was so much artificial smoke that he considered himself lucky to get in with his small ships and back to Le Havre safely again. From that time on, relations with the Norwegian navy improved.

14. According to the war log of the USS *Corry*, the ship was sunk by a mine. The Fort Saint-Marcouf battery report, however, indicates that the U.S. destroyer was hit by a 210-mm salvo at the same time.

15. Actually, they often detonated too early or homed on noisemaking buoys towed by the Allied destroyers.

16. This type of craft was, in effect, one torpedo suspended from another. From the upper one, which was for propulsion only and capable of a top speed of four knots, was hung the detachable missile torpedo. The operator sat astride the upper torpedo enclosed in a watertight casing, with his head above the surface in a transparent plastic dome eighteen inches in diameter. Samuel E. Morison, *The Invasion of France and Germany* (Boston: Little, Brown, 1957), 11: 192.

Chapter 8. The Air Campaign

1. As cited in Milton Shulman, *Defeat in the West* (London: Secker & Warburg, 1948), 118, and Chefs des Generalstabes Ob. West, Ia Nr. 356/44 g.Kdos.Chefs, "Meldung," 9 Jun 1944, Microcopy No. T311, Roll 25, Frame 7029402, National Archives (NA).

2. Basil H. Liddell Har (ed.), *The Rommel Papers*, trans. Paul Finley (New York: Harcourt Brace, 1953), 491; Air Ministry Translation, VII/40, "Effects of Air Power as Stated by German Leaders in Extracts from Original Documents and Allied Interrogation Reports," 1947, U.S. Air Force Historical Research Agency (USAFHRA) 512.621 VII/40; Williamson Murray, *Luftwaffe* (Baltimore: Nautical and Aviation Publishing, 1985), 267; and Panzergruppe West, Ia Nr. 2532/44 g.Kdos., "Verlaufe Eindrucke von Westkampf," 13 Jun 1944, T311/25/7029549, NA.

3. John S. D. Eisenhower, *Strictly Personal* (Garden City, N.Y.: Doubleday, 1974), 72.

4. Carlo D'Este, *Decision in Normandy*, reprint (New York: HarperCollins, 1983), 212; Sir Arthur Tedder (Lord Tedder), *With Prejudice* (London: Cassell, 1966), 564–72; Gen. Elwood R. Quesada interview, Jun 1977, K239.0512-1485, USAFHRA; and W. A. Jacobs, "Operation OVERLORD," in B. F. Cooling (ed.), *Case Studies in Air Superiority* (Washington, D.C.: GPO, 1993), 300–302.

5. As cited in D'Este, *Decision in Normandy*, 216.

6. Gen. Elwood R. Quesada interview, 12–13 May 1975, K239.0512-838, USAFHRA; D'Este, *Decision in Normandy*, 218–31; John Terraine, *A Time for Courage: The Royal Air Force in the European War, 1939–1945* (New York: Macmillan, 1985), 609; Tedder, *With Prejudice*, 573; and Vincent Orange, *Coningham: A Biography of Air Marshal Sir Arthur Coningham* (London: Methuen, 1990), 244.

7. Prime Minister Personal Minute, Serial No. M(5) 1/3, Prime Minister to Chief of the Air Staff, 15 Nov 1943, AIR 8/1187, Public Record Office (PRO); CPS, 86th meeting, 25 Oct 1943, CAB 88/51, PRO; and Wesley F. Craven and James L. Cate (eds.), *The Army Air Forces in World War II*, vol. 3, *ARGUMENT to V-E Day, January 1944 to May 1945* (Chicago: University of Chicago Press, 1951), 80–81.

8. W. A. Jacobs, "The Battle for France, 1944," in B. F. Cooling, ed., *Case Studies in the Development of Close Air Support* (Washington, D.C.: GPO, 1990), 240–45; Quesada interview, K239.0512-838, Tape 2, Side 2, pp. 4–5, USAFHRA; and Eighth Air Force (8AF), "The Tactical Use of Heavy Bombardment in the Normandy Invasion," 1947, 520.04-10, USAFHRA.

9. Allied Expeditionary Air Forces (AEAF), "Minutes of Allied Air Commanders' Conferences, 1 Jul to 31 Jul 1944 (31st to 59th Conferences)," 505.25-8, USAFHRA.

10. Jacobs, "Battle for France," 251. It is difficult to pinpoint when American aviators truly accepted close air support doctrine, but they were moving in that direction in 1943 during the North African campaign and finally used it effectively in early 1944 in southern Italy. Its development in the West awaited D-day. See David Syrett, "The Tunisian Campaign," and Alan F. Wilt, "Allied Cooperation in Sicily and Italy 1943–1945," in Cooling *Case Studies*, 167, 205.

11. Craven and Cate, *Army Air Forces*, 3: 72–78.

12. CAS/Misc/61(Final), "Final Minutes of a Meeting Held on Saturday March 25th to Discuss the Bombing Policy in the Period before 'OVERLORD,'" 28 Mar 44, 512.318-1, USAFHRA; Air Ministry, "Plan for Employment of Strategic Bombing

Force," 4 Apr 44, 512.318-1, USAFHRA; and David R. Mets, *Master of Airpower: General Carl A. Spaatz* (Novato, Calif.: Presidio, 1988), 204, 211.

13. DO(44), 5th–9th Meetings, 5 Apr to 3 May 1944, CAB 69/6, PRO; Prime Minister to President, 7 May, 1944, in Warren F. Kimball (ed.), *Churchill and Roosevelt: The Complete Correspondence*, (Princeton, N.J.: Princeton University Press, 1984), 3: 122; and President Roosevelt to Prime Minister, 11 May 1944, AIR 8/1190, PRO.

14. Supreme Headquarters Allied Expeditionary Forces (SHAEF), Office of the Deputy Supreme Commander, "Alternative Plans for Employment of Strategic Bomber Forces, Minutes of Meeting, 3 May 1944," 505.25-9, USAFHRA.

15. The best general discussion of preinvasion operations remains Alfred Goldberg, "Air Campaign OVERLORD: To D-Day," in Eisenhower Foundation, *D-Day: The Normandy Invasion in Retrospect* (Lawrence: University Press of Kansas, 1971), 57–78. For specifics, see Craven and Cate, *Army Air Forces*, 3: 155–71; Stephen L. McFarland and Wesley P. Newton, *To Command the Sky: The Battle for Air Supremacy over Germany, 1942–1944* (Washington, D.C.: Smithsonian Institution Press, 1991), 231; Jacobs, "Operation OVERLORD," 303–4; AEAF, "Daily and Weekly Target Summaries," 15 May-8 Jun 1944, 505.25-22, USAFHRA; and Army Air Forces Evaluation Board—European Theater of Operations, "Summary Report on Effectiveness of Air Attack Against Rail Transportation in Battle of France," 1 Jun 1945, 138.4-37A, USAFHRA. The total number of targets per category (rail centers, airfields, and so on) varied from day to day, as targets were added or deleted on the basis of new intelligence.

16. Jacobs, "Operation OVERLORD," 297–99; and Murray, *Luftwaffe*, 251–52, 257–59.

17. SHAEF, "A Review of Air Operations Preparatory to and in Support of Operation 'Neptune,'" 1945, 29–30, 506.306A, USAFHRA.

18. Craven and Cate, *Army Air Forces*, 3: 139; SHAEF, "Review of Air Operations," 36; Jacobs, "Operation OVERLORD," 305–6; McFarland and Newton, *To Command the Sky*, 241; and Sir Arthur Tedder, *Air Power in War* (London: Hodder and Stoughton, 1948), 42.

19. Quesada interview, 12–13 May 1975, Tape 2, Side 2, p. 34.

20. Ralph Bennett, "Ultra and Some Command Decisions," *Journal of Contemporary History* 16 (Jan 1981): 140–42.

21. SHAEF, "Review of Air Operations," 55, 58; and Edward Mark, *Aerial Interdiction: Air Power and the Land Battle in Three American Wars* (Washington, D.C.: GPO, 1993), 251.

22. SHAEF, "Review of Air Operations," 56–57; and S. Zuckerman (Lord Zuckerman), "Times for Reestablishment of Traffic Through Bombed Rail Centers and Junctions and Across Bridges," 11 Aug 1944, 505.26-38, USAFHRA.

23. SHAEF, "Review of Air Operations," 60–62; AEAF, "Daily Int/Ops Summaries Nos. 137 and 147," 8 Jun and 13–14 Jun 1944, 506.3071, USAFHRA.

24. W. A. Jacobs, "Tactical Air Doctrine and AAF Close Support in the European Theater, 1944–1945," *Aerospace Historian* 27 (May 1980): 43; and First Army G-3 (Air), "Air Support Report," 6 Aug 1944, 580.4501-1, USAFHRA.

25. Jacobs, "Battle for France," 254–58.

26. Ibid., 260; and Richard P. Hallion, *Strike from the Sky: The History of Battlefield Air Attack, 1911–1945* (Washington, D.C.: Smithsonian Institution Press, 1989), 197.

27. SHAEF, "Review of Air Operations," 45.

28. Jacobs, "Battle for France," 245–51, and Hallion, *Strike from the Sky*, 202.

29. Ibid., 203; Craven and Cate, *Army Air Forces*, 3: 549–50, 563–65; SHAEF, "Review of Air Operations," 73; and Tedder, *With Prejudice*, 555–56.

30. Hallion, *Strike from the Sky*, 224; and Quesada interview, 12–13 May 1975, Tape 2, Side 2, p. 34.

31. Craven and Cate, *Army Air Forces*, 3: 279; Tedder, *With Prejudice*, 552; and Terraine, *A Time for Courage*, 650–58.

32. Hallion, *Strike from the Sky*, 206–12; 8AF, "Statistical Summary," Aug 1943–Oct 1944, 520.308-7, USAFHRA; and Craven and Cate, *Army Air Forces*, 3: 232–38.

33. Jacobs, "Operation OVERLORD," 266; Ninth Air Force (9AF), "Air Support and Results," May-Oct 1944, 533.4501-10, USAFHRA; Craven and Cate, *Army Air Forces*, 3: 200; and Martin Blumenson, *Breakout and Pursuit (United States Army in World War II, The European Theater of Operations)* (Washington, D.C.: GPO, 1961), 232.

34. Craven and Cate, *Army Air Forces*, 3: 209; and AAF Eval Bd—ETO, "Report of Tactical Committee on the Subject of Doctrine, Organization, Tactics and Techniques of AAF in the ETO," 26 Sep 44, 138.4-36B, USAFHRA.

35. Compiling air totals is a risky undertaking. The totals in Sir Charles K. Webster and Noble Frankland, *The Strategic Air Offensive Against Germany*, vol. 4, *Annexes and Appendices* (London: HMSO, 1961), 433–34, 456, are based on a different source and are lower than those in Martin Middlebrook and Chris Everitt, (eds.), *The Bomber Command War Diaries: An Operational Reference Book, 1939–1945* (London: Penguin, 1985), 517–54. Given Everitt's extensive work in the Public Record Office, I used the latter's figures. Though helpful for getting an idea of the types of missions on a day-to-day basis, the totals in AEAF, "Daily Int/Ops Summaries," for Jun and Jul are incomplete. The figures in AEAF, "Historical Data," 15 Oct 1944, 48–49, 506.01, USAFHRA, are close to those I have assembled and may well be correct, but it has been impossible to ascertain from where the data were derived.

36. Lyle F. Ellis, *Victory in the West, 1944–45*, vol. 1, *The Battle of Normandy* (London: HMSO, 1962), 487–88; and AEAF, "Historical Data," 50.

37. Murray, *Luftwaffe*, 268–69; Air Ministry Translation, VII/32, "Air Operations over the Invasion Front in Jun 1944," 27 Aug 1944, 512.621 VII/32, USAFHRA; Jacobs, "Battle for France," 277; and Jacobs, "Operation OVERLORD," 306.

38. Ellis, *Victory in the West*, 1: 305–6; Murray, *Luftwaffe*, 290; 8AF, "Statistical Summary," 14–15; 9AF, "Statistical Summary of Operations, 1943–1945," 533.308, USAFHRA; Jacobs, "Operation OVERLORD," 275–76; Mets, *Master of Airpower*, 193; and Quesada interview, 12–13 May 1975, Tape 2, Side 2, p. 11.

39. Terraine, *A Time for Courage*, 619.

Chapter 9. Special Operations and the Normandy Invasion

The author wishes to thank Dr. Theodore A. Wilson of the University of Kansas; Clay Laurie, Dale Andrade, Andrew Birtle, and Jim Knight of the Army Center of Military History; Herb Mason of U.S. Air Force Special Operations Command; Richard Stewart and Stan Sandler of U.S. Army Special Operations Command; John Partin of U.S. Special Operations Command; Ed Reese and John Taylor of the

National Archives; Cathy Lloyd of the Naval Historical Center; and Jim O' Dell for their help in connection with this project.

1. Department of Defense, *Department of Defense Dictionary of Military and Associated Terms*, Jt. Pub. 1-02 (Washington, D.C.: Department of Defense, 1989), 339; Alfred H. Paddock, Jr., *U.S. Army Special Warfare: Its Origins: Psychological and Unconventional Warfare, 1941–1952* (Washington, D.C.: National Defense University Press, 1982), 25; M. R. D. Foot, *SOE in France* (London: HMSO, 1966), xviii, 11–12; Kermit Roosevelt, *War Report of the OSS*, 2 vols. (New York: Walker, 1976), 1: 16, 80, 206; War Department, *Dictionary of United States Army Terms*, TM 20–205 (Washington, D.C.: War Department, 1944); Max B. Garber, *A Modern Military Dictionary*, 2d ed. (Washington, D.C.: P. S. Bond, 1942), 232. For a discussion of the problem of definition, see Maurice Tugwell and David Charters, "Special Operations and the Threats to United States Interests in the 1980s," in Frank R. Barnett, B. Hugh Tovar, and Richard H. Shultz (eds.) *Special Operations in U.S. Strategy* (Washington, D.C.: National Defense University Press, 1984), 29–41.

2. See John M. Collins, *Green Berets, SEALs and Spetsnaz: U.S. and Soviet Special Military Operations* (Washington, D.C.: Pergamon-Brassey's, 1987), for a description of present-day American special operations forces and their roles.

3. David W. Hogan, Jr., *Raiders or Elite Infantry? The Changing Role of the U.S. Army Rangers from Dieppe to Grenada* (Westport, Conn.: Greenwood Press, 1992), 1–7; David F. Trask, *The War with Spain in 1898* (New York: Macmillan, 1981), 209–10, 322; Allan R. Millett and Peter Maslowski, *For the Common Defense: A Military History of the United States of America* (New York: Free Press, 1984), 281, 291, 294, 318–21, 343; Allan R. Millett, *Semper Fidelis: The History of the United States Marine Corps* (New York: Macmillan, 1980), 147–211, 236–63; Russell F. Weigley, *History of the United States Army*, 2d ed. (Bloomington: Indiana University Press, 1984), 274, 278; G. G. Bruntz, "Allied Propaganda and the Collapse of German Morale in 1918," and H. D. Lasswell, "Organization of Psychological Warfare Agencies in World War I," in William E. Daugherty and Morris Janowitz (eds.), *A Psychological Warfare Casebook* (Baltimore: Johns Hopkins University Press, 1958), 97, 122. Several books describe the American experience with small wars in the early twentieth century; see especially Dana G. Munro, *Intervention and Dollar Diplomacy in the Caribbean, 1900–1921* (Princeton, N.J.: Princeton University Press, 1964), and *The United States and the Caribbean Republics, 1921–1933* (Princeton, N.J.: Princeton University Press, 1974); John M. Gates, *Schoolbooks and Krags: The United States in the Philippines, 1898–1902* (Westport, Conn.: Greenwood Press, 1973); Brian M. Linn, *The U. S. Army and Counterinsurgency in the Philippine War, 1898–1902* (Chapel Hill: University of North Carolina Press, 1989); David Healy, *The United States in Cuba, 1898–1902* (Madison: University of Wisconsin Press, 1963); Hans Schmidt, *The United States Occupation of Haiti, 1915–1934* (New Brunswick, N. J.: Rutgers University Press, 1971); and Neil Macauley, *The Sandino Affair* (New York: Quadrangle Books, 1967). See also the forthcoming study by Andrew Birtle on the development of doctrine for low-intensity conflict in the pre-World War II army, to be published by the U.S. Army Center of Military History.

4. See Roger Keyes, *Amphibious Warfare and Combined Operations* (Cambridge: Cambridge University Press, 1943); J. W. Fortescue, *A History of the British Army*, 13 vols. (London: Macmillan, 1899–1930), 2: 348–51, 4: 153, 6: 300; Brian Bond, *Victorian Military Campaigns* (New York: Praeger, 1967); E. B. Potter and Chester W. Nimitz (eds.), *Sea Power* (Englewood Cliffs, N.J.: Prentice-Hall,

1960), 53, 471–72; Cyril Falls, *The Great War* (New York: Perigee Books, 1959), 362; Robert B. Asprey, *War in the Shadows: The Guerrilla in History*, 2 vols. (Garden City, N.Y.: Doubleday, 1975), 1: 125–34, 257–71; Forrest C. Pogue, *The Supreme Command* (Washington, D.C.: Office of the Chief of Military History [OCMH], 1954), 76; Foot, *SOE in France*, xvii, 1–5; Thomas A. Bailey, *A Diplomatic History of the American People*, 9th ed. (Englewood Cliffs, N. J.: Prentice-Hall, 1974), 566; Bruntz, "Allied Propaganda," 96–105.

5. Alistair Horne, *To Lose a Battle: France, 1940* (Boston: Little, Brown, 1969), 85–87, 110, 114, 161, 164, 212–15, 220–23, 241, 454–57; James Lucas, *Kommando: German Special Forces of World War II* (New York: St. Martin's Press, 1985), 24; Gordon Wright, *The Ordeal of Total War, 1939–1945* (New York: Harper & Row, 1968), 66–68; Hideya Kurnata and Wilbur Schramm, "Propaganda Theory of the German Nazis," and Paul W. Blackstock, "German Use of Psychological Warfare in 1940," in Daugherty and Janowitz, *Psychological Warfare Casebook*, 48, 418–23.

6. J. R. M. Butler, *Grand Strategy*, 3 vols. (London: HMSO, 1957), 2: 19, 258–61, 3: 38–48; Hogan, *Raiders or Elite Infantry?* 13; Gordon A. Harrison, *Cross-Channel Attack*, (Washington, D.C.: OCMH, 1951), 5, 200–201; Pogue, *Supreme Command*, 152; Foot, *SOE in France*, 15, 144, 148, 165; Wright, *Ordeal of Total War*, 73–74.

7. David W. Hogan, Jr., *U.S. Army Special Operations in World War II* (Washington, D.C.: Center of Military History [CMH], 1992), 7–8, 65; Paddock, *U.S. Army Special Warfare*, 24–26; Kermit Roosevelt, *War Report of the OSS*, 2 vols. (New York: Walker, 1976), 1: 5–7; Clayton D. Laurie, "Ideology and American Propaganda: The Psychological Warfare Campaign Against Nazi Germany, 1941–1945," Ph.D. dissertation, American University, 1990, 344–49; James Ladd, *Commandos and Rangers of World War II* (New York: St. Martin's Press, 1978), 95.

8. Maurice Matloff and Edwin M. Snell, *Strategic Planning for Coalition Warfare, 1941–1942* (Washington, D.C.: CMH, 1953), 184–90; Hogan, *Raiders or Elite Infantry?* 11, 14–17; Foot, *SOE in France*, 30, 32, 195; Roosevelt, *War Report of the OSS*, 1: 257, 2: 3–4; R. Harris Smith, *OSS: The Secret History of America's First Central Intelligence Agency* (Berkeley: University of California Press, 1972), 166.

9. Hogan, *Raiders or Elite Infantry?* 19–20, 36; Lord Lovat, *March Past: A Memoir* (New York: Holmes and Meier, 1978), 273; Brian Loring Villa, "Unauthorized Action: Mountbatten and the Dieppe Raid," *Journal of Military History* 54 (Apr 1990): 214. Among other things, the raid clearly demonstrated the need for flexible plans, more rehearsals, better communications, more fire support, and intelligence from sources other than air photographs, but its horrendous cost—3,400 casualties among 5,000 participants—has made it a subject of great controversy, most recently through Brian Loring Villa's intriguing, though probably unprovable, argument that Lord Mountbatten of COHQ ordered that the raid proceed without any authorization from the British Chiefs of Staff; see Brian Loring Villa, *Unauthorized Action: Mountbatten and the Dieppe Raid* (New York: Oxford University Press, 1989).

10. "Operations on the Continent in the Final Phase: Report by the Joint Planning Staff," 9 Dec 1941, U.S. War Department, Operations Division, ABC Files, 381 BOLERO (3–16–42), sec. 1, Modern Military HQ Branch, Record Group (RG) 165, National Archives (NA); Hogan, *Raiders or Elite Infantry?* 24, 36; Ladd, *Commandos and Rangers*, 60–65, 124, 131–32, 139–41, 271–74; Francis Douglas Fane and Don Moore, *The Naked Warriors* (New York: Appleton, 1956),

11–13; Pogue, *Supreme Command*, 57; Laurie, "Ideology and American Propaganda," 436; Harry L. Coles and Albert K. Weinberg, *Civil Affairs: Soldiers Become Governors* (Washington, D.C.: OCMH, 1964), 30, 159, 188. Laurie has effectively illustrated the clash in ideologies on the American side between the idealistic, New Deal OWI and the more conservative and realistic OSS.

11. Harrison, *Cross-Channel Attack*, 205; Hogan, *U.S. Army Special Operations*, 51; "Call to Arms for French Patriots," in Stanley N. Cannicott, *Journey of a Jed*, unpublished memoir held by Dr. Samuel J. Lewis, Combat Studies Institute, Fort Leavenworth, Kans.; John Keegan, *The Second World War* (New York: Viking, 1989), 487.

12. Hogan, U.S. *Army Special Operations*, 48; Harrison, *Cross-Channel Attack*, 198–200; Pogue, *Supreme Command*, 152; Smith, *OSS*, 167–69, 180; Roosevelt, *War Report of the OSS*, 2: 177–78; Allied Force Headquarters, "History of Special Operations, Mediterranean Theater, 1942–5," unpublished manuscript, p. 151, Modern Military HQ Branch, NA; Foot, *SOE in France*, 182, 229–30, 233, 237, 240, 283, 351, 359–61.

13. Coles and Weinberg, *Civil Affairs*, 653–55, 661; Robert Dallek, *Franklin D. Roosevelt and American Foreign Policy* (New York: Oxford University Press, 1979), 406–9; Roosevelt, *War Report of the OSS*, 2: 197; Arthur L. Funk, "American Contacts with the Resistance in France," *Military Affairs* 34 (Feb 1970): 15–19; Foot, *SOE in France*, 133, 141–42, 221, 360, 444; Francois Kersaudy, *Churchill and De Gaulle* (New York: Atheneum, 1982), 76, 218, 287, 319; U.S. State Department, *Foreign Relations of the United States [FRUS]: Diplomatic Papers, 1942*, 7 vols. (Washington, D.C.: GPO, 1962), 2: 512–18; U.S. State Department, *FRUS: Diplomatic Papers, 1943* (Washington, D.C.: GPO, 1964), 2: 24–25, 116, 185; Cordell Hull, *The Memoirs of Cordell Hull*, 2 vols. (New York: Macmillan, 1948), 2: 1132.

14. Foot, *SOE in France*, 136, 152, 231–32, 240, 358, 384; James MacGregor Burns, *Roosevelt: The Soldier of Freedom, 1940–1945* (New York: Harcourt Brace Jovanovich, 1970), 480; Stephen E. Ambrose, *The Supreme Commander: The War Years of General Dwight D. Eisenhower*, 2d ed. (Garden City, N.Y.: Doubleday, 1970), 380.

15. U.S. Navy, Commander, Task Force 122, "Report of Naval Combat Demolition Units, Operation NEPTUNE," 19 Jul 1944, 65, Naval Historical Center; Coles and Weinberg, *Civil Affairs*, 671; Foot, *SOE in France*, 182–83; Pogue, *Supreme Command*, 53, 60, 80, 85, 153; Harrison, *Cross-Channel Attack*, 52; Frederick Morgan, *Overture to OVERLORD* (Garden City, N.Y.: Doubleday, 1950), 174–76, 225–29; Morgan to Secretary, Chiefs of Staff Committee, 2 Oct 1943, 091.411 Vol. I SOE/OSS Activities, Box 9, SHAEF Office of the Chief of Staff, Secretary of the General Staff, Decimal File, May 1943–August 1945, RG 331, NA; Laurie, "Ideology and American Propaganda," in Michael Balfour, *Propaganda and War, 1939–1945: Organisations, Policies, and Publics in Britain and Germany* (London: Routledge and Kegan Paul, 1979), 101–2; "Coordination of Reconnaissance," COS (43) 624 (0), 13 Oct 1943, Box 131, SHAEF, Office of the Secretary of the General Staff, Staff Conferences, 1942–1944, RG 331, NA; "Proposals for Control by COSSAC of SOE/SO Activities in Northwest Europe," in Lt. Gen. Walter B. Smith, Chief of Staff, SHAEF, to Brig. Gen. E. E. Mockler-Ferryman and Col. Joseph F. Haskell, SOE/SO, 23 Mar 1944, 091.411 Vol. I SOE/OSS Activities, Box 9, SHAEF, Secretary of the General Staff, Decimal File, May 1943—August 1945, RG 331, NA.

16. Harrison, *Cross-Channel Attack*, 200–202.

17. Foot, *SOE in France*, 13, 63, 66, 75, 82, 234; Bernard V. Moore, "The Secret Air War Over France: USAAF Special Operations Units in the French Campaign of 1944," Master's thesis, Air University, 1992, 16–23, 28–31, 36–42; Harrison, *Cross-Channel Attack*, 201–2.

18. Foot, *SOE in France*, 11, 321, 329, 347, 350, 386.

19. Ibid., 13, 352; Hogan, *U.S. Army Special Operations*, 6; Michael Carver, "Montgomery," in John Keegan (ed.), *Churchill's Generals* (New York: Grove Weidenfeld, 1991), 149; Russell F. Weigley, *Eisenhower's Lieutenants: The Campaigns of France and Germany, 1944–1945* (Bloomington: Indiana University Press, 1981), 80–83; Hogan, *Raiders or Elite Infantry?* 14; Fane and Moore, *Naked Warriors*, 41–42; Morgan, *Overture to OVERLORD*, 174–76; D. K. R. Crosswell, *The Chief of Staff: The Military Career of General Walter Bedell Smith* (Westport, Conn.: Greenwood Press, 1991), 96, 147.

20. Smith, *OSS*, 105; see also Hogan, *U.S. Army Special Operations*, 8–9, 12–13, 41, 49–50; Foot, *SOE in France*, 49; Moore, "The Secret Air War Over France," 24–25, 51, 55–56; Office of Strategic Services, OG Missions, Caserta OG-OPS-5, Box 11, Entry 143, RG 226, NA; Fane and Moore, *Naked Warriors*, 18–22; Coles and Weinberg, *Civil Affairs*, 10–11; "Demolition Units of the Atlantic Theater of Operations," 1–2, in Dale Andrade Papers, CMH.

21. Peter Lyon, *Eisenhower: Portrait of the Hero* (Boston: Little, Brown, 1974), 248, 280; Ambrose, *Supreme Commander*, 97, 252, 321, 323, 325, 376; Pogue, *Supreme Command*, 84; Weigley, *Eisenhower's Lieutenants*, 36. On American policy, see Gaddis Smith, *American Diplomacy During the Second World War, 1941–1945* (New York: John Wiley, 1965), 57.

22. Eisenhower to CCS, 19 Jan 1944, Eisenhower to D'Astier, 17 Mar 1944, memorandum, 22 Mar 1944, and Eisenhower to CCS, 11 May 1944, in Alfred D. Chandler, Jr. (ed.), *The Papers of Dwight David Eisenhower*, 9 vols. (Baltimore: Johns Hopkins University Press, 1970), 3: 1540, 1668, 1687, 1771–72, 1784–85, 1857–59; Pogue, *Supreme Command*, 150; Coles and Weinberg, *Civil Affairs*, 656, 665–70.

23. Foot, *SOE in France*, 32–33, 385; Bull to SFHQ, 9 May 1944, 3704–5 Unorg Civ Resistance, and Minute 7 of Chiefs of Staff Conference, 25 Feb 1944, 3704–7 Coordination of Underground Agencies Working in France, Box 130, SHAEF G-3 Division, C Section, Decimal File, RG 331, NA; Roosevelt, *War Report of the OSS*, 2: 191–92; Air Ministry to Britman, 30 Mar 1944, and Smith to Brig. Gen. E. E. Mockler-Ferryman and Col. J. F. Haskell, 23 Mar 1944, in 091.411 SOE/OSS Activities, Box 9, SHAEF, Secretary of the General Staff, Decimal File, RG 331, NA; Funk, "American Contacts with the Resistance in France," 20; Pogue, *Supreme Command*, 154; Smith, *OSS*, 179, 182–83, 188; memorandum, 3 Jun 1944, in Chandler, *Eisenhower Papers*, 3: 1904.

24. Pogue, *Supreme Command*, 75–88; "Psychological Warfare Branch: Composition, Functions, and Relations to Other Agencies or Departments," 30 Dec 1943, and SHAEF Operations Memorandum No. 8, 11 Mar 1944, in 322.01 P&PW, Publicity and Psychological Warfare Division, Box 46, SHAEF Secretary of the General Staff, Decimal File, RG 331, NA; Laurie, "Ideology and American Propaganda," 436–41; Coles and Weinberg, *Civil Affairs*, 671–73, 721; Brig. Gen. Julius C. Holmes, DACOS, G-S Division, SHAEF, to Smith, 5 Apr 1944, 014.1 Vol. I—Civil Affairs in Northwest Europe, Box 6, SHAEF, Office of the Chief of Staff, Secretary of the General Staff, Decimal File, May 1943–August 1945, RG 331, NA.

25. Maj. Gen. Harold R. Bull, G-3, SHAEF, to Smith, 4 Mar 1944, Morgan to Secretary, Chiefs of Staff Committee, 20 Mar 1944, and Smith to Air Chief Marshal

Sir Trafford Leigh-Mallory, 11 Apr 1944, 091.412 Propaganda Vol. I, SHAEF, Secretary of the General Staff, Decimal File, RG 331, NA; Moore, "The Secret Air War Over France," 44; Foot, *SOE in France*, 352–56; Harrison, *Cross-Channel Attack*, 203; Anthony Cave-Brown, *The Last Hero: Wild Bill Donovan* (New York: Times Books, 1982), 524–26.

26. Foot, *SOE in France*, 111, 387–88; Eisenhower to CCS, 8 May 1944, in Chandler, *Eisenhower Papers*, 3: 1852–1853; Brig. Gen. Arthur S. Nevins, Chief, Operations Section, SHAEF, to McClure, 1 Jun 1944, Col. Earle M. Jones, G-3 section, to SFHQ, 19 May 1944, and Bull to Smith, 14 May 1944, in 00077-1 BBC Warning to Resistance, Box 122, SHAEF, G-3 C Section, Decimal File, RG 331, NA; "21 Army Group Plan for Combat Zone Propaganda in Connection with Operation OVERLORD Covering Period 1st April to D+60," 322.01 P&PW, Publicity and Psychological Warfare Division, Box 46, SHAEF, Secretary of the General Staff, Decimal File, RG 331, NA; Hogan, *U.S. Army Special Operations*, 51.

27. Hogan, *Raiders or Elite Infantry?* 68–69; Morgan to Chief, Publicity and Psychological Warfare Branch, 19 Jan 1944, McClure to Smith, 31 Jan 1944, McClure to Smith, 17 Feb 1944, McClure to Smith, 14 Mar 1944, and Lt. Cmdr. James E. Reid to Smith, 16 Mar 1944, 322.01 P&PW, Publicity and Psychological Warfare Division, Box 46, SHAEF Secretary of the General Staff, Decimal File, RG 331, NA; Bradley to Smith, 2 Jun 1944, and Smith to Bradley, 5 Jun 1944, 014.1 Vol. I: Civil Affairs in Northwest Europe, Box 6, SHAEF Secretary of the General Staff, Decimal File, RG 331, NA.

28. Smith to Mockler-Ferryman and Haskell, 23 Mar 1944, 091.411 Vol. I SOE/OSS Activities, Box 9, SHAEF Secretary of the General Staff, Decimal File, RG 331, NA; correspondence in 370-4-5 Unorg Civilian Resistance, and Maj. N. B. J. Hulisman, Operations A Subsection to G-4 (Osmanski), 20 Apr 1944, and SOE/SOHQ to G-3 (LTC Alms), 17 Apr 1944, 370-31 (1) Prevention of Demolitions by the Enemy, Box 133, SHAEF G-3 Division, Ops C Section, Decimal File, RG 331, NA; Roosevelt, *War Report of the OSS*, 2: 191; Foot, *SOE in France*, 350; Harrison, *Cross-Channel Attack*, 202, 205; Allied Force Headquarters, G-3, Special Projects Operations Center, "Plan for Coordination and Use of Resistance Movements in Connection with Operation OVERLORD," May 1944, in AFHQ, "History of Special Operations," unpublished manuscript, pp. 170–74, 179–81, NA; "The French Forces of the Interior: Their Organization and Participation in the Liberation of France," unpublished manuscript, 2: 394g, Historical Services Branch, CMH.

29. "Standing Directive for Psychological Warfare Against Members of the German Armed Forces," 16 Jun 1944, 091.412/3 Psychological Warfare Against Germany, Box 10, SHAEF Secretary of the General Staff, Decimal File, RG 331, NA; Bull to Chief, G-6 Division, Mar 1944, McClure to Wilson, 2 Jun 1944, "21st Army Group Plan for Combat Zone Propaganda for Operation OVERLORD Covering Period 1 April to D+60," 091.412 Propaganda Vol. I, SHAEF Secretary of the General Staff, Decimal File, RG 331, NA; SHAEF Psywar Div, "Psychological Warfare to Foreigners Serving in the German Armed Forces in Support of OVERLORD," Box 11, 091.412/4 Propaganda Directed to Non Germans Serving in the Wehrmacht, Box 11, SHAEF Secretary of the General Staff, Decimal File, RG 331, NA; Pogue, *Supreme Command*, 87–88.

30. F. S. V. Donnison, *Civil Affairs and Military Government Northwest Europe, 1944–1946* (London: HMSO, 1961), 37–38, 59–61, 67–69; Coles and Weinberg, *Civil Affairs*, 655.

31. Hogan, *Raiders or Elite Infantry?* 68–69; L. F. Ellis, *Victory in the West: The Battle of Normandy* (London: HMSO, 1962), 175; Ladd, *Commandos and*

Rangers, 181; Commander, Assault Force O, Western Naval Task Force, "Action Report: Assault on Colleville-Vierville Sector, Coast of Normandy," 27 July 1944, 98, Naval Historical Center; "Operation OVERLORD: Report of Naval Commander, Western Task Force (Comdr. TF 122): Rear Admiral A. G. Kirk's Report on Amphibious Operation NEPTUNE in Baie de la Seine During the Invasion of Normandy France. Report Covers the Period from 9 November 1943 to 3 July 1944," 25 Jul 1944," N-1, Naval Historical Center; "Report of Naval Combat Demolition Units, Operation NEPTUNE," 19 Jul 1944, 66–67, 71, Naval Historical Center; Michael G. Welham, *Combat Frogmen* (New York: Arco, 1984), 43.

32. Wesley F. Craven and James Lea Cate, *The Army Air Forces in World War 11*, vol. 3, *Europe: ARGUMENT to V-E Day, January 1944 to May 1945* (Chicago: University of Chicago Press, 1951), 493, 498, 499–502; Roosevelt, *War Report of the OSS*, 2: 141, 192; Foot, *SOE in France*, 357, 365–67; Ladd, *Commandos and Rangers*, 174–76; Moore, "The Secret Air War Over France," 47, 58; Laurie, "Ideology and American Propaganda," 495–99; Welham, *Combat Frogmen*, 42; Wallace Carroll, "Where Is the Luftwaffe?" in Daugherty and Janowitz, *Psychological Warfare Casebook*, 373–80.

33. Hogan, *Raiders or Elite Infantry?* 69; Ellis, *Victory in the West*, 169, 175, 183, 186, 202, 205, 209; NCDU report, 73–78; Kirk's report, N-1; Welham, *Combat Frogmen*, 43–44; Ladd, *Commandos and Rangers*, 178, 180–93.

34. "OWI in the ETO: A Report on the Activities of the Office of War Information in the European Theater of Operations, January 1944–January 1945," 22, Hoover Institution on War, Revolution, and Peace, Stanford, Calif.; Laurie, "Ideology and American Propaganda," 513–15; Coles and Weinberg, *Civil Affairs*, 721–26; Ellis, *Victory in the West*, 571–72; Donnison, *Civil Affairs and Military Government*, 73–78; Pogue, *Supreme Command*, 336–37, 343–45.

35. See reports in 370.2–3 Ops "C" Summaries of Resistance and SAS Activities, Box 135, SHAEF G-3 Division, Ops "C" Section, Decimal File, RG 331, NA; Moore, "The Secret Air War Over France," 60–62; Foot, *SOE in France*, 387–90, 397–407, 411; Roosevelt, *War Report of the OSS*, 2: 198, 204, 215; Harrison, *Cross-Channel Attack*, 206; Pogue, *Supreme Command*, 237; Hogan, *U.S. Army Special Operations*, 51.

36. Hogan, *U.S. Army Special Operations*, 57–58; Foot, *SOE in France*, 87, 433, 436; Kirk report, N-2; Hall report, 99; NCDU report, 79–83; Laurie, "Ideology and American Propaganda," 523; Coles and Weinberg, *Civil Affairs*, 673.

37. "The Value of SOE Operations in the Supreme Commander's Sphere," 091.411 Vol. I, SOE/OSS Activities, and McClure to Smith, 4 Aug 1944, 091.412 Propaganda, Vol. I, Box 9, SHAEF Secretary of the General Staff, Decimal File, RG 331, NA; Patton quoted in S. J. Lewis, *Jedburgh Operations in Support of the 12th Army Group, Aug 1944* (Fort Leavenworth, Kans.: Combat Studies Institute, 1991), 64; Hogan, *U.S. Army Special Operations*, 57; Foot, *SOE in France*, 387–90, 397, 408–9, 434–41; Moore, "The Secret Air War Over France," 63–65, 69; Pogue, *Supreme Command*, 132; Harrison, *Cross-Channel Attack*, 203–6; Laurie, "Ideology and American Propaganda," 489, 512, 530.

Chapter 10. D-day 1944

1. This chapter is based first of all on my own observations as a combat historian with U.S. First Army and on scores of interviews held with men of the 29th

and 1st Infantry Divisions beginning on 7 Jun 1944. For example, this and follow-ing paragraphs on the lieutenant come from an interview by the author with Spalding, 9 Feb 1945. I also drew on entries in a diary I kept at the time. In addi-tion, I consulted material used in my *The Supreme Command* (Washington, D.C.: GPO, 1954), the official account of General Eisenhower's command in northwest Europe, 1944–45, which was written under Eisenhower's directive and based on his personal files, Diary of the Office Commander in Chief, War Department files, minutes of the great conferences, and interviews in Europe and the United States with more than 100 of his wartime associates. Other volumes I consulted were Gordon A. Harrison, *Cross-Channel Attack* (Washington, D.C.: GPO, 1951), the official army volume on D-day, which is based on U.S. and British official files, captured German documents, and hundreds of interviews conducted within a few days of the action. This is the most complete and authoritative account of the subject. Other important official volumes are Charles H. Taylor, *Omaha Beach* (Washington, D.C.: GPO, 1945), and R. G. Ruppenthal, *Utah Beach to Cherbourg* (Washington, D.C.: GPO, 1947). The Department of the Army volume, *Small Unit Actions* (Washington, D.C.: GPO, 1946), contains Charles H. Taylor's account of Ranger actions on D-day. Samuel E. Morison, *The Invasion of France and Ger-many*, vol. 11 (Boston: Little, Brown, 1962), gives an excellent navy account based in part on eyewitness material and a narrative furnished by Lt. George M. El-sey. The British official volume on this period is L. F. Ellis, *Victory in the West: The Battle of Normandy*, vol. 1 (London: HMSO, 1962). Accounts by participants in-cluded Dwight D. Eisenhower, *Crusade in Europe* (New York: Doubleday, 1948); Omar N. Bradley, *A Soldier's Story* (New York: Henry Holt, 1951); Montgomery of Alamein, *Memoirs* (New York: New American Library, 1959); Marshal of the Royal Air Force Sir Arthur Tedder, *With Prejudice* (Boston: Little, Brown, 1966); Sir Frederick E. Morgan, *Overture to* OVERLORD (New York: Doubleday, 1950); and Forrest C. Pogue, "Political Problems of a Coalition Command," in Harry L. Coles (ed.), *Total War and Cold War* (Columbus: Ohio State University Press, 1962), 108–28.

2. Bernard Fergusson, *The Watery Maze* (New York: Holt Rinehart and Win-ston, 1961), 87–88, 350.

3. Ibid., 302–4; interview with Rear Adm. George E. Creasy, Lt. Gen. Sir Fred-erick E. Morgan, and Maj. Gen. Ray W. Barker.

4. Montgomery to Eisenhower, W-9418, 10 Jan 1944, Bernard L. Montgomery Correspondence File, Personal Papers of Dwight D. Eisenhower, 1916–52 (PPDDE), Eisenhower Library (EL), Abilene, Kans.

5. Eisenhower to Marshall, B-320, 21 Mar 1944, Cable File, PPDDE, EL.

6. Leigh-Mallory to Eisenhower, 29 May 1944, and Eisenhower to Leigh-Mal-lory, 30 May 1944, Leigh-Mallory Correspondence File, PPDDE, EL.

7. Interview by author with Marshal of the Royal Air Force Sir Charles Portal, 1947.

8. Eisenhower to Marshall, W-8550, 25 Dec 1943, Cable File, PPDDE, EL.

9. Interview with Portal, 1947.

10. Sir Charles Webster and Noble Frankland, *The Strategic Air Offensive Against Germany*, vol. 2 (London: HMSO, 1961), ch. 2; Pogue, *Supreme Com-mand*, 125; Tedder, *With Prejudice*, 501–15.

11. Combined Chiefs of Staff to Eisenhower, W-19763, 7 Apr 1944, SHAEF SGS 373/1 Policy re: Control and Employment of USSTAF and Bomber Com-mand, National Archives (NA).

12. "Minutes of Meeting Held on Saturday, March 25 [1944] to Discuss the

Bombing Policy in the Period before OVERLORD," CAS misc. 61, U.S. Air Force Historical Division, Aerospace Studies Institute, Maxwell Air Base, Ala. (filed as "Minutes of OVERLORD Bombing Plan," 519, 3171–78); Wesley F. Craven and James L. Cate (eds.), *Europe: ARGUMENT to V-E Day, January 1944 to May 1945* (Chicago: University of Chicago Press, 1951), 78 n. 62.

13. Eisenhower to Marshall, 29 Apr 1944, George C. Patton Correspondence File, PPDDE, EL.

14. Churchill to Tedder note, quoted in Pogue, *Supreme Command*, 132; Smith to Marshall, S-51984, 17 May 1944, Eyes Only Cables, Walter B. Smith Collection, EL.

15. Eisenhower to Secretary, Chiefs of Staff Committee, 6 Mar 1944, Gen. Leslie C. Hollis to Eisenhower, 11 Mar 1944, SHAEF SGS 380.01/4 Security for Operations, NA.

16. Eisenhower to Brooke, 9 Apr 1944, and Brooke to Eisenhower, 17 Apr 1944, Alan Brooke Correspondence File, PPDDE, EL.

17. Eisenhower to Combined Chiefs of Staff, S-51678, 11 May 1944, and Roosevelt to Eisenhower, W-e6054, 13 May 1944, SHAEF SGS 092 France, French Relations, vol. I, NA.

18. Sir Robert Bruce Lockhart, *Comes the Reckoning* (London: Putnam, 1947), 299–305; and interview by the author with Lockhart, London, 1946.

19. In Sep 1943, COSSAC adopted a special procedure, known as BIGOT, by which all papers relating to the OVERLORD operations that disclosed the target area or the precise dates of the assault were limited in circulation to a small group of officers and men and subjected to stringent safeguards. Pogue, *Supreme Command*, 162.

20. These paragraphs relating to the decision to go are summarized from my account in *Supreme Command*, 168–70, which was based on various published accounts by participants, on interviews with several of them, and on two unpublished contemporary reports—one by Maj. Gen. Harold R. Bull, "Memo for Record," 5 Jun 1944, OVERLORD Misc. File, SHAEF Files of General Bull, microfilm copy, NA and EL; and the other by Air Vice Marshal James M. Robb, report written on morning of 5 Jun 1944, copy in possession of author. Gen. W. Bedell Smith's remarks are in Walter Bedell Smith, *Eisenhower's Six Great Decisions* (New York: Longmans, Green, 1956), 55.

Chapter 12. Deposited on Fortune's Far Shore: The 2d Battalion, 8th Infantry

1. The attached units included Company B of the 87th (4.2) Chemical Mortars, Company A, 237th Engineers, Company B and a detachment of Company C, 70th Tank Battalion, the 65th Armored Field Artillery Battalion, and two Naval Fire Control Parties, "Narrative History of the 4th Infantry Division, 1940–46," Adjutant General Records, Combined Arms Research Library Files (CARL) (microfilm), Fort Leavenworth, Kans. (hereafter "4th ID Narrative History").

2. Quoted in Max Hastings, *OVERLORD: D-Day and the Battle for Normandy 1944* (London: Michael Joseph, 1984), 51.

3. Ibid., 52.

4. The compilation by Royce L. Thompson, "Personal Loads," U.S. Army Center of Military History (1951), convincingly documents how overloaded the as-

sault troops in Normandy were. The comments by survivors make for harrowing reading.

5. "4th ID Narrative History."

6. Ibid.; George L. Mabry, Jr., "The Operations of the 2nd Battalion, 8th Infantry (4th Inf. Div.) in the Landing at UTAH Beach, 6–7 Jun 1944: Personal Experience of a Battalion S-3," unpublished paper, 3.

7. "4th ID Narrative History," 2–3; the conversion to triangular organization—with three regiments rather than four—reflected a commitment to maneuverability over staying power. For the effects of blitzkrieg, see Christopher Gabel, *The U.S. Army GHQ Maneuvers of 1941* (Washington, D.C.: Center of Military History, 1991), 28 29.

8. Dulic. O. Omith statement, Apr 1993, in author's possession.

9. Kent R. Greenfield et al., *The Organization of Ground Combat Troops* (Washington, D.C.: Historical Division, U.S. Army, 1947), 177, 277–78.

10. "4th ID Narrative History," 7–8.

11. This issue is dealt with in engaging fashion by Lee Kennett, *GI: The American Soldier in World War II* (New York: Warner Books, 1987).

12. Documents attached to "4th ID Narrative History," AG Historical Files (CARL microfilm).

13. This analysis derives from data in "History of the 4th Infantry Division, 1 January-31 December 1943," Hdq, 4th Infantry Division, Fort Jackson, S.C., 8 Jan 1944 (AG 314.7), documents attached to "4th ID Narrative History."

14. These issues are dealt with in some detail in Robert R. Palmer et al., *The Procurement and Training of Ground Combat Troops* (Washington, D.C.: Office of the Chief of Military History, 1948).

15. Memorandum for Assistant Chief of Staff (G-3), War Department, "Readiness of Divisions for Combat," 20 Dec 1941, AG Section–General Headquarters File (GHQ) (D.F. 353), Box 71, Records Group (RG) 337, National Archives (NA).

16. "History of the 4th Infantry Division, 1 January-31 December 1943," Hdq, 4th Infantry Division, Fort Jackson, S.C., 8 Jan 1944 (AG 314.7), documents attached to "4th ID Narrative History."

17. "4th ID Narrative History," 4.

18. Memorandum for the Chief of Staff, "Training Fitness of Divisions for Battle," 4 Dec 1943, Army Ground Forces (AGF) files (D.F. 353.22), Box 664, RG 337, NA.

19. "4th ID Narrative History: England," 7–8; BOLERO Base Plan, AG Historical Files (CARL microfilm).

20. Ibid., 8.

21. Beryl E. Clove to author, 10 Sep 1983, in author's possession.

22. J. Lawton Collins, *Lightning Joe: An Autobiography* (Baton Rouge: Louisiana State University Press, 1979), 180–81; see also Chapters 10 and 16 in this volume.

23. The mission orders given to Barton contrasted sharply with those received by Maj. Gen. Charles H. Gerhardt, commanding the 29th Division, when he first met with Lt. Gen. Jacob Devers in Jul 1943: "1. To prepare the Division to go ashore and stay ashore; 2. To get along with Lady Astor, the Mayoress of Plymouth; and 3. To correct the situation of too many men in the guardhouse." Charles H. Gerhardt memoir (Jul 1964), U.S. Army Military History Institute (MHI), Carlisle Barracks, Pa., 39.

24. Harry C. Butcher, *My Three Years with Eisenhower* (New York: Simon & Schuster, 1946), 487–88.

25. Collins, *Lightning Joe*, 182–83; the mixup has been cited by Martin Blumenson as exemplifying the highly centralized, often whimsical system controlled by Gen. George C. Marshall. Blumenson, "America's World War II Leaders in Europe: Some Thoughts," *Parameters*, 29, 4 (Dec 1989): 6. Van Fleet's subordinates judged him a fearless, aggressive leader "with moral as well as physical courage." Col. John H. Meyer to Gen. Richard G. Stillwell, 26 July 1988, in author's possession.

26. "History of the 12th Infantry," AG Records, RG 407, NA.

27. SHAEF, G-1, AG Records, Historical Section, n.d., documents attached to "4th ID Narrative History."

28. Collins, *Lightning Joe*, 186–87.

29. "4th ID Narrative History: England," 7.

30. Baker Smith statement, 14 Apr 1993, in author's possession.

31. "4th ID Narrative History: England," 8–9; Collins, *Lightning Joe*, 187–89.

32. Among these are Nigel Lewis, *Channel Firing: The Tragedy of Exercise Tiger* (London: Viking, 1989), and Edwin P. Hoyt, *The Invasion before Normandy: The Secret Battle of Slapton Sands* (New York: Military Heritage Press, 1985).

33. In this entry for 28 Apr 1944, Butcher noted at the bottom of the page, "This is one of the passages I was most tempted to delete since history made a monkey of me." Butcher, *My Three Years with Eisenhower*, 529–31.

34. "Action against Enemy, Period 15 May–3 July 1944," Headquarters 8th Infantry, 21 Jul 1944, Box 791, U.S. Army Records, Dwight D. Eisenhower Library, Abilene, Kans.

35. Mabry, "Operations of the 2nd Battalion," 7; Roland G. Ruppenthal, *Utah Beach to Cherbourg* (Washington, D.C.: Historical Division, U.S. Army, 1947), 3–4.

36. "4th ID Narrative History," 9–10; Mabry, "Operations of the 2nd Battalion," 12–13.

37. Mabry, "Operations of the 2nd Battalion," 14; "After-Action Report," 21 July 1944.

38. G-3 Reports, 4th Division, 1–8 Jun 1944 (CARL microfilm).

39. William B. Breuer, *Hitler's Fortress Cherbourg: The Conquest of a Bastion* (New York: Stein and Day, 1984), 87.

40. Mabry, "Operations of the 2nd Battalion," 18.

41. Quoted in Cornelius Ryan, *The Longest Day* (New York: Simon & Schuster, 1959), 167.

42. Ruppenthal, *Utah Beach to Cherbourg*, 43. This study, based on a variety of official records and after-action interviews, remains the most complete narrative history of VII Corps operations from 6 Jun to the capture of Cherbourg on 27 Jun 1944.

43. Ruppenthal, *Utah Beach to Cherbourg*, 44.

44. Mabry, "Operations of the 2nd Battalion," 19–20.

45. The 2d Battalion's aid station was in operation by late morning. Beginning in late afternoon of D-day, wounded were evacuated by LCT to a hospital LST, which remained off Utah Beach for four days before returning to Britain. "When the wounded were going out to sea in the afternoon there was heavier shelling of the boats than there had been on the landing and quite a number of wrecked small boats could be seen in the water. . . . The LCTs would tie up alongside (on one occasion there was an LCT on each side of the ship) and the casualties be hoisted by rope and pulley. This operation was quite difficult due to the heavy swells," Col. William T. Gayle, "Supplementary Notes to 4th Division Day-by-Day Account, 6–30 June 1944," CARL Files, 4–5.

46. Ruppenthal, *Utah to Cherbourg*, 44–45.

47. Col. William T. Gayle, "4th Infantry Division Day-by-Day Account, 6–30 Jun 1944," CARL Files, 2.

48. Chester Hansen diary, 6 Jun 1944, MHI.

49. Gayle, "Supplementary Notes," 1.

50. Mabry, "Operations of the 2nd Battalion," 21, 30–31.

51. Ruppenthal, *Utah Beach to Cherbourg*, 45; Gayle claims that "a change was made at the last minute because the fire was so heavy on the planned landing beaches." "Day-by-Day Account," 1.

52. Annette Tapert (ed.), *Lines of Battle: Letters from American Servicemen, 1941–1945* (New York: Pocket Books, 1987), 154.

53. General Collins later observed that although Exit 4 through the inundated area was left uncovered, the shift south "avoided a heavily defended area, with many beach obstacles, east of St. Martin-de-Varreville." Collins, *Lightning Joe*, 200.

54. Ruppenthal, *Utah to Cherbourg*, 48–50.

55. G-3 Reports, 1–8 Jun 1944, 4th Division (CARL microfilm).

56. Interview with 1st Lt. John Rebarchek, 2 Jul 1944, 4th ID Files (CARL microfilm).

57. Mabry, "Operations of the 2nd Battalion," 20. Gayle's narrative confirmed this information: "The Nazis had a considerable number of doodlebugs (automatic tankettes loaded with 300 pounds of TNT) emplaced among the dunes. Their holes were cut into the seaward side of the dunes where they sloped downward to the beach, evidently designed to run down to the water and explode among the disembarking troops. But none of them were ever launched; they remained in their holes until removed by our engineers." Gayle, "Supplementary Notes," 3.

58. Mabry, "Operations of the 2nd Battalion," 22–23.

59. Ryan, *Longest Day*, 226.

60. Mabry, "Operations of the 2nd Battalion," 24.

61. Rebarchek interview, 2.

62. Capt. John E. Galvin, Jr., "Unit Report No. 1, 8th Infantry," 0630–1200, 6 Jun, G-3 Reports, 1–8 Jun 1944 (CARL microfilm). Galvin noted that the troops had one D ration on hand and a C ration coming in on an LST; they averaged 50 percent of the basic load of ammunition.

63. Omar N. Bradley and Clay Blair, *A General's Life: An Autobiography* (New York: Simon & Schuster, 1983), 249.

64. "G-3 Periodic Report, 6 Jun," G-3 Reports, 4th Division, 1–8 Jun 1944 (CARL microfilm).

65. Ruppenthal, *Utah to Cherbourg*, 199.

66. Mabry, "Objectives of the 2nd Battalion," 31.

67. The report of the 8th Regiment executive officer concluded: "In reviewing the action of the first day, the outstanding feature was the low rate of casualties in relation to the resistance which was met, and can be ascribed to the skill, training and courage of the average soldier in the assault units," 8th Regiment "After-Action Report," 21 July 1944. A number of the AGF observers reports on the Normandy invasion offered similar conclusions. See also Joseph Balkowski, *Beyond the Beachhead: The 29th Infantry Division in Normandy* (Harrisburg, Pa.: Stackpole Books, 1989), 124–30.

Chapter 13. Caught in the Middle: The French Population in Normandy

1. Jean Quellien, *La Normandie au coeur de la guerre* (Rennes: Editions Ouest-France, 1992), 18.
2. Jeanne Grall, *Le Calvados dans la guerre, 1939/1945: La vie quotidienne sous l'occupation* (Le Coteau: Editions Horvath, 1986), 65–68.
3. For conditions in France during the occupation, see also Henri Amouroux, *La vie des français sous l'occupation* (Paris: Laffont, 1961); Robert Aron, *Histoire de la libération de la France* (Paris: Fayard, 1959), translated into English as *France Reborn* (New York: Scribner's, 1964); Henri Michel, *Histoire de la Résistance* (Paris: PUF, 1950); Henri Noguères, *Histoire de la Résistance en France*, 5 vols. (Paris: Laffont, 1981); David Schoenbrun, *Soldiers of the Night: The Story of the French Resistance* (New York: Dutton, 1980); John Sweets, *Choices in Vichy France: The French under Nazi Occupation* (New York: Oxford University Press, 1986).
In 1984, a conference at Caen on OVERLORD devoted fourteen papers to conditions in Normandy. The proceedings, edited by François Bédarida, have been published as *Normandie 44: Du débarquement à la libération* (Paris: Albin Michel, 1987).
4. Quellien, *Normandie*, 13–23.
5. Grall, *Calvados*, 87.
6. Amouroux, *La vie des français*, 524–38.
7. Marcel Baudot, "La contribution de la Résistance à la libération de la Normandie," in Bédarida, *Normandie 44*, 168. See also Marcel Baudot, *Libération de la Normandie* (Paris: Hachette-Littérature, 1974).
8. Schoenbrun, *Soldiers of the Night*, 177, 366–67.
9. Charles-Louis Foulon, *Le pouvoir en province à la libération* (Paris: Armand Colin, 1975), 61–84.
10. Aron, *Histoire de la libération*, 252–53.
11. M. R. D. Foot, *SOE in France* (London: HMSO, 1966), 80–88. Foot described SOE missions affecting the Normandy area, such as PROSPER, SALESMAN, HELMSMAN, and SCIENTIST, but they are outside the scope of this chapter.
12. A good example is Raymond Ruffin, *La résistance normande face à la Gestapo* (Paris: Presses de la Cité, 1977), which lists many sabotage acts. See also works referred to in n. 1, 2, and 3.
13. Charles de Gaulle, *Complete War Memoirs* (New York: Simon & Schuster, 1967), 592–93; Forrest C. Pogue, *The Supreme Command* (Washington, D.C.: GPO, 1954), 146–57, 236–37.
14. Grall, *Calvados*, 42–45, 123–24; Ruffin, *Résistance normande*, 251; Michel de Bouard, "La repression allemande dans le Calvados durant l'occupation," in Bédarida, *Normandie 44*, 127–42.
15. Jean Quellien, *Résistance et sabotages en Normandie* (Condé-sur-Noireau: Editions Corlet, 1992).
16. Foot, *SOE in France*, 273; Baudot, "Contributions de la Résistance," 167–68. Ruffin, in *Résistance normande*, describes at length the collaboration of Rouen police inspector Louis Alie with the occupiers. He enumerates 50 specific operations leading to the death of over 100 resistance members (131–32).
17. Baudot, "Contributions de la Résistance," 169–73; Quellien, *Normandie au coeur*, 18–22; Grall, *Calvados*, 114–20; Jean Quellien, "Le département du Calvados à la veille du débarquement," in Bédarida, *Normandie 44*, 157–58.

18. Louis Blouet, "L'action des FTP dans la Manche," in Bédarida, *Normandie 44*, 229.

19. Marcel Baudot, *Libération de la Bretagne* (Paris: Hachette-Littérature, 1973), 110.

20. Blouet, "L'action des FTP," 229–30.

21. Baudot, *Libération de la Normandie*, 141; Aron, *Histoire de la libération*, 160–62; Ruffin, *Résistance normande*, 107–10.

22. Baudot, *Libération de la Normandie*, 140–47; Grall, *Calvados*, 142; Foot, *SOE in France*, 409. On SUSSEX, see Anthony Cave-Brown (ed.), *The Secret War Report of the OSS* (New York: Berkley, 1976), 442.

23. Baudot, "La contribution de la Résistance," 173.

24. Dwight D. Eisenhower, *Crusade in Europe* (Garden City, N.Y.: Doubleday, 1948), 296. Why no specific plans had been developed for use of the FFI in Normandy is analyzed by Bradley F. Smith, "L'OSS, l'armée américaine et la Résistance pendant la bataille de Normandie," in Bédarida, *Normandie 44*, 111–20.

25. Winston S. Churchill, *The Second World War*, 6 vols. (Boston: Houghton Mifflin, 1948–53), 6: 5, 12.

26. De Gaulle, *Complete War Memoirs*, 561–63; Harry L. Coles and Albert K. Weinberg, *Civil Affairs: Soldiers Become Governors* (Washington, D.C.: GPO, 1964), 707–9. On the liaison officers, see Foulon, *Pouvoir en province*, 99–101. When de Gaulle ordered no cooperation, 80 men of the 412 in training had already left for France.

27. De Gaulle, *Complete War Memoirs*, 563–66.

28. Coles and Weinberg, *Civil Affairs*, 709–18; Foulon, *Pouvoir en province*, 103–15.

29. Quellien, *Normandie au coeur*, 172.

30. Raymond Coulet, *Vertu des temps difficiles* (Paris: Plon, 1967), 249–50.

31. "Survey of Attitudes of the Normans to the Allied Landings," 061.2 Public Opinions 17W4.13/16A, Box 47, Record Group (RG) 331, National Archives (NA). A copy of the questionnaire (in Coulet Papers, French Archives Nationales) was made available to the author by Jean Quellien. See also Pogue, *Supreme Command*, 520–21; "Report, Civil Affairs Detachment A1A1, Jun-Aug 44," in Coles and Weinberg, *Civil Affairs*, 730–38.

32. The plight of the Norman populace is described throughout the books already cited: Quellien, *Normandie au coeur*; Grall, *Calvados*; Ruffin, *Résistance normande*. See also Aron, *Histoire de la libération*, 162–75; Amouroux, *La vie des français*, 349–79; André Heinz, "Caen pendant la bataille," in Bédarida, *Normandie 44*, 161–65; Etienne Fouilloux and Dominique Veillon, "Mémoires du debarquement en Normandie," in Bédarida, *Normandie 44*, 214–27; André Gosset and Paul Lecomte, *Caen pendant la bataille* (Caen: Ozanne, 1946); Maurice Lantier, *Saint-Lô au bûcher* (Saint-Lô: Imprimerie Jacqueline, 1969).

33. Aron, *Histoire de la libération*, 169.

34. Quellien, *Normandie au coeur*, 160–61.

35. Ibid., 163.

36. Bernard Lebrun, "La presse du Calvados à la Libération," in Bédarida, *Normandie 44*, 196.

37. Quoted in Quellien, *Normandie au coeur*, 233.

38. Ibid., 233–34; Grall, *Calvados*, 163; Max-André Brier, "La reconstruction," in *La Normandie de 1900 à nos jours* (Toulouse: Privat, 1978), 309–18; "Le Calvados Martyr" (anonymous pamphlet, 1946). Most authoritative are the figures tabulated by the INSEE (Institut National de la Statistique et des Etudes

Economiques) published in *L'annuaire statistique régional* in 1966. An analysis of civilian deaths is still under way (1993).

39. Jean-Marie Girault, "Des ruines à la reconstruction," in Bédarida, *Normandie 44*, 240–45.

40. On Norman reconstruction in general, see Brier, "La reconstruction," 318–25. For France as a whole, see Danièle Voldman (ed.), "Images, discours, et enjeux de la reconstruction des villes françaises après 1945," *Cahier* (Institut d'Histoire du Temps Présent) 5 (Jun 1987).

41. Comments presented at the laying of the Mémorial's cornerstone, 10 Sep 1986.

Chapter 14. Two Armies in Normandy: Weighing British and Canadian Military Performance

1. The first major barrage in the postwar paper battle over the Normandy campaign was Chester Wilmot's *The Struggle for Europe* (New York: Harper, 1952). Wilmot, an Australian war correspondent, had a great deal of help from Montgomery who made his personal papers available. Wilmot's intensely readable book (biased, of course, toward Montgomery), although now dated, remains influential. The relevant volume of the British official history, L. F. Ellis, *Victory in the West*, vol. 1, *The Battle of Normandy* (London: HMS0, 1962), "leans over in favor of Montgomery," as A. J. P. Taylor noted at the time. Montgomery's own notorious *Memoirs* (New York: World Publishing, 1958) are perhaps best regarded as a self-inflicted wound. The case for Montgomery in Normandy is best made in the second volume of Nigel Hamilton's official biography, *Monty: Master of the Battlefield 1942–44* (London: Hamish Hamilton, 1983). There are two Canadian official versions, C. P. Stacey's *The Canadian Army 1939–45: An Official Historical Summary* (Ottawa: Queen's Printer, 1948), and the same author's massive *The Victory Campaign: Operations in North-West Europe, 1944–45* (Ottawa: Queen's Printer, 1960). John English's *The Canadian Army and the Normandy Campaign: A Study in Failure in High Command* (New York: Praeger, 1992) is also essential reading on the Canadian role. Secondary accounts of the fighting in Normandy appear constantly. I would single out the following as particularly illuminating: Carlo D'Este's *Decision in Normandy* (New York: Dutton, 1983), is an evenhanded, carefully analytical account. Max Hastings's *Overlord: D-Day and the Battle for Normandy* (New York: Simon & Schuster 1984) is more conventional but highly readable. Finally, there are several books dealing with larger themes that put the campaign in Normandy into perspective. Tim Travers's *How the War Was Won: Command and Technology in the British Army on the Western Front, 1917–18* (New York: Routledge, 1992) discusses the techniques of 1918 that affected British military thinking for the next twenty years. Shelford Bidwell and Dominic Graham's *Firepower: British Army Weapons and Theories of War 1904–45* (London: Unwin Hyman, 1982) is crucial to understanding the British way of war in the first half of the twentieth century. John Ellis, *Brute Force: Allied Strategy and Tactics in World War Two* (New York: Viking, 1990), argues that the Allies needed (and had) little tactical or operational flair because they could rely so heavily on quantitative superiority. Correlli Barnett's *The Audit of War: the Illusion and Reality of Britain as a Great Nation* (London: MacMillan, 1986) is a devastating account of the industrial (and social) base of the British war effort and

should be read by anyone who wants to understand modern Britain. I have also drawn liberally on a manuscript in preparation entitled "Winston's Generals: British Military Leadership in World War II," to be published by the University Press of Kansas.

2. Hastings, *Overlord*, 46–50, offers a succinct statement of this argument. The quotation is from p. 48.

3. Winston Churchill, *Their Finest Hour* (Boston: Houghton Mifflin, 1949).

4. Communicated to the author by Lt. Gen. Sir Ian Jacob. The commandant was the future Field Marshal Lord Wilson.

5. The quotation is from Shelford Bidwell and Dominic Graham, *Tug of War: the Battle for Italy 1943–44* (London: Hodder and Stoughton, 1986), 100. Both authors are retired British army officers.

6. Bernard Fergusson, *The Trumpet in the Hall* (London: Collins, 1970), 278. This is a beautifully written, passionate defense of the regimental system.

7. The phrase is Correlli Barnett's, *Audit of War*, 190 .

8. Stacey, *The Victory Campaign*, 275.

9. English, *Canadian Army and Normandy*, 13–62, surveys Canadian military development between the wars. I have drawn heavily on this excellent study. English is particularly critical of McNaughton. Ibid., 41–47.

10. Carlo D'Este, in *Decision in Normandy*, 268–70, argued that more British infantry replacements were available in the United Kingdom than were released to 21st Army Group. He strongly implied that Churchill was instrumental in holding them back in order to minimize British casualties, although he concedes that further research is necessary on the point. Absent further evidence, this seems a serious misreading of Churchill's whole approach to war. The man who faced national bankruptcy wihtout flinching was unlikely to blanch at the unsparing use of other national assets.

11. Despite much writing on Montgomery, there is no satisfactory study. Ronald Lewin's *Montgomery as Military Commander* (London: Batsford, 1971) is still perhaps the most balanced, though now dated. Nigel Hamilton's massive three-volume official biography *Monty* (London, Hamish Hamilton, 1981–86), although essential reading, is also a sustained piece of advocacy. A. J. P. Taylor observed many years ago that what was needed was less concentration on Montgomery's personality and more detailed study of his battles. So far, only Michael Carver, *Alamein* (London: Batsford, 1982), has done this.

12. Bidwell and Graham, *Firepower*, 289.

13. Ibid., 288.

14. Miles ("Bimbo") Dempsey is a slightly mysterious figure in the history of the British army in World War II. Rising from lieutenant colonel to army commander in four years, he retired after the war, wrote no memoirs, and has, so far, escaped the attention of biographers. Until we have a full study of Dempscy, there will be some intriguing blanks in the record, including the record of GOODWOOD.

15. Brig. James Hargest, notes on the fighting in Normandy, dated Jun 1944, quoted in English, *Canadian Army and Normandy*, 206. Hargest was taken prisoner during the "Crusader" battles of Nov 1941, escaped in 1943, and was killed while observing action in Normandy in Aug 1944.

16. Wilmot, *Struggle for Europe*, 398.

17. English, *Canadian Army and Normandy*, 208.

18. David Fraser, *And We Shall Shock Them: The British Army in the Second World War* (London: Hodder and Stoughton, 1983), 52–53. Fraser notes of the Normandy fighting that "the enemy had acquired more convincingly than some

of the British" facility in "the intimate cooperation of tanks and infantry." Ibid., 329.

19. Ellis, *Brute Force*, 345-88. This is a very shrewd analysis if perhaps too prone to assume that quantities of material translate inevitably into battlefield success.

20. Churchill to Air Chief Marshal Sir Charles Portal, 7 Oct 1941, Winston S. Churchill, *The Grand Alliance* (Boston: Houghton Mifflin, 1950), 508-9.

Chapter 15. Assessing American Military Leadership:
Two Postinvasion Corps Commanders

1. Significant studies of Allied command in the post–Normandy invasion include Martin Blumenson, *Breakout and Pursuit* (Washington, D.C.: GPO, 1961); Carlo D'Este, *Decision in Normandy* (New York: Dutton, 1983); John Keegan, *Six Armies in Normandy* (New York: Viking, 1982); Forrest C. Pogue, *The Supreme Command* (Washington, D.C.: GPO, 1954); and Russell F. Weigley, *Eisenhower's Lieutenants: The Campaigns of France and Germany, 1944–45* (Bloomington: Indiana University Press, 1981).

2. On Bradley, see his autobiography, *A Soldier's Story* (New York: Holt Rinehart and Winston, 1951); Charles Whiting, *Bradley* (New York: Ballantine Books, 1971); and Pogue, *Supreme Command*. On Patton, see Martin Blumenson, *The Patton Papers*, 2 vols. (Boston: Houghton Mifflin, 1972, 1974), and Hubert Essame, *Patton: A Study in Command* (New York: Charles Scribner's Sons, 1974).

3. Robert H. Berlin, "U.S. Army World War II Corps Commanders: A Composite Biography," *Journal of Military History* 53 (Apr 1989): 147–67. In World War II the corps was the key army headquarters for employing all combat elements properly in battle, particularly division-size tactical formations. The corps was an elastic unit that controlled divisions, which were standardized units.

4. See J. Lawton Collins, *Lightning Joe: An Autobiography* (Baton Rouge: Louisiana State University Press, 1979).

5. Russell F. Weigley, *Eisenhower's Lieutenants: The Campaigns of France and Germany, 1944–45*, 2 vols. (Bloomington: Indiana University Press, 1981), 2: 1061.

6. Martin Blumenson, "America's World War II Leaders in Europe: Some Thoughts," *Parameters* (Dec 1989): 2–13.

7. List reproduced in Weigley, *Eisenhower's Lieutenants*, 2: 1098. Eddy was 18 and Brooks 24 in Bradley's assessment.

8. Memorandum for General McNair, 1 Dec 1942, in Larry I. Bland and Sharon Ritenour Stevens (eds.), *The Papers of George Catlett Marshall* (Baltimore: Johns Hopkins University Press, 1991), 3: 463–64.

9. Matthew B. Ridgway, *Soldier: The Memoirs of Matthew B. Ridgway* (New York: Harper, 1956), 18. Sadly, Ridgway, the last living U.S. Army World War II corps commander and one of America's finest soldiers and patriots, died in his sleep at age 98 on 26 Jul 1993 as this chapter was being finalized.

10. Biographical data on Eddy can be found in *Current Biography 1951* (New York: H. W. Wilson Company), "Eddy, Manton S(prague), 176: 178. My primary source for data on Eddy was his military personnel records (MPR) jacket (201 file originally kept by the adjutant general's office) at the National Personnel Records

Center (NPRC), National Archives and Records Administration (NA), St. Louis, Missouri.

11. Eddy, "Summary of Efficiency Reports," 1917, MPR, NPRC, NA.

12. "Statements of Military Service," MPR, NPRC, NA.

13. Edward Hale Brooks, MPR, NPRC, NA. Richard Pearson, "Lt. Gen. Edward Brooks," *Washington Post* 14 Oct 1978.

14. Letter from Brig. Gen. B. A. Poore, Commanding General 7th Infantry Brigade, AEF, to President Examining Board, Germany, 1 May 1919 in Eddy, MPR, NPRC, NA.

15. Col. William M. Cruikshank to the adjutant general, 30 Mar 1920, Brooks, MPR, NPRC, NA.

16. For a thorough treatment of the U.S. Army in World War I, see Edward M. Coffman, *The War to End All Wars: The American Experience in World War I* (Madison: University of Wisconsin Press, 1986).

17. Brooks and Eddy, MPR, NPRC, NA.

18. Col. Paul B. Malone, Eddy officer efficiency report (OER), 30 Jun 1921, MPR, NPRC, NA.

19. Col. F. W. Rowell, Eddy OER, 10 Jun 1926, MPR, NPRC, NA.

20. Marshall, Eddy OER, 10 Jun 1930, MPR, NPRC, NA.

21. Col. George C. Gatley, Brooks OER, 6 Sep 1921, MPR, NPRC, NA.

22. Lt. Col. W. P. Ennis, Brooks OER, 30 Jun 1926, MPR, NPRC, NA.

23. 30 Jun 1928, OER, MPR, NPRC, NA.

24. Ben M. Sawbridge to Brooks, 21 Jan 1930, MPR, NPRC, NA.

25. Quotations from Timothy K. Nenninger, "Creating Officers: The Leavenworth Experience 1920–1940," *Military Review* (Nov 1989): 58–68.

26. Col. W. B. Burt, Brooks and Eddy OERs, 30 Jun 1933, MPR, NPRC, NA.

27. Maj. Andrew J. McFarland, Brooks OER, 25 Sep 1933, MPR, NPRC, NA.

28. Russell F. Weigley, *History of the United States Army* (Bloomington: Indiana University Press, 1967, 1984), 402. Charles William Johnson, "The Civilian Conservation Corps: The Role of the Army," doctoral dissertation, University of Michigan, 1968, assesses the benefits of the CCC for the U.S. Army.

29. Brooks OER, 8 Jul 1936, MPR, NPRC, NA.

30. Brig. Gen. W. S. Grant, Brooks OER, 30 Jun 1937, MPR, NPRC, NA.

31. Lt. Gen. Eddy (ret.), lecture on corps operations at U.S. Army Command and General Staff College, 16 Mar 1954, in Archives, Combined Arms Research Library, Fort Leavenworth, Kans. (hereafter cited as Eddy lecture).

32. Eddy, MPR, NPRC, NA.

33. Marshall to Lt. Gen. Stanley D. Embick, 29 Apr 1940, in Bland and Stevens, *Marshall Papers*, 2: 203.

34. Brooks OERs, 30 Jun 1940 and 30 Jun 1941, MPR, NPRC, NA.

35. Brooks OER, 7 Jul 1942, MPR, NPRC, NA.

36. Eddy OERs, MPR, NPRC, NA.

37. Eddy OER, 7 Jul 1944, MPR, NPRC, NA.

38. Dispatch from France, 1944, as cited in *The New York Times*, 10 Apr 1962.

39. Eddy OER, 7 Sep 1944, MPR, NPRC, NA.

40. Donald E. Houston, *Hell on Wheels: The 2d Armored Division* (San Rafael, Calif.: Presidio, 1977), 209.

41. Handwritten note signed by Dwight D. Eisenhower, Brooks OER, 5 Aug 1944, MPR, NPRC, NA.

42. Houston, *Hell on Wheels*, 268; and General Orders Number 39, "Award of the Silver Star Medal (Oak Leaf Cluster) 5 Sep 1944, in Brooks MPR, NPRC, NA.

43. Eddy lecture.

44. Eddy diary, 2 Sep 1944, Infantry School Archives, Fort Benning, Ga.

45. Hanson W. Baldwin, *Tiger Jack* (Fort Collins, Colo.: Old Army Press, 1979), is a biography championing Wood. Wood's nickname, "P for professor," came from Wood's tutoring fellow cadets at the Military Academy.

46. Eddy lecture.

47. Ibid.

48. Hugh M. Cole, *The Lorraine Campaign* (Washington, D.C.: Historical Division, U.S. Army, 1950), 525.

49. A. Harding Ganz, "Patton's Relief of General Wood," *Journal of Military History* 53 (Jul 1989): 272.

50. Christopher R. Gabel, *The 4th Armored Division in the Encirclement of Nancy* (Fort Leavenworth, Kans.: Combat Studies Institute, 1986), 25.

51. Eddy diary, 24 Mar 1945.

52. Charles B. MacDonald, *The Last Offensive* (Washington, D.C.: Office of the Chief of Military History, 1973).

53. G. C. Marshall to Brooks, 22 Oct 1945, Box 16, Folder 10, George C. Marshall Papers, Marshall Library, Lexington, Va.

54. Brooks, MPR, NPRC, NA.

55. Eddy, MPR, NPRC, NA.

56. Antoine-Henri Jomini, *Summary of the Art of War* (Harrisburg, Pa.: Stackpole, 1987), 449.

Chapter 16. Dwight D. Eisenhower: Architect of Victory

1. Arthur Bryant, *Triumph in the West: A History of the War Years Based on the Diaries of Field-Marshal Lord Alanbrooke, Chief of the Imperial General Staff, 1943–1946* (Garden City, N.Y.: Doubleday, 1959), 139. See also Bryant's first volume, *The Turn of the Tide* (Garden City, N.Y.: Doubleday, 1957), 430, 454. For a brief summary and refutation of these criticisms, see Martin Blumenson and James L. Stokesbury, *Masters of the Art of Command* (Boston: Houghton Mifflin, 1975), 287–315. See also E. K. G. Sixsmith, *Eisenhower as Military Commander* (New York: Stein and Day, 1973). The historiographical debate is summarized in Colin F. Baxter, *The Normandy Campaign, 1944: A Selected Bibliography* (Westport, Conn.: Greenwood Press, 1992), 36–39.

2. In the major War Department reorganization of Mar 1942, the old General Headquarters and War Plans Division (WPD) were replaced by a new and powerful Operations Division (OPD) to plan strategy, staff the wartime interservice and interallied committees, and serve as General Marshall's Washington command post. Eisenhower had been appointed head of WPD in mid-Feb and, in the following month, became OPD's first chief. See Ray S. Cline, *Washington Command Post: The Operations Division* (Washington, D.C.: GPO, 1951).

3. See Louis Morton, "Germany First: The Basic Concept of Allied Strategy in World War II," in Kent Roberts Greenfield (ed.), *Command Decisions* (Washington, D.C.: GPO, 1960), 11–47.

4. Maurice Matloff and Edwin M. Snell, *Strategic Planning for Coalition Warfare, 1941–1942* (Washington, D.C.: GPO, 1953), 97–119. For conference documents, see U.S. Department of State, *Foreign Relations of the United States*

[FRUS]: The Conferences at Washington, 1941–1942, and Casablanca, 1943 (Washington, D.C.: GPO, 1968), 3–415.

5. Matloff and Snell, *Strategic Planning*, 102–14.

6. Alfred D. Chandler, Jr. (ed.), *The Papers of Dwight David Eisenhower: The War Years* vol. 1 (Baltimore: Johns Hopkins University Press, 1970), 30, 39. See also Robert H. Ferrell (ed.), *The Eisenhower Diaries* (New York: Norton, 1981), 40–41. Eisenhower had been specifically assigned the task of coordinating and directing reinforcements to the Philippines. See Louis Morton, *Strategy and Command: The First Two Years* (Washington, D.C.: GPO, 1962), 151.

7. Actually, Eisenhower realized the hopelessness of the effort on the very day he proposed it to Marshall, 14 Dec, which was also his first day in Washington. He maintained that the effort to save the U.S. garrison had to be made anyway for psychological reasons. Marshall agreed. "Do your best to save them," he had replied after hearing Eisenhower's assessment of the situation. See Dwight D. Eisenhower, *Crusade in Europe* (Garden City, N.Y.: Doubleday, 1948), 17–21; Forrest C. Pogue, *George C. Marshall: Ordeal and Hope, 1939–1942*, vol. 2 (New York: Viking, 1966), 238–39; and Stephen E. Ambrose, *The Supreme Commander: The War Years of Dwight D. Eisenhower* (Garden City, N.Y.: Doubleday, 1970), 4–6.

8. Ferrell, *Eisenhower Diaries*, 44; Chandler, *Eisenhower Papers*, 1: 66. According to Stephen Ambrose, *Eisenhower: Soldier, General of the Army, President-Elect, 1890–1952* (New York: Simon & Schuster, 1983), 1: 147, Eisenhower's experiences at the ARCADIA conference, combined with "Marshall's persuasive abilities, hard military facts, and broadened responsibilities," all "caused him to change his mind" at this time.

9. Chandler, *Eisenhower Papers*, 1: 66.

10. Ibid., 75, 118–19.

11. Ibid., 149–55. See 145–48 for the original version of this memorandum, undated and unsigned but apparently edited if not written by Eisenhower between 16 and 28 Feb. See also Ambrose, *Supreme Commander*, 30–35; and Matloff and Snell, *Strategic Planning*, 157–59.

12. Chandler, *Eisenhower Papers*, 1: 149–55.

13. Ibid; emphasis in original.

14. Ferrell, *Eisenhower Diaries*, 48.

15. Chandler, *Eisenhower Papers*, 1: 149–55.

16. WPD War Department Strategic Estimate, Oct 1941, WPD 4510, Records of the War Department General and Special Staffs, Record Group (RG) 165, National Archives (NA), Washington, D.C.

17. Memorandum by Lt. Col. Edwin E. Schwien, "An Essential Strategic Diversion in Europe," Aug 1941, WPD 4402–77, RG 165, NA, discussed in Matloff and Snell, *Strategic Planning*, 177.

18. USSR Ministry of Foreign Affairs, *Russia: Correspondence Between the Chairman of the Council of Ministers of the U.S.S.R. and the Presidents of the U.S.A. and the Prime Ministers of Great Britain During the Great Patriotic War of 1941–1945* (Moscow: Foreign Languages Publishing House, 1957), 1: 20–22.

19. Memorandum, Lee, Assistant Chief of Staff, G-2, to Chief of Staff, "Possibility of a Negotiated Russo-German Settlement," 12 Feb 1942, Russia Folder, Box 105, Harry Hopkins Papers, Franklin D. Roosevelt Library, Hyde Park, N.Y.

20. Matloff and Snell, *Strategic Planning*, 26–28; Robert Sherwood, *Roosevelt and Hopkins: An Intimate History*, rev. ed. (New York: Grossett and Dunlap, 1950), 415. See also Chapter 1 in this volume; Charles E. Kirkpatrick, *An Unknown Future and a Doubtful Present: Writing the Victory Plan of 1941* (Wash-

ington, D.C.: Center of Military History, 1990); Russell F. Weigley, *The American Way of War: A History of United States Military Strategy and Policy* (New York: Macmillan, 1973), 312–59; and Michael Howard, *The Mediterranean Strategy in the Second World War* (London: Weidenfeld Nicolson, 1968).

21. Henry L. Stimson diary, 24 Feb and 5–6 Mar 1942, Stimson Papers, Sterling Memorial Library, Yale University, New Haven, Conn.; memorandum, Arnold to Chief of Staff, "Employment of Army Air Forces," 3 Mar 1942, Box 39, SOF, 1941–1945, Henry H. Arnold Papers, Library of Congress, Washington, D.C. Ambrose emphasizes Marshall's role, noting in *Supreme Commander*, 22, 30, that "there was never any doubt, throughout the war, that Marshall's was the guiding hand behind the broad policies" and that he "set the goals, while OPD prepared the studies that showed how they could be accomplished." In Feb 1942, Marshall wanted "a coherent statement" for the president and Combined Chiefs of Staff that would "outline a general strategy for the war. Eisenhower prepared it for him." See also Ambrose's comments in *Eisenhower*, 1: 147.

22. Chandler, *Eisenhower Papers*, 1: 112–13; Matloff and Snell, *Strategic Planning*, 154–56.

23. Memorandum, King to president, 5 Mar 1942, in Thomas B. Buell, *Master of Seapower: A Biography of Fleet Admiral Ernest J. King* (Boston: Little, Brown, 1980), 503–5.

24. See n. 20.

25. Richard W. Steele, *The First Offensive, 1942: Roosevelt, Marshall and the Making of American Strategy* (Bloomington: Indiana University Press, 1973), 81–93.

26. Warren F. Kimball (ed.), *Churchill and Roosevelt: The Complete Correspondence* (Princeton, N.J.: Princeton University Press, 1984), 1: 398–99; Matloff and Snell, *Strategic Planning*, 165–68; Chandler, *Eisenhower Papers*, 1: 174–76.

27. JPS covering letter in JCS 23 and memorandum, Smith to Dykes, "Strategic Deployment of the Land, Sea and Air Forces of the U.S.," 14 and 16 Mar 1942, Combined Chiefs of Staff (CCS) 381 (1–30–42) (1), RG 225, NA; Matloff and Snell, *Strategic Planning*, 159–61, 167–68; Kimball, *Churchill and Roosevelt*, 1: 411–14.

28. "The principle to be observed in strategic deployment," he continued, "is merely that *minima* should be diverted to secondary or merely desirable objectives, while *maxima* are to be striven for in primary, essential operations." Chandler, *Eisenhower Papers*, 1: 151.

29. Chandler, *Eisenhower Papers*, 1: 205–8; Matloff and Snell, *Strategic Planning*, 181–82. See also Eisenhower's 12 Apr memorandum in Chandler, *Eisenhower Papers*, 1: 241–44.

30. Stimson diary, 25 Mar 1942; Henry L. Stimson and McGeorge Bundy, *On Active Service in Peace and War* (New York: Harper & Brothers, 1947), 416–17; Chandler, *Eisenhower Papers*, 1:207.

31. The final memorandum is reproduced in J. R. M. Butler, *Grand Strategy*, vol. 3, pt. 2 (London: HMSO, 1964): 675–81. All quotes are from this version. For the evolution of the memorandum, see Matloff and Snell, *Strategic Planning*, 183–87, 383. Ambrose, *Supreme Commander*, 38, concludes that the final memorandum was "a staff product, but throughout it carried Eisenhower's personal touch. The main conclusions were his and of course they represented Marshall's thought."

32. Kimball, *Churchill and Roosevelt*, 1: 437, 441, 448–49.

33. The operational codenames actually belonged to much more limited oper-

ations that were then being considered by British planners. See Chapter 2 in this volume; Gordon A. Harrison, *Cross-Channel Attack* (Washington, D.C.: Office of the Chief of Military History, 1951), 6–12; and Butler, *Grand Strategy* 3(2): 566–71.

34. Chandler, *Eisenhower Papers*, 1: 183–84, 260; Ferrell, *Eisenhower Diaries*, 50–51, 53.

35. Appendix 2 to JPS 2/6 in JCS 23, "Strategic Deployment of the Land, Sea and Air Forces of the U.S.," 14 Mar 1942, CCS 381 (1–30–42) (1), RG 225, NA.

36. Chandler, *Eisenhower Papers*, 1: 205–8; see also 241–44.

37. Bryant, *Turn of the Tide*, 285–90; James Leasor, *War at the Top: Based on the Experiences of General Sir Leslie Hollis* (London: Michael Joseph, 1959), 184.

38. Mark A. Stoler, *The Politics of the Second Front: American Military Planning and Diplomacy in Coalition Warfare, 1941–1943* (Westport, Conn.: Greenwood Press, 1977), 36–49; Kimball, *Churchill and Roosevelt*, 1: 494.

39. Incoming message 3457, Marshall to McNarney, 13 Apr 1943, OPD Exec. 1, item 5c, RG 165, NA; Matloff and Snell, *Strategic Planning*, 198–232.

40. Sherwood, *Roosevelt and Hopkins*, 577; Stoler, *Politics of the Second Front*, 48–49.

41. Chandler, *Eisenhower Papers*, 1: 328.

42. Ibid., 292–96, 327–28. Eisenhower recommended the appointment of General Mark Clark as ground commander and General Joseph T. McNarney as theater commander, rather than General James E. Chaney, who was at that time the commanding general of U.S. Army forces in Britain.

43. Ibid., 292–96, 318–27; Pogue, *George C. Marshall*, 2: 339. Eisenhower's proposals regarding organization and unity of command were accepted. With only minor modifications they would govern Allied command relationships in the North African, Mediterranean, and European theaters.

Marshall incorrectly recalled that Churchill's reaction to Eisenhower was positive, whereas neither he nor Eisenhower met with the prime minister at this time. More likely was a positive reaction from the British Chiefs of Staff relayed through General Sir John Dill, head of the British Joint Staff Mission in Washington. See Ambrose, *Supreme Commander*, 48.

44. Butler, *Grand Strategy*, 3(2): 627; Kimball, *Churchill and Roosevelt*, 1: 520–21. For Eisenhower's participation in the Anglo-American discussions just prior to his departure for London, see Ambrose, *Supreme Commander*, 49; and Chandler, *Eisenhower Papers*, 1: 346–49.

45. Telegram, Marshall to Eisenhower, 16 Jul 1942, OPD Exec. 5, item 9, RG 165, NA; Mark A. Stoler, "The 'Pacific First' Alternative in American World War II Strategy," *International History Review* 2 (Jul 1980): 437–43.

46. Chandler, *Eisenhower Papers*, 1: 378–81, 388–96, 400–414; Eisenhower, *Crusade in Europe*, 68–71; Chapter 2 in this volume, n. 11. Eisenhower's staff had originally favored Le Havre as the landing site but shifted to Cherbourg between 17 and 20 Jul, with members of Admiral Lord Louis Mountbatten's Combined Operations Staff providing a detailed and optimistic outline plan; Eisenhower's original pessimistic estimates referred to the Le Havre operation. See Ambrose, *Supreme Commander*, 71; and Joseph L. Strange, "Cross-Channel Attack, 1942: The British Rejection of Operation SLEDGEHAMMER and the Cherbourg Alternative," Ph.D. dissertation, University of Maryland, 1984, 425–45.

47. Chandler, *Eisenhower Papers*, 1: 378–81, 388–96, 400–414.

48. Ibid., 406.

49. Alex Danchev, *Establishing the Anglo-American Alliance: The Second World War Diaries of Brigadier Vivian Dykes* (London: Brassey's, 1990), 178.

50. Harry C. Butcher, *My Three Years with Eisenhower* (New York: Simon & Schuster, 1946), 29; Matloff and Snell, *Strategic Planning*, 278–84. U.S. Army support for SLEDGEHAMMER may not have been as strong as it appeared at this time. According to Dykes's diary, Eisenhower had felt before his departure from Washington that SLEDGEHAMMER "was probably *not* a sound move"; General Walter Bedell Smith was "relieved" over its final defeat, "never having felt that it was really on," and played a critical role in getting Marshall and King to accept North Africa instead. See Danchev, *Establishing the Anglo-American Alliance*, 178–80.

51. Ambrose, *Supreme Commander*, 77–79. Actually, Eisenhower's command at first included North African *and* cross-Channel operations, for Marshall was trying to postpone a final decision on SLEDGEHAMMER versus TORCH until mid-Sep and had not yet accepted Roosevelt's refusal to do so.

52. See Chapter 1 in this volume and Maurice Matloff, *Strategic Planning for Coalition Warfare, 1943–1944* (Washington, D.C.: Office of the Chief of Military History, 1959), 18–243. See also Robert Beitzell, *The Uneasy Alliance: America, Britain and Russia, 1941–1943* (New York: Knopf, 1972), 76–123; and *FRUS: The Conferences at Washington and Casablanca* and *The Conferences at Washington and Quebec*.

53. See *FRUS: The Conferences at Cairo and Tehran*; Keith Eubank, *Summit at Teheran* (New York: William Morrow, 1985); and Keith Sainsbury, *The Turning Point: Roosevelt, Stalin, Churchill and Chiang-Kai-Shek, 1943: The Moscow, Cairo, and Teheran Conferences* (New York: Oxford University Press, 1985).

54. *FRUS: Washington and Quebec*, 483–98; Harrison, *Cross-Channel Attack*, 46–82.

55. See sources cited in n. 54 above and in Chapter 1 of this volume.

56. See Chapter 17 in this volume and Stoler, *Politics of the Second Front*, 85–123.

57. *FRUS: Cairo and Tehran*, 533–52.

58. See Forrest C. Pogue, *George C. Marshall: Organizer of Victory, 1943–1945*, vol. 3 (New York: Viking, 1973), 263–78, 297–325. See Chapter 17 in this volume for a possible additional and intriguing reason for the Eisenhower appointment.

59. Chandler, *Eisenhower Papers*, 3: 1713–15. See also Harrison, *Cross-Channel Attack*, 99, 165–66; and Forrest C. Pogue, *The Supreme Command* (Washington, D.C.: Office of the Chief of Military History, 1954), 106–8.

60. See Chandler, *Eisenhower Papers*, 3: 1775–79; Pogue, *Supreme Command*, 108–21; Harrison, *Cross-Channel Attack*, 166–74; Maurice Matloff, "The Anvil Decision: Crossroads of Strategy," in Greenfield, *Command Decisions*, 383–400; Bryant, *Triumph in the West*, 125–34, 157–68; Winston S. Churchill, *The Second World War: Triumph and Tragedy*, vol. 6 (Boston: Houghton Mifflin, 1953), 57–71, 716–23. See also Chapter 17 in this volume.

61. "From the outset," General Lord Ismay of the British Chiefs of Staff noted in relating this and other stories regarding Eisenhower and Allied relations, "he regarded Anglo-American friendship as a religion." See *The Memoirs of General Lord Ismay* (New York: Viking, 1960), 258–59, 263.

62. Butcher, *My Three Years with Eisenhower*, 8.

63. Harrison, *Cross-Channel Attack*, 79.

64. See Chapter 17 in this volume for a reassertion of OVERLORD's centrality to Allied victory.

Chapter 17. D-day: Analysis of Costs and Benefits

1. L. F. Ellis, *Victory in the West*, vol. 2, *The Defeat of Germany* (London: HMSO, 1968), 407.

2. Dieter Ose, *Entscheidung im Westen: Der Oberbefehlshaber West und die Abwehr der Invasion* (Schriftenreihe des Militärgeschichtlichen Forschungsamtes) (Stuttgart: Deutsche Verlags-Anstalt, 1982), 266–67.

3. Keith Sainsbury, *The Turning Point: Roosevelt, Churchill, and Chiang Kaishek, 1943; The Moscow, Cairo, and Teheran Conferences* (Oxford and New York: Oxford University Press, 1985), 96.

4. James J. Sadkovich, "Of Myths and Men: Rommel and the Italians in North Africa, 1940–1942," *International History Review* 13, 2 (May 1991): 284–313, and "Understanding Defeat: Reappraising Italy's Role in World War II," *Journal of Contemporary History* 24, 1 (Jan 1989): 27–61.

5. Walter S. Dunn, Jr., *Second Front Now—1943* (University: University of Alabama Press, 1980).

6. See the table in Jürgen Rohwer and Eberhard Jäckel (eds.), *Die Funkaufklärung und ihre Rolle im Zweiten Weltkrieg* (Stuttgart: Motorbuch, 1979), 165.

7. Dunn, *Second Front Now*, 100–102.

8. The specific references for this and most other statements in this piece are in Gerhard L. Weinberg, *The Greatest War* (Cambridge: Cambridge University Press, forthcoming).

9. There is a vast literature on the subject; the most recent treatment is Michael Howard, *British Intelligence in the Second World War*, vol. 5, *Strategic Deception* (New York: Cambridge University Press, 1990).

10. Ose, *Entscheidung im Westen*, 266. As of 6 Aug 1944, German intelligence had ten extra divisions in the Allied armies on the front in northern France.

11. See, for example, Josef Schröder, *Italiens Kriegsaustritt 1943* (Göttingen: Musterschmidt, 1969).

12. See Chapter 8 in this volume.

13. See W. W. Rostow, *Pre-Invasion Bombing Strategy: General Eisenhower's Decision of Mar 25, 1944* (Austin: University of Texas Press, 1981), 44–46.

14. Note Churchill's expression at the final briefing of 15 May 1944: "I am hardening on this enterprise." There are numerous accounts of the conference; Churchill is quoted in Martin Gilbert, *Winston S. Churchill*, vol. 7, *Road to Victory 1941–1945* (Boston: Houghton Mifflin, 1986), 771.

15. Harry C. Butcher, *My Three Years with Eisenhower* (New York: Simon & Schuster, 1946), 610.

16. The quotation from the diary of Field Marshal Brooke is in Weinberg, *The Greatest War*; it was omitted in Sir Arthur Bryant's edition.

17. Thomas Parrish, in his book *Roosevelt and Marshall* (New York: William Morrow, 1989), seems to be unduly influenced by the quantity of surviving records and other information pertaining to political factors in Roosevelt's decision that Eisenhower rather than Marshall should command the invasion. There were excellent reasons, beyond the president's usual reticence about such matters, not to put anything about keeping Marshall in reserve for a second invasion on paper. Historians must always be careful not to confuse the volume of surviving records with their significance. Certainly Eisenhower would never have been appointed to command a second attempt. Who other than Marshall could have been chosen?

18. See David Stafford's discussion in "Britain Looks at Europe 1940: Some

Origins of the SOE," *Canadian Journal of History* 10 (1975): 231–48, and *Britain and European Resistance 1940–1945: A Survey of the Special Operations Executive, with Documents* (Toronto: University of Toronto Press, 1980), ch. 2.

19. See Rostow, *Pre-Invasion Bombing*, 46–47; Forrest C. Pogue, *The Supreme Command* (Washington, D.C.: GPO, 1954), 274. See also Chapter 8 in this volume.

20. See Sir Michael Howard's comments in Richard H. Kohn (ed.), "The Scholarship on World War II: Its Present Condition and Future Possibilities," *Journal of Military History* 55, 3 (Jul 1991): 379–80. On the problems of the Canadian army, see the study by John A. English, *The Canadian Army and the Normandy Campaign: A Study of Failure in High Command* (New York: Praeger, 1991).

21. On this whole subject, see the study by Alfred C. Mierzejewski, *The Collapse of the German War Economy, 1944–1945: Allied Air Power and the German National Railway* (Chapel Hill: University of North Carolina Press, 1988); and the review article " 'Bomber' Harris in Perspective," *Journal of the United Services Institute for Defence Studies* 130, 2 (1985): 62–70.

22. The map is reproduced photographically in Maurice Matloff, *Strategic Planning for Coalition Warfare, 1943–1944* (Washington, D.C.: GPO, 1959), facing p. 341. See also Earl F. Ziemke, *The U.S. Army in the Occupation of Germany, 1944–1946* (Washington, D.C.: GPO, 1975), 116–22.

Glossary

AAF	Army Air Forces (U.S.)
ABC	American-British conversations (January–March 1941)
AEAF	Allied Expeditionary Air Force
AGF	Army Ground Forces (U.S.)
ANCXF	Allied Naval Commander, Expeditionary Force
ANVIL	planned 1944 Allied invasion in the Toulon-Marseille area of southern France
Anzio	small port on the west coast of Italy; site of the Anglo-American amphibious assault in January 1944
ARCADIA	U.S.-British conference in Washington, December 1941–January 1942
ASF	Army Service Forces (U.S.)
ASP	Air support party
ASTP	Army Specialized Training Program (U.S.)
ASW	antisubmarine warfare
Atlantic conference	secret meeting of Roosevelt and Churchill off the coast of Newfoundland, August 1941
bangalore	torpedo used primarily for clearing barbed wire and detonating land mines
BAR	Browning automatic rifle
BBC	British Broadcasting Corporation
BC	Bomber Command (British)
beachmaster	person who oversaw troop and equipment movements onto and off the beaches
Beaufighter	Bristol Beaufighter, a British torpedo bomber of 1943
BEF	British Expeditionary Force
Belgian gates	barricadelike gates (German) constructed of steel angles and plates on concrete rollers placed in rows on the beach causeways

BIGOT	special security procedure to protect OVERLORD plan
Black Widow	large, fast, radar-equipped American night-fighter that flew at low altitudes from May 1944
bocage	hedgerow country in Normandy
BODYGUARD	generic codename for a series of Allied deception plans designed to cloak the timing and location of OVERLORD
Bofors gun	Allied light, rapid-firing 40-mm antiaircraft cannon with a range of 12,500 feet
bogey	enemy aircraft
BOLERO	buildup of troops and supplies in the United Kingdom in preparation for a cross-Channel attack
BONIFACE	ULTRA material
Bren-gun carrier	derivative of the tankette that carried the .303 Bren automatic rifle
BUCO	Build-up Control Organization
C elements	Belgian gates
CARPETBAGGER	project to drop supplies and agents to the French resistance
CCC	Civilian Conservation Corps (U.S.)
CCS	Combined Chiefs of Staff (U.S.-British)
CHARNWOOD	British operation to seize Caen, launched 8 July 1944
CIGS	Chief of the Imperial General Staff (British)
COBRA	Operation launched by First U.S. Army on 25 July 1944, designed to break out of the Normandy lodgment
COHQ	Combined Operations Headquarters
COI	Coordinator of Information (later OSS) (U.S.)
Combined Bomber Offensive	POINTBLANK
COPP	Combined operations assault pilotage party
COS	Chiefs of Staff (British)
COSSAC	Chief of Staff to the Supreme Allied Commander designate

DD	American duplex-drive flotation system fitted on various types of tanks used in amphibious landings
Dieppe raid	amphibious assault by British and Canadian troops on the coast of France in August 1942
DOD	Department of Defense (U.S.)
DRAGOON	Later codename of Operation ANVIL
DUKW	six-wheel 2 1/2–ton amphibian truck
Dunkirk	northern French seaport from which British and Allied forces were withdrawn in a last-minute escape in May 1940 after a German breakthrough
DZ	dropping zone (paratroopers)
EMFFI	Etat Major, Forces Françaises de l'Intérieur
ETO	European Theater of Operations
EUREKA	Tehran conference, November–December 1943
F section	SOE section that operated agent networks
Falaise Gap	pocket of land between Falaise and Argentan in northern France from which 300,000 German soldiers escaped in August 1944
FCNL	French Committee of National Liberation
fifth column	subversive organization working in a country for an invading army
flail	tank fitted with heavy chains on a revolving drum that beat the ground in front of the tank, clearing land mines
flimsies	ULTRA evaluations from intelligence analysts to decision makers
Force U	American naval force connected with Utah Beach
FORTITUDE	OVERLORD deception operations
funnies	special armored assault teams developed under Maj. Gen. Sir Percy Hobart that operated unusual vehicles such as flail tanks
FUSAG	First United States Army group
FW-190	Focke-Wulf 190, German fighter aircraft
G-2	Military Intelligence Division (U.S.)

G-3	operation and training section of divisional or higher staff (U.S.)
Garand	M-1 semiautomatic rifle, standard issue to U.S. Army infantrymen by 1941
gee	radio navigational aid
glide-bomb	German remote-controlled bomb carrying a 1,100-pound warhead, launched from a plane
GOODWOOD	British attack to break out of the Normandy lodgment in late July 1944, coinciding with the U.S. Operation COBRA
Gooseberry	harbor constructed of sunken ships used to shelter small craft
Grand Alliance	World War II coalition of the United States, Great Britain, and the Soviet Union
Grasshopper	support craft to the rear of the landing craft that fired rockets in an attempt to destroy mines and obstacles
green books	works in the official history of the U.S. Army in World War II
GYMNAST	Anglo-American invasion and occupation of French North Africa; renamed TORCH
H-hour	exact minute for the beginning of a military operation
hedgerow rocket	bazooka with a sensitive fuse that blew apart hedgerows and other obstacles
HMSO	Her Majesty's Stationary Office
Hollerith card	punch card containing coded alphanumeric information
hunter-killer group	naval task force overseeing antisubmarine operations
HUSKY	Allied invasion of Sicily in July 1943
IFF	identification friend or foe
impregnated clothing	uniforms in which charcoal was sewn in order to prevent chemicals and gas from reaching the skin
interdiction	cutting an enemy's line of communication by firepower to halt the enemy's advance
IX Tactical Air Command	U.S. air unit that supported ground forces in operations such as COBRA
JCS	Joint Chiefs of Staff (U.S.)

Jedburgh team	specially trained units of Allied officers and men dropped behind enemy lines to aid resistance groups
JIC	Joint Intelligence Committee
JSM	Joint Staff Mission
JUPITER	Proposed operation in Norway
LCI	landing craft, infantry
LCM	landing craft, mechanized
LCT	landing craft, tank
LCVP	landing craft, vehicle and personnel
Leigh light	searchlight used for antisubmarine operations
lend-lease	act passed in March 1941 allowing Roosevelt to sell, transfer title to, exchange, lease, lend, or otherwise dispose of equipment to any country on which U.S. defense was thought to depend
Liberty ships	Mass-produced U.S. cargo vessels
London controlling station	Headquarters of the British Royal Air Force defense system
LSD	landing ship dock
LST	landing ship, tank
Maginot Line	line of static concrete and steel defenses stretching between Luxemburg and Switzerland along France's border with Germany, built by the French between 1930 and 1935
magnetic mines	also known as influence mines, planted on the seabed and detonated by the pull of a ship's magnetic field
Maquis	guerrilla fighter in the French resistance
MARKET GARDEN	airborne operation intended to establish a bridgehead across the Rhine in the Netherlands, September 1944
ME-262	first operational jet fighter, first employed in substantial numbers by the Luftwaffe in fall 1944
MI6	British secret intelligence service
Midway	key naval battle between the U.S. Pacific Fleet and Japan's Combined Fleet on 4 June 1942

MOI	Ministry of Information (British)
Mosquito	fastest aircraft in the RAF from 1941 to 1943, made mostly of wood and used as both a bomber and a fighter
MTB	motor torpedo boat
Mulberry	artificial harbor developed from 1942 to 1944 for use in OVERLORD; built of sunken ships and concrete caissons that formed a 200-foot breakwater for mooring facilities
musette bag	small canvas or leather bag with a shoulder strap
MWT	Ministry of War Transport (British)
NA	National Archives
NATO	North Atlantic Treaty Organization
Naval Gruppe West	German coastal artillery located in Normandy
NCDU	Naval combat demolition unit
NEPTUNE	operation to transport assault troops and equipment across the sea to Normandy
OB	order of battle; composition and disposition of forces
OCMH	Office of the chief of Military History
OG	ordnance group
Omaha	eastern landing beach of U.S. forces in Normandy
OPD	Operations Division, U.S. War Department
OSS	Office of Strategic Services (U.S.)
OVERLORD	plan for the invasion of northwest Europe in the spring of 1944
OWI	Office of War Information (U.S.)
Panzer Group West	established by the Germans, (U.S.) November 1943, to control armored units in any large-scale counterattack against Allied landings
Passchendaele	battle in Flanders in World War I
Phoenix floating caisson	hollow concrete barges that formed part of the Mulberry
pillbox	low-roofed concrete emplacement for machine gun or antitank gun

POE	Port of embarkation
POINTBLANK	long-range bombing program from Britain against Germany
POM	preparation for overseas movement.
PRO	Public Records Office (British)
PROSPER circuit	British espionage network in France
PRU	photographic reconnaissance unit
PSP	Perforated steel plate
PWE	Political Warfare Executive (British)
PX	post exchange
QUADRANT	first Quebec conference of Roosevelt, Churchill, and CCS, August 1943
RAINBOW	various plans prepared between 1939 and 1941 to meet Axis aggression involving more than one enemy
rations—C, D, and K	C was a balanced meal in a can; D was a fortified chocolate bar; K was a box meal more nourishing and compact than C rations
RN	Royal Navy
ROUNDHAMMER	original codename for OVERLORD
ROUNDUP	various 1941–43 Anglo-American plans for a cross-Channel attack that projected an all-out assault
SAS	special air service
SEAL	sea-air-land special operation team
Second Front	invasion of Europe by Anglo-American forces to relieve the Eastern (first) Front
SEELOEWE	planned German invasion of England, 1940–41
SEXTANT	Cairo conference, 22–26 November 1943
SFHQ	Special Forces Headquarters
SHAEF	Supreme Headquarters Allied Expeditionary Force
shingle	rough section of beach on the edge of the water
Siegfried Line	see Maginot Line
sigint	signals intelligence
SIS	Secret Intelligence Service (British)
slave station	secondary part of the complex radar systems on airplanes

SLEDGEHAMMER	Plan for a limited-objective attack across the Channel in 1942, designed either to take advantage of a German collapse or as a "sacrifice" operation to aid the Soviets
SOE	Special Operations Executive (British)
SS	Nazi unit originally created to serve as Hitler's bodyguard; later expanded to oversee intelligence and security
Supreme Headquarters	established in London in February 1944 after two years in development
tactical air force	Generic name for the Allied ground support air forces and air commands
tetrahydra	Part of the German obstacles on the beaches of Normandy.
TIGER	U.S. VII Corps full-dress rehearsal for Utah assault, Slapton Sands, England, April 1944
Tobruk	Libyan port that fell to the British, January 1941, and became a vital supply base for Allied desert operations
Todt organization	German organization for military construction
TOE	table of organization and equipment
TORCH	Allied invasion of North and northwest Africa, November 1942
TRIDENT	Washington conference, May 1943
U-boat	German submarine
ULTRA	British operation to intercept and decrypt German radio communications
USN	United States Navy
Utah	western landing beach for U.S. forces in Normandy
V-1 buzz bombs	also known as the V-1 missile, built between June 1942 and December 1943 with a one–ton warhead and a range of 150 to 250 miles
V-weapons	German secret weapons planned as revenge for the bombing of Germany; the V-1 missile and V-2 rocket.
VLR	very long range
VT proximity fuse	fuse that contained a small radio transmit-

	ter that detonated a shell on interference from a nearby aircraft; used in Allied anti-aircraft guns
WAAF	Womens's Auxiliary Air Force (British)
WSA	War Shipping Administration
XX Committee	Secret committee of British officials that dealt with counterintelligence

About the Contributors

Robert H. Berlin is a faculty member and dean of the Advanced Military Studies Program in the U.S. Army Command and General Staff College, Fort Leavenworth. Berlin earned his Ph.D. in history at the University of California–Santa Barbara and has taught at Mansfield College, the University of Kansas, and the Combat Studies Institute, CGSC. Among other works, he is the author of *U.S. Army World War II Corps Commanders: A Composite Biography* (1989).

Omar N. Bradley graduated from West Point in 1915. In 1941 he was promoted to brigadier general, the first member of his class to receive a general's star. In February 1943, Bradley was assigned to the North African theatre, where he first served as field aide to Eisenhower. In May he became commanding officer of II Corps, which distinguished itself in North Africa and Sicily. In September 1943 he took over the First Army, which participated in the D-day invasion and the subsequent Normandy campaign, and in August 1944 he was appointed commander of the Twelfth Army Group, which helped sweep the German forces from France to final defeat in Germany. After the war, Bradley served as administrator of Veterans Affairs (1945–48), Army chief of staff (1948–49), and chairman of the Joint chiefs of Staff (1949–53). General Bradley died in 1981.

Raymond Callahan, professor of history, University of Delaware, received his Ph.D. from Harvard University. He served as John F. Morrison Professor of Military History at the U.S. Army Command and General Staff College, Fort Leavenworth, in 1982–83. Among Callahan's numerous works on Britain's conduct of World War II are *The Worst Disaster: The Fall of Singapore* (1977), *Burma, 1942–1945* (1978), and *Churchill: Retreat from Empire* (1984). He is currently completing a book on Churchill and British military leadership in World War II.

Alexander S. Cochran is associate professor of history at the Air War College. He edited the first major collection on MAGIC and has written numerous articles on intelligence and strategy in World War II. He also wrote the volume on planning in an authoritative study of the U.S. Air Force and the Gulf War. Cochran earned his Ph.D. at the University of Kansas. He is presently at work on a study of the Mediterranean theater of operations in World War II.

Alex Danchev is professor of international relations at the University of Keele. Educated at Oxford, Cambridge, and London University, he served for some years in the Royal Army Educational Corps. Danchev has held fellowships in the Department of War Studies, King's College, and the Woodrow Wilson International Center for Scholars. He is the author of *Very Special Relationship* (1986), *Establishing the Anglo-American Alliance: The Second World War Diaries of Brigadier Vivian Dykes* (1990), *Oliver Franks: Founding Father* (1993), and numerous articles on World War II British military topics and Anglo-American relations.

John S. D. Eisenhower graduated from West Point on D-day, 6 June 1944. He served with the U.S. 1st Army in World War II and the Army of Occupation, Germany and Austria. He then served with the 15th Infantry Regiment and with the 3d Infantry Division during the Korean War. He retired from the army as a brigadier general. He served as assistant staff secretary in the White House, 1958–61, and as U.S. ambassador to Belgium from April 1969 to October 1971. He assisted in the writing of *White House Years* (1965), edited *Letters to Mamie* (1977), and has written *The Bitter Woods* (1969), *Strictly Personal* (1974), *Allies: Pearl Harbor to D-Day* (1982), and *So Far from God* (1989), a history of the Mexican War.

Arthur L. Funk, professor of history emeritus at the University of Florida, earned his Ph.D. from the University of Chicago in 1940. He served for many years as president of the American Committee for the History of the Second World War, now the World War II Studies Association. Known for his scholarship on modern French history and World War II, Funk is the author of *Charles de Gaulle: The Critical Years, 1943-44* (1959), *The Politics of Torch: The Allied Landings and the Algiers* Putsch, *1942* (1974), and *Hidden Ally: The French Resistance, Special Operations, and the Landings in Southern France, 1944* (1992), among other works.

Robin Higham, professor of history at Kansas State University, served in the Royal Air Force from 1943 to 1947. He earned his Ph.D. at Harvard University and taught at the University of Massachusetts and the University of North Carolina. He has edited the journals *Military Affairs* and *Aerospace Historian.* He is the author of numerous books and articles, among which are *Britain's Imperial Air Routes, 1918–1939* (1961), *The Military Intellectuals in Britain: 1918–1939* (1966), *Diary of a Disaster* (1986), and *Air Power: A Concise History* (3d rev. ed., 1988).

David Hogan is a research historian at the U.S. Army Center of Military History, Washington, D.C. He earned his Ph.D. from Duke University. Hogan has written widely on special operations and is the author of *Raiders or Elite Infantry? The Changing Role of the U.S. Army Rangers from Dieppe to Grenada* (1992). He is now completing a study of the U.S. First Army during World War II.

Maurice Matloff is retired deputy chief historian in the Department of the Army Office of Military History. He received his Ph.D. from Harvard University and has held numerous visiting teaching posts. He served as an intelligence officer and historian in the U.S. Army Air Forces in World War II. Matloff coauthored, among other works, *Strategic Planning for Coalition Warfare* (2 vols., 1953–59).

Forrest C. Pogue, noted military historian and former director of the George C. Marshall Research Library, served as assistant historian for the Second Army in 1943–44. As a combat historian, he accompanied units of the First Army from Omaha Beach to Pilzen, Czechoslovakia. Among numerous studies of the World War II period, Pogue wrote *The Supreme Command* (1954) and a massive four-volume biography of General George C. Marshall.

Friedrich Ruge, Vice-Admiral, Federal German Navy (ret.), entered the German Imperial Navy in 1914. As Senior Officer, Minesweepers, during World War II, he participated in North Sea and English Channel operations. In November 1943, he was appointed naval adviser to Field Marshal Erwin Rommel and served in that capacity during the Allied invasion of Normandy. In 1956, Ruge became Chief of Naval Operations in the Federal German Navy. After his retirement in 1961, he served as professor of political science at the University of Tubingen. He authored, among other works, *Der Seekrieg: The Story of the German Navy in World War II* (1967) and *Rommel und die Invasion* (1959). Ruge died in 1982.

Max Schoenfeld, professor of history, University of Wisconsin–Eau Claire, earned his Ph.D. at Cornell University. He has taught European and military history at Eau Claire since 1964. Schoenfeld has published widely, including *The War Ministry of Sir Winston Churchill* (1972), *Sir Winston Churchill: His Life and Times* (2d rev. ed., 1986), and *U.S. Army Air Force Antisubmarine Operations in the Eastern Atlantic in World War II* (1994). He is now completing research for a comprehensive study of the naval war in the Atlantic in World War II.

Kevin Smith is assistant professor of history, Ball State University. He earned his Ph.D. at Yale University, working with Gaddis Smith and Paul Kennedy. He is currently revising his dissertation, "The Causes and Consequences of Dependence: British Merchant Shipping and Anglo-American Relations, 1940–1943," and wrote "Logistics Diplomacy at Casablanca: The Anglo-American Failure to Integrate Shipping and Military Strategy," published in *Diplomacy and Statecraft*.

Mark A. Stoler is professor of history at the University of Vermont, specializing in twentieth-century U.S. military and diplomatic history. He received his Ph.D. from the University of Wisconsin–Madison and has held visiting appointments at the Naval War College and the University of Haifa. Stoler is the author of *The Politics of the Second Front* (1977), *George C. Marshall: Soldier-Statesman of the Twentieth Century* (1989), and numerous articles on World War II strategy and diplomacy. He is currently at work on a study of the Joint Chiefs of Staff and national policy.

Gerhard L. Weinberg is William Rand Kenan Professor of History at the University of North Carolina–Chapel Hill. He is the author of numerous scholarly books and articles, including *The Foreign Policy of Hitler's Germany: Starting World War II, 1937–1939* (1980), *World in the Balance: Behind the Scenes in World War II* (1981), and *The Greatest War* (1993).

Don Whitehead, free-lance writer and newspaperman, joined the Associated Press in 1935. During World War II, he covered both the North African and European campaigns. Whitehead accompanied the 1st Division's D-day assault on Omaha Beach. He was awarded the Medal of Freedom for his work covering the war. The recipient of two Pulitzer prizes, he wrote several books on FBI operations and organized crime. Whitehead died in 1981.

Theodore A. Wilson is professor of history at the University of Kansas. He earned his Ph.D. at Indiana University. Wilson served as the John F. Morrison Professor of Military History, U.S. Army Command and General Staff College, in 1983–84, and as Senior Research Fellow at the U.S. Army Center of Military History during 1989–91. Among his various publications are *The First Summit: Roosevelt and Churchill at Placentia Bay, 1941* (rev. ed., 1991), *WW2: Critical Issues* (1974), *Makers of American Diplomacy* (1975), and *Building Warriors: The Selection and Training of American Ground Combat Forces in World War II* (forthcoming).

Alan Wilt is professor of history at Iowa State University. He earned his Ph.D. at the University of Michigan. He is the author of several books on

World War II strategy and military operations, including *The Atlantic Wall: Hitler's Defenses in the West, 1941–1944* (1975), *The French Riviera Campaign of August 1944* (1981), and *War from the Top: German and British Military Decision Making during World War II* (1990), and contributed the chapter on close air support in the ETO for the recently published Air Force History official volume.

Index